Venice and the Veneto

Further titles available
in the
Phaidon Cultural Guides
series:

Athens and Attica
Austria
Florence and Tuscany
France
Germany
Great Britain and Ireland
Greece
Holland
Italy
Jerusalem and the Holy Land
The Loire Valley
London
Paris and the Ile de France
Provence and the Côte d'Azur
Rome and Latium
Spain
Switzerland

Edited by Marianne Mehling

Venice and the Veneto

A Phaidon Cultural Guide

with over 340 colour illustrations
and 7 pages of maps

Phaidon

Contributors: Dr Marianne Albrecht-Bott, Martin Locher, Dr Marianne Mehling, Valentine Wassermann

Photographs: Fratelli Fabbri Editori S.p.A., Mailand, Alexandra Hertlein, Joachim Hertlein, Franz N. Mehling, SCALA Istituto Fotografico Editoriale, Florenz, Anita Schmid-Eggar

Phaidon Press Limited, Littlegate House, St Ebbe's Street, Oxford OX1 1SQ

First published in English 1988
Originally published as *Knaurs Kulturführer in Farbe: Venedig und Venetien*
© Droemersche Verlagsanstalt Th. Knaur Nachf. Munich 1986
Translation © Phaidon Press Limited 1988

British Library Cataloguing in Publication Data

Venice and the Veneto.—(A Phaidon cultural guide)
   1. Venice (Italy)—Description—
Guide-books
I. Mehling, Marianne II. Albrecht-Gott,
Marianne
914.5'31   DG672

ISBN 0-7148-2505-0

Translated and edited by Babel Translations, London
Typeset by WM Print Ltd, Walsall
Printed in West Germany by Druckerei Appl, Wemding

Cover illustration: Santa Maria della Salute, from the Grand Canal
(photo: © The Photo Source, London)

Preface

The Veneto, that land of many forms, is linked by name with Venice, the capital of the province. The city of Venice dominates this land. It is perhaps the most wonderful and magical city in the world, while at the same time being the city most threatened by transience. The winged lions which are still to be found in all parts of the province bear witness to the rule of Venice. They are embroidered on flags, carved in sculptures and reliefs, painted on pictures and incorporated in coats-of-arms. The lions are the emblems of St.Mark, the patron saint of this city, which was built on piles and islets in the sea in early Christian times and has stood here ever since. Its location made it unconquerable. Neither the Goths, nor the Huns, nor the foraying hordes of the Barbarian Invasions, were able to reach it. It continued to develop and preserve its power as the centuries passed. Venice's hegemony, ranging from the Dolomites as far as Milan and Cyprus, was based on the most powerful navy in the West and on its monopoly of sea trade. It was not until 1797 that Venice's power was broken, when it fell to Napoleon.

Today the Veneto is one of the twenty regions of Italy. It has the most varied landscape and an unbelievably rich artistic heritage. It includes the provinces of Venice, Treviso, Belluno, Padua, Vicenza, Verona and Rovigo. Its territory extends from the high mountains (Marmolata: 10,965 ft.), with the enormous, bizarre massifs of the Dolomites and their glaciers, the ski resort of Cortina d'Ampezzo (Winter Olympics of 1956), and deep mysterious mountain lakes (Lago di Misurina), and through mountain villages in the Val di Cadore as far as Belluno. It continues through small, charmingly situated towns such as Asolo, which nestle in the foothills and have a rich history, and extends to Lake Garda in the west and the Euganean Hills further to the south, where the natural thermal springs in Abano and Montegrotto have been in use since the time of the Romans. It ends in Rovigo and Adria in the south, where ruins and villas testify to the riches of the Roman period and to the perfection of Venetian architecture during the Renaissance. Cities such as Verona, Vicenza and Padua contain an almost infinite profusion of famous buildings, historical monuments and, in particular, splendid paintings. The Adriatic coast in the south-west of the Veneto is one of the most popular bathing areas in Europe, and so is the stretch from Eraclea Mare through Venice to Chioggia and the region shortly before Ravenna further to the south. This is an area full of old history. Visible efforts are now being made here to plant new forests and to care for the sandy beaches in order to put a brake on the spread of industry which occurred throughout the last century and in the first half of this one.

Owing to its favourable position, the Veneto was inhabited in prehistoric times, some 150,000 years ago. The Bronze Age finds (7−6C BC) are now mostly in the Museo Atestino in Este. It was inhabited by Eugans (Indoeuropeans), Rhaeti and Etruscans, and also, in c. 1000 BC by the Heneti (later called Venetians). The Heneti were a tribe originating from a region on the Black Sea. The museums of Este and Pieve di Cadore display some finds from that culture, the so-called 'Cività Atestina'. It was at that time that Padua, Vicenza, Feltre, Treviso and the town which preceded Vittorio Veneto were founded. The Romans pursued their expansion in the Veneto from 250 BC onwards and built roads in the region. Some of the Roman buildings, such as the famous Arena in Verona, survive to the present day. The conversion of the population to Christianity began from Aquileia in AD 400. During the Barbarian Invasions, the region suffered the inroads of the Marcomanni, Goths, Visigoths, Huns and Lombards. Frankish hegemony in Italy began with Charlemagne; but Venice was able to resist this and gradually brought the whole surrounding region under its power.

In its culture, Venice produced a combination, unique in Europe, of the medieval and Byzantine styles. This cultural amalgam spread out to the surrounding region, which in turn, over the centuries, was influenced by styles such as the Gothic from the north and by the advances of the Renaissance from the south. From this melting pot, art blossomed anew. Of artists who worked in the Veneto, Giotto was active in Padua, Gentile da Fabriano in Venice, Pisanello in Verona, Filippo Lippi and Mantegna in Padua, and finally the Bellini and Vivarini families in Venice and Murano. It was here that Carpaccio, Giorgione, Titian and Tintoretto evolved an art of painting which spread to Germany and Spain and achieved a perfection never attained since. The style was continued by Bassano, Lotto, Cina da Conegliano, Pordenone, Veronese, Palma Vecchio and his nephew Palma Giovane. Then, in the 18C, came Tiepolo, Piazzetta, Longhi, Canaletto and Guardi amongst a whole host of lesser known painters. Their art and their command of technique was renowned throughout Europe.

In the Middle Ages, architecture and sculpture in Venice displayed a charming combination of Romanesque, Gothic and Byzantine influences. The early Renaissance began as far back as c. 1420 in the Veneto, and produced such famous architects and sculptors as Donatello, Verrocchio, Rizzo, Lombardo, Coducci, Sansovino, Scamozzi, and finally Andrea Palladio (1508–80). The latter worked mainly in Vicenza and Venice. In addition to churches, palaces and theatres, it was at this time that the famous country villas were built in the Veneto. Baldassare Longhena was one of the outstanding baroque architects. Although the 18C was a period of political decline for the Veneto, rococo art became increasingly refined, and in Napoleonic times Venice produced the celebrated sculptor Canova.

Besides the visual arts, Venice has also been a home to literature. The poet Petrarch (1304–74) lived and died in Arquà, now known as Arquà Petrarca. Aretino was active in Venice in the Renaissance and in the 18C the city boasted such writers as Goldoni, Gozzi, Casanova and da Ponte.

Music, too, was of great importance. It was performed in St.Mark's in Venice from the early Middle Ages onwards and in the 16C Flemish influence became apparent in church music. Such names as Andrea Gabrieli, Claudio Monteverdi and, in particular, Antonio Vivaldi, speak for themselves. Tartini and Perosi continued in their footsteps, and the works of Ermanno Wolf-Ferrari, Gian Francesco Malipiero and Luigi Nono have been well received in the 20C. The theatre has played an active part in the life of the Veneto since the time of the commedia dell'arte. Today the most celebrated theatrical events are the large-scale

The lion is the emblem of both city and region ▷

operatic performances in the Arena in Verona, and the first nights of classical and modern plays and operas in Venice. The universities of Padua and Venice have played a prominent role in the natural sciences ever since the Middle Ages.

The Veneto is a region of such varied character, such rich history, and such prominence in art, that it cannot be compared with any other region in the world. It is not surprising that it is one of the most popular of all tourist destinations.

As with other guides in the series, the text is arranged in alphabetical order of place name for easy reference. The link between places which are geographically close but separated in the text because of the alphabetical arrangement is provided by the maps. They show all the principal towns described in the text, and also, in the same colour, those subsidiary places mentioned in the environs section at the end of each entry.

The heading to each entry gives the town and postal code and, below, its geographical region and a reference to the map section, giving page number and grid reference. Within each entry the sights are printed in bold type: less significant objects of interest appear under the heading **Also worth seeing** and places in the vicinity under **Environs.** At the end of the book is an index of the sights of Venice, as well as an index of other places mentioned in the text, an index of artists and a glossary of architectural and artistic technical terms used in the text.

'Piazzetta' by Canaletto

Venice

Map of Venice: p. 10/11 and 32/33

'Other cities possess works of art, but Venice is a work of art in itself.'

Thomas Mann

This city resembles a fairy-tale and is so magical that it will at some time, perhaps when least expected, so captivate even its harshest critic that he will never again be entirely free of its spell. Sensitive souls are precisely those whom this city initially repels, and this impression may persist for a long time. But sooner or later they will fall under its spell and sensitive natures, more easily affected than others, are of course the very ones to be captivated by the magic of the art of Venice, art which is often hidden and with a character all its own, in the glow of a Venetian chandelier flickering across the water from one of the succession of beautiful palaces on the Grand Canal, along with the mystery of the branching, labyrinthine alleys with

Sunset in Venice

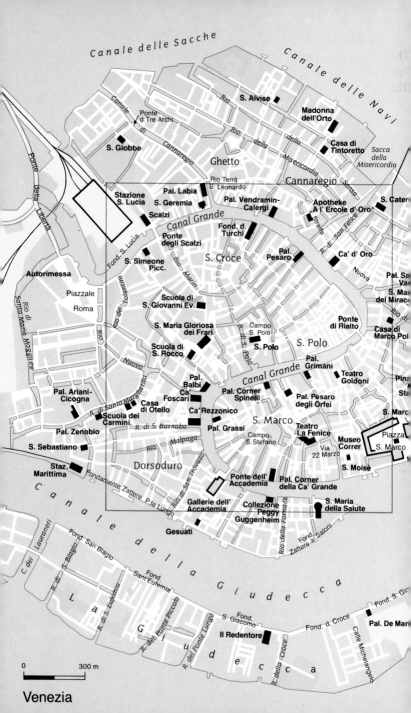

Venezia

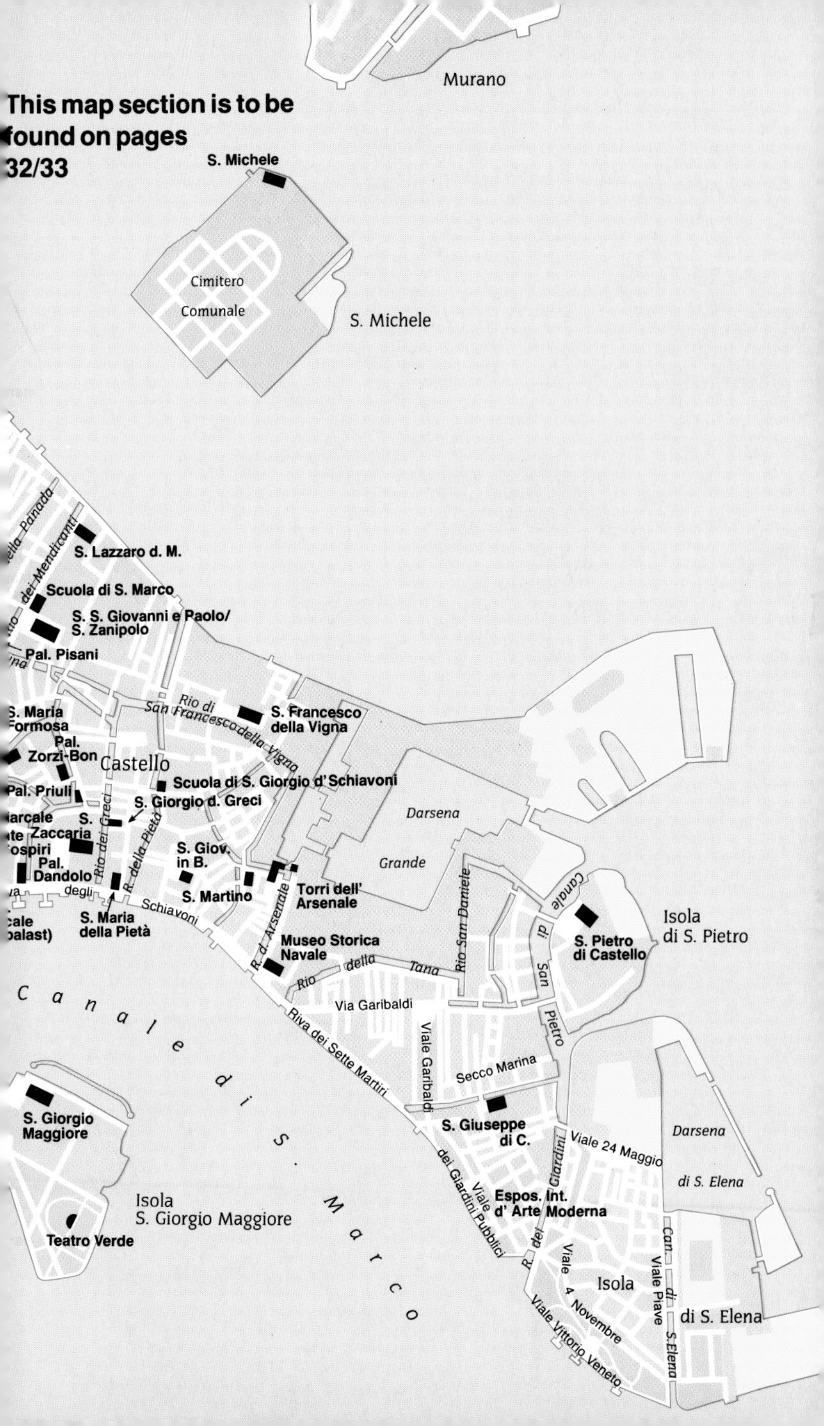

Murano

This map section is to be found on pages 32/33

S. Michele

Cimitero
Comunale

S. Michele

S. Lazzaro d. M.

Scuola di S. Marco

S. S. Giovanni e Paolo/
S. Zanipolo

Pal. Pisani

S. Maria
Formosa
Pal.
Zorzi-Bon

Castello

Pal. Priuli

Scuola di S. Giorgio d'Schiavoni

S. Giorgio d. Greci

arcale
te
Zaccaria
ospiri

Pal.
Dandolo

S. Giov.
in B.

degli

S. Martino

Schiavoni

Torri dell'
Arsenale

cale
palast)

S. Maria
della Pietà

Museo Storica
Navale

Rio   della   Tana

Via Garibaldi

Riva dei Sette Martiri

S. Francesco
della Vigna

Rio di
San Francesco della Vigna

Darsena
Grande

Canale   di   San   Pietro

S. Pietro
di Castello

Isola
di S. Pietro

Canale   di   S.   Marco

S. Giorgio
Maggiore

Isola
S. Giorgio Maggiore

Teatro Verde

Viale Garibaldi

Secco Marina

S. Giuseppe
di C.

Viale 24 Maggio

Espos. int.
d' Arte Moderna

Viale dei Giardini pubblici

Viale
Piave

Viale 4 Novembre

Viale Vittorio Veneto

Darsena
di S. Elena

Isola
di S. Elena

Can. di S. Elena

their myriad of bridges, the black gondolas, accompanied perhaps by the magic of the city's aromas: salt water, perfume, fish and the many different spices which the Venetians use to such effect in their cuisine. It was from spices, especially pepper, that Venice derived its wealth. In the early Middle Ages, spices, works of art, silk, and even relics, were brought on Venetian ships from the Far East, Arabia, China, India, Russia and Africa, and the rest of Europe gave gold in exchange for them.

Originally there were only fish and salt. Venice, the Serenissima, as the Venetians respectfully called their city, became wealthy through trade, and it was this wealth which allowed the arts to flourish—the arts which have made this city so beautiful, so enchanting and which have so enriched its surrounding region. The Doges governed this city within the framework of a firm constitution for 1100 years, showing political cunning, finesse and intrigue, greed and worldly wisdom, cruelty, energy and even self-castigation. But Venice has been dying since before Napoleon took it over from the Doges, as one trading monopoly after another was broken, and especially since the industrial

development of Mestre and Marghera. Venice stinks of decay. It is dying because the enormous amount of ground water pumped up by industry means that the ground level is falling, and also because high tide, mass tourism, motor boats and environmental pollution are destroying the city. Venice has sunk 10 ft. since its foundation, 3.5 inches of this subsidence having occurred in the relatively short period from 1945 onwards. The air, suffused with the smoke of the chemical factories, eats away at the architectural monuments, frescos and façades. It has become necessary to restore many of the buildings, which are therefore now boarded up. Some of the works of art, such as the famous horses of S.Marco, have had to be replaced by copies to protect them from decay. International efforts to rescue Venice are constantly being made.

Venice did not develop like other cities. It came into existence because the inhabitants of the upper Adriatic, north of the mouth of the Po, who lived mainly by fishing, were a people of reason and imagination. When the Barbarian Invasions burst into north-eastern Italy, the Venetians found an escape route which Alaric's Visigoths and, thirty years later,

View N. from San Marco

the Huns, were unable to follow. They built themselves huts on the islands in the lagoon. The predecessors of today's gondoliers, who are so skilful at steering their vessels through the narrow waterways, used their knowledge of the sea to save their lives. They knew all the shoals and shallows in the lagoon, and they alone were able to manoeuvre the boats there. Their enemies either had no boats or else had such a poor knowledge of the lagoon that their boats ran aground or sank. The island of *Malamocco*, which lay before the Lido and later sank below the waves in the floods of 1102, was the Venetians' first refuge. They then moved to Torcello and finally to the 118 islands which form today's Venice. Over the centuries these islands were linked together by the 400 arching bridges which still make it impossible for any wheeled vehicle to travel in the city. Houses, palaces and churches were built on countless numbers of piles driven into the mud. Entire forests in northern Italy were cut down to supply the timber, and 177 canals had to be shored up.

Venice consists of six districts or Sestieri: *San Marco, Castello, Dorsoduro, San Polo, Santa Croce* and *Cannaregio*. The houses are numbered by districts. Apart from this, in addition to a large number of small uninhabited islands, there are also *Lido*, now essentially a resort and dormitory suburb; *San Michele*, cemetery; *San Lazzaro*, monastery; *San Francesco*, the so-called wedding island; *San Clemente*, hospital; *Vignole*, market garden; *Murano*, glass-blowers'; *Burano*, an island of fishermen and lace-makers; and the wonderful island of *Torcello*, where the Venetians lived before they were driven out by malaria and founded today's city. There still stand in isolation on Torcello a few buildings of great antiquity.

Venice had no fixed link with the coast until 1846. This made the city so impregnable that in the Middle Ages it needed neither to be fortified nor to have a wall. Venice grew and flourished through shipping and trade. It was only slowly and gradually that Venice began to suffer when America was discovered, when Vasco da Gama discovered the sea route to India in 1498, when increasingly distant and better trade links became possible, and when the other cities banded together against Venice. The city declined in importance after the Renaissance. However, the Venetians still had their art and culture, an art

The lagoon

and culture which had originally been imported but which developed here an originality of its own. This culture enticed the first visitors in the early 18C, and finally resulted in the mass tourism which almost chokes the city today but earns it a considerable income. For example, the art of glass-blowing on Murano had almost died out, as had netting and lace-making on Burano. But in the late 19C these arts were revived through tourism and an industry has developed to satisfy this market. 17 million foreigners visit Venice every year. But only half of them stay for longer than one day. 200 hotels are full from spring to autumn. However, three times as many people now live in Mestre and Marghera as in Venice itself. The reason for the decline is that most of the jobs are in the factories of Mestre and Marghera. Mestre has now become Venice's main problem. Venice would be poor if Mestre were not there, but Mestre's presence is killing Venice.

I. General history

1&2C: Roman villas on Torcello, destroyed during a flood in the 5&6C.
3C: The Venetians, Illyrians settling on the Adriatic coast N. of the Po, were conquered by the Romans.
395: Emperor Honorius made Ravenna the capital of the Western Roman Empire.
402: The Visigoths under King Alaric I conquered Aquileia.
421: 25 March 421, the traditional date of Venice's foundation, corresponds fairly closely to historical reality. The Visigoths, led by Alaric, attacked not only Aquileia but also Altinum and other coastal towns. The inhabitants escaped to the islands in the lagoon. Some of them returned, while others remained on the islands and settled there.
476: Odoacer, the Germanic mercenary leader, toppled the Western Roman Empire.
493: The Germanic prince Odoacer, who had deposed Romulus Augustulus, the last Western Roman Emperor, was defeated by Theoderic's Ostrogoths.
523: Cassiodorus reported on the Venetians' skill in navigating the lagoons.

539: Ravenna became part of the Byzantine Empire, and subsequently the seat of the exarch.
552: The inhabitants of the lagoon were brought under Byzantine rule by the Byzantine general Narses.
568: The Lombards, led by Alboin, invaded Italy. More and more Venetians settled on the lagoons.
580: The patriarch of Aquileia moved his seat to Grado.
602: The Byzantine army rebelled.
638: After the Lombards conquered Altinum, Christians led by Bishop Paolo fled from there to the island of Torcello, where a basilica, part of which survives, was erected by Bishop Mauro in 639 under the protectorship of Ravenna. Torcello was a bishopric until 1818 when it joined the patriarchate of Venice.
640: Oderzo, the outermost bulwark on Venetian soil, was conquered by the Lombards. Since the 7C the islands have served as a distribution centre for cereals and sea salt.
697: The exarch of Ravenna appointed Paoluccio Anafesto, a 'dux' (duca-Doge) elected by the twelve maritime tribunes, to rule the settlement on the lagoon in Heraclea.
726: The second Doge, Duca Marcello Tegaliano, leant towards Byzantium. There was a revolt supported by the Lombards.
737: The next Doge was elected under Byzantine pressure.
742: The Doge moved his official seat from Heraclea on the edge of the mainland to the island of Malamocco, which was then known as Metamauca, and sank beneath the sea in 1102.
756: Pepin III, the son of Charles Martel and father of Charlemagne, bequeathed Rome and the exarchate of Ravenna to the Pope (beginning of the Papal State).
810: Pepin, the second son of Charlemagne, made a vain attempt to conquer the lagoon. He died on the site where Venice later stood.
811: The 10th Doge moved his seat of government to the island of rivo alto

Gondola ▷

(Rialto), after Pepin had destroyed Malamocco in 800. The 'civitas rivi alti', which spread from here to the neighbouring islands, gradually developed into what later became the city of Venice.

812: Treaty of Aachen.

827: The island of Olivolo (today S.Pietro di Castello) was elevated to a bishopric.

828: The legendary relics of St.Mark, after being removed from Alexandria, were brought to the Rialto.

830: The first church of St.Mark was built in 830−6. It was a structure worthy of housing the bones of the holy Evangelist, and also served as a State church and a chapel of the Doges.

840: A treaty with the Emperor Lothar I ensured free trade on the Po.

c. 850: Venice possessed the most powerful naval force in the Mediterranean.

864: The Doge Pietro Tradonico was assassinated for attempting to appoint his son as his successor.

950: Tradition relates that Otto I, the Holy Roman Emperor, was himself responsible for ordering the building of SS.Maria e Donato in Murano.

976: The Doge Pietro Candiano was murdered along with his young son.

990: The Venetian navy was expanded.

c. 1000: Venice is still called 'Civitas Rivoalti'. The republic was the main trading partner of Byzantium and the Levant (spices, wine, olives, weapons), and was in fact independent despite its supposed dependence on Byzantium.

1000: The Doge Pietro Orseolo conquered Zara (Zadar), Trau and Spalato (Split), and was referred to as 'Dux Dalmatiae'. The Doge's marriage to the sea was celebrated every Ascension Day from then on. The power of Venice constantly increased thanks to trade and shipping. Venice dominated the coasts of Istria and Dalmatia, established trading posts, and defeated the Normans in southern Italy.

1008: Bishop Orso Orseolo II, the son of Doge Pietro Orseolo, enlarged the already existing basilica on Torcello (it still survives).

1080: Venice saved Byzantium from the Normans and, in reward, was granted privileges which consolidated its position as the major trading power.

1083: Emperor Alexius I Comnenus exempted Venice from all taxes.

1094: The new church of St.Mark was consecrated in the presence of Emperor Henry IV.

1100: Venice obtained privileges in Jerusalem.

1102: Malamocco sank in the floods.

1104: Work began on building the arsenal.

1111: Revolt in Zara.

1123: Victory of the Venetian navy, together with the Crusaders, over the Egyptians before Ascalon.

1124: Victory over Tyre.

1167: Venice, along with the Pope, joined the Lombard League against the Emperor Frederick Barbarossa, but then remained neutral.

1172: The Great Council, which ensured aristocratic rule until the end of the Republic, was formed.

1177: Conflict with Genoa, with Byzantium siding with Genoa.

1201: Venice conducted negotiations over the Fourth Crusade, and joined it.

1202−4: Fourth Crusade.

1202: Zara was recaptured.

1204: The Peloponnese and most of the Greek islands came under the sway of Venice.

1229: The Senate was formed. Initially it only had six members representing the six districts of Venice; later it had 60 members.

1232: The Quarantia (40 members) was created in addition to the Great Council and the Senate.

1271: The brothers Niccolò and Maffeo Polo, accompanied by Niccolò's 17-year-old son Marco, undertook their second journey to Mongolia.

1289: The people rebelled in vain against their exclusion from the election of the Doge.

1290: Jews were granted the right of residence in Venice.

1292: Marco Polo returned to Venice. It was from the 13C onwards that the city became known as 'Venezia'.

1297: Only the members of 287 noble families recorded in the 'Golden Book' were permitted to join the 'Great Coun-

Carnival in Venice ▷

cil' (Consiglio maggiore), which elected not only the Doge, who retained the post for the rest of his life, but also his six advisers, known as the 'Privy Council' (Consiglio minore).

1299: A sumptuary law (against excessive luxury in clothing etc.) was passed.

1306: The sumptuary law was repealed.

1310: Rebellion by the families who were excluded from electing the Doge; the Council of Ten was established as a kind of secret police.

1334: The sumptuary law was re-introduced and made tougher.

1339: Spring tides.

1348: The plague was introduced from the Orient.

1359: 2nd epidemic.

1361: 3rd epidemic.

1378–81: Venice defeated Genoa in the War of Chioggia.

1381: Venice's inhabitants numbered 200,000.

1386: The Jewish cemetery on the Lido was founded. It still survives.

1392: Trade with England further increased the city's fortunes.

14C: Torcello declined in importance so

The Pope giving the sword to the Doge—Palazzo Ducale, Tintoretto

much that it gradually fell into oblivion. This was due to the rise of Venice, and also to the effects of malaria and other contagious diseases which drove the inhabitants away.

1406: Padua, Vicenza and Verona rejoined Venice.

1418: The Venetians occupied Friuli.

1425: Venice and Florence concluded an alliance against Milan.

c. 1430: The territory of Venice extended as far as the Alps, Milan and Cyprus. It was a centre of art and science. Trade links had developed as far as England and Flanders (sugar, spices and other goods from the Orient).

1432: Venice engaged condottieri for its wars. The first was Carmagnola (Francesco Bussoni) who scored some successes, but was then suspected of espionage and was executed on the Piazzetta in 1432.

1441: Gattamelata (Erasmo da Narni), a condottiere, fought against Milan and regained Cremona and Ravenna for Venice.

1453: Peace between Venice and Milan. Venice had reached its greatest extent, and sent diplomatic representatives to various European courts.

1454: In the peace of Lodi, Venice had to refrain from further expansion in northern Italy.

1455: Bartolomeo Colleoni became a condottiere.

Giosafat Barbaro undertook expeditions to Russia. Other Venetian seafarers travelled as far as the Lofoten Islands, the Canary Islands and Senegal. Venice traded with the whole world.

1466: Venice lost parts of the Peloponnese.

1470: Loss of Euboea.

1472: The Venetian lady Caterina Cornaro married James II of Cyprus, who died shortly thereafter (he may have been murdered). Their little son died not long afterwards. Caterina was received in Venice with great pomp and was then removed to Asolo. Cyprus belonged to Venice.

1479: Various areas which had been under the control of Venice fell to the Turks.

1492: Jews were expelled from Spain and settled in Venice.

1498: After the discovery of America in

1492, the sea route to India was discovered in 1498, and this led to a decline in Venice's power.

1509: Dispute with the Fuggers (Augsburg banking family).

1510: Doge Leonardo Lordean reached an agreement with the Pope.

1511: The Holy League against France was concluded in Venice under Pope Julius II. France was defeated in the battle of Novara. Venice was saved, but lost Verona, Vicenza and Padua.

1516: The district of the city formerly occupied by the foundrymen (gheto) includes a lagoon, which is surrounded by canals and which can be sealed off, and the island known as the Ghetto. The lagoon and island were assigned to the Jews and this district survives to the present day. The word 'ghetto' derives from here and later came to be used all over the world.

1517: The Turks conquered Egypt, depriving Venice of one of its most important trading partners.

1522: The Turks conquered Rhodes, and later some other Venetian colonies. Portugal became Venice's rival in the pepper trade.

1523: Lodovico Gritti, the son of Doge Andrea Gritti, was captured by the Turks in Candia and taken to Turkey. Venice had to promise to resolve its dispute with France, to declare war on Charles V, and to supply cannons to Turkey. In return, the Venetians were allowed to sail unhindered in the Black Sea in order to trade with Russia.

1562: The city authorities forbade the pageantry which the Venetians longed for. The colourfully decorated gondolas used until that time could now only be painted black.

1565: The Turks besieged Candia (Crete) and were defeated.

1569: The Arsenale was destroyed in a gunpowder explosion.

1571: The Turks conquered Cyprus, but broke their promise to permit Captain Marcantonio Bragadin and his troops to make an honourable withdrawal from Famagusta, murdering them instead. After this, Pius V joined with Venice and Spain to form a holy league which, on 7 October, won a triumphant victory at the naval battle of Lepanto.

1573: Loss of Cyprus.

1574: Henry III of France visited Venice.

1603: The Venetian navy lost twelve ships in this year alone due to piracy.

Equestrian statue of Bartolomeo Colleoni outside S.Zanipolo

The Doges of Venice
1. Paoluccio Anafesto 697–717.
2. Marcello Tegaliano 717–26.
3. Orso Ipato 726–37.
4. Maestro dei Militari 737–42.
5. Diodato Ipato 742–55.
6. Galla Gaulo 755–6.
7. Domenico Monegario 756–64.
8. Maurizio Galbaio 764–87.
9. Giovanni Galbaio 787–804.
10. Obelerio Antenorio 804–09 or –10.
11. Agnello Partecipazio 810–27.
12. Giustiniano Partecipazio 827–9.
13. Giovanni Partecipazio I 829–36 or –37.
14. Pietro Tradonico 836 or 837–64.
15. Orso Partecipazio I 864–81.
16. Giovanni Partecipazio II 881–7.
17. Pietro Candiano I 887.
18. Pietro Tribuno 888–912.
19. Orso Partecipazio II 912–32.
20. Pietro Candiano II 932–9.
21. Pietro Partecipazio 939–42.
22. Pietro Candiano III 942–59.
23. Pietro Candiano IV 959–76.
24. Pietro (S.) Orseolo I 976–8.
25. Vitale Candiano 978–9.
26. Tribuno Memmo 979–91.
27. Pietro Orseolo II 991–1009.
28. Ottone Orseolo 1009–26.
29. Pietro Centranico 1026–32.
30. Domenico Flabanico 1032–42.
31. Domenico Contarini 1043–70 or –71.
32. Domenico Selvo 1070 or 1071–84.
33. Vitale Falier 1084 or 1085–96.
34. Vitale Michièl I 1096–1102.
35. Ordelaffo Falier 1102–18.
36. Domenico Michiel 1118–29.
37. Pietro Polani 1130–48.
38. Domenico Morosini 1148–56.
39. Vitale Michiel II 1156–72.
40. Sebastiano Ziani 1172–8.
41. Orio Malipiero 1178–92.
42. Enrico Dandolo 1192–1205.
43. Pietro Ziani 1205–29.
44. Iacopo Tiepolo 1229–49.
45. Marino Morosini 1249–53.
46. Raniero Zen 1253–68.
47. Lorenzo Tiepolo 1268–75.
48. Iacopo Contarini 1275–80.
49. Giovanni Dandolo 1280–9.
50. Pietro Gradenigo 1289–1311.
51. Marino Zorzi 1311–12.
52. Giovanni Soranzo 1312–28.
53. Francesco Dandolo 1329–39.
54. Bartolomeo Gradenigo 1339–42.
55. Andrea Dandolo 1343–54.
56. Marino Falier 1354–5.
57. Giovanni Gradenigo 1355–6.
58. Giovanni Dolfin 1356–61.
59. Lorenzo Celsi 1361–5.
60. Marco Corner 1365–8.

61. Andrea Contarini 1368–82.
62. Michele Morosini 1382.
63. Antonio Venier 1382–1400.
64. Michele Steno 1400–13.
65. Tomaso Mocenigo 1414–23.
66. Francesco Foscari 1423–57.
67. Pasquale Malipiero 1457–62.
68. Cristoforo Moro 1462–71.
69. Nicolò Tron 1471–3.
70. Nicolò Marcello 1473–4.
71. Pietro Mocenigo 1474–6.
72. Andrea Vendramin 1476–8.
73. Giovanni Mocenigo 1478–85.
74. Marco Barbarigo 1485–6.
75. Agostino Barbarigo 1486–1501.
76. Leonardo Loredan 1501–21.
77. Antonio Grimani 1521–3.
78. Andrea Gritti 1523–38.
79. Pietro Lando 1539–45.
80. Francesco Donato 1545–53.
81. Marcantonio Trevisan 1553–4.
82. Francesco Venier 1554–6.
83. Lorenzo Priuli 1556–9.
84. Girolamo Priuli 1559–67.
85. Pietro Loredan 1567–70.
86. Alvise I Mocenigo 1570–7.
87. Sebastiano Venier 1577–8.
88. Nicolò da Ponte 1578–85.
89. Pasquale Cicogna 1585–95.
90. Marino Grimani 1595–1605.
91. Leonardo Donato 1606–12.
92. Marcantonio Memmo 1612–15.
93. Giovanni Bembo 1615–18.
94. Nicolò Donato 1618.
95. Antonio Priuli 1618–23.
96. Francesco Contarini 1623–4.
97. Giovanni I Corner 1625–9.
98. Nicolò Contarini 1630–1.
99. Francesco Erizzo 1631–46.
100. Francesco Molin 1646–55.
101. Carlo Contarini 1655–6.
102. Francesco Corner 1656.
103. Bertuccio Valier 1656–8.
104. Giovanni Pesaro 1658–9.
105. Domenico Contarini 1659–75.
106. Nicolò Sagredo 1675–6.
107. Alvise Contarini 1676–84.
108. Marcantonio Giustinian 1684–8.
109. Francesco Morosini 1688–94.
110. Silvestro Valier 1694–1700.
111. Alvise II Mocenigo 1700–09.
112. Giovanni II Corner 1709–22.
113. Alvise III Mocenigo 1722–32.
114. Carlo Ruzzini 1723–35.
115. Alvise Pisani 1735–41.
116. Pietro Grimani 1741–52.
117. Francesco Loredan 1752–62.
118. Marco Foscarini 1762–3.
119. Alvise IV Mocenigo 1763–78.
120. Paolo Renier 1779–89.
121. Lodovico Manin 1789–97.

Previous page:
Doge Francesco Foscari kneeling,
S.Marco

1605: The Pope excommunicated Venice
for the third time.
1619: State Bank established.
1633: 500 Jews living in the Ghetto.
1645: The Turkish invasion of Candia
began. Sultan Suleiman the Great wished
to become emperor of both Byzantium and
Rome.
1663–99: Great Turkish War.
1684: Alliance against Turkey.
1699: Some areas were recaptured.
1714–18: Turkish War.
1716: Imperial Count von der Schulen-
burg, whom the Venetians had elected as
their military commander, prevented the
Ionian Archipelago from being conquered
in the Turkish onslaught.
1718: After the peace of Passarowitz,
Venice was forced to relinquish for good
its position as a great political power in
the eastern Mediterranean.
c. 1720: People with an interest in culture began to visit Venice; it rose to social
and cultural importance during the rococo
period.
1744–82: Construction of the 'murazzi',
a long wall built of blocks of Istrian granite
to keep floods at bay. It runs along the
Lido of Pellestrina.
1796–1815: Napoleonic Wars.
15 May 1797: Lodovico Manin, the last
Doge, handed the city of Venice over to
Napoleon.
1798: The French ceded Venice to
Austria.
1805: Venice once again came under
French rule.
1815: Venice became part of the Habsburg
kingdom of Lombardy-Venetia.
1846: Joined to the mainland by a railway
bridge.
1848: Revolution. Daniele Manin became
president of the new republic.
1849: Venice conquered by the Austrians.
The Austrian General Radetsky entered
Venice.
22 Oct. 1866: A plebiscite was held in the
Veneto concerning the province's
affiliation.
7 Nov. 1866: Vittorio Emanuele II

entered the city. Venice was united with
Italy.
1869: The port of Venice regained its
importance after the opening of the Suez
Canal. The Arsenale was re-equipped.
However, it was not large enough, and the
industrial ports of Mestre and Marghera
were therefore built. Venice increased in
importance and became a major tourist
resort.
1879: Flooding in Venice.
1933: The gigantic causeway was built as
a route to the mainland.
1945: Work was started on refineries and
chemical factories in Mestre and
Marghera.
1959: Flooding.
Nov. 1966: Disastrous floods in several
parts of Italy; Venice and Florence were
especially badly affected.
1970: Venice became the capital of the
Veneto region.
1973: A special law controlled the amount
of water drawn off by the industrial zone.
1980: A group of artists revived the Venetian carnival, which had fallen into oblivion in the 19C.
1981: Research undertaken by the Minis-
try of Public Buildings resulted in a
project to save Venice from destruction in
which three steel gates would be used to
regulate the water level.
1983: The USA withdrew from
UNESCO and consequently no longer felt
any responsibility to help meet the cost
of this immensely expensive project.

II. Cultural chronology

1&2C: Remains of Roman villas from the
1&2C AD, which were destroyed in a
flood in the 5 or 6C, have been discovered
on Torcello.
5C: Venetians settled on the lagoon
islands, especially on Malamocco, which
was flooded by the sea in 1102.
568: Paolino the patriarch moved his seat
from Aquileia to Grado.
6C: Settlements were built on the 118
islands around the rivo alto (later Rialto).
A small church, initially pre-Romanesque

Doge Alvise Mocenigo, ▷
Galleria dell'Accademia, Tintoretto

in style, but influenced by early Christian and later by Byzantine elements, was built on almost every one of these islands. The following were founded in the 6C in what were to become the Sestiere Castello: *San Antonin* and *San Lorenzo;* in Cannaregio: *San Geremia* and *San Giovanni Cristoforo;* and in San Marco: *San Geminiano.*

c. 600: The remains of Roman glass vessels dating from *c.* 600 have been excavated in Aquileia and on Torcello.

635: Paolo I, bishop of Altino, moved his seat to Torcello.

639–41: The cathedral of *Maria Assunta,* with a nave and two aisles, was built on Torcello in a style showing a Byzantine influence derived from Ravenna. The attached baptistery also dates from this time.

7C: At a later date, in the 13C, the islands were united and subdivided into six districts or sestieri. The following churches were founded in the 7C in what later became the Sestiere Castello: *Santa Giustina, Santa Maria Formosa, San Martino;* and in the future Sestiere Dorsoduro: *Angelo Raffaele* and *San Nicolo dei Mendicoli.*

Only a few of these old buildings survive. However, many of those which were destroyed by fire or had become decayed were later restored or rebuilt.

742: The Doge moved across to Malamocco.

774: An archbishopric was established on the island of Olivolo, being a suffragan of the patriarchate of Grado.

788–812: The effects of iconoclasm (destruction of images) were felt on the islands.

8C: The following churches were built in what later became the district of Castello: *San Giovanni in Bragora* and *San Daniele. Santa Croce* was erected in the sestiere which later took its name from it, and *San Zan Degolà* was also built there. In San Marco: *San Moisè.*

c. 800: More and more people settled on the group of islands around the rivo alto. By now the islands were linked by some 100 wooden bridges. The wooden houses were supported by piles driven into the mud.

811: The 10th Doge moved his seat of government to the group of islands where

Venice now stands.

c. 820: The first *castle* was built for the Doge next to what was originally a *palace chapel* of St.Theodore, the settlement's first patron Saint, later replaced by St.Mark.

828: The relics of St.Mark were brought to Venice.

830–6: The first *church of St.Mark* was built to serve both as a Doges' chapel and a State church. It was of wood, consequently nothing of this structure survives.

9C: Apart from the church of St.Mark, the following buildings in what is now the Sestiere San Marco also date from the 9C: *San Bartolomeo, Ascensione* (Santa Maria in Broglio), *San Mauricio, San Paternian* and *San Zulian.* In Castello: *San Zaccaria, San Severo, San Provolo, San Pietro* and *San Lio.* In San Polo: *San Giovanni Elemosinario, San Silvestro* and the church of *San Polo* which later gave the district its name. In Dorsoduro: *San Trovaso, San Pantalon, Santa Margherita* and *San Barnaba.* In Cannaregio: *San Cassiano, Santi Apostoli, San Marcuola, San Marziale* and *Santa Sofia.* Finally, in Santa Croce: *San Cassiano* and *San Giacomo dell'Orio.*

976: When the Doge was murdered, the first church of St.Mark, which was mainly of wood, was completely burned down.

10C: The following churches were built in the Sestiere San Marco in the 10C: *Sant' Angelo, San Fantin, Santa Maria del Giglio, San Samuele* and *San Giorgio Maggiore.* In Castello: *San Giovanni Novo,* and in Santa Croce: *San Simeon Grande, San Simeon Piccolo, S.Staè* and *Santa Maria Mater Domini.* In San Polo: *San Tomà, San Stin, San Giovanni Evangelista, San Baldo* and *Sant'Agostin.* In Dorsoduro: *Sant'Agnese, San Basegio* and *S.Vio.* In Cannaregio: *Santa Maria Nova, Misericordia, Santa Fosca* and *San Felice.* And on Giudecca: *SS. Biagio e Cataldo* and *Sant'Eufemia. Santa Fosca,* first mentioned in 1011, was built on the island of Torcello.

999: The architecture of this period is Romanesque. Under the influence of the Byzantine churches, bricks were also employed. An example of surviving build-

St.Christopher, by Titian, ▷
in the Palazzo Ducale

ing of this period is the beautiful cathedral, begun in 999, of *SS.Maria e Donato* on the island of Burano. The old floor mosaics are among the original features which survive.

c. 1000: Benedictine monks on San Giorgio Maggiore were mentioned as glass-blowers. They brought this art from the mainland to the islands, and later passed it on to the craftsmen who moved the glass factories to Murano in 1291.

1091: From now on the bishops called themselves Castellani after the cathedral of San Pietro di Castello.

11C: The arsenal was set up as a permanent installation for fitting out the Venetian navy; the campanile of Santa Maria Assunta was erected on Torcello. The area which later became Venice was coalescing more and more into a single unit at that time. Other churches built there in the 11C include: in the future Sestiere San Marco: *San Vidal, San Salvador, San Luca, San Benedetto* and *San Basso.* In Castello: *Santa Marina, San Giovanni di Malta* (or *dei Furlani*), *San Biagio* and *Santa Ternita.* In San Polo: *Sant'Aponal;* and in Dorsoduro: *San Gregorio, Santa Caterina* and *Trinità.* Finally, in Cannaregio: *San Leonardo.*

The relics and spoils which the Venetians brought back with them from their innumerable trading journeys and military expeditions had to be given a worthy home. Numerous remains of martyrs were brought from Alexandria and the building of churches was scarcely able to keep up with this influx.

1094: A second *church of St.Mark*, built of stone, was erected as a cruciform domed church on the model of the 6C church of the Apostles in Constantinople. It still survives as the core of the present building.

11C: The architectural style of the 11C and even the 12C was Romanesque, but it was influenced by Byzantine art.

1131: Enrico Dandolo, the patriarch of Grado, moved his seat to Venice.

1204: After the capture of Constantinople, the bronze horses of St.Mark's and sundry architectural features including columns were incorporated in Venetian buildings.

1205: Silk factories.

12&13C: The mosaics in the cathedral of S.Maria Assunta on Torcello date from this period.

13C: Veneto-Byzantine palaces were constructed in a style all their own, examples being: *Palazzo Farsetti, Palazzo Loredan, Palazzo Zorzi* and the *Fondaco dei Turchi.* The following were built in Castello: *Sant'Anna, Ca' di Dio, San Francesco di Paola, San Francesco della Vigna Vergini.* In San Marco: *Santo Stefano.* In Dorsoduro: *Carmini.* In Santa Croce: *Santa Chiara.* In Cannaregio: *Gesuiti* and *Maddalena. Santa Croce* on Giudecca. In San Polo: *Frari* which, like *Santi Giovanni e Paolo* in the 14C, was built in the form of a Gothic cathedral.

1284: Gold coins were minted and used in trade.

1291: The glass factories were moved from the Rialto to Murano.

1292: Return of Marco Polo.

1301: Work on the *Doges' Palace* was begun. Philippo Calendario and Giovanni and Bartolomeo Bon (Ca' d'Oro, Doges' Palace, Santa Maria della Carità, San Rocco and Scuola di San Rocco) worked as architects and sculptors.

1365: What was probably the first musical competition in Europe was organized under Doge Lorenzo Celsi, with Petrarch, the poet, participating.

14C: Venice turned to the Gothic style, and broke from established traditions in art.

1381: Venice's population reached 200,000.

1388: The brothers Jacobello and Paolo dalle Masegne worked here from 1388 on.

1409: The painter Gentile da Fabriano from Umbria, and his co-worker Antonio Pisano, known as Pisanello, came to Venice.

1421–40: *Ca' d'Oro.*

1429: Jacopo Bellini the painter was a pupil of Fabriano's, but did not himself work in Venice. However, his sons Gentile (b. 1429) and Giovanni (b. 1430) founded the Venetian style of painting. Jacopo Bellini also had an influence on the Vivarini (they were members of the

Triumph of Venice, Palazzo Ducale, ▷
Veronese

Murano school, which painted in early Renaissance style). The Bellini had the same effect on Venice as Giotto had on the whole of Italy.

1436: Birth of Pietro Lombardo who, as sculptor and architect, continued Antonio Rizzo's work on the courtyard of the Doges' Palace. Pietro Lombardo was a proponent of the Renaissance style which had already won favour in the rest of Italy. Birth of Andrea Verrocchio in Florence.

1440: Birth of Mauro Coducci, the architect who was to become a leading representative of the Venetian Renaissance.

1450: Painting school in Murano. The Vivarini, a Venetian family of painters, attempted to break away from the purely Byzantine style and to move towards realism.

1451: Venice became a patriarchate. The first patriarch was Lorenzo Giustiniani, who was later canonized.

1463: *Doges' Palace.*

1465: Birth of Vittore Carpaccio, the painter who later became Gentile Bellini's great pupil.

1468: Nicolas Jenson studied printing under Johannes de Spirra in Venice, and worked as a printer in his own right from 1470 onwards. He is thought to have invented the Roman style of type (1468).

1469: Letterpress printing in Venice.

1470: *San Giobbe* was rebuilt and enlarged by Pietro Lombardo and Antonio Gambello.

1474: The right to patent one's inventions was introduced.

1477: Birth of Titian (real name: Tiziano Vecellio) in Pieve di Cadore in the mountains of the Veneto. Titian was the most famous of the Venetian painters, and was in demand as a portrait painter all over Europe.

1478: Birth of Giorgione, who was the first to produce non-religious works of art in Venice.

1480: Adrian Willaert was born in Flanders. He was later appointed musical director at St.Mark's, where he worked for 35 years.

1481: Coducci continued the work on *S.Zaccaria* which had been begun by Antonio Gambello.

1481–9: Pietro Lombardo and his sons built *Santa Maria dei Miracoli*, the first early Renaissance masterpiece in Venice.

1483: The Renaissance reached Venice when Antonio Rizzo of Verona was appointed architect for the courtyard façade of the Doges' Palace.

1488: Until 1488, shortly before his death in Venice, Verrochio worked on the *equestrian statue of Colleoni*. This monument was completed by Alessandro Leopardi in 1496. It now stands outside Zanipolo.

1495: This is probably the year in which Mauro Coducci produced the plans for the clock tower on the Piazza.

1495: The works of Aristotle were printed in Venice.

1500: The *Procuratie Vecchie*, the *Palazzo Vendramin Calergi*, and probably the *Palazzo Spinelli*, were built after 1500.

1507–34: *S.Salvatore* was built by Giorgio Spavento, Tullio Lombardo and Jacopo Sansovino.

1508: Birth of Andrea Palladio.

1510: Birth of Andrea Gabrieli in Venice. As a pupil of Willaert, he became organist at San Marco at the age of 46, and also made a name for himself as a composer.

1512: Birth of Antonio da Ponte. This pupil of Sansovino later beat Palladio in the competition to rebuild the Doges' Palace. He also constructed the *Bridge of Sighs.*

1515: Birth of Jacopo Bassano the painter. He and his sons Francesco (b. 1549) and Leandro (b. 1557) continued the Venetian painting tradition.

1516: The Ghetto was assigned to the Jews.

1516–18: Titian painted his Assunta for the Frari.

1518: Birth of the painter Jacopo Tintoretto in Venice.

1526: At the age of 40, Jacopo Sansovino came from Florence and Rome to Venice, where he had a decisive effect upon sculpture and architecture.

1537: Sansovino built the Old Library on the Piazzetta, and also the *Palazzo Corner.*

1552: Birth of Vicenzo Scamozzi in Vicenza. Scamozzi was influenced by the baroque style. In Venice, he built the *Palazzo Corner-Mocenigo* on the Campo San Polo, completed the *Old Library,* and began building the *Procuratie Nuove.*

1556: Death of the Mannerist painter Lorenzo Lotto.

1557: Birth in Venice of Giovanni Gabrieli, who was a nephew of Andrea Gabrieli and later became an important composer. He was also one of the greatest organ virtuosi of his time.

1557: The painter Paolo Veronese (Paolo Caliari from Verona) came to Venice.

1565–87: Tintoretto painted the Scuola di S.Rocco (see 'Schools').

1566–1610: *San Giorgio Maggiore:*

1573: Veronese painted the 'Feast in the House of Levi' (Accademia).

1576: Death of Titian during an epidemic of plague in Venice.

from 1577: Palladio built *Il Redentore.*

1583–1640: *Procuratie Nuove.*

1588: Death of Veronese in Venice.

1588–91: *Rialto Bridge.*

1588–90: Tintoretto (Jacopo Robusti) worked on the ceiling painting of Paradise in the Doges' Palace.

1593: Tintoretto painted the Last Supper for San Giorgio Maggiore.

1598: Birth of Baldassare Longhena in Venice. It was here that he created his masterpiece, the church of *Santa Maria della Salute.* He built the *Ca' Rezzonico* on the Grand Canal and completed the *Procuratie Nuove.*

La Tempesta, by Giorgione, Galleria dell'Accademia

1602: Birth of Francesco Cavalli, the Venetian opera composer.

1606: Papal bull of excommunication and interdict against Venice, which was in dispute with the Church.

1613: Claudio Monteverdi was summoned from Mantua and appointed musical director of St.Mark's. Opera, the new art form, achieved a breakthrough with Monteverdi's 'Orfeo'. Monteverdi died in Venice in 1643.

1619: *State Bank.*

1623: Birth of the Venetian composer Antonio Cesti.

from 1631: *Santa Maria della Salute* was built to designs by B.Longhena.

1637: *San Cassiano,* the first opera house in the world, was opened in Venice.

1660: *Ca' Rezzonico* was begun by Longhena.

1667: 'Arcadia in Brenta', a collection of novellas by the Venetian poet Giovanni Sagredo, was published in Venice.

1669: Birth of Antonio Vivaldi in Venice. He later became a priest, a virtuoso violinist and a world-famous composer.

1675: Birth of Rosalba Carriera, the portrait painter.

1676: B.Longhena began building the *Palazzo Pesaro.*

1678: The *S.Giovanni Crisostomo,* the seventh opera house in Venice, was opened.

1682: Birth of Giambattista Piazzetta, who became the pioneer of Venetian rococo painting.

1696: Birth of Giambattista Tiepolo, that master of Venetian painting, who later also worked in Germany and Spain. Giorgio Massari, the Venetian architect, was born the same year.

1697: This is the year in which Antonio Canaletto was born.

18C: Venice: the uncrowned capital of rococo art.

1702: The year in which Pietro Longhi was born.

1707: Birth in Venice of Goldoni, who later became a lawyer and a famous writer of comedies. His 'commedia nuova' was his answer to the 'commedia dell'arte', the extempore comedy which was particularly popular in Venice.

1712: Birth of Francesco Guardi. Like

Canaletto, he later concentrated on painting enchanting Venetian vedute.

1720: Birth of Carlo Gozzi, the poet who attacked Goldoni's efforts at reform and wrote very successful fairy-tale comedies.

1720: Printing of 'Il teatro alla moda', the work by Benedetto Marcello, the Venetian politician and musicologist.

1723: St.Mark's Square was paved.

1724: Birth of the painter Gian Domenico Tiepolo, a son of Giambattista.

1725: Birth of Giacomo Girolamo Casanova in Venice. He later became world famous as a philosopher, idler, gallant, and poet.

1757: Wall painting by Giambattista Tiepolo in the *Palazzo Labia.*

1758: Frescos by Giambattista Tiepolo in the *Ca' Rezzonico.*

1790–2: Antonio Selva built the *Teatro la Fenice.*

1807: Venice became a bishopric.

1810: St.Mark's Square altered by Napoleon. The granaries and San Geminiano were razed. The *Ala Nuovissima* (Napoleonica) was built opposite the Basilica, to complete St.Mark's Square.

1818: The patriarch of Venice was given authority over the bishoprics of Caorle and

Triptych by Jacobello Alberegno, Accademia

Torcello.

1826: The *university* was founded in the Palazzo Foscari.

1846: *Santa Lucia,* one of Palladio's churches, was torn down to make room for the railway bridge from the mainland.

1854: The architect Nevelli designed the *Accademia Bridge.*

1858: The Scalzi Bridge near the railway station was built by Nevelli.

1875: Various dilapidated towers and churches, including *San Paternian,* were pulled down.

1882: Gian Francesco Malipiero, the Italian composer, was born in Venice.

1882: The *Stucky mill* was built on Giudecca.

1891: A plan to preserve the city was drawn up.

1895: The *Biennale,* an international exhibition of modern art, was founded. Since then it has been held in the exhibition halls of the Giardini Pubblici every two years.

1902: The campanile of S.Marco collapsed.

1903–12: The 12C campanile was rebuilt.

1907: Construction of the neo-Gothic *fish market.*

1912: Thomas Mann wrote the novella 'Death in Venice', which captures the city's atmosphere.

1916: Venice was bombed by Austria, *Santa Maria Formosa* being one of the buildings to be damaged.

1920: Bruno Maderna, the Italian composer and conductor, was born in Venice.

1924: Birth in Venice of Luigi Nono, the Italian composer.

1932: The international *film festivals* were established. They are held annually on the Lido.

1951: The *Centro Internazionale delle Arti e del Costume* was founded in the Palazzo Grassi.

1951: Stravinsky's 'The Rake's Progress', produced by the composer, had its world première in Venice.

1954: World première in Venice of Benjamin Britten's 'The Turn of the Screw'. The first Italian performances of Alban Berg's 'Lulu' and of Gershwin's 'Porgy and Bess' were also given in Venice.

1969: Albino Luciano (who became Pope John Paul I in 1978) was appointed archbishop in Venice.

1973: Benjamin Britten's opera 'Death in Venice' was given its first performance in Aldeburgh.

III. One day in Venice

The best time to visit Venice is in the spring or autumn, but one should if possible avoid going on 25 April (Liberation Day), at Easter or on 1 May, because of the congestion in the city.

Car-drivers will normally end up in one of the enormous garages on the Piazzale Roma. From here, porters, gondolieri and taxi drivers offer their services. But the much more reasonably priced municipal 'vaporetti' (boats plying the canals and operating to a timetable, like buses) are only a few steps away.

If you only have a day in Venice, the best thing to do is to take a vaporetto on Line 1 heading for S.Marco along the Grand Canal, with its splendid backdrop of palazzi and churches.

Map: Odd numbers in squares refer to buildings on the left bank, even numbers to those on the right bank (beginning at S.Lucia railway station) (pp. 75 ff). Numbers in circles refer to churches (pp. 39 ff.).

Along the Grand Canal to St.Mark's Square
Buildings which can be seen during the ride from the Piazzale Roma to S.Marco are marked on the map on the facing page. The façade of the Scalzi church appears on the left immediately after the railway station. The Fondaco dei Turchi follows on the right, opposite San Marcuola, followed by the Palazzo Vendramin Calergi (9) on the left, the façade of San Staè (8) and of the Palazzo Ca' Pesaro (22) on the right and the splendid Ca' d'Oro (25) which then follows on the left. Shortly afterwards the boat passes under the Rialto. The beauty of the façades of the palazzi makes one overlook the advanced state of decay which many have fallen into. Diagonally opposite Palazzo Loredan and Palazzo Farsetti, after which comes the Palazzo Grimani, there follows the San Silvestro landing stage on the right, and the S.Angelo landing stage on the left. The S.Tomà halt on the right is next, opposite the Palazzi Mocenigo (69). Immediately after the broad Rio Nuovo on the right, which the taxi drivers like to use as

Palaces on the Canal Grande

Having reached St.Mark's, the visitor is spoilt for choice as regards buildings to visit and routes to follow but here, as a guide, are six suggestions.

1

A visit to the Basilica of St.Mark and then a guided tour of the Doges' Palace; strenuous but highly informative and rich in history.

2

Turn to the left and walk through the Ala Napoleonica, heading west across the Frezzeria, a narrow street, stopping here and there to shop and passing by San Moisè. Turn right off the Calle Larga 22. Marzo and visit the Teatro la Fenice. There are some pleasant restaurants in this area.

3

Cross the Piazzetta Leoncini N. of the Basilica and walk to S.Maria Formosa. Further on in the same direction are the magnificent Gothic Zanipolo (church of SS.Giovanni e Paolo) and the Scuola Grande di S.Marco, with Verrochio's equestrian statue of Colleoni standing outside it.

4

If your main interest is the old historic trading centre follow the signposts (arrows on the walls of buildings) from St.Mark's Square through the innumerable alleyways to the Rialto and possibly also the Fondaco dei Tedeschi. A considerable volume of business is still done in this area, especially in the shops on the bridge. There are eating-places all over Venice: expensive, high-class, distinguished restaurants, and low-priced little trattorie and osterie where it is often possible to eat well from a varied selection of dishes.

5

Atmospheric trips by gondola within the city start from a number of places. The trip from the Campo San Moisè along the Rio dei Barcaroli can be recommended.

6

To visit the islands of the lagoon from S.Marco take a Line 5 vaporetto for the Arsenale and to go via the Fondamenta Nuova to Murano, the glassblowers' island, then take a Line 12 to Burano, whose inhabitants are fishermen and the world's most skilled embroiderers and lace-makers. There are excellent restaurants on Burano. If time permits, continue to Torcello on Line 12. This is one of the most beautiful and mysterious of the islands, lonely and deserted when the tourists have gone, covered with brushwood and overrun with macchia. Two wonderful churches, which pre-date the foundation of present day Venice, are to be found only a few yards from the shore. Return by Line 12 to the Fondamenta Nuova, and from there to the Piazzale Roma by Line 5.

a short cut from the station, comes the Palazzo Foscari (66), and then the campanile of S.Samuele on the left, while on the right, after the Palazzo Nani, there follows the Ca'Rezzonico (72). Ca' is an abbreviation for Casa (house); but Casa is an understatement to say the least where these gorgeous buildings are concerned. There now follows the Accademia landing stage on the right. After the S.Maria del Giglio halt on the left, the boat heads towards Santa Maria della Salute (38), an impressive baroque church. S.Giorgio Maggiore comes into view in the background, while on the left, after the short stretch of greenery in the Giardinetti Reali, there follows S.Marco, with the splendid Piazzetta. The newcomer is greeted by the two historic columns crowned by S.Teodoro and S.Marco, the city's patron Saints. On the right is the Doges' Palace, and behind it St.Mark's Basilica.

The landing stage is a little further to the E., on the Riva degli Schiavoni. To double back to the Basilica cross the Ponte della Paglia with its many steps (the famous Ponte dei Sospiri, the Bridge of Sighs, is to be seen in the background), pass the Doges' Palace and then turn into the Piazzetta and walk the length of the W. façade of the Palace. This brings you to the Basilica of St. Mark, with the campanile to the left and the clock tower opposite. Between the two, in front of the façade of the Basilica, is St. Mark's Square, flanked by the long range of buildings of the Procuratie Nuove and Procuratie Vecchie and closed by the Ala Napoleonica.

The full beauty of the famous Square, together with its sense of theatre, are best enjoyed from a table outside the famous Caffè Florian, sipping tea or an espresso and gazing at the Basilica and Square with its countless people. The components of the Square have been gathered from all over the world, but have been combined into a unique, magnificent and perfect work of art.

There are many ways of spending a day in Venice. The tourist who does not venture out of St. Mark's Square will be able while there to sense what Venice is, but he should know that this city has many faces, and that one day in Venice can only display a single facet of a jewel.

IV. Piazza and Piazzetta

The Venetians refer to their famous St. Mark's Square simply as the 'Piazza' (in English: 'square') and 'Europe's drawing room', as Napoleon referred to it, is indeed amongst the world's most beautiful squares. It is the only square in Venice to be called a 'piazza', all the others being known as 'campi'. To reach it from the Canal Grande one has first to cross the Piazzetta (little square), which is flanked by the Doges' Palace and the Old Library.

The two columns: The visitor arriving by boat is greeted from afar by the two columns in the Piazzetta which bear the symbols of Venice. These are St. Theodore, who is the church's former patron Saint, and the lion of St. Mark. Legend relates that these enormous granite columns were brought by ship from the Orient to Venice in 1172 and were set up there as symbols of power. The figures on the columns are also from the Orient. The bronze lion probably originates from 4C China. Its wings and book were added later. The figure of St. Theodore was a Roman marble statue dating from the period of Hadrian. In the Middle Ages, this was the spot where the power of the city of Venice and the cruelty with which it was ruled were demonstrated. Criminals were executed between the two columns

St. Mark's Square

including the Doge Marino Falier who was accused of subversion. Not the least reason for the power of Venice was the harshness and ruthlessness of its politics.

Biblioteca Marciana (also known as Libreria Vecchia). In 1175, the Piazzetta, which until then had been a harbour basin, was filled in and laid out as a square. Work began on the library opposite the Doges' Palace in 1537 under the supervision of Jacopo Sansovino. The ceiling fell down in 1545; but the library was completed in 1554, having an arcaded lower storey and an enclosed upper storey with columns and arches. In 1582–8, Scamozzi widened and lengthened the building, including the arcades, as far as the Molo. Shops and a café are now to be found under the arcades, and behind the library is the Museo Archeologico. The library owes its origins to a valuable collection bequeathed by Cardinal Bessarione to the Republic in 1468. Today the library's contents are very extensive (manuscripts, early printed books with miniatures from 1477 onwards). It is open to the public from 9 a.m. to 7 p.m. during the week, and also on Saturday mornings, but it is closed on Sundays. The splendid public rooms on the upper storey are entered through a portal (1553/4, by A.Vittoria and L.Rubini) flanked by two caryatids above a fine staircase with paintings from the 2nd half of the 16C. There is a ceiling painting by Titian in the vestibule, which is by Scamozzi. Recessed medallions painted by famous Venetian artists occupy the ceiling. The wall paintings, including some portraits of philosophers, are by Jacopo Tintoretto.

Zecca: The façade of the former State mint faces the lagoon. It was begun by Sansovino in 1537 and a third storey was added in *c.* 1570. In 1870 it ceased to be used as a mint and since 1905 part of the *Biblioteca Marciana* has been housed here.

St.Mark's Square: The Piazzetta opens into the *Piazza S.Marco*, St.Mark's Square proper. Together the Piazza and Piazzetta form an L and at first sight the Piazza appears rectangular. However, it is actually trapezoid, being broader at the end with the magnificent Basilica façade (270 ft. against the 185 ft. of the Ala Napoleonica; the sides measure 575 ft.). There was originally a monastery garden on this site. A square was laid out in the 13C, using a layer of brick paving which was continually renovated by adding new layers of bricks.

Campanile and Loggetta: The massive free-standing campanile rises on the left, opposite the entrance to the Doges' Palace. It was built in the late 12C on the foundations of an early-medieval 9C structure. The belfry and spire are early-16C and the Archangel Gabriel at the top dates from 1517. 310 ft. in height, the tower fell down in 1902, but was faithfully rebuilt in 1903–12. The campanile acts as a kind of focal point to the Piazza and the Piazzetta, and this was emphasized when the multicoloured marble Loggetta di S.Marco was built to the E. at its base by Sansovino in 1537–40. The Loggetta was also rebuilt in 1912. It is decorated with figures and reliefs by G.Lombardi, D.Cattaneo and T.Minio, while the four bronze statues in niches are by Sansovino, as is the terracotta group with the Virgin Mary and St.John in the interior.

Three *flagpoles*, which used to fly the flags of the subject kingdoms of Cyprus, Candia and Morea, stand in front of the W. façade of the Basilica. Their bronze bases were cast by A.Leopardi in 1505. Before the S. façade of the basilica there are two *marble pillars* from Constantinople (*c.* 6C). The *Pietra di bando*, the stump of a porphyry column taken from Acre, stands in front of the SW corner of St.Mark's Basilica. New laws were proclaimed from this column.

Clock Tower (Torre dell'Orologio): The famous clock tower faces the NW corner of St.Mark's Basilica. The *Merceria*, Venice's best-known shopping street, is entered through the broad central arch at the base of the tower. The clock tower is a Renaissance building and on its terrace two bronze giants strike the hours.

Old library with campanile ▷

These were cast by P.Savini in 1497.

Ala Napoleonica: St. Mark's Square is flanked by the two long Procuratie and at the end opposite the Basilica it is closed by the *Ala Napoleonica* (Napoleonic Wing). The church of *S. Geminiano,* built in 1098 and rebuilt by Sansovino in 1557, stood on this site but it was pulled down in 1807 at Napoleon's command. The present classical structure, which has two storeys and an attic and is also known as the *Ala Nuovissima,* was built in its stead. It houses the entrance to the *Museo Civico Correr,* which occupies the Procuratie Nuove, and the ballroom on the first floor is now used for public events.

Procuratie Vecchie: If you look towards St.Mark's Basilica from the Ala Napoleonica the building on your left which runs along the full length of the Piazza is the *Procuratie Vecchie* (Old Procurators' Office). Today the famous Caffè Quadri is on the ground floor. Next to it there have always been shops. Private and public offices are housed on the upper storeys. From the very earliest times, the procurators of S.Marco were responsible for maintaining and administering the Doge's chapel. Their office and responsibilities were later extended to include the administration of the entire Republic, so that a kind of atrium for the procurators was built as early as *c.* 1172 on the site of today's Old Procurators' Office. One of the tasks given to the procurators was that of supervising all public building projects. They retained their own architect, known as a 'Proto'. Work on the Procuratie Vecchie was begun in *c.* 1500. After a fire in 1512, the work was continued by Bartolomeo Bon and Gugliemo Grigi. It was completed by Sansovino in 1532.

Procuratie Nuove: The *New Procurator's Offices* were begun in 1583 under the supervision of V.Scamozzi. They stand opposite the Procuratie Vecchie, on the site of an earlier medieval building. Completed by B.Longhena in *c.* 1640, they originally also housed the procurators. Beginning in 1918, alterations were made to the interior of the upper storeys and today they house the *Museo Civico Correr.* Like the Procuratie Vecchie, there have always been shops on the ground floor and the famous *Caffè Florian,* which was opened in 1720 and is thought to be the oldest café in Italy, is to be found here.

Domes of San Marco

V. Churches in Venice: Map: p. 32

St.Mark's Basilica/Basilica di S.Marco:

History: St.Mark's, probably the richest church in the whole of the West, stands on the site of the ancient *palace chapel* dedicated to St.Theodore, the original patron saint of Venice. Two sailors brought the relics of St.Mark the Evangelist from Alexandria to Venice in 828/9. In 836 these relics were interred in a church founded especially for the purpose and after this original church had been destroyed, the Doge Pietro Orseolo I ordered a second one to be built in 976. All that remains of this today are the small walled-up crypt below the crossing, and some fragments in the masonry. The cruciform, domed structure of the church and narthex evidently derive from the building of 836, and the core of this design still survives. The present St.Mark's Basilica was begun under the Doge Domenico Contarini in the 2nd half of the 11C and the major sections of this building still survive. It was completed by 1094. Western Romanesque elements, such as the hall-shaped crypt below the sanctuary, were added to the Byzantine model, and an original Vene-tian architectural style evolved. The five domes arranged in a cross were still fairly flat in this two-storeyed building. A new phase of building began in 1204. The interior was decorated with mosaics throughout. The colonnaded W. façade was built, and a new narthex to the N. The height of the domes was raised to good effect by the addition of exterior domes. The façades of the N. narthex and the S. end of the W. narthex were added to in the 13&14C. The *baptistery* (31) also dates from this period and so do the bronze doors on the W. front, the Gothic tracery windows on the W. and N. façades, and the Cappella di S.Isidoro (39). A new phase began in 1385 which saw the addition of a late Gothic crown to the clerestory walls, with figures in tabernacles and statues on the points of the gables. The new sacristy (36) and the Cappella di S.Teodoro were built in the late 15C, while the Cappella Zen (30) is early 16C. **The present structure: W. façade** (facing St.Mark's Square): The lower storey is formed by five *portals* (1–5) with arches supported by columns, capitals some of which are Byzantine, and rectangular doorways. Between these there are areas of wall with 13C Veneto-Byzantine reliefs.

San Marco

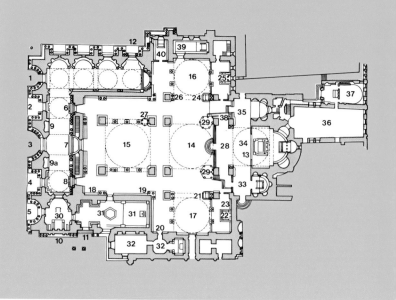

St.Mark's Basilica, Venice: 1 to 5 Portals 6 Porta di S.Pietro 7 Main portal 8 Porta di S.Clemente 9 and 9 a Tomb of Doge Vitale Michièl and his wife (9a) 10 arch with columns to the Zen chapel 11 Portal with columns leading to baptistery 12 Porta dei Fiori 13 Choir dome 14 Ascension dome 15 Pentecost dome 16 St.John's dome 17 St.Leonard's dome 18 Deesis, Byzantine relief, 11C 19 Madonna del Bacio, devotional relief, 12C 20 Man of Sorrows, c. 1400 21 St.James altar, wall altar, 15C 22 Altar of the Sacrament (17C) with modern baldacchino in the chapel of the sacrament 23 Byzantine icon in relief (Virgin Mary, 13C) 24 St.Paul altar, the counterpart to the St.James altar (21), 15C; statue of St.Peter, 16C 25 Virgin Mary altar, 1617, with Byzantine devo-

tional image, c. 10C; next to it are 3 relief icons, 13C, 9C and 17C 26 Madonna dello Schioppo, large, very beautiful Veneto-Byzantine relief icon, 13C 27 Annunciation altar, 14C; statues, 13C; painted crucifix, brought from Constantinople in 1205; said to have miraculous properties 28 Iconostasis (1394-1404) by Jacobello and Pierpaolo dalle Masegne and their studio; a large bronze crucifix by Jacopo di Marco Bennato above the steps to the sanctuary 29 Early-14C pulpits built with spoils 30 Cappella Zen 31 Baptistery 32 Treasure chamber 33 Cappella di S.Clemente 34 Sanctuary 35 Cappella di S.Pietro 36 Sacristy 37 Cappella S.Teodoro 38 Steps to crypt 39 Cappella di S.Isidoro 40 Cappella dei Mascoli

The 1st portal (1), the Porta di S.Alippio, has 13C reliefs above the portal and the oldest surviving mosaic on the façade, which dates from c. 1265 and depicts the Translation of the Body of St.Mark. The 2nd portal (2) is 14C, with a traceried window and bronze door dating from 1300. The decoration above the door is from the 2nd quarter of the 13C; the mosaic showing St.Mark's relics being transferred dates from 1728. In the upper tympanum of the

3rd portal (3) there is an enormous mosaic from 1836 showing Christ in Judgement. 13C bands of relief on the archivolts are reminiscent of French portal sculpture. 4th portal (4): Bronze door and traceried window as in the 2nd portal (above this is a mosaic from 1660, showing St.Mark's relics being venerated). 5th portal (5): Reduced in size, because of the Cappella Zen. The door is blocked off. Fine inlay work and carving, no later than the 11C.

San Marco, façade detail

Above this is a mosaic, *c.* 1660, showing St.Mark's relics being removed from Alexandria. Mosaics (1616/17) by A.Gaetano occupy the tympana on the façade's upper storey, which rises from a terrace (it can be reached by stairs to the right and left of the main portal [7]). In the centre of the upper storey is a large window with reliefs on the archivolt, and above this is the enormous statue of St.Mark offering a blessing (*c.* 1419), flanked by four statues on the points of the other gables (16C). There are six figures in tabernacles and below these there are four water-carriers (*c.* 1400) between the arches. Four massive *bronze horses* (copies) stand on the terrace above the central portal, below the figure of St.Mark. The originals dating from the time of the Roman Empire were taken to Constantinople in the 4C, shipped from the hippodrome in Constantinople to Venice in 1204, carried off to Paris by Napoleon in 1797, and finally installed again on St.Mark's Basilica in 1815 (they

are now housed in a room in the Museo Marciano (q.v.) behind the terrace).

S. façade (its first section faces the Piazzetta, and its second section runs alongside the Doges' Palace): It is essentially similar in arrangement to the W. façade. The wall of the second section, which projects further forward because of the Tesoro (32), is encrusted with old stone fragments and it is pierced at ground-floor level by a 14C double-arched window. Until the Capella Zen was built, the first arch (10) contained an entrance, now blocked, leading into the W. narthex. The old portal and the 13C tympanum mosaic may still be seen inside the chapel. The next arch (11), which has a doorway and a 14C traceried window, leads into the ante-room of the baptistery, and beside this on the right is a Gothic double-arched window. Like the W. façade, the upper storey of the S. façade has a terrace, late Gothic gables crowned with statues, and figures in tabernacles.

N. façade (on the Piazza dei Leoncini): Like the W. façade, this has an arcaded lower storey surmounted by a terrace and the clerestory, with statues on the gables and figures in tabernacles. A rectangular section adjoins the N. transept, and this forms the outer wall of the Mascoli chapel (40), the Cappella di S.Isidoro and, to the E., abuts the Patriarch's Palace. Again the first part of the lower storey is covered with reliefs, some are Byzantine in origin. The Porta dei Fiori (12) is from the 3rd quarter of the 13C. The archivolts are carved, and there are large icons in relief above the Porta and the adjoining transept wall.

Narthex: The W. and N. narthexes form a single unit but they were built at different times, the W. one dating from the 11C, the N. one from the 13C. In the W. narthex, the pairs of marble columns in front of the inner façade, and the vaulted ceiling (with pendentive domes and tunnel vaults), were very likely built at a later date (probably 13C). The inlaid floor of the W. narthex might be late 11C, while that of the N. one is perhaps 13C. The bronze leaves (1st half of 12C) of the main portal are inlaid with silver and are based on the Byzantine door-leaves of the Porta di S.Clemente (8). The angels to the right and left of the portal are 12C. The mid-16C St.Mark in the vault is by the brothers F. and V.Zuccato, as are the mosaics (also mid-16C) in the pozzo (light shaft). A mosaic (1532) by Zuccato is above the Porta di S.Clemente. To its right is the door of the Cappella Zen. The impression of solemn wealth created by the narthexes is the result of the mosaics which completely cover the vaults; a late Romanesque cycle of mosaics (13C) on a gold background begins at the S. end. The tombs of the Doge Vitale Michièl and his wife Felicità (9), dating from *c.* 1100, are also in the W. narthex. In the N. narthex there are further monuments from the 13–15C, some with spoils from early Christian sarcophagi.

Interior: The inside of the church makes a sombre impression, despite the 16 small round-arched windows in the dome vaults, the large round window in the S. transept, and the W. windows. The interior appears to be divided into a nave and two aisles because of the arcades between the pillars. The gallery running above these arcades dates from the 11C. The pavement, which is inlaid with mosaics, is uneven. The main attraction of the church, like the narthex, is its *mosaics,* which form the largest area of mosaics in the world, covering a total of 43,000 sq.ft. They date mainly from between the 11C and 14C, and were restored in various places from the 15C onwards. Cycles of mosaics, seen against an uninterrupted gold background, cover the entire upper part of the church, the five domes, and all the tunnel vaults in between (the best cycle is that depicting the story of Christ). Here, the dome in the choir (13) depicts Christ blessing, the Dome of the Ascension shows the Risen Christ (*c.* 1200), and the Dome of the Pentecost (15) has the twelve Apostles enthroned with the Holy Ghost (*c.* 1150). The Dome of St.John (16) is covered with scenes from the lives of the Evangelists (13C), while the Dome of St.Leonard (17) displays four Saints (13&17C). Other splendid features include the *iconostasis* (28) and the *Pala d'Oro* in the sanctuary (34; q.v.). The fine *iconostasis* (1394–1404), by Jacobello and Pierpaolo dalle Masegne and their workshop, stands on top of the front wall of the crypt. It consists of a row of columns supporting a series of splendid late Gothic marble statues and, in the centre, a large bronze crucifix by Jacopo di Marco Bennato, beneath which a flight of steps leads up to the sanctuary. Further details of these features are given on the ground plan and the associated text.

Cappella Zen (30): In 1503/4–15, an existing part of the narthex and a portal was converted into today's chapel (restored in 1604) in order to house the tomb of Cardinal Giambattista Zen, the nephew of the Venetian Pope Paul II. The monument (early-16C) has a large recumbent figure of the Cardinal, and six allegories. The statues of the altar and the bronze baldacchino are by Paolo Savini and Pietro Campagnato to designs by A.Lombardi, who was also responsible for the figure of

San Marco ▷

the Virgin Mary (1515). The two lions beside the altar are 13C, and so are the icons in relief on the right-hand wall and the standing figure of the Virgin Mary to the left of the altar.

Baptistery/Cappella di S.Giovanni (31): Became a baptistery in 1312–20. Fine mosaics (mid-14C). Hexagonal font, probably designed by J.Sansovino in *c.* 1545 and made by T.Minio and D.da Firenze, with eight pictorial reliefs on the bronze cover. The bronze figure of the Baptist is by Segala (1565). **Tesoro/ Treasury (32):** Some sections of the thick walls of the Tesoro date from the 1st millennium AD and were probably part of a corner tower of the Doges' Palace. The church treasure has been kept here since 1209. The structure was rebuilt and strengthened in the 15C. Despite theft and the melting-down of some objects in 1797, the treasury still houses over 300 precious items and, culturally, it is one of the most important collections of treasure in the West. It is divided into three rooms: the anti-tesoro, the sanctuary (with 110 reliquaries in 11 niches), and the tesoro proper. The Byzantine works seized when Constantinople was taken form a particularly fine group amongst the relics, garments, pieces in gold, glasses, icons in relief and other works of art, including the so-called *throne of St.Mark,* an Alexandrian marble reliquary (6C or 7C).

Cappella di S.Clemente (33): This was originally directly connected to the Doges' Palace and was reserved for the Doges alone. The iconostasis (14C), with its columns, is from dalle Masegne's workshop. A very fine 12C mosaic in the apse. The altar is adorned by various 15&16C figures.

Sanctuary (34): The old pews from the area in front of the choir and some tapestries (1551) are now in the Museo Marciano and the Museo Correr. But the *singing galleries* by J.Sansovino are still in position on either side. The gallery on the left dates from 1537, that on the right from 1541–4. Late Gothic tabernacles, and wall retables containing relics, the work of the dalle Masegne workshop, are borne by the pillars on both sides. Four statues of Evangelists (mid-16C, by Sansovino) stand on the late Gothic colonnaded balustrades of coloured marble. The four statues of the Fathers of the Church (on the left) were added by Gabriele Orlandini and B.Nicolini in 1614. The high altar was rebuilt in 1834–6, using old fragments.

San Marco, portal tympanum mosaics

The bronze candlesticks are 16C, while the baldacchino with its statues and columns decorated with images dates from the 13C. However, the rear pair of columns may in fact be from 5C or 6C Byzantium. The famous *Pala d'Oro*, an enormous golden altarpiece covered with carved figures and precious stones, was begun in 976 and completed in 1345 (Byzantine and Venetian enamelled gold). It stands on a marble pedestal behind the high altar. In the central niche of the apse there is a 16C tabernacle with turned columns. On the door of the tabernacle is a bronze relief by Sansovino. The bronze door in the apse wall, leading to the sacristy, is a late work by the same artist.

Cappella di S.Pietro (35): Contains an iconostasis (*c.* 1397) from the Dalle Masegne workshop.

Sacristy (36): A broad Renaissance room (1471), with 16C mosaics in the vault and sumptuous inlaid cupboards (15&16C). The sacristy is adjoined by two rooms, the *Sagrestia Capitolare* (with a Nativity by G.B. Tiepolo on the altar) and the *Antisagrestia*. There then follows the *Cappella S.Teodoro* (37), built in 1486 as a new chapel for the Doges.

Crypt (38): The 11C hall crypt is below the sanctuary, of the Cappella di S.Pietro and the Cappella di S.Clemente (the old 10C crypt, now walled up, is to the W. of this crypt).

Cappella di S.Isidoro (39): The relics of St.Isidore were brought from Chios to Venice in 1125. This richly decorated chapel was built in 1354–5 to house them.

Cappella dei Mascoli/Cappella Nova (40): Built in 1430, and dedicated since 1618 to the brotherhood of unmarried men. The locked door to the Piazzetta dei Leoncini is from the 14C, as are the sculptures of the altar and the mosaics.

Museo Marciano: The museum is housed above the narthexes and displays items from the church treasure, including the four original bronze horses.

Other churches: Map: p. 32
Most of Venice's many churches are either artistically important or else simply beautiful. Only the main ones are described below, in as much detail as possible.

(1) **S.Alvise** (in the extreme N. of the city, by the Rio S.Alvise): Founded in 1388, it was originally a convent church from 1388. After the 17C rebuilding, only the

San Marco, portal tympanum detail

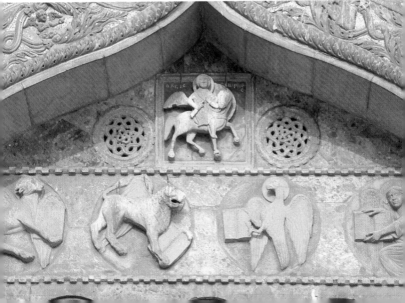

façade, parts of the sanctuary, and the campanile survived. The nuns' gallery (barco) and two early works by Tiepolo (Crown of Thorns and Scourging) are to be seen on the long right-hand side. 'Christ on the Road to Calvary' is on the right wall of the sanctuary.

(2) **SS.Apostoli** (Campo SS.Apostoli): Parish church founded in the 9C and rebuilt several times. Painting of a guardian angel by F.Maffei (2nd half of 17C) on the altar in the left side-choir. Remains of frescos (1300) in the right side-choir. The *Cappella Corner* (Venetian early Renaissance), with an altarpiece by G.B. Tiepolo depicting the communion of St.Lucy, was added in the late 15C. Caterina Cornaro (d. 1510), the queen of Cyprus, was originally buried here.

(3) **S.Bartolomeo** (SE of the Rialto): Founded in the 12C as a private church for German merchants. Rebuilt with a nave and two aisles in the 18C. It contains some panel paintings which are masterpieces of the Venetian early Renaissance and include four works by Sebastiano del Piombo (1507–9, originally the organ doors).

(4) **S.Benedetto** (further S., towards the Grand Canal): Built in 1685. A St.Sebastian by B.Strozzi, a masterpiece of the Venetian baroque, is at the 2nd side altar on the right, and at the 1st side altar on the left there is an altarpiece by Tiepolo.

(5) **Carmini/S.Maria del Carmelo** (in the SW of the city, near the Rio di S.Barnaba): 13&14C. Choir, façade and interior altered in the 16C. The *rich contents* of this colonnaded basilica with a nave and two aisles date from this period: late-16C painting in the clerestory. In the right aisle: a medieval bronze relief of the Lamentation by Francesco di Giorgio Martini; statues by G.Campagna and Antonio Corradini, 1721; fine carved 16C organs, with paintings by Marco Vincentino and A.Schiavone. In the left side aisle: a panel painting by L.Lotto (*c.* 1523); 15C sacristy; 16C cloister.

(6) **S.Cassiano:** Originally 10C, it was enlarged into a hall church with a nave and two aisles in the early 17C. The 15C campanile is notable. Dominated inside by the two rows of columns. Particular attention should be paid to the decoration. The *ceiling paintings* are by Constantin Cedini.

San Marco, Pala d'Oro

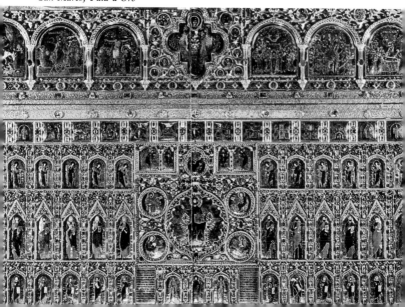

There is a *panel painting* by Rocco Marconi at the 1st side altar on the right. The *Visitation* at the altar of the right-hand choir chapel is by Leandro Bassano. In the sanctuary there are three paintings by Jacopo Tintoretto: 'Resurrection' above the high altar; 'Crucifixion' on the left (*c.*1637); 'Christ in Limbo' on the right.

(7) **S.Caterina** (in the N. of the city): Originally a 9C convent church, rebuilt several times. 15C nuns' gallery. At the high altar: a copy of a Veronese, and paintings by Tintoretto of the legend of St.Catherine.

(8) **S.Eustachio/S.Staè** (Grand Canal): A fine façade by Domenico Rossi (1709). Inside fine paintings by Tiepolo (St.Bartholomew), G.A. Pellegrini (St.Andrew), and G.B. Piazzetta (St.James).

(9) **S.Fantin** (near St.Mark's Square, opposite the Teatro La Fenice). A Renaissance church dating from 1507. Sanctuary (1564) to a design by J.Sansovino. Fine contents, including the monument to V.Dandolo (*c.* 1517) above the sacristy door, and a Romanesque font.

(10) **S.Felice** (Strada Nuova): Founded in the 10C, it was rebuilt as a Renaissance church; restored in 1957. The altarpiece at the right side altar is an early Tintoretto (1547).

(11) **S.Francesco della Vigna** (in the E. of the city): A monumental church begun in 1534 to a design by J.Sansovino and completed when Palladio finished the façade in 1572. On the altar in the right transept is a panel painting (1450–60) of the Virgin Mary enthroned, the work of Antonio da Negroponte. The *Cappella Giustinian,* with fine sculptures (*c.* 1500) and a retable (also *c.* 1500), is next to the left-hand choir chapel. The fifth chapel in the left aisle has an altarpiece (1562) by P.Veronese, while the third chapel has ceiling paintings by G.B. Tiepolo.
Cloisters (15C) and chapels. The *Cappella Santa,* by the transept, has a painting by G.Bellini (1507).

(12) **Frari/S.Maria Gloriosa dei Frari** (to the W. of the Grand Canal): This vaulted colonnaded basilica with a nave and two aisles is popularly referred to simply as 'I Frari' (Franciscan brothers). Together with SS.Giovanni e Paolo, it is

San Marco, Pala d'Oro, detail

the finest of Venice's late Gothic churches. It is an impressive brick structure with a very tall transept having only one aisle, seven choir chapels (a large central one, flanked by three smaller chapels on each side), a tripartite, almost plain façade (having a single portal with 15C statues of the Virgin Mary, St.Francis and Christ; round windows; three Gothic pinnacles), and the second highest campanile in the city after San Marco.

The Franciscans were given a plot of land by the Doge Jacopo Tiepolo prior to 1250. On it they built the original church, completing it in *c.* 1338. But this was completely demolished in 1415.

The present structure was built in several phases. The earliest part is the choir (1340), followed by the transept. The campanile dates from 1361–96. Finally, the nave (1420–43) was built on the site of the old church which was torn down in 1415. Thus, the Frari is a combination of a tall choir full of light (and a transept) from the 14C and a compact, hall-like nave from the quattrocento (15C). Besides Titian's *Assunta*, which is undoubtedly the chief attraction, the church houses such an abundance of fine altarpieces, monuments and other works, that some can only be briefly described below (the numbers in brackets refer to the ground plan). The baroque *monument to Girolamo Garzoni*, (2) who fell in battle against the Turks in 1688, is on the end wall, above the portal. The standing figure of the deceased is overlooked by a guardian angel, an unusual feature for a Venetian monument; the alternation of white and black marble is another interesting feature. To the left of this is L.Bregno's *tomb of A.Pasqualino* (3), the procurator of S.Marco who died in 1522. To the right, the *tomb of P.Bernardo* (1) who died in 1538; parts of the figures by T.Lombardo on the burial chest; and the excellent group by an unknown artist, showing Christ, St.Peter and the deceased kneeling. *St.Anthony's altar* (4), by B.Longhena, has an altarpiece by F.Rosa (1670). After this, in the 2nd bay of the right aisle, there follows the *monument to Titian* (6), who is said to have been buried here in 1576. The monument (1838–52) was built by L. and P.Zandomeneghi, who were pupils of Canova, in the manner of a triumphal arch. The reliefs in the background are reproductions of paintings by Titian: in the middle is the 'Assunta', on the right is the 'Pietà', and on the left is the copy of the paint-

San Marco, Treasury, glass bowl, 4C

ing, destroyed by fire in SS.Giovanni e Paolo in 1867, depicting the murder of Peter the Martyr, the Dominican friar, in 1252. Next to this is the *Zeno-Valier altar* (7), with paintings (Presentation in the Temple) and frescos by G.Salviati (about 1560). Only the figures from the pediment and the marble statue of St.Jerome (8) survive from the stucco reliefs of A.Vittoria's altarpiece of 1560.

Next come the *Pesaro altar* (10), two baroque monuments (11, 12), the *tomb* of the scholar *B.Brugnolo di Legnago* (13) by G.M. Mosca, and, immediately before the transept, the door (14) to the cloister. The frame of this door has a decorative terracotta frieze dating from 1420. Just round the corner in the transept is the *wall tomb of Jacopo Marcello* (15; d. 1484), the work of P.Lombardo and his workshop. The statue of the deceased, standing on the sarcophagus holding the banner of St.Mark in his hand, is accompanied by two armour bearers. The *wall tomb of Beato Pacifico Bon* (16) has interesting reliefs and a decorated base, and dates from *c.* 1435. Legend relates that Beato Pacifico designed the nave of the Frari. The wooden *equestrian monument to Paolo Savelli* (18) is the first Venetian equestrian monu-

ment to a condottiere. Dating from *c.* 1410, it has fine statuettes in the niches. In between the previous two monuments, and pierced by the round—arched doorway to the sacristy, is the two-tiered *monument to Admiral Benedetto Pesaro* (17), who died in 1503, with a statue of the deceased, by L.Bregno, standing between Neptune and Mars.

The sacristy (19) has Veronese frescos on the vault and walls. On the entrance wall is a painting, by P.Veneziano, of the Virgin Mary Enthroned. A few decades after being built, the sacristy passed to the Pesaro family, who ordered the little Pesaro choir to be built in 1488 and commissioned Giovanni Bellini to paint an altar triptych (23), the *Pesaro altar*, the central panel of which shows the Madonna seated on a raised throne in a niche, with the Christ-child standing on her thigh. In accordance with the rules of the early Renaissance, the figures are arranged in a triangle. The gilded vault above the Madonna's head symbolizes the halo customarily seen in medieval paintings. The much smaller panels at the sides depict St.Nicholas and St.Peter in a very confined space, and to the right are St.Benedict and St.Mark; only St.Benedict

Carmini church, portal

San Francesco della Vigna

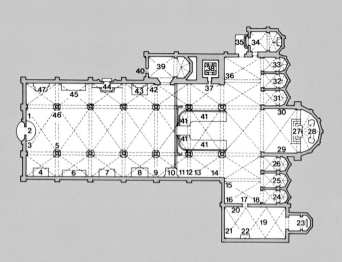

Venice, S.Maria Gloriosa dei Frari 1 Tomb of Pietro Bernardo (d. 1538), partly by T.Lombardo **2** Baroque monument of Girolamo Garzoni (d. 1688), above the portal. A rectangular door with 15C tympanum and statues leads into the church **3** Monument of Alvise Pasqualino (d. 1528), procurator of S.Marco, by L.Bregno **4** Altar by B.Longhena, 1663; altarpiece by Franc.Rosa, 1670 **5** Bronze statuette by G.Campagna, 1593 **6** Titian monument (Titian is said to have been buried here in 1576) by L. and P.Zandomeneghi, 1838-52 **7** Zeno-Valier altar with painting and frescos by G.Salviati, c. 1560 **8** Only the two gable figures and the marble statue of St.Jerome still survive from the former stuccoed retable relief, 1560, by A.Vittoria; altarpiece by G.Nogari, 1763 **9** 16C Tomb **10** Pesaro altar with altarpiece by Jac. Palma **11** and **12** Two baroque monuments **13** Monument to Benedetto Brugnolo di Legnago (d. 1505) by G.Maria Mosca **14** Door to cloister (closed) with terracotta frieze, 1420; above is an urn containing the ashes of the Count of Carmagnola, 1432 **15** Wall tomb of Jacopo Marcello (d. 1484) by Pietro Lombardi and his studio **16** Wall tomb of Beato Pacifico, who legend relates was the architect of the Frari, c. 1435 **17** Round-arched portal leading to sacristy, with monument to Benedetto Pesaro (d. 1503) **18** Wooden equestrian monument to Paolo Savelli, a Roman (d. 1405) **19** Sacristy, 1450, with Veronese paintings on vault and walls; painting (Virgin Mary Enthroned) by P.Veneziano on the entrance wall **20** 15C tabernacle containing the relics of Christ's Blood **21** Door to 14C chapterhouse with monument to

Doge Francesco Dandolo (d. 1339) **22** Relic altar, 1711 **23** Altar with triptych by G.Bellini, 1488 **24** Cappella Bernardo with panel painting by B.Vivarini, 1482; on the right, wall tomb with sculptures from 1370-80 **25** Chapel of the Sacrament with wall tomb from 1336 on the right and a mid-14C wall tomb on the left **26** Florentine chapel; national chapel of the Florentines, with altar from 1436. The central niche of the retable is the wooden figure of John the Baptist by Donatello, c. 1451, in a modern frame **28** Assunta by Titian, 1516, behind the high altar; an enormous retable flanked by a pair of Corinthian columns **29** Monumental tomb of Doge Francesco Foscari (d. 1457), built by P. and A.Bregno in 1460, with beautiful figures and coats-of-arms from 1473 **30** Monumental tomb of Doge Niccolò Tron (d. 1473) by A.Rizzo, with good statues by Rizzo **31** St.Francis chapel, with early-16C altarpiece by B.Licinio. 14C wall monument on the right. Frescos by J.Palma Giovane and Vicentino. **32** Trevisan chapel. On the right, a wall tomb to Melchiore Trevisan (d. 1500) with a statue by L.Bregno and good frescos. Mid-14C Gothic coffin on the left, with a ceiling painting fragment by Tiepolo above **33** Milanese chapel. To the left, in the pavement there is the tomb slab of Claudio Monteverdi (d. 1643). Altar, 1503, panel painting by A.Vivarini and M.Basaiti **34** Cappella Corner (1422), with holy-water stoup crowned by a marble statue of John the Baptist by J.Sansovino (1545). Wall frescos (c. 1460) and reliefs on the front of the bench are by the Mantegna circle of artists. Triptych by B.Vivarini (1474) on the altar. Colourful stained-glass (15C) **35** Fine tympanum relief, c. 1440, above the outer chapel portal **36** Wall tomb of Generosa Orsini-Zen and her son Maffeo, beneath which there are late-Gothic stalls from the 15C **37** Tympanum relief, 1390, above the door to the campanile; above this is a painting by P.Negri, 1670 **38** Campanile **39** Cappella Emiliana (S.Pietro), 1434. Marble polyptych with figures from various periods on the altar. Niche figures, c. 1440. Wall tomb on the left, 1464 **40** Entrance to the church, with statue of St.Peter in the tympanum outside, and late-15C painted crucifix on the inside **41** Marble choir screens, begun under B.Bon in 1468 and completed by Pietro Lombardo in 1475, surrounded by choir screens; choir stalls by German wood carvers under supervision of Marco Cozzi, 1468 **42** Monument to Jacopo Pesaro (d. 1547) **43** Side altar to Madonna di Ca' Pesaro, with a Titian painting; Pesaro Madonna (1519-26) **44** Mausoleum of Doge Giovanni Pesaro (d. 1659), built in 1669 to a design by B.Longhena, with figures mostly by M.Barthel **45** Monument to Antonio Canova (d. 1822) by Canova's pupils Ferrari, Rinaldi, Zandomeneghi and Bosa, 1827 **46** Two holy-water stoups with bronze figures by G.Campagna **47** Side altar of the Holy Cross, with statues by Giusto Le Court; wall tomb (1360) on the right

Frari church, portal

(who, like St.Nicholas, occupies a dominant position in the foreground) faces the onlooker. Dürer undoubtedly used these four Saints as a model when painting his 'Four Apostles' in 1526. The solemn harmony which characterizes this masterly work is intensified by the splendid frame by J.da Faenza. The articulation and forms (cf. the capitals) of this frame are repeated in detail in Bellini's painting. In the sacristy there are also a 15C tabernacle with Christ's blood (20), a Pietà above it from the same period, a richly decorated altar with a reliquary (22) dating from 1711 with large angels by A.Brustolon, and a 17C wall clock to the left of the Pesaro altar. A door (21) leads into the 14C *chapterhouse* containing the tomb of the Doge Francesco Dandolo (d. 1339).

A panel painting (Virgin Mary and Saints) by B.Vivarini (1482), and a wall tomb with sculptures (1370−80), are to be found in the *Cappella Bernardo* (24), which is the outermost of the three chapels in this transept. The *Chapel of the Sacrament* (25) has the wall tomb of Duccio degli Alberti (d. 1336). Finally, the *Chapel of the Florentines* (26) contains an altar from 1436 with a wooden John the Baptist shown preaching by Donatello (1451) in the central niche. This figure has a modern mount. Titian's *Assunta*, the finest individual

piece in the church, is to be found in the *sanctuary* behind the high altar. It is an enormous *altarpiece*, framed by an imposing pair of Corinthian columns and it broke new ground both in respect of the monumental baroque design of the altar, which dominates the space, and in certain aspects of the way in which the Virgin was depicted; innovations which were to exert an influence for several centuries. It is a very large panel painting (22 ft. 8 in. x 12 ft. 10 in.) with a semicircular upper edge and the events it depicts are divided into three zones. At the bottom are the Apostles looking upwards in excitement, amazement or disbelief; some of them are in dark shadow. On the other hand, the Apostles standing at the edges are brightly lit by the light emanating from the Assunta. In the dominant middle zone, the Virgin Mary, clad in heavenly colours, with a red garment and a flowing blue mantle, is seen ascending into Heaven, floating on clouds and framed by angels, against a background glowing with a golden colour. In the upper zone is God the Father, only half of whose figure is shown.

The monumental tomb (29) on the right wall of the choir was built by Paolo and Antonio Bregno in 1460 for the great Doge Francesco Foscari (d. 1457), who extended Venice's possessions on the mainland and who, as a patron of architecture, had the Doges' Palace enlarged and the Ca'Foscari built on the Grand Canal. His tomb is among the finest Venetian monuments from the transitional stage between late Gothic and early Renaissance. The Doge is seen recumbent on the sarcophagus underneath a canopy of fabric held by two armour bearers. He is surrounded by allegorical figures and on the front of the sarcophagus is a bust of St.Mark. At the base and at the top of the tomb there are several fine figures of Christ, the Virgin Mary and others, as well as two coats-of-arms of doges.

Opposite this is another tomb of a doge. This one (30), which is already early Renaissance in style, is divided into four tiers and and was built by A.Rizzo for Niccolò Tron who died in 1473.

Next to this there are three choir chapels in the left transept: the early-16C altar-piece in the *Chapel of St.Francis*, depicting the Virgin Mary Enthroned with Saints, is by B.Licinio; on the right-hand side there are frescos by Palma Giovane and Vicentino, and also a 14C wall tomb. The *Trevisan chapel* (32) houses the wall tomb of Melchiore Trevisan (d. 1500) with the statue in his honour by L.Bregno and some good frescos; a Gothic sarcophagus (*c*. 1350); and a fragment of a ceiling painting by Tiepolo. The third of the left-hand choir chapels is the *Chapel of the Milanese* (33), containing the tombstone of Claudio Monteverdi, the composer and director of music who died in 1643, and an altar (1503) with a panel painting of the Coronation of the Virgin Mary, begun by A.Vivarini and completed by M.Basaiti. The *Cappella Corner* (34) was added to the left transept in 1422. It is usually closed, but some of its fine decorations can be observed through the grille of the door. The holy-water stoup is crowned by a marble statue of John the Baptist (1545) by J.Sansovino. Other features include: the frescos (*c*. 1460) by the school of Mantegna, the reliefs on the front of the stalls, the altar triptych (1474) by B.Vivarini showing St.Mark between John the Baptist, St.Jerome, St.Nicholas and St.Paul,

Frari church. Right: Monument to Titian by L. and P. Zandomeneghi

and the brightly coloured stained-glass 15C windows. The excellent relief on the tympanum (35) above the outer portal of the chapel dates from *c.* 1440 and is a transitional work between the late Gothic and the Renaissance. By an anonymous but probably Venetian artist, it depicts the Madonna and Child between two angels. The wall monument to Generosa Orsini-Zen and her son Maffeo (36) is in the left transept, with the 15C late-Gothic choir stalls below it. A tympanum relief (37) dating from 1390, and above it a painting by P.Negri from 1670, are seen in the left aisle, above the door to the campanile. A pointed arch next to this leads into the *Cappella Emiliana* (39) built in 1434, where there are a mid-15C marble polyptych with figures and half-figures in niches and a wall tomb from 1464. The entrance (40) to the church is also in this chapel (on the outside, on the tympanum, is a statue of St.Peter, and on the inside is a late-15C painted crucifix).

The only marble choir surrounds (41) to survive in Venice occupy the fifth bay of the nave. They were begun under Bartolomeo Bon in 1468, and completed by Pietro Lombardo in 1475. The reliefs of Prophets are late Gothic, but the reliefs

of the Fathers of the Church clearly belong to the early Renaissance.

To the left of the monument (42) to Jacopo Pesaro (d. 1547) is the *Pesaro Madonna* (43), which was donated by the same Jacopo Pesaro. It was painted by Titian in 1519–26 shortly after the Assunta. It shows some decisive and influential iconographic innovations. For the first time, the Madonna has been moved from the centre of the picture to its right-hand edge, and portraits of Jacopo Pesaro the donor (bottom left) and some members of his family are included (Jacopo's brother Francesco is seen at the bottom right). Another new feature is the diagonal which directs one's view from the kneeling donor, past the standard-bearer (the Papal coat-of-arms on the standard, and the captive Turk, refer to Jacopo's battle against the Turks in the service of the Pope) and St.Peter, to the Madonna and Child. St.Francis, the name saint of Jacopo's brother Francesco, is also shown. Like St.Peter, he is standing close to the Madonna and is interceding with her.

The sumptuous baroque monument (44) to Doge Giovanni Pesaro (d. 1659) incorporates the side portal and was built in 1669 to a design by B.Longhena. Most of

Frari church, monument to Giovanni Pesaro (left), John the Baptist by J.Sansovino

the figures, including that of the Doge (beneath a fabric canopy), are by the German artist Melchior Barthel. To the left of it, opposite the Titian monument, is the monument to Antonio Canova, the neoclassical sculptor, who died in 1822. His heart is preserved within the pyramid. The monument is the work of his pupils Bosa, Ferrari, Rinaldi and Zandomeneghi. Canova had himself already designed an unusual monument in the Augustinian church in Vienna, and also a monument to Titian which was never actually built. Other items of interest in the church are: the *side altar of the Holy Cross* (47), with fine statues by Giusto Le Court; to the right of this is the wall tomb of Simone Dandolo (d. 1360), and also two holy-water stoups with late-16C bronze figures (46) by Girolamo Campagna.

The *former Franciscan monastery* attached to the Frari encloses two 16C cloisters. Today the *State archive* (Archivo di Stato) is housed here, with imperial documents, Papal Bulls, letters written by Doges, autographs, Senate files and other historical documents.

(13) **S.Geremia** (in the N. of Venice, on the Grand Canal): A domed church built by Corbellini in 1753. The relics of *St.Lucy*, which many visitors come to see, are housed here. They were transferred from Palladio's S.Lucia, which was pulled down in the 19C when the railway was built. There is a memorial tablet in the paving of the railway station forecourt.

(14) **Gesuati/S.Maria del Rosario** (on the Canale della Giudecca): Built by the Dominicans in 1726–36, it stands on the spit of land at the end of which S.Maria della Salute is situated. S.Maria del Rosario has a massive and beautifully articulated façade, a bright interior with an interesting dome, and fine paintings: altarpieces by Piazzetta, Ricci, Tintoretto and Tiepolo; the latter also frescoed the ceiling.

(15) **Gesuiti/S.Maria Assunta** (in the N. of the city, near the landing stage for boats from Murano): The Crociferi were active on this site from 1200 onwards but a small

oratory, decorated in the late 16C, is all that survives of their monastery. Inside there is a cycle of paintings by Palma Giovane. Today's church was begun in 1714 to designs by Domenico Rossi and the façade is especially impressive. The interior is clad in marble and stucco, painted with gold and other bright colours, and frescoed by Francesco Fontebasso. Sculptures by G.Torretti occupy niches in the pillars of the crossing and at the high altar. The altar of the Virgin Mary in the left transept has an altarpiece by J.Tintoretto. The church's main attraction is the large Titian altarpiece of the *Martyrdom of St.Lawrence*. Dating from before 1559, it is in the last chapel on the left of the nave. Paintings by Palma Giovane and Fumiano hang in the sacristy.

(16) **S.Giacomo dell'Orio/S.Giacomo de Lupio:** This parish church is picturesquely situated on the Campo of the same name in the NW of the city, and dates originally from 1225 (campanile and transept). The nave and aisles were added in the 15C, and the fine sanctuary with its dwarf gallery in the 16C. It contains works by Tizianello, Palma Giovane and Lotto (high altar, 1546). Paintings by Palma Giovane in the old sacristy (1575). In the Cappella di S.Lorenzo: more works by Palma Giovane, and an altarpiece by G.B. Pittoni. In the baptismal chapel (1566): Palma Giovane again, and Francesco Zugno. The new sacristy has ceiling paintings by Paolo Veronese, and also a collection of fine paintings by Veronese, Buonconsiglio, Francesco da Ponte (*c.* 1570), and Palma Giovane.

(17) **S.Giacomo di Rialto** (on the Grand Canal): A cruciform domed church dating back to the 12C. Rebuilt in the 16&17C, although the original ground plan was retained (similar to S.Marco). The columns and capitals inside are 12C, while the colonnaded W. portico is late 14C.

(18) **S.Giobbe/SS. Giobbe e Bernardino** (in the NW of the city): Begun

Gesuiti, portal

S.Giobbe, portal

as a flat-roofed structure in 1450, rebuilt and enlarged in 1470. The sanctuary was enlarged to house a dome, and contains a monument to the Doge Cristoforo Moro. There are a number of good chapels on the N. side of the nave. The best of these is the Cappella dei Martini (the fourth chapel from the choir), which is decorated in Tuscan style, with majolica tiles and a dome supported by pendentives.

(19) **S.Giorgio dei Greci** (near to S.Zaccaria): The church of the Greek colony, built between 1539 and 1561 (the dome is from 1571, the campanile is later than 1587). The long, vaulted, rectangular interior is arranged according to the Greek rite. The iconostasis has a fine 14C icon of Christ Pantocrator.

(20) **S.Giorgio Maggiore** (Isola di S.Giorgio Maggiore in the S. of Venice): This church, visible from afar, stands only a few yards from the bank of the Grand Canal. Along with the Doges' Palace and the 17C church of S.Maria della Salute, it is one of the landmarks of Venice.

Part of an old Benedictine monastery, whose origins went back to the 10C, the church was rebuilt by Palladio in 1566–80 as a cruciform basilica with a nave and two aisles. It is Palladio's largest church and it has semicircular transepts, a dome supported by a drum over the crossing and a square sanctuary followed by a monk's choir. The campanile, which is 195 ft. in height, was rebuilt by Burati in 1791 after falling down. The white *façade* is intended to be viewed from afar. It was built in 1597, 17 years after Palladio's death, but probably to his design, although slight alterations may have been made. It is divided into three sections, corresponding to the nave with its two aisles. The central section is reminiscent of classical temples: four massive Corinthian three-quarter columns, standing on a pedestal, support a pediment crowned by an 18C

S.Giorgio dei Greci

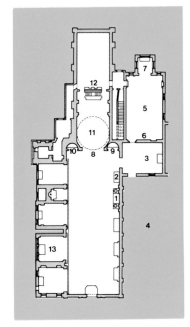

statue of Christ by A.Tarsia and two angels; there are statues of St.George and St.Stephen by G.del Moro; and a square panel above the portal. This central section is accentuated by the two lower and narrower side sections, which have flat pilasters rising from the ground, monuments to the Doge Tribuno Memmo (d. 991) and the Doge Sebastiano Ziani (d. 1178), and sculptures which are probably by G.del Moro. It is not certain whether the lower sections on both sides are by Palladio. Despite certain inconsistencies, such as the varying height of the pedestal, the façade of S.Giorgio Maggio served as a model for the façades of several churches in the 17&18C.

The white *interior* is decorated with great restraint, but it makes a very festive impression. Palladio probably based his design on classical Roman models. Ponderous pillars with engaged semi-columns form the arcades of the nave and thermal windows light both the nave and transept.

San Giobbe 1 Monument to Renè de Voyer de Palmy, executed after 1651 to a design by Claude Perrault **2** Side altar with painting of St.Peter by Paris Bordone **3** Cappella Contarini with a Nativity painting by Gerolamo Savoldo (c. 1540) **4** Cloister **5** Sacristy **6** Portrait of Doge Moro in the style of Gentile Bellini **7** Altar (1445) with triptych by Antonio Vivarini **8** Triumphal arch with fine sculptures by Pietro Lombardo (after 1470) **9** and **10** Side altars **11** Splendid early-Renaissance dome and pendentives **12** Monument to Doge Cristoforo Moro (1470) **13** Cappella dei Martini

Pilasters are used in the semicircular transepts and at the corners of the crossing, which is surmounted by the drum and dome. The sanctuary has four free-standing columns, one in each corner. *Contents:* The high altar stands in the sanctuary and has a group of the four Evangelists (1591-3) by G.Campagna, which shows the Evangelists bearing a globe of the world, on which there stands a splendid statue of Christ blessing. Next to this, on the side walls, are two paintings by Tintoretto (1594): on the left is the Shower of Manna, whose subject is not so much

33

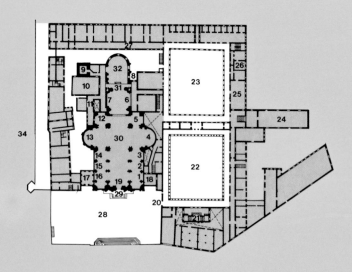

San Giorgio Maggiore 1 Altar with a Nativity by
J.Bassano (1592) **2** Altar with wooden crucifix **3** Altar
with painting from Tintoretto's studio **4** Altar with
Coronation of the Virgin Mary, by Tintoretto **5** Vir-
gin Mary and Saints by S.Ricci (1708) **6** Tintoretto:
Last Supper **7** Tintoretto: Shower of Manna **8** Monu-
ment to Doge Domenico Michièl in the corridor **9**
Campanile, originally 1470, but rebuilt in 1791 after
it collapsed (lift up to the platform; superb view) **10**
Sacristy with paintings by J.Palma and Tintoretto
(St.George) **11** Corridor leading to Cappella dei Morti
and Cappella Superiore **12** Altar with a painting from
Tintoretto's workshop **13** Altar with painting of
St.Stephen by Tintoretto **14** Altar with a painting
by M.Ponzone **15** Altar with marble group by
G.Campagna **16** Altar with painting by Leandro Bassano **17** Monument to Marcantonio Memmo (1615)
18 Monument to Lorenzo Venier (1625) **19** Monument to Doge Leonardo Donà above the portal **20**
Access to monastery, to Fondazione Cini and to
library of Baldassare Longhena **21** Stairs by Baldassare Longhena (library on upper storey) **22** Chiostro
degli Allori (1579-1614) **23** Chiostro dei Cipressi
(1516-40) **24** Refectory by Palladio **25** Chapterhouse
26 Abbot's house **27** Dormitory **28** Forecourt **29**
Church façade **30** Dome on drum **31** Organ gallery
32 Monks' choir **33** Teatro Verde in the park
34 Bacino; in the former monastery buildings behind
it: Centro Marinaro and Centro Arti e Mestieri

the miracle of the manna as the significance of the nourishment granted by
God through the fertile soil; several groups
of people are shown casually arranged in
an idyllic landscape; they represent human
society and are thus dependent on the
grace of God. The Last Supper on the
right was painted shortly before Tintoretto's death. The dramatic contrasts in
this painting are particularly effective and
convey a sense of the artist's unusual and
deep religiosity: the middle-aged servants
in the foreground are contrasted with the
spirits of light at the top right and with
the Christ surrounded by light in the
centre, and the Apostles in excited discussion at the front of the table as compared
with the Apostles grouped quietly around
the mild, self-sacrificing Christ. Other
works from Tintoretto's workshop are:
'Resurrection' at the altar to the left of the
sanctuary, 'Martyrdom of St.Stephen' (left
transept), 'Coronation of the Virgin Mary'
(right transept), and 'St.Cosmas and

St.Damian' (3rd altar of right aisle). In the monks' choir behind the sanctuary there are 48 stalls by G.Gatti (1594–8) with reliefs from the life of St.Bernard, and a lectern by Albert de Brulle. In the left aisle there is a marble group of the Coronation of the Virgin Mary (1595) by G.Campagna at the 2nd altar, and a painting of St.Lucy by L.Bassano at the 3rd altar. In the right aisle: a 'Nativity' painted by J.Bassano (1st altar), and a crucifix, probably by Hans von Judenburg (*c.* 1400), at the 2nd altar. In the right transept (near the presbytery): a 'Virgin Mary with Saints' (1708) by S.Ricci. Three early-17C monuments on the W. wall. The sacristy has a painting by Palma Giovane, statues of St.Mark and St.George, and a St.George by Domenico Tintoretto. The *Cappella dei Morti* (a Pietà by Tintoretto). The *Cappella Superiore* (with 'St.George and the Dragon' by Carpaccio), where the conclave for Pope Pius VI was held in 1799.

The adjoining *monastery* was used as a barracks following its secularization. Since 1951, the Benedictine monastery has once again been housed here, as has most of the 'Fondazione Giorgio Cini' (cultural centre; school and educational centre for orphans and children of socially deprived families; not normally open to visitors), the buildings having been restored by Count Vittorio Cini as a memorial to his only son and heir, Giorgio. To the right of the church there are two cloisters, which can be seen from the campanile. The cloister at the rear, built by G.Buora and his son Antonio in 1516–40, has broad arches supported by powerful columns, and groin vaults over the walks. The arcades of the front cloister (1579–1614) use sets of twin columns. The former *refectory* (1559–64) by Palladio is a long rectangular hall with an interesting vault (groin and barrel vaulting). This building formerly housed the 'Marriage at Cana' by P.Veronese, now in the Louvre, and its place in the refectory has been taken by the 'Betrothal of the Virgin Mary' by Domenico Tintoretto. The baroque staircase (1641–3) with its two flights of stairs, and the two-storeyed library (1641) with its articulated tunnel vault, are both by B.Longhena.

The two-storeyed dormitory (late 15C) has a tripartite façade with a relief of St.George and the Dragon by G.B.Bregno (1508).

(21) **S.Giovanni in Bragora:** An 8C parish church; some of the columns in today's church are original. In 1475–9 it was enlarged into a late-Gothic basilica with a nave and two aisles. A new sanctuary was added in 1485–94. Inside: a large canvas painting by Jacopo Palma Giovane on the W. wall; remains of frescos on the wall and chancel arch; a 15C Pietà in the 1st side chapel on the right. A 15C wooden shrine on the left side wall. 13C marble icons above the sacristy door. Four 15C panel paintings to the right of the portal. A large wooden crucifix (*c.* 1490/1) by Leonhard the German artist in the sacristy. The old altarpiece on the rear wall of the apse has a painting (1492–4) of the Baptism of Christ by Cima da Conegliano. Paintings by Bartolomeo and Alvise Vivarini in the choir chapels and side chapels. The baptismal chapel has a 15C octagonal font of red marble.

(22) **S.Giovanni Crisostomo** (NE of the Rialto): A domed Renaissance church begun by M.Codussi in 1497, with a very fine, clear ground plan and structure. Inside: a high altar painting by Sebastiano del Piombo (1509–11). An altarpiece by Giovanni Bellini in the 1st side chapel on the right. A relief of the Coronation of the Virgin Mary (1502) by T.Lombardo in the 1st side chapel on the left.

(23) **S.Giovanni Decollato:** This colonnaded basilica by the Fondaco dei Turchi has a nave and two aisles and was founded after 1000. The walls, clerestory, and columns in the nave, date from as early as the 11C. The remains of 13C frescos in the N. side-choir are the oldest surviving frescos in Venice.

(24) **S.Giovanni Elemosinario** (to the W. of the Rialto Bridge): First mentioned in 1051. Rebuilt by Scarpagnino in 1527–39, retaining the original arrangement. The campanile is from 1398–1410. The sombre interior has paintings by Tit-

ian (high altar, 1545), Pordenone (altarpiece in the right-hand choir chapel, 1535), Palma Giovane (in the left transept) and G.B. Pittoni (altarpiece in the 18C sacristy). A 14C marble Pietà at the altar of the left-hand choir chapel, and a fragment of a 6C (?) relief in the left transept.

(25) SS.Giovanni e Paolo/S.Zanipolo

(Rio dei Mendicanti): This cruciform Dominican church, like the Frari, is one of the finest Italian Gothic buildings. It is popularly referred to with affection as 'Zanipolo', an abbreviated combination of the names Giovanni and Paolo, the two mid-13C martyrs who are the church's patron saints.

It has no campanile but it is the largest church in Venice, with a high nave of five bays, flanked by an aisle on each side, a vault rising to 115 ft. over the crossing, a broad transept, and a high apse housing the choir, with two narrower chapels on each side. The tabernacles on the façade were added later; the main portal dates from c. 1460.

Although the Doge Jacopo Tiepolo granted a plot of land to the Dominicans shortly before the middle of the 13C, it was probably not until c. 1330 that building could begin in earnest, owing to the lack of funds, which had to be obtained from donations (the design of the nave and the lower parts of the façade probably dates from the late 13C). The nave was completed in 1369, and the transept and parts of the chapels in the 14C, while the choir (c. 1445) and the crossing (1450) are of later date.

Inside the church there is a basilican nave with a rib vault and arches supported by imposing round pillars, and the choir at the end of the church is flooded with light. Taken as a whole, the interior appears more uniform than that of the Frari, and its features are more distinctly Gothic. This uniformity was heightened after the choir screens below the crossing were removed in 1648.

There are some good altarpieces and sculptures, but the most interesting items in the church are undoubtedly the numerous tombs of the Doges interred in S.Zanipolo from the 2nd half of the 14C onwards (before this they were buried in S.Marco). Thus this church provides an almost complete picture of the development of Venetian funerary monuments, particularly in the 15&16C. The numbers in brackets in

Isola di S.Giorgio Maggiore

the following description refer to the numbers on the ground plan.

The splendid tomb (11) of the Doge Alvise Mocenigo (d. 1577) and his wife is on the W. wall, straddling the portal. Begun in 1580 but not completed until 1646, it has, on its second tier, a sarcophagus and the two recumbent figures of the deceased beside a statue of the Saviour, with reliefs underneath. To the right of this, following a small early Renaissance tomb, is the tomb (12) of the Doge Giovanni Mocenigo

Venice, SS.Giovanni e Paolo/Zanipolo 1 Late Gothic Cappella dell'Addolorata converted to baroque, with wall paintings and stuccoed soffitto by G.B. Lorenzetti, c. 1639 **2** Cappella della Pace/St. Hyacinth chapel with Byzantine miraculous image **3** Cappella di S.Domenico with beautiful ceiling painting by G.B. Piazzetta, 1727 **4** Cappella del Crocifisso with baroque altar; to its left and right are bronze statues by A.Vittoria **5** Cappella della Maddalena with 16C altar retable **6** Sanctuary with baroque high altar **7** Cappella della Trinità **8** Cappella Cavalli **9** Cappella del Rosario, 1582; burnt down in 1867, along with paintings by Tintoretto, Palma, Titian; restored in 1913, it now has works by Veronese and his school; the original statues by A.Vittoria and G.Campagna survive **10** Sacristy, 16&17C, with ceiling painting by M.Vecellio; painting by Palma Giovane on the altar **11** Portal with monuments to Doge Alvise Mocenigo (d. 1577) and his wife **12** Monument to Doge Giovanni Mocenigo (d. 1485) by T.Lombardo **13** Monument to Doge Pietro Mocenigo (d. 1476) by P.Lombardo **14** 13C relief, epitaph to Doge Ranieri Zeno (d. 1268) **15** Side altar with retable by F.Bissolo **16** Early-baroque wall tomb to Marcantonio Bragadin **17** Side altar with fine retable, c. 1475-80 **18** Baroque marble mausoleum of Doges Bertuccio and Silvestro Valier (d. 1658 and 1700) **19** Panel painting by Alvise Vivarini (1474) and Coronation of the Virgin Mary by G.Martini da Udine (early 16C); above, an equestrian monument of Nicola Orsini (d. 1509) **20** Altar with a painting by Lorenzo Lotto, 1542; above, to the left, is a large stained-glass window, later than 1470 **21** Wall tomb, 1510, above the door **22** Altar with Christ, St.Peter and St.Andrew, by R.Marconi **23** Monument to Doge Michele Morosini (d. 1382) **24** Monument to Doge Leonardo Loredan (d. 1521) with statue of the doge by G.Campagna **25** The famous late-15C monument to Doge Andrea Vendramin is a Venetian Renaissance masterpiece designed by T.Lombardo with bas relief by P. and A.Lombardo and statues by T.Lombardo **26** Gothic monument to Doge Marco Corner (d. 1368) with statue of the Madonna by N.Pisano **27** Monument to Doge Sebastiano Venier (d. 1578) **28** Monument to Doge A.Venier (d. 1400) **29** Early-15C wall tomb of Agnese and Orsola Venier **30** Monument to Leonardo Prato da Lecce (d. 1511) **31** Marble altar, 16C; above the sacristy is a monument to Jacopo Palma Vecchio and Giovane (father and son), 1621 **32** Above: monument to Doge Pasquale Malipiero (d. 1462) by P.Lombardo **33** Monument to Senator G.B. Bonzo (d. 1508) by G.M. Mosca, 1525 **34** Above: monument to Pompeo Giustinian, 1616 **35** Important monument to Doge T.Mocenigo (d. 1423) by P.Lamberti and G.di Martino da Fiesole **36** Monument to Doge Niccolò Marcello (d. 1474) by P.Lombardo **37** Altar with copy of the original Titian painting (destroyed by fire) **38** Monument to Orazio Baglioni (d. 1617) **39** Renaissance altar with statue of St.Jerome, a leading work by A.Vittoria **40** 19C monument, with a late-15C monument above

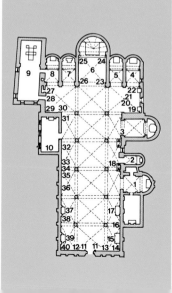

(d. 1485). Carved from Carrara marble by Tullio Lombardo in *c.* 1500, it takes the form of a triumphal arch. Here too, the deceased is depicted recumbent on a sarcophagus. The transition from early Renaissance to High Renaissance is seen in the monument to the Doge Pietro Mocenigo (13; front of right aisle), who died in 1476. This is probably Pietro Lombardo's masterpiece. For the first time, the tomb and its base (which has scenes from the legend of Hercules) are at ground level, and, also for the first time, the Doge is seen standing on the sarcophagus (between two armour bearers). Christian and heathen themes are intertwined in the iconography. A monument to the Doge Ranieri Zeno with a 13C relief (14). A side altar with a retable by F.Bissolo (15). An early baroque monument (1596) to Marcantonio Bragadin (16) who defended Famagusta (Cyprus) against the Turks in 1571 and was tortured to death by them. After this, in an original frame, there follows an altarpiece (17) painted in 1475–80. Contrary to what is sometimes claimed, this is most probably not by Giovanni Bellini. It depicts scenes from the life of Vincent Ferrer the Dominican Saint (predella), St.Vincent between

St.Sebastian and St.Christopher (central panel), and a Pietà and the Annunciation on the outer leaves.

The *Cappella dell'Addolorata* (1) by G.B. Lorenzetti, with its wall paintings and stuccoed ceiling (*c.* 1639), was originally late Gothic but it has been altered and is now baroque. It contains the tombstone, let into the floor, of Ludovico Diedo who died in 1466. The baroque mausoleum (18) to the Doges Bertuccio and Silvestro Valier (d. 1658 and 1700) is the last monument to the Doges in Venice, and has some excellent statues and reliefs. It stands between the Cappella dell'Addolorata and the *Cappella della Pace* (2), formerly the Chapel of St.Hyacinth, which is named after a Byzantine wonder-working image on the altar.

The *Cappella di San Domenico* (3), added in front of the right transept in the early 18C, contains the 'Glory of St.Dominic' by G.B. Piazzetta (1727). This outstanding example of Venetian rococo is surrounded by a golden frame. The bronze reliefs by G.Mazza show scenes from the life of St.Dominic.

The right transept (19) has an altarpiece of 'Christ bearing the Cross' by Alvise Vivarini (1474), an early-16C 'Coronation

SS.Giovanni e Paolo. Right: 'St.Antoninus' by Lorenzo Lotto

of the Virgin Mary' by G.Martini da Udine and, above this, an equestrian monument to Nicola Orsini (d. 1509). The large, four-part stained-glass window from the Murano glass works dates from shortly after 1470. It depicts St.Theodore and the church's two patron Saints in the lower row, and Fathers of the Church and symbols of the Evangelists in the quatrefoils. The altar below this window and to the right of it has 'St.Antoninus giving alms' by Lorenzo Lotto (1542). St.Antoninus, a Dominican, was the archbishop of Florence and this altarpiece is the best panel painting in the church. It is divided into three zones: at the bottom are the almsfolk, there are two clergymen in the middle, and at the top is St.Antoninus who, being the main figure, is treated with special emphasis.

The *Cappella del Crocifisso* (4), the outer of the two right-hand choir chapels, has a baroque altar (*c.* 1684) of black marble, with two excellent bronze statues by A.Vittoria, a 14C tomb, and the wall tomb of E.Windsor, the English ambassador (d. 1574). The *Cappella della Maddalena* (5) has a 16C altar retable, the wall tomb of Marco Giustinian (d. 1347), and a baroque

monument to Melchiore Lanza, the painter, who died in 1674.

The monumental high altar (1619) by Baldassare Longhena in the adjoining sanctuary (6) is in the form of a classical triumphal arch. John and Paul, the church's eponymous Saints standing underneath, are by F.Cavrioli (1662), while the seated figures of the Virgin Mary, St.Dominic and St.Theresa are by B. Falcone (*c.* 1659). The wall tomb (23) of the Doge Michele Morosini (d. 1382) is to the right of the entrance to the sanctuary. The recumbent statue of the deceased lies on the sarcophagus. There are also two tall tabernacles at the sides, a pointed arch, and a mosaic (Crucifixion with the founders). Behind this tomb, on the floor, there stands the tomb (24) of the Doge Leonardo Loredan (d. 1521). It has four colossal columns and is in the form of a peace monument, with the seated figure of the Doge being depicted by G.Campagna mediating between two estranged parties, who are the personifications of the Republic of Venice, depicted in the person of Venezia, and the League of Cambrai.

Opposite this is the *tomb* of the Doge

SS.Giovanni e Paolo, 'Assunta' by Veronese (left), Christ bearing the Cross, by Alvise Vivarini

Andrea Vendramin (25), who died in 1478. Designed by Tullio Lombardo, it is a tripartite structure on a stepped base. It is one of the masterpieces of the Venetian Renaissance, and is probably the most famous of all the Doges' tombs. Here too, the iconography is a mixture of Christian and heathen-classical motifs: the Doge is seen on a bier supported by eagles, and there are personifications of Virtues in the niches, a Virgin Mary, an Annunciation, warriors, sea-horses, Perseus and Medusa, and other works. Pietro (the reliefs in the lunette) and Antonio Lombardo (the Annunciation) also contributed to the monument. But the best figures are by Tullio Lombardo himself, as are the two young warriors in the side niches.

To the left of this is the tomb of the Doge Marco Corner (26), who died in 1368. A retable with statues is positioned above the recumbent figure of the deceased on the sarcophagus. The superb Virgin Mary by the Tuscan sculptor Nino Pisano is the earliest purely Gothic sculpture in Venice. Next come the left-hand choir chapels. The *Cappella della Trinità* (7) contains a panel painting by L. Bassano (1622) and two 14C tombs. In the *Cappella Cavalli* (8) is the wall tomb of Jacopo Cavalli who died in 1384 (a recumbent figure of the deceased, busts in the tall oval niches by the sarcophagus) and, on the left, the tomb, consisting only of a sarcophagus, of the Doge Giovanni Dolfin (d. 1361), with reliefs by Andrea da S.Felice.

Three monuments to the Venier family are seen on the W. wall of the left transept. The tomb (28) of the Doge Antonio Venier (d. 1400), with excellent sculptures by various artists, is between the wall tombs of the Doge Sebastiano Venier (27; d. 1578) and Agnese and Orsola Venier (29; d. 1410 and 1411).

A door below the monument to Antonio Venier leads into the *Cappella del Rosario* (9), built in 1582 to commemorate the naval victory at Lepanto (1571). After a fire in 1867 had destroyed the interior and the contents, which included paintings by Titian, Tintoretto, L.Bassano and Palma Giovane, the chapel was restored, the work being completed in 1913. Statues in niches by A.Vittoria and G.Campagna survive in the sanctuary, and there are Paolo Veronese's ceiling paintings the 'Adoration of the Magi', 'Assumption', 'Annunciation', 'Adoration of the Shepherds'. The 'Nativity' on the rear wall is also by him. The Virgin Mary by C.Lorenzetti on

SS.Giovanni e Paolo, 'S.Agnano' by T.Lombardo

the free-standing altar tabernacle is after an original by A.Vittoria.

A 16C marble altar (31) and three altarpieces by Vivarini (1473) are to the right of the sacristy entrance. Back in the left transept, there is a monument (30) to Leonardo Prato da Lecce (d. 1511). Above the sacristy door there are busts (31) of Jacopo Palma the elder and the younger (1621) and also, between them, of Titian. In the late-16C sacristy itself (10), which retains its original decoration, there are a ceiling painting by M.Vecellio, an altarpiece by Palma Giovane, and wall decoration.

The tabernacle-like monument (32) to the Doge Pasquale Malipiero (d. 1462) is surmounted by a lunette and comprises a sarcophagus with a recumbent figure of the deceased beneath a fabric canopy. It is Pietro Lombardo's earliest work in Zanipolo and the statues personify the Virtues rather than Saints. Underneath the monument (33) to Senator G.B. Bonzio (d. 1508) there are two 15&16C monuments. After these comes the equestrian monument (34) to P.Giustinian (d. 1616). This is followed by the notable wall tomb (35) of Tommaso Mocenigo (d. 1423), who is famous for his 'Speech to the Nation'.

This tomb was built by the Tuscan artists P.Lamberti and G.di Martino da Fiesole and is transitional in style between the late Gothic and early Renaissance. The fabric canopy, the first such example to be found on a Doge's tomb, falls from the retable to the sarcophagus, where the figure of the deceased lies. The tomb also has conch-shaped niches.

This tour of the interior ends with the following works: the monument (36) to the Doge Nicolò Marcello (d. 1474); an altar with a copy of Titian's painting of 'St.Peter Martyr' (37), which was destroyed by fire in the Cappella del Rosario in 1867. An equestrian monument (38) to O.Baglioni the condottiere (d. 1617). Finally, a Renaissance altar with the kneeling marble statue of St.Jerome (No. 39), one of A.Vittoria's masterpieces.

On the façade, in the arcade on either side of the main portal (1460), are the tombs of the Doges Jacopo Tiepolo (d. 1249) and Lorenzo Tiepolo (d. 1275), and also M.Michièl and the Buono brothers.

The *equestrian monument to Bartolomeo Colleoni*, the condottiere, stands on a marble base surrounded by columns immediately to the right of the church. It was modelled in wax by the Florentine

Madonna dell'Orto

Madonna dell'Orto, portal detail

artist Andrea Verrocchio before being cast in bronze by Alessandro Leopardi, a local artist. This monument is among the outstanding achievements of Italian Renaissance sculpture. The rider and horse convey a feeling of dynamism and strength and the rider, full of proud self-assurance, appears as an ideal 15C condottiere. Colleoni, who was born near Bergamo in 1400 and died at his Malpaga castle in 1475, was in fact one of the most successful and wealthy mercenary leaders of his time. He served the republic of Venice from 1448 onwards, after previously being employed by Naples and Milan. In his will, Colleoni called upon the Signoria (State council) to build a monument in his honour outside San Marco in gratitude for his abundant bequests (100,000 gold ducats) to the republic. The Signoria found this demand unacceptable and could not carry it out. However, the problem was finally solved after five years: the Signoria kept the bequests and Colleoni was given his monument, but outside the Scuola di San Marco, and not outside St.Mark's Basilica, which was the building to which the will was intended to refer, although the will did not specify the Basilica, referring merely to San Marco.

S.Maria della Fava, tower

(26) **S.Giuliano** (N. of St.Mark's Square): An old parish church rebuilt in 1553, with J.Sansovino designing the fine façade and the figure over the portal. Inside: statues by A.Vittoria who, along with Sansovino, was responsible for the entire building. High altar by Palma Giovane. The altarpiece in the 1st right-hand side altar is by P.Veronese.

(27) **S.Giuseppe di Castello** (in the SE): A convent church rebuilt in the 16C. The 17C painted ceiling gives an illusion of depth. On the left side wall is a late-16C monument to the Doge Marino Grimani and his wife (designed by V.Scamozzi, with figures and reliefs by G.Campagna).

(28) **S.Lazzaro dei Mendicanti:** This undivided rectangular church was built as a hospice church in 1601–31 to designs by V.Scamozzi. It stands to the N. of Zanipolo. The façade was designed by Giuseppe Sardi in 1673. A late-baroque monument on the portico. An altarpiece by P.Veronese in the 1st side altar on the right, and another by J.Tintoretto in the 2nd side altar on the left.

(29) **S.Lio/S.Leone** (E. of the Rialto Bridge): An 11C church dedicated to St.Leo, the Pope. Rebuilt in the 18C. Inside: A ceiling painting by D.Tiepolo. St.James, by Titian, at the 1st side altar. On the right: the 15C Cappella Gussoni, possibly by P.Lombardo. 17C Crucifixion by P.della Vecchia.

(30) **Madonna dell'Orto:** This flat-roofed colonnaded basilica (one nave, two aisles) in the N. of the city was begun in 1350, and has been rebuilt several times. Its 15C façade is decorated with beautiful sculptures (the Twelve Apostles by Paolo and Pierpaolo dalle Masegne). Inside the church is the tomb of J.Tintoretto, and there are also some paintings by him above the door to the Maurus Chapel and in the sanctuary. Paintings by Cima da Conegliano and Palma Giovane in the Cappella di S.Mauro. A fine *cloister*, and a *campanile* with a dome (*c.* 1500).

(31) **S.Marcuola/SS.Ermagora e For-**

tunato (in the N. of the city, on the Grand Canal): Founded in the 9C, the present church was built by G.Massari between 1728 and 1736, using existing sections. Inside there are paintings in the manner of Titian and Tintoretto around the pulpits, as well as a famous Tintoretto (the Last Supper, left side of the sanctuary), with carved groups including works by G.M. Morlaiter.

(32) **S.Maria della Fava** (E. of the Rialto): Built by Antonio Gaspari in 1711. The domed sanctuary was added by G.Massari in 1750–3. An altarpiece by G.B. Tiepolo in the 1st side chapel on the right. One of Piazzetta's masterpieces (*c.* 1725) is at the 2nd side altar on the left. A tabernacle with two angels by G.M. Morlaiter.

(33) **S.Maria Formosa:** Tradition relates that this church was founded in the 7C. It was rebuilt as a domed cruciform church in the 11C, and rebuilt again by Mauro Codussi in 1493–1500 as a basilica with a nave, two aisles and a transept. The fine façades were only added in the 16C (towards the Rio) and 17C. The campanile is 17C. Inside there are paintings by

S.Maria del Giglio, façade detail

Vivarini (1473, 1st chapel on right), Bassano (2nd chapel on right) and Palma Vecchio (*c.* 1520, 1st chapel of right transept). The mosaics in the vault of the apse are to a design by Palma Giovane. On the altar of the small *Oratorio della Purificazione* there are good marble statues (1400) and an altarpiece by G.B. Tiepolo.

(34) **S.Maria del Giglio/S.Maria Zobenigo:** This 17C single-aisled rectangular church near the Teatro la Fenice has an imposing baroque façade to a design by G.Sardi, with figures by G.Le Court. The panel on the pedestal has relief maps of Venetian military bases and Italian towns. Inside the church: Paintings by Giuseppe Salviati on the W. wall. Paintings (1552–7) of the Four Evangelists by J.Tintoretto on what were the organ doors. In the sacristy is a work by P.P. Rubens.

(25) **S.Maria Mater Domini** (SE of the Fondaco dei Turchi): A small, originally Romanesque parish church, rebuilt in Renaissance style in 1502–40 by J.Sansovino amongst others.

(36) **S.Maria dei Miracoli:** The first Renaissance building in Venice, with an

S.Maria dei Miracoli

inimitably clear architectural arrangement, the small 'Miracoli' is simple and harmonious in form. The geometrical patterns of inlaid marble on its outer walls give it the appearance of a jewel casket and the left flank stands directly on the canal. It was built by P.Lombardo and his sons in 1481–9 for a wonder-working icon of the Virgin Mary which had been discovered in an old house; it is now on the high altar. Originally part of a small convent, the rectangular church is single-aisled and tunnel-vaulted. It is faced with polychrome marble both inside and out. There is a domed sanctuary. The paintings, and especially the sculptures which are here almost overshadowed by the architecture, are of a high standard (Titian's workshop; Tullio Lombardo, Antonio Lombardo, Pietro Lombardo. A.Vittoria).

(37) S.Maria della Pietà/S.Maria della Visitazione (Riva degli Schiavoni): Built by G.Massari (1745–60). The marble façade, which was designed by Massari and is built into the front of the former hospice, was not completed until 1906. Inside: ceiling paintings by G.B. Tiepolo (1754–60). The altarpiece on the late-baroque high altar is by Piazzetta and

G.Angeli. Marble statues by Gai and Marchiori at the high altar. The tabernacle angel is by M.Morlaiter.

(38) S.Maria della Salute: This imposing church of gleaming white marble, stands diagonally opposite the Piazzetta on the other side of the Grand Canal. It is the finest baroque building in Venice and, with its two domes and its façade approached up a flight of stone steps, it, together with the Doge's Palace and S.Giorgio Maggiore, is one of the landmarks of Venice.

The Salute was founded by the Senate in 1630 after an epidemic of the plague had ended. Baldassare Longhena (1630–87) was the architect, and it is regarded as his masterpiece. It is a centrally-planned, octagonal building with six chapels around its circumference and it is crowned by an enormous drum and dome. Inside the church, the dome rests on eight massive pillars with engaged three-quarter columns facing towards the centre. The sanctuary, with a smaller dome and two semicircular exedrae at the sides, adjoins the main body of the church, and so too does the rectangular monks' choir with its two sacristies at either end. The exterior is decorated

S.Maria dei Miracoli, carved detail

with gables, massive volutes (known as orrechioni), balustrades and marble statues. The façade, which faces the Grand Canal, is conceived in the manner of a triumphal arch, with four giant columns standing on pedestals flanking the main portal. The outsides of the adjoining chapels (pilasters, figures in niches, large thermal windows, volutes) are also in the form of small façades. The Renaissance inheritance is seen in the ground plan (an octagonal centrally planned structure), in the exterior (design of the façade), and in the interior (which has a clear, rational articulation arranged around the centre). In the following description of the *contents*, the figures in brackets refer to those of the ground plan. The panel of the 'Presentation', 'Ascension' and 'Birth of the Virgin Mary' at the altars of the three right-hand chapels (3/4/5) are by L.Giordano (from 1667 onwards). Paintings (1687) by P.Liberi in the first two left-hand chapels (14/15). The 'Descent of the Holy Ghost' at the 3rd left-hand altar (13) is by Titian. An excellent group of statues by Giusto le Court is to be seen at the high altar (8): Venezia kneeling at the feet of the standing Madonna and Child, while on the right the plague in the shape of an

ugly old woman is being driven away by a putto; underneath this are St.Mark and St.Lorenzo Giustinian, and a 12C or 13C Byzantine miraculous image in the middle of a marble shrine. Two ponderous columns taken from the ancient theatre of Pola (9) open the way into the monks' choir (10), with carved stalls and three ceiling paintings by G.Salviati.

Numerous works of art taken from churches in Venice which were deconsecrated in the 19C are preserved in the *Great Sacristy* (11) to the left of the monks' choir. The altarpiece of St.Mark, who is seen enthroned above St.Cosmas, St.Damian, St.Roch and St.Sebastian, is an early work (1511/12) by Titian, but the main figure is already emphasized and a certain asymmetry is implied in the position of the columns. Other works by Titian in the sacristy are the ceiling paintings (1540–2) of 'Cain and Abel', 'Abraham's Sacrifice' and 'David and Goliath', and also the eight tondi on the walls, with depictions of Evangelists and Fathers of the Church. The enormous 'Marriage at Cana' (1561) by Jacopo Tintoretto opposite the entrance impresses by its perspective effect. The sacristy also houses some paintings by G.Salviati

S.Maria della Salute

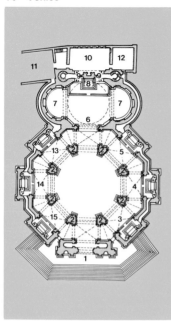

Venice, S.Maria della Salute 1 Triumphal arch façade 2 Colossal composite columns with statues on the volutes 3, 4 and 5 Altar chapels with altarpieces by Luca Giordano, from 1667 6 Sanctuary 7 Exedra 8 High altar with statue group by Giusto le Court, Byzantine Madonna and Child, bronze candelabras and Easter candlestick, 1570. Two campaniles to the right and left of the altar outside 9 Ancient columns from the theatre of Pola 10 Monks' choir with carved pews and 3 ceiling paintings by Giuseppe Salviati 11 Great sacristy with art assembled from various churches in the 19C, including an altarpiece, by Titian (1511/12), with St.Mark; icon of the Virgin Mary (1115) in the altar tabernacle; an antependium tapestry designed by Jacopo Bellini; 8 tondi on the walls with paintings by Titian; other paintings by Giuseppe Salviati; an enormous painting by Jacopo Tintoretto (1561) opposite the entrance; more good paintings and sculptures in the antisagrestia, including a Pietà by Tullio Lombardo 12 Small sacristy (usually closed) with sarcophagus (c. 1500) and portal tympanum (c. 1443) 13 Chapel with altarpiece (Descent of the Holy Ghost) by Titian 14 and 15 Altar chapels with paintings by P.Liberi, 1687

(including 'Last Supper', 'David's Triumph'), an altarpiece of 'St.Sebastian' by M.Basaiti, an icon of the Virgin Mary from 1115, and an antependium in the shape of a tapestry designed by Jacopo Bellini. The *Small Sacristy* (12) has the sarcophagus (*c.* 1500) of Antonio Cornaro, and a tympanum from a portal with a Coronation of the Virgin Mary (*c.* 1443).

(39) **S.Martino** (in the E. of the city): Rebuilt in 1550 to designs by J.Sansovino, altered and redecorated in the 17&18C. Inside are a monument to the Doge Francesco Erizzo (1633), and an altar (2nd half of 15C) with figures by T.Lombardo in the large left-hand side chapel.

(40) **S.Michele in Isola** (on the cemetery island between Venice and Murano): This is an early work by Mauro Codussi (1469, nave and choir completed in 1499). The façade (1477), with its Ionic capitals and carved stone, was later regarded as a model of monumental Renaissance architecture. Inside there are finely carved arcades and a monks' choir. To the left of the façade is the *Cappella Emiliana* (*c.* 1530) by G.Bergamasco, a centrally-planned structure.

(41) **S.Moisè** (SW of St.Mark's Square, on the Rio di Barcaroli): This church was

S.Maria della Salute, painting by Titian

S.Maria della Salute ▷

S.Michele

originally 8C. The present structure is a single-aisled rectangular church, built from 1632 onwards. The façade (1688) is by A.Tremignon. Inside there are paintings, including some by Tintoretto. The sacristy contains an antependium (1633) by Niccolò and Sebastiano Roccatagliata.

(42) **S.Nicolò da Tolentino** (on the Rio Tolentini by the Giardino Papadopoli in the W. of the city): This Theatine church (1591–1601) is by V.Scamozzi (partly to plans by Palladio). The portico is 18C. Baroque paintings by Bernardo Strozzi (St.Lawrence) and Johannes Liss (St.Jerome).

(43) **S.Pantalon/S.Pantaleone** (on the Rio Ca' Foscari): Built by Fr. Comino in 1668–86 on the site of a 13C church. Inside, the vaults were painted by G.Fumiani in 1680–1740. High altar by G.Sardi. Left choir chapel: Coronation of the Virgin Mary, paintings by Giovanni d'Alemagna and Bartolomeo Vivarini. The altar has a marble relief (earlier than 1400).

(44) **S.Pietro in Castello** (on the Isola di S.Pietro): The former patriarchal church has a campanile by M.Codussi, 1482–8. The church's new façade (1596) was built by F.Smeraldi to plans by Palladio. The interior was altered by G.Grapiglia from 1619 onwards. The high altar is to a design by B.Longhena. The marble throne of St.Peter (*c.* 13C) in the right aisle has fragments of Islamic carving. Paintings by P.Veronese, P.Liberi, P.Ricchi and M.Basaiti, and an Immacu-lata by G.M. Morlaiter. Mosaic icons by A.Zuccato (1570).

(45) **SS.Redentore** (on the Giudecca, in the S. of the city): After the city's liberation from the plague, the Signoria ordered a votive church to be built here in 1577–92 to plans by A.Palladio. It is a masterpiece of the transition from the

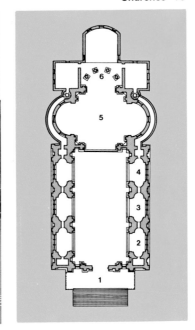

S.Moisè

Renaissance to the baroque. The façade is in the form of a classical temple. The enchanting, harmonious interior proceeds smoothly from nave to sanctuary and then retro-choir. There is a Crucifixion group by G.Campagna at the baroque high altar.

(46) **S.Rocco:** The sanctuary dates from the original church (1489–1508). Today's single-aisled rectangular church was rebuilt by Giovanni Scalfurotto in the mid 18C. On the upper storey of the façade (1765–77) are statues and a large relief by G.M. Morlaiter. Inside there are fine paintings by Tintoretto, Ricci and Trevisan.

(47) **S.Salvatore/S.Salvador** (near the Teatro Goldoni): The buildings which previously stood here were 7&12C. The present church (1507–34) was built by Giorgio Spavento with the assistance of T.Lombardo and J.Sansovino. The façade (1663) is to a design by G.Sardi. The

architecturally well-balanced interior harbours the following works: sculptures and reliefs by Sansovino, G.Campagna and A.Vittoria; paintings by P.Bordone, F.Vecellio and, in particular, Titian (high altar). A 14C silver reredos is occasionally placed on the altar. The *sacristy* from the period when the church was originally built is architecturally interesting, and has *trompe l'oeil* paintings.

(48) **Scalzi/S.Maria di Nazareth** (near the railway station by the Grand Canal): This single-aisled Carmelite church was begun by Longhena in 1670, and its façade (1683–9) was built under G.Sardi's supervision. The fine late-baroque interior had

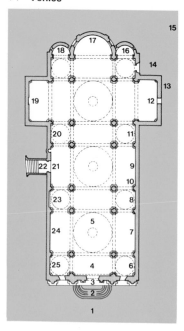

S.Simeone Piccolo

S.Salvatore/S.Salvador 1 Campo S.Salvador **2** Steps up to the main entrance **3** Baroque façade (from 1663) designed by Giuseppe Sardi **4** Marble pavement (1604), laid in multicoloured geometric patterns, covers the whole church **5** Three large domes above the nave and 8 smaller domes above the aisles, produce interesting architectural and lighting effects **6** Altar of the cross (later than 1650) **7** Wall monument to Andrea and Benedetto Dolfin by Girolamo Campagna (c. 1600); figure of Christ by Giulio del Moro **8** Altar with statues by Girolamo Campagna **9** Excellent monument to Doge Francesco Venier by Jacopo Sansovino (c. 1556) **10** Fine statues of women by Sansovino, particularly the 'Allegory of Belief' **11** Altar with Titian's famous 'Annunciation' (1560-6) **12** Monuments to the Cornaro family on the transept walls. Above the sacristy, an epitaph to Caterina, Queen of Cyprus, by B.Contino (1580-4) **13** Narrow passage to the sacristy **14** Early-16C sacristy. Large hall with blind arches whose wall panels are painted with trompe l'oeil trees and birds to give the illusion of a view outdoors. Two domed chapels with good paintings **15** Cloister **16** Right choir chapel with altarpiece by Paris Bondone (St.Theodore) **17** High altar (1534) by Guglielmo dei Grigi, with famous Resurrection painting by Titian. 14C silver-gilt altar retable depicting Saints in four rows, one above the other, framed by pillars and arches with delicate decorations, is displayed only on high holidays and from 3-15 August each year **18** Mosaic decorations in the apse vault (1523) **19** Monuments to the Cornaro family on the transept walls **20** Altar with sculptures by A.Vittoria **21** Organ front (1530) with paintings by F.Vecellio, a brother of Titian, on the organ doors **22** Side exit to the Merceria S.Salvador **23** Altar with architecture by Guglielmo dei Grigi (1540-50) **24** Double monument to Doges Lorenzo and Gerolamo Priuli (2nd half of 16C) with statues of St.Laurence and St.Jerome by G.B. Piazzetta **25** Altar with a painting begun by Giulio da Moro and completed in 1754 by D.Maggiotto

ceiling frescos by G.B. Tiepolo which were destroyed in World War 1. But the high altar by G.B. Viviani and G.Pozzo survived.

(49) **S.Sebastiano** (in the W. of the city): A convent church built by A.Scarpagnino between 1505 and 1546. The paintings and frescos by P.Veronese (after 1553) are the main reason why the church is world famous. The statues on the parapet in the gallery are by G.Campagna.

(50) **S.Simeone Piccolo** (Grand Canal): A late-baroque domed church (1718–38)

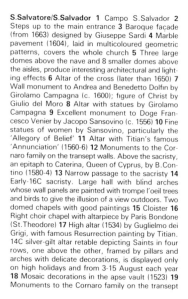

S.Trovaso, tower (left) and façade (right)

by Giovanni Scalfurotto. A Pietà by Palma Giovane.

(51) S.Trovaso/SS.Gervasio e Protasio (Campo S.Trovaso): A large single-aisled church (1584–1657) with paintings by Tintoretto (Last Supper, *c.* 1555), M.Giambono (before 1440), Giovanni Bellini (Virgin Mary) and three fine marble reliefs (*c.* 1460/70).

(52) S.Zaccaria (E. of S.Marco): The previous 10C building was attached to the most important convent in Venice. The crypt (10&11C), which is below the Cappella S.Tarasio (1440; in the S., to the right of the choir), has three fine late-Gothic carved altars and frescos by Andrea da Castagno, 1442. This church is among the finest examples of Venetian early-Renaissance architecture. It was begun by A.Gambello, whose work was continued by M.Codussi in 1481 and completed in *c.* 1500. Inside there are a nave and two aisles. On the walls of the nave are 17&18C paintings depicting scenes from Venetian history. Columns with early-Renaissance capitals. A choir, an ambulatory and chapels are grouped around the sanctuary. Paintings of Christ's Passion by Palma Giovane are seen at the high altar. In the left aisle there is an altar of the Madonna, with one of Giovanni Bellini's finest paintings (1505) to be seen in situ in Venice. (See ground plan on p.76.)

VI. Palaces: Map: p. 32

Palaces and other secular buildings along the Grand Canal: Such a series of buildings, spanning the 13C to the 19C, is to be found nowhere else in the world, numbering as it does both outstanding examples of and a myriad of variants on the architectural styles of these centuries (Romanesque-Byzantine, with the city's earliest stone buildings; Gothic; Renaissance; baroque, neoclassical and, finally,

San Zaccaria 1 Campo S.Zaccaria, is reached from San Marco via the Salizzada S.Provolo. At the point where the Salizzada enters the Campo at its NW corner, the Salizzada is framed by a late-Gothic portal with a fine mid-15C tympanum relief **2** Façade of the so-called 'Chiesa Vecchia', late-Gothic façade of the earlier San Zaccaria church **3** Pre-Gothic campanile, one of the oldest surviving church towers in Venice **4** Entrance to the parlatory **5** Façade of the so-called Chiesa Nuova, today's San Zaccaria. Lower part of façade (1st and 2nd storeys) by A.Gambello (after 1450), upper part by M.Codussi (from 1481) **6** The vault is supported by six monumental columns with fine capitals by Giovanni Buora (from 1476) **7** Dome on pendentives **8** Holy water stoup with small statue of John the Baptist by A.Vittoria **9** Side altar with altarpiece by J.Palma Giovane. The wall painting above shows the church's function as Venice's Easter church, which the Doge and the Signoria attended at Easter. The church which survives today was founded by Doge Pasquale Malipiero as an Easter church in 1457 **10** The 2nd side altar, donated by A.Vittoria in 1599, preserves the relics of St.Zacharias in a baroque shrine. The painting above the altar is by G.A.Fumiani (1469) **11** 'Adoration of the Shepherds', a painting by A.Balestra **12** Large wall painting by Bernardo Strozzi hangs above the portal (1599) **13** Cappella di S.Atanasio, built in 1595 as the nuns' choir above the nave of the former church of San Zaccaria. Pews from 1455-65 **14** Altar by A.Vittoria with an early J.Tintoretto altarpiece depicting John the Baptist **15** Lectern (15C) **16** Organ door painted by Palma Giovane **17** 'Mount of Olives' by M.Desubleo (17C), and 'Sacra Conversazione' by Palma Vecchio **18** 'Christ in Limbo' by Domenico Tintoretto, and paintings by Leandro Bassano **19** Door to a corridor leading to the Cappella di S.Tarasio and, via a staircase, to the 10C Romanesque colonnaded crypt which lay beneath the choir of the old San Zaccaria chapel and which can still be visited today **20** Cappella di S.Tarasio. Built in its present form from 1458 onwards by Antonio Gambello on the site of the original choir of the pre-Gothic church of S.Zaccaria **21** The splendid frescos in the apse are by Andrea Castagno (1442) **22** High altar with multi-storeyed retable, carved by Ludovico da Forlì in 1443-4. Three panels in the middle date from 1385 **23** Altar of St.Sabina (1443) **24** Corpus Christi altar (1443) by Giovan and Andrea da Murano **25** Wall of the ambulatory (2nd half of 15C) **26** High altar with domed ciborium (16C) **27** Vault frescos in the choir by Giovanni Antonio Pellegrini **28** Ambulatory with fine architecture from the 1st half of the 16C **29** Monument to A.Vittoria, begun by Vittoria himself and finally decorated by his pupils (completed 1604) **30** Sacristy (1562) **31** Altar with famous painting of the Virgin Mary (1505) by Giovanni Bellini **32** Side altar with retable by Giuseppe Salviati **33** Holy water stoup with a small statue of Zacharias by A.Vittoria **34** 'Secondo Chiostro', a cloister with double-storeyed arcades **35** 'Primo Chiostro', the cloister of the old Zaccaria church, also with double-storeyed arcades

neo-Gothic). Thus a trip down the Grand Canal offers a survey of how the specifically Venetian form of palazzo, at once residence and place of business, developed. Beginning with the Gothic, the basic scheme of the *Venetian palace façade* is a tripartite vertical division into a central, main section flanked by narrower side sections (torriselle), corresponding to the arrangement of the interior. Asymmetrical façades occasionally occur, such as

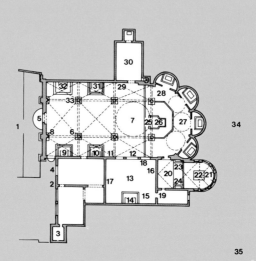

when one of the side sections was not built due to lack of space or funds (likewise, there are also examples of unfinished buildings where, although they have been laid out in full, work has ceased before they have reached full height). In the Renaissance this division into three sections began to give way to articulation extending across the entire width of the façade, but nevertheless it continued to exist in principle. A further feature is the first floor loggia of the central section, which gave emphasis to the piano nobile, the most elegant of a palazzo's floors with its central public rooms. Technical advances during the Gothic period—for example the tremendous work of driving the piles in the lagoon—then made it possible to erect taller buildings, and thus also a second piano nobile.

The Grand Canal, Venice's main artery, is over 2 miles long and has been described as 'the most beautiful "road" in the world'. Its width varies between 100 ft. (at the Rialto Bridge) and about 230 ft. (at the mouth), and it links rather than divides the three districts (sestieri) on the W. bank (S.Polo, S.Croce, Dorsoduro) with those on the E. bank (Cannaregio, S.Marco, Castello). It is flanked by the façades of the buildings along its banks and it forms the backbone of the whole city both as regards its commerce and transport. There are also instances where the individual buildings facing each other across the water are designed so as to relate to one another. From the 15C onwards, there are countless views of Venice in the works of Vittore Carpaccio, Giovanni and Gentile Bellini, including the cycle of the 'Miracles of the Holy Cross' (c. 1500; in the Gallerie dell'Accademia, q.v.), Giovanni Antonio Canal and his nephew Bernardo Bellotto, and Francesco Guardi (18C); to name but a few. Not only are these works charming in themselves but they provide an invaluable record of Venice's past appearance.

Left bank: Map: p. 32
(1) **Palazzo Flangini** (17C): An impressive baroque building by Giuseppe Sardi with an asymmetrical façade (the left-hand section, which should also have a corner window, is missing). The massive ground floor, built of rusticated ashlars, includes the portal, and is divided into the lower zone where the shops formerly were, and the offices on the raised ground floor. The columns of the two main storeys are Ionic

Palazzo Flangini

Palazzo Erizzo

and Corinthian, and have been a popular element of Venetian façades since the Renaissance.

Behind *S. Geremia*, on the Canale di Cannaregio, stands the Palazzo Labia.

(3) **Pal. Labia** (regional headquarters of RAI, the Italian broadcasting company): Begun in the late 17C, and continued by Andrea Cominelli from about 1720 onwards. The façade (*c.* 1750) is by Alessandro Tremignon. In the ballroom there are frescos by Giovanni Battista Tiepolo, assisted by Girolamo Mengozzi-Colonna, the architectural painter. Cleopatra's banquet and her embarkation for Rome are seen on the walls. The ceiling paintings depict allegories of love, the art of poetry, and Pegasus. This massive palace belonged to a family of Catalan merchants who had become naturalized in the 17C, and it stood in what was the heart of the city, near the then Spanish Embassy and at the point where two main waterways crossed.

(5–7) **Pal. Correr-Contarini** (17C).

(7) **Pal. Gritti:** 17C, incorporating late Gothic fragments.

(9) **Pal. Vendramin-Calergi** (Venice Casino): This is one of the earliest Renaissance buildings in the city, and had an enduring effect on Venetian architecture. Begun by Mauro Coducci in 1481, and completed by Tullio Lombardo in 1504–9. The traditional tripartite Gothic division of the façade is here only hinted at by the doubling of the columns around the pairs of windows at the sides, the corresponding arrangement of the eagles and coats-of-arms on the cornice frieze, and the balcony. The design of the windows (twin windows with engaged semi-column, and an oculus in the surrounding arch) introduces some Tuscan Renaissance elements (some related forms are seen on the Pal. Corner-Spinelli, No. 65). The garden wing (*c.* 1600) by Vicenzo Scamozzi was rebuilt in 1660 immediately after it had been destroyed. Private gardens were an expensive luxury, since land prices in Venice have always been very high. Richard Wagner died in this palazzo on 13th February 1883. The sadness felt in Venice at his death was reflected in literature in Gabriele D'Annunzio's novel 'Il fuoco' ('The Fire', 1900).

(11) **Pal. Erizzo** (2nd half of 15C): This late-Gothic building has a loggia of four arches set within a rectangle, as was usual at this period. Baroque alterations by Giorgio Massari in 1717.

Ca' d'Oro

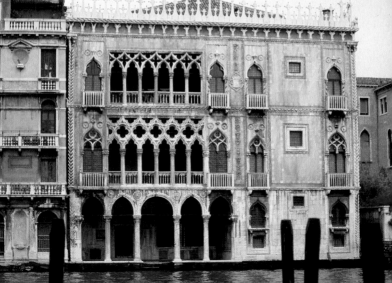

(13) **Pal. Emo** (1st half of 17C).

(15–19) **Pal. Barbarigo** (3rd quarter of 16C): There are some slight traces of Camillo Ballini's paintings on the façade, which date from the time when the palazzo was built. **Pal. Zulian** (17C). **Pal. Ruoda** (17C). To the left of the mouth of the *Rio di Noale:*

(21) **Pal. Gussoni-Grimani** (*c.* 1548–56): Several prints show the Canal façade decorated with frescos by Jacopo Tintoretto. Today the frescos have gone but the harmonious façade, with its two loggias (four arches), remains.

To the right of the mouth of the *Rio di S.Felice:*

(23) **Pal. Fontana:** Typical 16C forms. This is the birthplace of Pope Clement XIII Rezzonico (1693–1769).

(25) **Ca' d'Oro** (houses the Galleria Giorgio Franchetti, cf. under Museums): The Ca' d'Oro (literally, the Golden House) is famous for its elegant ornament, which was once gilded. Built for Marino Contarini, the procurator, in 1421–40 on the site of a 12C Romanesque-Byzantine building. The decoration of the asymmetrical canal façade is mostly by Matteo Raverti, working under the supervision of Giovanni and Bartolomeo Bon. Raverti

also had a hand in Milan cathedral and in the Doges' Palace. Late-Gothic elements (fine tracery, marble inlay and decorative battlements) are impressively combined with early-Renaissance features (the breaking-down of separate sections of wall into large, flat rectangles). This façade influenced the development of forms in Venetian secular architecture right up until the 19C. However, it derives two of its features, the open arcade on the ground floor, which was already uncommon in the Gothic period, and the rather heavy right-hand section, with rectangular windows in Oriental style from the previous building on the site. The building was thoroughly restored in 1969–84. There then follow:

(27) **Pal. Pesaro** (1st half of 15C): On the two main floors there are relatively simple but harmonious Gothic loggias and individual windows, each framed by stone dressings. Immediately adjoining this:

(29) **Pal. Sagredo:** This 13C Romanesque-Byzantine building retains its original ground floor, and also the beautiful series of windows on the piano nobile (columns of multi-coloured stone). In *c.* 1500, extra storeys were added and the right-hand annex, with its ogee-arched

Palazzo Pesaro

Palazzo Foscari

windows and elegant quadripartite loggia, typical features of Gothic palazzi. An interior staircase was installed in 1734 instead of the Gothic external staircase, with walls and ceilings painted by Pietro Longhi (Crushing of the Giants, 1754). To the right, on the *Campo S.Sofia*:

(31) **Pal. Foscari:** Typical High Gothic building (*c.* mid 15C), with a six-arched loggia. Multi-coloured columns.

(33) **Pal. Michiel dalle Colonne** (2nd half of 17C), with a particularly tall ground-floor arcade (hence the name). Decorative busts in relief at the points of the window arches.

To the left of the mouth of the *Rio dei SS.Apostoli*:

(35) **Pal. Mangilli-Valmarana:** Built by Antonio Visentini in 1740−51, using Gothic fragments. Enlarged in 1784. Giovanni Antonio Selva's ornaments, dating from the period when it was built, were brought to Paris at Napoleon's command.

(37) **Ca' Da Mosto:** One of the oldest surviving buildings (late 12C) on the Grand Canal, with extra storeys added in the 17C. There are reliefs with Christian motifs and late Veneto-Byzantine stylistic features (pointed upper sides of the arches). This is the house where Alvise da Mosto (1432−88), the voyager who discovered the Cape Verde Islands, was born.

(39) **Pal. Sernagiotto** (19C). A good ground floor façade.

(41) **Pal. Civran:** Early-18C, possibly by Giorgio Massari. A typical Venetian feature is the use of an arch flanked by rectangular, pedimented windows to emphasize the large portal and the central window.

(43) **Fondaco dei Tedeschi** (main post office): Standing close to the Rialto Bridge, this used to be a centre for German merchants. It was used both for trade (ground floor) and to house the merchants, who were organized into a monastery-like community. It was probably founded shortly after the capture of Constantinople during the Fourth Crusade (1204) and it is the oldest trading post of a foreign nation in Venice. Renaissance in style and arranged around a square courtyard, it was rebuilt in 1505−8 by Giorgio Spavento and Antonio Abbondio, immediately after the original 13C building had burnt down. The proportions of the tripartite façade facing the canal were much disfigured in 1836 when the corner sections were reduced in height to the level of the cen-

Fondaco dei Tedeschi

Palazzo Farsetti

tral part. Its exterior was once covered with paintings by artists such as Giorgione and the young Titian but these have been completely destroyed and it today appears rather plain, since the walls have deliberately been left without ornament in order to emphasize the paintings. Napoleon dissolved the institution in 1806, after which the building fell into decay and its decorations were scattered. It was restored in *c.* 1940 and its interior was enlarged for its new role.

Rialto Bridge. On the left of the mouth of the *Rio di S.Salvador:*

(45) **Pal. Dolfin-Manin** (Banca d'Italia): A Renaissance palace to plans by Jacopo Sansovino (1532–45), with a courtyard, which is unusual in private Venetian buildings. Because of the site it occupied, the public is allowed to walk along the massive ground-floor arcade. Lodovico Manin, the last Doge, had the interior refurbished in the late 18C in neoclassical style by Giovanni Antonio Selva.

There then follow:

(47) **Pal. Bembo:** A noble late-Gothic building (*c.* 1460). It is well proportioned despite its width, and the façade, with symmetrical five-arched loggias, retains its traditional division into three sections.

(49–51) **Ca' Loredan** (part of the city administration) and **Pal. Farsetti** (town hall): Despite much evidence of 19C restoration, the ground floor and piano nobile of these two 13C buildings are well-preserved examples of Romanesque-Byzantine architecture with its characteristic series of arches and windows across the whole façade. The rhythm of this harmonious progression is subtly controlled by the use of different capitals and by doubling the columns. The second storey, based on the style of the piano nobile, was added in the 16C, and so too was the attic which is typical of Venetian palazzi.

(53) **Pal. Martinengo** (18C): To the left of the mouth of *Rio di S.Luca:*

(55) **Pal. Grimani** (court of appeal): Renaissance; the powerful façade, a masterpiece by the Veronese architect Michele Sanmicheli, is vividly articulated both horizontally and vertically throughout. Begun in *c.* 1540, Giangiacomo dei Grigi, the successor to Sanmicheli, continued work on the 2nd main storey after Sanmicheli's death. Completed by Giovanni Rusconi in 1575. Two Victories by Alessandro Vittoria in the spandrels of the monumental portal.

Ca' Loredan

Palazzo Bembo

There now follow:

(57) **Pal. Corner-Contarini dei Cavalli:** Gothic ground floor and piano nobile, *c.* 1445–50. Characteristic, six-part loggia and corner windows with a trefoil arch and half quatrefoils above, all enclosed within a typical rectangular frame. Extra storey added in the 17C. Adjoining the building:

(59–61) **Palazzetto Tron** (15C). This is followed by the **Pal. Martinengo-Volpi** (mid 16C).

To the left of the mouth of *Rio S.Michele:*

(63) **Pal. Benzon:** Artists and men of letters who were involved in politics, such as Antonio Canova and Ugo Foscolo, met in the drawing-room during the difficult period of foreign rule after the end of the Venetian republic (1797).

To the right of the mouth of the *Rio dell'Albero:*

(65) **Pal. Corner-Spinelli:** A Renaissance palace (1490–1510) by Mauro Coducci, resembling the Pal. Vendramin-Calergi (No. 9). For the first time in a Venetian palazzo, the massive lower storey is rusticated, a feature which emphasizes the horizontal axis, in lively contrast to the vertically accentuated large windows, also derived from the Florentine Renaissance.

Another feature in the façade's powerful articulation is that these 'extraneous' elements merge with the traditional Venetian division into three parts and the solid frame of friezes and pilasters at the corners. Michele Sanmicheli reworked the interior in classical Renaissance style in 1542 and the courtyard was built at the same time. The ceiling paintings from that period by Giorgio Vasari, the Tuscan painter, architect and art historian, have been lost.

(67) **Pal. Corner-Gheltoff** (1st half of 17C): The central windows are typical examples of the Venetian window or serliana: a central arch between two lower openings crowned by horizontal architraves. This form of window first appeared in the 2nd half of the 16C.

Directly adjoining this:

(69) **Palazzi Mocenigo:** A series of four palaces. The first was built in the 17C and incorporated part of an existing Gothic building. The adjacent, severely articulated 18C double façade (Venetian windows) was once painted. There is a tablet in memory of Lord Byron who stayed here in 1818–19. The following façade (1579) is rather a conservative example of late Renaissance style in a Venetian mould, but

Palazzo Corner-Gheltoff

Palazzo Contarini dalle Figure

has fine decorative details. Giordano Bruno the philosopher lived here in 1592 (the Inquisition had him burned to death in Rome in 1600). Seven members of the Mocenigo family were Doges between 1414 and 1778.

Adjoining this:

(71) **Pal. Contarini dalle Figure:** Begun in 1504, probably by Giorgio Spavento, and completed by Antonio Abbondio in 1546. The tripartite Renaissance façade bears decorative carvings from which the palace takes its name. The striking pediment above the central window of the piano nobile may have been suggested by Andrea Palladio, the architect from Vicenza, whose patron was Jacopo Contarini. The building is followed by the Gothic **Pal.Erizzo** and **Pal. Da Lezze** (15C).

(73) **Pal. Moro-Lin:** Two existing buildings, rising on the inside of the bend of the Grand Canal, were joined together (*c.* 1650–70) to produce a long Florentine Renaissance façade with a uniform series of arches.

On the left, by the *Campo S.Samuele:*

(75) **Pal. Grassi** (Centro Internazionale delle Arti e del Costume, temporary exhibitions): The city's largest 18C palazzo was begun in 1718 by Giorgio Massari, later than most of the other buildings along the canal. Completed after his death. The remote, impressive façade uses Venetian arches as well as classical forms and it contrasts with the interior, which displays a late-baroque expansiveness, with typical Venetian decoration (staircase probably painted by Alessandro Longhi; individual rooms painted by Jacopo Guarana and Fabio Canal).

(77) **Pal. Malipiero** (1st quarter of 17C). To the left of the mouth of *Rio del Duca:*

(79) **Ca' del Duca:** The corner section on the Rio del Duca and the two columns give an idea of the intended mass and dimensions of this building, which was begun by Bartolomeo Bon in *c.* 1450. However, work was discontinued after some years, perhaps as a result of objections by the municipal building authorities, who laid down precise limits for area and elevation in order to ensure the structural safety of foundations and building, and general hygiene. Titian had his studio here at times. The other buildings in this complex were erected in the 17C or 19C on the old foundations. It houses the *Raccolte d'Arte Orientale e di Porcellane* (cf. Museums).

Palazzo Malipiero

Palazzo Giustinian-Lolin

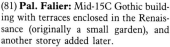

Palazzo Bàrbaro

Palazzo Cavalli-Franchetti

(81) **Pal. Falier:** Mid-15C Gothic building with terraces enclosed in the Renaissance (originally a small garden), and another storey added later.

(83) **Pal. Giustinian-Lolin:** This elegant palace (1623) is believed to be the earliest work of Baldassare Longhena, who designed several magnificent baroque buildings for the city. Old fashioned elements include the overall composition of the façade and the Venetian windows, a feature from the 2nd half of the 16C (cf. No. 67). But the masks on the keys of the arches and the garlands stretched like cloths are examples of baroque ornament.

(85) **Pal. Cavalli-Franchetti:** Outstanding late-Gothic façade (c. 1565; restored in the late 19C) with fine tracery. The individual windows have prominent frames, and the corners are decorated with slender twisted columns. At the rear there is a neo-Gothic addition.
Following this:

(87) **Palazzi Bàrbaro:** The left-hand section (1425) is a good example of a Gothic palazzo; note the polychrome roundels. The half storey on the ground floor (mezzà) can be seen clearly and it was in use from the 15C, housing the bookkeeping department above the shops. The right-hand extension (1694–8) is by Antonio Gaspari.

(89) **Casa Stecchini:** Two buildings, one 16C (with two double windows) and one 18C.
Next:

(91) **Casino delle Rose:** Plain 17C house, where the neoclassical sculptor Antonio Canova had his first studio in Venice.

(93) **Pal. Corner della Ca' Grande** (Prefettura): This, the greatest of the Renaissance palazzi in Venice, was begun by Jacopo Sansovino in 1537 for a nephew of the queen of Cyprus. Elements of Roman and Florentine Renaissance are combined in this building which, after taking 30 years to build, was probably com-

Palazzo Gritti

pleted by Vicenzo Scamozzi. On the one hand are the square courtyard, the façade with the contrast between the massive ground floor and the vertically accentuated main storeys, and the classical order of Ionic and Corinthian columns. On the other hand there is the rusticated pedestal and cylinders and the triple arches of the portal. Venetian features include the lightly indicated tripartite division of the façade, the paired columns and the arches. One reason why the canal façade is so elegant is that the windows rise through two storeys, as can be seen by comparing the façade with the side walls.

This palazzo is followed by:

(95) **Pal. Minotto:** 15C Gothic palace. The roof terrace (liagò), which can be seen in paintings of Carpaccio and Canaletto, has always been popular on Venetian houses, since the narrow canals and alleyways and the lack of lawns left little opportunity to spend time in the sun.

(97) **Pal. Gritti-Pisani** (Gritti Palace Hotel): 1st half of 15C. The base of the canal façade is 19C and dates from the restoration of the palazzo and its conversion into a hotel. The walls are conspicuously bare today, but were originally frescoed. The hotel provided the setting for Ernest Hemingway's short novel 'Across The River And Into The Trees' (1950).

This is followed by:

(99) **Pal. Flangini-Fini** (17C): Adjoined by the mid-15C Gothic **Pal. Manolesso-Ferro,** with later alterations.

Next comes:

(101) **Pal. Contarini-Fasan:** Graceful late-Gothic house (*c.* 1470). Beautiful façade contrasting with dressings of bright Istrian stone and charming, traceried balconies. Legend relates that it is the house of Desdemona, who was murdered by her husband Othello out of jealousy. (Casa Otello: see Scuola Grande dei Carmini; cf. The Schools).

The 'Regina-Europa' hotel now follows,

comprising several buildings of different date and quality, among them:

(103–105) **Pal. Contarini:** Gothic buildings from the 2nd half of the 15C, rebuilt and converted in the 19C in line with the taste and opinions then current. After some more modern buildings there follows: **Pal.Tiepolo** (17C), with 19C alterations.

There follow:

(107) **Pal. Treves-Bonfili:** 3rd quarter of 17C; radically restored.

To the right, on the mouth of the *Rio di S.Moisè:*

(109) **Hotel Bauer-Grünwald:** Neo-Gothic, carefully designed to blend in stylistically and built in 1901 using Gothic masonry as far as the piano nobile. Its style and ornament are based on the following:

(111) **Pal. Giustinian** (seat of Biennale di Venezia with an information bureau for all cultural events): Gothic (3rd quarter of 15C), with later alterations. Multicoloured façade, inlaid and dressed with bright Istrian stone.

(113) **Fontego della Farina** (Capitaneria di Porto/port administration): Old flour storehouse built in 1483; until 1806 was the seat of the academy of arts founded in 1750.

Palazzo Contarini-Fasan

Right bank: Map: p. 32

(2–6) **Palazzo Gritti:** Late-16C, but now rebuilt throughout. Next to it is **Pal. Corner.** The ground floor is the only section surviving from the building of *c.* 1595. Followed by **Pal.Donà-Balbi** (17C).

(8) **Pal. Giovanelli-Dorigo:** *c.* 1460–80. The harmonious façade combines Gothic and Renaissance elements.

(10) **Fondaco dei Turchi** (Museo di Storia Naturale; cf. Museums): The symmetrical arrangement of the façade into a two-storeyed central section and tower-like sides follows the Romanesque-Byzantine scheme of 13C Venetian palazzo architecture. Typical features include the arcade opening on to the canal through a series of narrow, round arches, and the reliefs on the elegant marble facing. However, it is difficult to be sure about the original form of this massive building with its rectangular courtyard, because after falling further and further into decay during the 18&19C it was extensively rebuilt in 1880, with some of the original materials being used in this work. Built for a private owner in the mid 13C, it changed hands several times before becoming the Turkish trading post from 1621–1838. This area was once at the heart of the city's diplomatic and business district.

The following buildings are on the left of the mouth of the *Rio del Fondaco dei Turchi:*

(12) **Deposito del Megio:** The republic's former granary. A functional 15C building, with a few, small windows, as befitted its purpose. The only decorations are the relief of the lion of St.Mark (reworked from drawings in the 19C) and the decorative battlements.

On the right, at the mouth of the *Rio Tron:*

(14) **Pal. Battagià-Belloni:** Baroque building, *c.* 1650–63, probably by Baldassare Longhena, whose façade, with its carved ornament and accentuated piano nobile, contrasts very effectively with the plain building adjoining to the right.

Neighbouring buildings:

(16) **Pal. Tron** (end of 16C). The adjoining Gothic **Pal. Duodo** (15C) was rebuilt in baroque style in the late 17C.

(18) **Pal. Priuli-Bon-Dandolo:** The nar-

row round arches on the ground floor, along with the water gate, were probably all joined together at a later date. They were part of a Romanesque-Byzantine building which was repeatedly altered over the following centuries. One of the changes was the addition of ogee arches in the Gothic loggia.

After the square in front of *S.Staè:*
(20) **Pal. Foscarini-Giovanelli** (*c.* 1550).
(22) **Ca' Pesaro** (Galleria Internazionale d'Arte Moderna and Galleria d'Arte Orientale; cf. Museums): This late work by Longhena is a high point of Venetian baroque architecture. It was only two storeys high at his death in 1682 but after a break of several years it was completed in 1710 under Antonio Gaspari's supervision. The animated façade is distinguished by an abundance of ornament and yet makes a harmonious overall impression due to the proportions of the three storeys, which are almost equal in height. The seven bays of the façade display the traditional tripartite arrangement, with the central section being accentuated by the use of paired columns. The diamond rustication of the ground storey is an unusual feature, as too are the carved masks.
(24) **Pal. Corner della Regina:** The

façade of this building, completed by Domenico Rossi in 1724, clearly refers to the dominant canal front of the nearby Ca' Pesaro (No. 22; between the two buildings are the 18C **Pal. Dona** and the 17C **Pal. Correggio**). But the ornament, which is more reticent in its variety of forms and more severe in its individual motifs (e.g. the flat rustication, and pediments on the 2nd main storey) already shows neoclassical influences. It takes its name from Caterina Cornaro, the queen of Cyprus, who was born in 1454 in the building which previously stood on this site.

This is followed by the early-Gothic **Casa Bragadin-Favretto** (14C).
(26) **Pal. Brandolin:** 15C Gothic building opposite the Ca' d'Oro, with the common Venetian motif of a row of quatrefoils between the extradoses of the upper loggia. A third upper storey was removed in the mid 19C.
(28) **Pescheria/fish market:** Built on a traditional site in 1907 in Gothic style by Domenico Rupolo and Cesare Laurenti, who also designed the statue of *St.Peter.*
(30) **Fabbriche Nuove:** A long, functional building to plans by Jacopo Sansovino (1552–5) housing storerooms and

Palazzo Flangini-Fini

Palazzo dei Camerlenghi

offices, it stands near the fruit and vegetable market. The rhythmic series of Tuscan and Ionic pilasters and the ground floor arcade help this sober complex to blend in with its surroundings relatively well. The pedimented window is a Roman Renaissance feature. Restored in 1860, when alterations to the original design were removed.

(32) **Fabbriche Vecchie:** Built by Antonio Abbondio in 1522 in still plainer forms than the immediately adjoining Fabbriche Nuove.

To the right, beside the *Rialto Bridge:*
(34) **Pal. dei Camerlenghi** (court of justice): The former seat of the Exchequer (1464) was rebuilt in its present form in 1525–8 after being severely damaged in the devastating Rialto fire of 1513. The ground plan and the richly ornamented façade of the imposing Renaissance building follow the curve of the canal.

To the left, at the foot of the *Rialto Bridge:*
(36) **Pal. dei Dieci Savi** (Magistrato alle Acque): The seat of the 'Ten Wise Men', who were responsible for taxation, stood in what was the heart of the Venetian administrative, financial and business centre around the Rialto Bridge. This building, also much damaged in 1513, was rebuilt by Scarpagnino, work being completed in 1521.

(38) **Pal. Barzizza:** Enlarged and partly rebuilt in the 17C, the building retains on its ground floor (portal) and its piano nobile several important traces of its 13C Veneto-Byzantine core.

This is adjoined by:
(40) **Pal. Buginello:** Probably a late-13C Romanesque-Byzantine structure with an extra storey added in the 17C. A ground-floor arcade (formerly, three open arches), and windows with narrow arches.

On the other side of the *Rio dei Meloni:*
(42) **Pal. Papadopoli** (university institute): High Renaissance building (*c.* 1555–60) by Giangiacomo dei Grigi. The **Pal. Donà** adjoins this.

Following this, on the right, at the mouth of the *Rio della Madonnetta:*
(44) **Pal. Donà della Madonnetta:** 13C Veneto-Byzantine structure with arcade running the full length of the façade, and later alterations. It takes its name from a relief of the Madonna on the 1st floor.

To the left of the mouth of the *Rio della Madonnetta:*
(46) **Pal. Bernardo:** The façade of this four-storeyed late-Gothic building (*c.* 1442) is a classic example of the Venetian

Fish market

style: central loggias, dressings of Istrian stone, twisted columns at the corners and a cornice beneath the roof. The upper loggia has a series of trefoil arches and quatrefoils and a balcony of dwarf balustrades alternating with taller ones. The two water gates lead into two separate courtyards, with a very fine external staircase to the 1st storey.

There now follow:

(48) **Pal. Querini** (17C). Adjoined by:

(50) **Pal. Grimani:** This noble Renaissance façade (1st half of 16C) has round arches and fine carved ornament, with marble tondi, ovals and rectangles in a variety of different colours.

Now come the:

(52) **Pal. Cappello-Layard:** The exterior was painted by Paolo Veronese and Giovanni Battista Zelotti (c. mid 16C) but their work was destroyed by a fire in the 17C.

To the left of the mouth of the *Rio di S.Polo:*

(54) **Pal. Barbarigo della Terrazza:** Only the left-hand section was built (completed 1569) to its full height, whilst the ground floor of the central and right-hand sections form a terrace, hence the name of the palace.

Followed by:

(56) **Pal. Pisani-Moretta:** The tracery of the upper loggia is a good feature in the fine façade of this late-Gothic palace (c. 1465). The formation of pointed arches by the intersection of semicircular arches is a popular motif in Italian Gothic.

There follow:

(58–60) **Pal. Tiepolo-Donà** (16C). The **Pal. Giustinian-Persico** is to the right of the mouth of the *Rio di S.Tomà:* Gothic buildings with an extra Renaissance storey. To the right of the mouth of the *Rio della Frescada:*

(62) **Pal. Civran-Grimani:** 17C, with interesting proportions to the façade (high piani nobili).

(64) **Pal. Balbi** (Giunta Regionale/regional administration): This impressive palace was built in 1582–90 to plans by Alessandro Vittoria. It occupies a prominent position on the outside of the wide left-hand sweep of the Grand Canal. Mannerist features on the façade include the pediments of the portals and side windows, and the pairs of columns in the arcades.

In an equally prominent position, on the other side of the mouth of the *Rio di Ca' Foscari*, a continuation of the *Rio Nuovo*, is the:

(66) **Ca' Foscari** (main building of the university, and seat of the *Biblioteca Generale di Venezia):* A masterpiece of Venetian architecture. Begun for Doge Francesco Foscari in 1452 on the site of an earlier building. It has an elegant, traditionally arranged façade, and displays glorious examples of the Gothic richness of form (arches and the clearly defined tracery). But the balconies and the frieze of putti and coats-of-arms in relief above the upper loggia reveal Renaissance elements and suggest that work continued until c. 1470. Restored in 1844–7 and rebuilt throughout at the rear. King Henry III of France stayed here in 1574. Immediately adjoining:

(68) **Palazzi Giustinian:** Also begun in 1451/2, probably under the supervision of Bartolomeo Bon. The buildings, initially separate, were joined to form the fine double façade, with a central portal and single windows above. The overall effect of

Palazzo Pisani-Moretta

this composition which is magnificent in its details is intensified by accentuating the central axes of what were the original middle sections. On the 2nd floor, the main piano nobile with the public rooms, the loggias are extended by two bays. In addition, what were originally the side windows are larger and more ornate than the other windows and have pendant tracery. These two palaces, together with the Ca' Foscari, form a continuous and majestic front on the broad curve of the canal. Richard Wagner composed the second act of 'Tristan' here in 1858−9.

(70) **Pal. Nani:** 16C Renaissance building.

(72) **Ca' Rezzonico** (see Museo del Settecento Veneziano; cf. Museums): A splendid baroque building by Baldassare Longhena (begun in 1667), and continued after his death in 1682 by Antonio Gaspari, up to and including the 1st floor. After the building had come into the possession of the Rezzonico family, it was completed by Giorgio Massari in 1756, probably to plans by Longhena. In contrast to Longhena's powerful façade of the Ca' Pesaro (No. 22), his articulation of the front of Ca' Rezzonico uses Renaissance elements from the Pal. Corner della Ca'

Grande (No. 93). The delicate 18C decoration and furnishings of the interior are very well-preserved and are the work of the period's leading artists. Robert Browning died here on 12 December 1889.

(74−76) **Pal. Contarini-Michiel** (17C). **Palazzetto Stern:** Fragments of an earlier Gothic building were incorporated into Giuseppe Berti's neo-Gothic palace (2nd half of 19C). To the left of the mouth of the *Rio Malpaga:*

(78) **Pal. Moro:** An imposing 16C Renaissance building. Adjoined by:

(80) **Pal. Loredan degli Ambasciatori:** A fine Gothic building (*c.* 1460−*c.* 1475) with a typical tripartite Venetian façade (the diagonals of the façade intersect at the main loggia). Clearly defined, bright stone dressings; trefoil arches with quatrefoils. The two late-15C figures of knights are striking features of the piano nobile, and are probably by one of the many followers of Pietro Lombardo. Restored in 1891 after fire damage. It owes its name to the fact that it was the Austrian embassy in the 18C.

To the left of the mouth of the *Rio di S. Trovaso:*

(82−84) **Pal. Contarini-Corfù:** 15C late-Gothic building with 19C alterations.

Ca' Rezzonico

Palazzo Contarini-Corfù

Adjoined by **Pal. Contarini degli Scrigni:** Early baroque, by Vicenzo Scamozzi (1608–9).

(86) **Former Scuola Grande della Carità** (see Galleria dell'Accademia, cf. Museums): Mid-15C Gothic, built at the same time as the church which stands at right angles to it. Neoclassical façade (1820). Today, as the Accademia, it houses the world's most important collection of Venetian paintings (14–19C).

Accademia Bridge. There follow:

(88) **Pal. Brandolin-Rota:** Robert Browning lived in this 17C building for a considerable time.

(90) **Pal. Contarini dal Zaffo:** Early-Renaissance (late 15C), possibly by Tullio Lombardo. Baroque balconies. Decorative façade with marble and porphyry ornament of various colours and outstanding carving (capitals and frieze above the ground floor).

(92–94) **Pal. Balbi-Valier:** Carved fragments from an earlier 13C Romanesque-Byzantine building were incorporated in the 17C palace.

To the right of the mouth of the *Rio di S.Vio:*

Pal. Loredan: Mid-16C Renaissance building. Its façade is plain today, but may formerly have been painted by Giuseppe Salviati.

To the left, by the *Campo S.Vio:*

(96) **Pal. Barbarigo** (offices of the Compagnia Vetri Muranesi): This 16C façade was decorated with mosaics in the late 19C, whose subject matter is connected with glassblowing. On the left, they depict Emperor Charles V in Titian's studio, and on the right is the visit to Murano of the French King Henry III. After this:

(98–102) **Pal. Da Mula-Morosini:** A typical 15C Gothic building; rococo interior (18C). **Pal. Centani** (18C). **Casa Biondetti** (18C): House where Rosalba Carriera, the painter and famous portrait artist, lived, and also died in 1758. Many fine pastel portraits in the Gallerie dell'-Accademia (rooms 15–17) and in the Museo del Settecento Veneziano (room 4; cf. Museums).

(104) **Pal. Venier dei Leoni** (Collezione Peggy Guggenheim; cf. Museums): This building by Lorenzo Boschetti faces the Pal. Corner della Ca'Grande (No. 93). Begun in 1748, work never proceeded beyond the ground floor, which is complete. It probably takes its name from the lions' heads on the canal façade. After repeatedly changing hands, the building,

Palazzo Corner-Contarini dei Cavalli

Palazzi Giustinian

Ca' Foscari (left) and Palazzo Balbi (right)

which has one of the city's largest gardens, came into the possession of Peggy Guggenheim in 1949 and from 1951 onwards it housed her magnificent and constantly expanding collection of modern art. This was bequeathed to the city in her will in 1979.

(106) **Pal. Dario:** A splendid testimony to the early Renaissance (*c.* 1480). Asymmetric façade displaying the architectural (round arches) and decorative (porphyry and marble inlay) hallmarks of the school of Pietro Lombardo, which had an enduring influence on Venetian architecture from the late 15C onwards (similar to Pal. Contarini dal Zaffo, No. 90). Its harmonious proportions, the variety of the inlaid roundels, and the fine details, make it a masterpiece of Venetian architecture. There then follow:

(108) **Pal.Barbaro:** Late-Gothic (*c.* 1445), with an extra storey added later.

(110) **Pal. Salviati:** Modern building, with traditional features and a mosaic (allegory of Venice), which stands out conspicuously from its surroundings.

(112) **Pal. Genovese:** A final delight to the eye in the chain of buildings on the right bank of the canal. This imposing Gothic-style reconstruction (1892) of a 15C Gothic building has unusually wide side sections but a number of other typical stylistic features: bright stone dressings, trefoil arches and quatrefoils and balconies.

Adjoining this are 14/15C Gothic sections of the former **Benedictine monastery of S.Gregorio.**

S.Maria della Salute

(114) **Seminario Patriarcale** (Raccolta del Seminario Patriarcale; cf. Museums): The deliberately plain, four-storeyed former monastery of the Trinitarians (from 1817 it was the diocesan seminary), built by Baldassare Longhena in 1670 to the N. of the baroque church of S.Maria della Salute, which was still being built at that time.

Palazzo Barbaro

Palazzo Dario

(116) **Dogana da Mar:** Customs house by Giuseppe Benoni (1672–82). It is a stumpy, functional building for the storage of goods and the administration of commerce, and its sobriety counters the arcaded E. front. The triangular building ends in a tower-like pavilion which stands at the point of the island and is crowned by two telamones supporting a large golden globe of the world on which the goddess Fortune turns in the wind. Despite the lack of uniformity, the complex forms an effective architectural unit on this prominent site.

Palazzo Ducale/Doges' Palace (Piazzetta S.Marco): This monumental Gothic palace, a symbol of Venetian power, stands between St.Mark's Basilica and the Molo and its façade dominates its surroundings. Superbly decorated and a showpiece for the mastery of Venice's stonemasons, woodcarvers and stucco artists, it represents the zenith of Venetian secular

architecture and at the same time provides a backdrop to a display of the inexhaustible power of Venetian painting. The *history* of the building of the palace can be divided into *four phases:* 1) 1340–1423: The S. wing on the Molo, with the Sala del Maggior Consiglio [17], was the first part of a new building. Carved façade ornament (capitals, corner sculptures [C, D], and narrow windows with a balcony [17a] (c. 1404). 2) 1424–83: W. wing rebuilt on the Piazzetta. 3) 1483–1574: The E. wing contains the doge's private apartments [9]. This wing was burnt down and rebuilt in Renaissance style. The Arco Foscari was completed [E]. Scala dei Giganti [F]. 4) After 1574 or 1577: Commencement of lengthy restoration or rebuilding of the interior to repair the damage caused by fires in the halls and adjoining rooms in the S. and W. wings. Exterior and interior façades of E. wing completed in the early 17C. New State prisons completed in 1614. The gorgeous decoration of the *interior*, the work of the city's leading artists, is mainly 16C. The paintings are by Giovanni Bellini, Vittore Carpaccio, Giorgione, Titian, Paolo Veronese, Jacopo Tintoretto and Palma Giovane and show all the traditional Venetian mastery of colour.

Façade:

The S. and W. *façades* with their wealth of carving (capitals) accentuate, in their strong horizontal articulation, the extreme length of the building's wings (235 and 245 ft.). Ground floor arcades are supported by rows of stumpy columns and in turn support first floor arcades of elegant trefoil arches (each occupying half the width of the lower openings) with quatrefoils inserted between the extradoses. Above these arcades rises the massive 2nd storey (the main floor with public rooms and almost twice the height of the lower storeys) faced with a two colour pattern of rhombi. The splendid capitals on the ground floor depict a French Gothic cycle (e.g. the Seasons; Ages of Man; Virtues and Vices; famous Biblical, historical and legendary figures; constellations; flora and fauna). The large, central W. window is similar to that on the S. side (17 a), but plainer (crowning Justice dating from 1579). A Justice on the lion's throne (allegory of Venice) above the 6th arch from the right (instead of the quatrefoil) and the thicker columns mark the back wall of the *Sala del Maggior Consiglio* (17) and the point from where the W. wing was rebuilt (work began in 1424). The 330 ft. long E. wing is four storeys high and houses the doge's private apartments. Its early-Renaissance marble *courtyard façade* is impressive both for its size and its abundant decorative details (e.g. polychrome inlay, reliefs); the right-hand section was not built until the 2nd half of the 16C.

Ground floor:

A) *Porta della Carta:* High Gothic main portal (1438–42) by Giovanni and Bartolomeo Bon, assisted by Lombard and Tuscan stonemasons. Above the door, the figure of Doge Francesco Foscari (1423–57), who commissioned this W. wing, kneels in front of the Lion of St.Mark. The original figure was smashed in 1797 and the present replacement dates from 1885. To the sides of this are four Statues of the Virtues. St.Mark appears above the window and Justice crowns all. *Corner sculptures:* B) Judgement of Solo-

Doges' Palace

mon; above this the Archangel Gabriel.
C) Fall of Man: the Archangel Michael
above. D) Drunkenness of Noah; above
this the Archangel Raphael with Tobias.
E) *Arco Foscari:* An impressive two-
storeyed building in the form of a triumphal arch which plays an important role
in the coronation of the Doge. St.Mark,
who is blessing the approaching Doge,
turns to the staircase (F) where the insig-
nia of worldly power are granted to the
Doge. The façade towards the courtyard
has a clock, and was completed by
Bartolomeo Manopola in 1618.
F) *Scala dei Giganti:* A splendid marble
staircase (1483) by Antonio Rizzo, conceived as a throne and aligned with the
Arco Foscari, it forms the setting for the
coronation of the Doge elect with his dis-
tinctive Cornu (Corno Ducale). Since 1554
it has been flanked by Jacopo Sansovino's
colossal statues of 'Mars' and 'Neptune'.
G) *Cortile dei Senatori/*Meeting place of
the Senators.
H) *Cappella di S.Nicolò:* Rebuilt by Giorgio Spavento in 1505–06 with a severe but
decorative Renaissance façade, the arcades
of which accord with those in the E. wing.
Titian's painting inside (1523/4) has been
lost. One altarpiece was transferred to
St.Mark's Basilica. A garden was laid out
on the roof terrace in the early 16C.
I) *Cortile/courtyard:* Two bronze well-
heads (1554–9) by Alfonso Alberghetti
and Niccolò dei Conti.
M) *Museo dell'Opera:* This museum of the
restoration work contains originals of the
carving which has had to be replaced on
the façade by copies, fragments of sculptures, and architectural features of various
kinds. The 19C plans and the model for
preserving the building are also on display
and they give an idea of the tremendous
pile foundations on which this monumental palace stands.

1st floor:

1) *Scala d'Oro:* Designed in 1530–59 by
J.Sansovino, and completed by Antonio
Abbondio. Sculptures at the entrance by
Tiziano Aspetti. It takes its name from
Alessandro Vittoria's gilded stucco vault
and it has mythological and allegorical
paintings by Giovanni Battista Franco. A
separate passage leads from the first flight
of stairs to the Doge's apartments on the
2nd floor.
3–5) *Former offices:* chancellery, public
prosecutor's office, and notary's office.
6) *Ponte dei Sospiri/Bridge of Sighs:* A
covered bridge completed by Antonino

Doges' Palace, façade detail

Doges' Palace, façade detail

The key events in the history of the palace:

811 – Seat of government moved from Malamocco (on today's Lido) to the Rialto. Building of fortifications, and also the castle of the Doge (Venetian 'doge' = Italian 'duca' = duke), initially wood.

832 – First church of St.Mark consecrated as the palace chapel.

976 and 1172–98 – Rebuilding of the palace after it had been burnt down.

1297 – Closing of the Maggior Consiglio (Great Council). From now on, only those citizens who were entered in the Golden Book of the City could become members of the Maggior Consiglio.

1335 – The oligarchic constitution of the Venetian republic was drawn up in its final form.

1340–67 – Extension and rebuilding of the *Sala del Maggior Consiglio* (17) in what is today the oldest part of the palace, on the Molo; 1404 window with balcony (17a).

1424 – Beginning of what was planned as the final phase: rebuilding of the *W. wing* on the Piazzetta; including:

1438 – *Porta della Carta* (A) and 1440–70 – Extension as the *Arco Foscari* (E).

From 1483 – Antonio Rizzo, and later Pietro Lombardo, largely rebuilt the *E. wing*, which had burnt down.

1505–6 – *Cappella di S.Nicolò* rebuilt (H).

From 1507 – *Sala del Maggior Consiglio* (17) painted by Gentile and Giovanni Bellini, Alvise Vivarini, V.Carpaccio, Giorgione and Titian (entirely destroyed by fire in 1577).

1521 – For the first time, a Doge (Antonio Grimani) was crowned on the completed *Scala dei Giganti* (F).

1530 – Work began on the *Scala d'Oro* (1) to a design by Jacopo Sansovino (completed 1559).

1553–4 – Ceiling paintings in the *Sala del Consiglio dei Dieci* (23) and the *Sala dei Tre Capi* (21) by Paolo Veronese, Giovanni Battista Ponchino and Giovanni Battista Zelotti.

1563–1614 – The *Prigioni Nuove/New State Prisons* built on the opposite side of the Rio del Palazzo by Giovanni Antonio Rusconi and later by Antonino and Tommaso Contin.

1574 – Serious fire damage; the *Sala delle Quattro Porte* (24) was immediately rebuilt by Andrea Palladio.

1575–7 – *Sala del Collegio* (26) painted by P. Veronese.

1577 – Devastating fire in the *Sala del Maggior Consiglio* (17) and *Sala dello Scrutinio* (19) on 20 December.

1577–80 – Four wall paintings by Tintoretto and 'Rape of Europa' by P.Veronese, together in the *Anticollegio* (25) since 1713.

1578–81 – Ceiling painting by Tintoretto in the *Sala delle Quattro Porte* (24).

1578–85 – Ceilings restored in the *Sala del Maggior Consiglio* (17) and *Sala dello Scrutinio* (19).

1581–4 – Four paintings by Tintoretto for the *Sala del Collegio* (26).

c. 1585 – Veronese's 'Triumph of Venice' for the ceiling of the *Sala del Maggior Consiglio* (17).

1587–94 – 'Last Judgement' by Palma Giovane in the *Sala dello Scrutinio* (19).

1588–90 – Tintoretto's 'Paradise' in the *Sala del Maggior Consiglio* (17).

1593 – Work began on the *palace chapel* (29).

1777 – *Courtyard* paved in stone (instead of brick).

1797 – End of the republic. The Palazzo Ducale was looted, with nearly all the furnishings being smashed or carried off.

1811–1904 – Temporary home of the *Biblioteca Marciana,* evacuated from the building opposite which was designed by J.Sansovino.

1875–87 – Extensive restoration, see the Museo dell'Opera (M).

Doges' Palace, Scala dei Giganti ▷

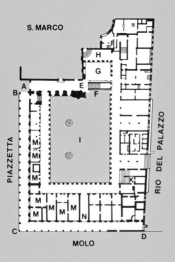
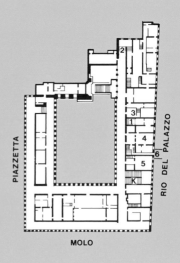

Contin in 1603 to a design by Antonio da Ponte. The bridge has separate passages going in each direction and links the palace and the rebuilt State prison (1563–1614). Its expressive name is a reminder of the horrors—which have sometimes been embroidered—of the State Inquisition. One description of them comes in the memoirs of Giacomo Casanova who, in 1757, managed to escape from the piombi (cells beneath the lead roof of the prison). Despite the torture and secret trials, the Venetian Inquisition, in contrast to comparable institutions in other countries, was itself subject to severe regulations to prevent arbitrariness and cruelty.

2nd floor:

7) *Sala degli Scarlatti:* Assembly room of the Doges' councillors who accompanied the Doge and, on ceremonial occasions, were clad in purple robes. Renaissance decoration (*c.* 1485–1510), and carving by several members of the Lombardo family. *Doges' apartments:* 8) The *Sala dello Scudo*

Palazzo Ducale/Doges' Palace: A Porta della Carta **B-D** Corner sculptures **E** Arco Foscari **F** Scala dei Giganti **G** Cortile dei Senatori **H** Cappella di S.Nicolò **I** Cortile/courtyard **K** Scala dei Censori **L** 'Pozzi' (fountains), prisons, parts of which are underground **M** Museo dell'Opera/Museum of the work on the palace (**N** Entrance)
1st floor 1 Scala d'Oro **2** Scala dei Senatori **3** Cancelleria/chancellery **4** Avogaria/lawyers' office **5** Censori/censors' office **6** Ponte dei Sospiri/Bridge of Sighs
2nd floor: 7 Sala degli Scarlatti **8-13** Doges' apartments **8** Sala dello Scudo **8a** Guard room **9** Pinacoteca/picture collection **10** Sala dei Filosofi **11** Camera degli Stucchi **12** Sala Erizzo **13** Sala Grimani **14** Quarantia Criminal **15** Quarantia Civil Vecchia **16** Sala di Guariento **17** Sala del Maggior Consiglio/Great Council **17a** Window and balcony **18** Quarantia Civil Nuova **19** Sala dello Scrutinio
3rd floor: 20 Sala degli Inquisitori **21** Sala dei Tre Capi **22** Sala della Bussola **23** Consiglio dei Dieci/Council of the Ten **24** Sala delle Quattro Porte **25** Anticollegio **26** Collegio/State council **27** Sala del Senato/Senate **28** Antichiesetta **29** Chiesetta/ Palace chapel **30** Archivio Segreto/former secret archive **31** Sala delle Armi/weapon collection

contained the heraldic shield (scudo) of the ruling Doge. The shield of Lodovico Manin, the last Doge, who abdicated in

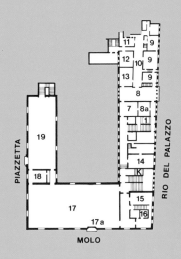

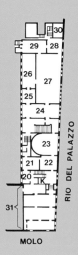

1797, is now on display. The maps in baroque frames are copies made by Francesco Grisellini in 1762 of works (1540) by Giovanni Battista Ramusio the cartographer. 8a) *Sala degli Scudieri/guard room:* Giovanni Battista Tiepolo's 'Neptune presenting the treasures of the sea to Venezia' (*c.* 1755) from the *Sala delle Quattro Porte* (24). 9) *Pinacoteca:* Fine collection of excellent paintings, mostly the palace's own. Room 1: 'Lamentation', probably by Giovanni Bellini. Room 2: Depictions of 'Hell' and 'Heaven' by Hieronymus Bosch. Room 3: Works by Jacopo da Ponte, known as Bassano, including 'Noah's Ark'. 10) *Sala dei Filosofi:* Passage connecting the apartments, named after a series of portraits of philosophers and scholars, temporarily hung here until 1762. 11) *Camera degli Stucchi:* Outstanding stucco from *c.* 1620 (doorway and vault) and the 18C (walls). The paintings set in the wall at that time include a copy of a portrait by Tintoretto

(it may be of the French King Henry III) beside the entrance. To the right of the exit a doorway opens on to a staircase, above the door there is the only Titian to have survived in the palace, his fresco of 'St.Christopher' (1523/4). 12) *Sala Erizzo:* Ceiling *c.* 1489. View over the roof terrace of the Cappella di S.Nicolò (H). 13) *Sala Grimani:* Intended for the Doge's private audiences. Named after the coat-of-arms of the Doge Marino Grimani (1595–1605), which is set in the Renaissance ceiling, the ceiling itself is probably by the Lombardi (*c.* 1487). The marble chimney piece is late 15C, with a late-16C upper part. Coat-of-arms of Doge Pasquale Cicogna (1585–95).

14–15) *Former courts of justice,* used by the Council of Forty (Quarantia) for hearing criminal and civil cases. 17C paintings are now on display.

16) *Sala di Guariento:* Former armoury. Fragments of the fresco of the Coronation of the Virgin, which was damaged by fire

in 1577. It was painted by Guariento, from Padua, in 1365-7 for the Sala del Maggior Consiglio (the remains were detached from underneath Tintoretto's 'Paradise' in 1903).

17) *Sala del Maggior Consiglio/Hall of the Great Council:* After the hall's destruction by the fire of 1577, a new council chamber was built (175 ft. long, 80 ft. wide, 44 ft. high), which at times held up to 1800 council members (the benches for the nobles ran lengthwise). The entire programme of the paintings on the walls and ceilings serves to glorify Venice: the city, the republic, and the mighty empire created by the republic. Behind the podium for the State Council (Signoria) and for the Doge's throne is the overwhelming 'Paradise' (much restored in the 18C) by Jacopo Tintoretto (1588-90; the details are mainly by his pupils), the largest canvas painting in the world (70 ft. long, 25 ft. high). The paintings on the other walls, some of them by Andrea Vicentino, Domenico Tintoretto, Palma Giovane, and the school of Paolo Veronese, depict events in Venice's history. On the wall looking on to the courtyard the 'Reconciliation between Emperor Frederick Barbarossa and Pope Alexander

Doges' Palace, courtyard

III' (with apocryphal details). This reconciliation (1177) was made possible by the mediation of Venice. Opposite this: the 'Fourth Crusade', with the capture and looting of Constantinople in 1204, a decisive event in the rise of Venice as a maritime and mercantile power. The end wall begins with a continuation of the previous cycle: 'Baldwin of Flanders' Coronation' as first Latin Emperor of Byzantium (the Latin Empire lasted until 1261). Followed by 'Defeat of the Genoese at Chioggia in 1379' and 'The victorious Doge Andrea Contarini returning to the city', one of Veronese's last works. *Ceiling paintings* with allegorical (centre) and historical (sides) subjects: Central rectangle: 'Homage to Venice' by Tintoretto. Arranged around the four corners: (some of the work is by the artist's workshop) Venetian conquests and victories (1438-82). In front of the 'Paradise': works by Veronese. In the oval: 'Triumph of Venice' (*c.* 1585). In the corners: 'Conquest of Smyrna in 1472' (left), 'Liberation of Scutari in 1474' (right). Rear oval: 'Coronation of Venezia' by Jacopo da Ponte the younger, flanked by the smaller paintings by Francesco da Ponte. 'Battle of Maclodio, 1426' on the left. 'Battle of Cadore, 1508' on the right. Before the front wall: on the left: Palma's 'Victory over Milan, 1427'. On the right: 'Reconquest of Padua, 1509'.

17a) *Window with balcony* (1404), donated by the Doge Michele Steno, a work by Piero Paolo and Jacobello dalle Masegne. Crowned by a Justice (1577) by Alessandro Vittoria.

18) *Sala della Quarantia Civil Nuova:* Court that dealt with civil law in the overseas possessions and colonies and on the mainland. 17C wall paintings, subject matter appropriate to the room's function. Byzantine icon of the Virgin in a 16C Renaissance frame.

19) *Sala dello Scrutinio:* Rooms where meetings were held to prepare for elections and count the votes. The ceiling, destroyed by fire, was rebuilt by Cristoforo Sorte in 1578-85. Triumphal arch by Antonio Gaspari (1694) to Francesco Morosini, who had defeated the Turks in Greece. Above the throne is a 'Last Judge-

ment' (1587–94) by Palma Giovane. The lively depictions of Venetian battles and victories in the paintings on the ceiling and walls include: Tintoretto's 'Capture of Zara, 1346' (1584–7) to the right of the entrance. Andrea Vicentino's 'Battle of Lepanto, 1571' (on the same side), a new version of Tintoretto's painting of the same subject which was destroyed by the fire of 1577. Interesting frieze with portraits of Doges which were painted from life, in contrast to most of the historical portraits in the Sala del Maggior Consiglio.

3rd floor:

20) *Sala degli Inquisitori:* Meeting room of the three State inquisitors appointed from 1539 onwards. 'The Prodigal Son', a ceiling painting by Tintoretto, echoes the room's function. At the sides are allegories of the 'Virtues'.

21) *Sala dei Tre Capi:* Meeting room of the three leaders of the Council of Ten.

22) *Sala della Bussola:* Ante-room of the Sala del Consiglio dei Dieci, waiting room for those summoned before the courts and, from the 16C onwards, for those called before the Inquisition. A door led to the prison. The main ceiling painting is Veronese's 'St.Mark with the Theologi-

cal Virtues' (copy; original in Paris). The paintings at the sides are by the artist's workshop. Wall paintings by Marco Vecellio and Antonio Vassilacchi, known as Aliense (early 17C).

23) *Sala del Consiglio dei Dieci:* Meeting room of the Council of Ten, which is responsible for protecting the Venetian Constitution and had to judge cases of high treason. Mid-16C decoration. The ceiling paintings (1553/4) by Veronese are his earliest works in Venice: 'Zeus hurling his thunderbolts at the Vices', a mythological description of the tasks performed by the Council which met here (central oval; original in Paris). 'Juno presenting the Doge's Cornu to Venezia' (left rectangle). 'Neptune' and 'Janus and Juno' (corner ovals on the window side). The other ceiling paintings are by Giovanni Battista Ponchino and Giovanni Battista Zelotti. Wall paintings, mostly by the same artists as in the previous room.

24) *Sala delle Quattro Porte:* This room named after the four doors has a vaulted ceiling and was rebuilt by Andrea Palladio in 1574 after being destroyed by fire. Stuccoes by Giovanni Battista Cambi, known as Bombarda. The ceiling paintings (1578–81) by Tintoretto and his workshop

Doges' Palace, tetrarchs. Right: Conquest of Constantinople

Doges' Palace, Sala del Maggior Consiglio

were much restored in the 19C. The large painting of the dedication of Doge Antonio Grimani was begun by Titian in *c.* 1523 and completed by Marco Vecellio in *c.* 1600. Opposite this is the 'Visit of the French King Henry III in 1574' by Andrea Vincentino. Above the door: 'Neptune presenting Venezia with the treasures of the Mediterranean' by Giovanni Battista Tiepolo.

25) *Sala dell'Anticollegio:* It took its present form in 1713 and it contains a number of 16C Venetian masterpieces. On each side of the door are two mythological wall paintings by Tintoretto; 'Venus, Bacchus and Ariadne' is regarded as one of his finest works. Also: 'Rape of Europa' by Veronese (*c.* 1580). 'Jacob's Return from Canaan' by Jacopo Bassano. Sculpture by Alessandro Vittoria above the entrance to the next room. Sumptuous stucco by Marco del Moro.

26) *Sala del Collegio:* The meeting room of the State Council (Signoria), it was com-

pletely rebuilt after the fire of 1574, and is one of the most splendid of the palace's halls. It was laid out by Antonio da Ponte; the carved and gilded ceiling is by Francesco and Andrea da Faenza (1576–7). The wall paintings by Tintoretto and his workshop (1581–4), and Veronese's ceiling paintings (1575–7), follow the official programme of paintings, which deals with Venetian State politics but is enlarged upon by Christian, mythological and allegorical motifs.

27) *Sala del Senato:* A room redesigned by Antonio da Ponte after 1574. On the ceiling, sumptuously gilded stuccoes to a design by Cristoforo Sorte form the framework to the paintings by Tintoretto and his workshop (1585–95), which once again serve to glorify Venice. Subjects include: 'Coins being minted in the Zecca' by Marco Vecellio (above the tribune). Opposite this, near the front of the room: the Doge Pasquale Cicogna 'Adoring the Eucharist' at the consecration of the

Doges' Palace, Sala delle Armi

Redentore, painted by Tommaso Dolabella (1592). 'Venus (= Venezia) in Vulcan's forge', an allegory of Venice's armed might, by Andrea Vicentino (before the entrance to the Sala del Collegio [26]). On the walls are votive paintings of the Doges, who traditionally had portraits of themselves painted for this purpose (two Doges in each painting on the front side). On the tribune side: 'The Body of Christ venerated by Pietro Lando and Marcantonio Trevisan' by Tintoretto. Opposite: 'Lorenzo and Girolamo Priuli adoring Christ between the Madonna and St.Mark' by Palma Giovane.

28) *Antichiesetta:* Ante-chamber to:

29) *Chiesetta/palace chapel* (usually closed to the public): Begun by Vicenzo Scamozzi in 1593. Ceiling painted by Jacopo Guarana (1766).

30) *Archivio Segreto/Former secret archive.*

31) *Sala delle Armi:* Armoury of the palace guard. Now used to display over 2,000 exhibits (weapons, coats of mail etc.) from the 15–18C, but most of them are not from the palace's original stock, which was looted in 1797.

Other important palaces in the city:
Palazzo Agnusdio (2060 S.Croce; Rio di S.Staè, Fondamenta Mocenigo): The palace displays a number of fine examples of 14C Gothic carving: the five-arched window with the symbols of the Evangelists between the extradoses, the water gate crowned by the patera of the Agnus Dei (Lamb of God), the feature from which the palace takes its name, the beautiful door leading to the bridge, and the cornice.

Pal. Ariani-Cicogna (2376 Dorsoduro; Rio Angelo Raffaele): Late-14C Gothic palace, the tracery of its loggia (six arches) is complex and delicate. A fine external staircase in the courtyard. Diagonally opposite towards the city centre, on the Rio dei Carmini: the broad *Pal. Zenobio* (q.v.).

Doges' Palace, 'Mercury with the Graces'   *Palazzo Centani-Goldoni*

Pal. Centani-Goldoni (2798 S.Polo; Calle Nomboli; site of the *Goldoni Museum* and the *Istituto di Studi Teatrali*): A Gothic building (*c.* 1440), with late-15C alterations. The elegant outdoor staircase supported by arches, and the fountain in the courtyard, are also late 15C. This is the house where the comic playwright *Carlo Goldoni* (1707–93) was born. With his comedies taken from everyday bourgeois life (initially, that of Venice), Goldoni reformed the traditional commedia dell'arte with its stylized roles, and sometimes encountered considerable resistance from Pietro Chiari and Carlo Gozzi. He was active in Paris with great success from 1762 onwards, and died there, having become increasingly isolated following the Revolution. *Museo Goldoni*, with mementoes and contemporary details, early editions of comedies, and records of the Venetian theatre. The *Goldoni monument* (1883) by Antonio dal Zotto is in the Campo S.Bartolomeo (also Campo Goldoni) near the Rialto Bridge.

Pal. Contarini dal Bovolo (4299 S.Marco; at the mouth of Rio dei Fuseri/Rio di S.Luca): A stately, tall mid-15C Gothic palace with an elegant spiral staircase by Giovanni Candi in its courtyard. Built around 1500, the effect of the early-Renaissance staircase is enhanced by the contrast between its diagonals and the arcades of the courtyard façade, by the articulation of the walls and by the contrast in colour between the red brick and white marble. The palazzo is one of the landmarks of the city when looking NW from the Campanile di S.Marco.

Pal. Corner-Mocenigo (2128 Campo S.Polo): Imposing Renaissance structure (*c.* 1545), possibly to plans by Michele Sanmicheli. Following a basic rule of Venetian secular architecture, applied from the 15C onwards, the main façade looks on to the canal, in this case the narrow Rio di S.Polo, rather than what is the largest campo in the city. *Pal. Soranzo*

View from San Marco on to the spiral staircase of the Palazzo Contarini dal Bovolo

and *Pal. Tiepolo-Maffetti* (q.v.) also both stand in this square.

Pal. Dandolo (part of the Hotel Danieli Excelsior, 4581 Castello; Riva degli Schiavoni): Mature Gothic building (*c.* 1425), the ground floor has been altered to suit its present use. The façade displays the traditional tripartite arrangement, which reflects the original layout of the interior. The corners and windows are dressed with white stone and there are balconies and dwarf balustrades.

Casa di Desdemona: See *Pal. Contarini-Fasan* on the Grand Canal (No. 101).

Pal. Giustinian-Faccanon (by the Ponte della Fava bridge): Late-Gothic building (*c.* 1460), with two loggias (six arches). Turned columns at the corners. 18C statuettes. Nearby is the fine **Pal. Gussoni,** built a little later (*c.* 1475–80) by Pietro Lombardo in early-Renaissance style.

'Al Ercole d'Oro' pharmacy (opposite S.Fosca; Strada Nuova): The city's oldest surviving pharmacy (17C), with the original furnishings almost intact. 18C vases.

Casa di Carlo Goldoni: See *Pal. Centani-Goldoni.*

Pal. Loredan (2945 S.Stefano; Campo Morosini, site of the *Istituto Veneto di Scienze, Lettere ed Arti*): A long Renaissance palace, it is the product of the rebuilding and amalgamation (*c.* 1540) of several earlier Gothic buildings, slight traces of which can still be seen in the front facing the Rio S.Vidal. The broad façade by Antonio Abbondio, looking on to the square, once bore contemporary frescos by Giuseppe Salviati, whereas the N. side (1618) by Giovanni Grapiglia has carved ornament and resembles a theatre backdrop, thus lending the spacious square an elegant tone. Opposite this, on the same square: *Pal. Pisani* (q.v.).

Casa di Aldo Manuzio (2311 S.Polo; Rio Terrà Secondo di S.Agostino): A good example of a Gothic house. *Aldus Manutius* (*c.* 1450–1515) lived here. He was the most important Humanist printer and publisher, and brought out numerous first editions of Greek and Latin classics. As such, he was one of the major figures of the heyday of printing and publishing in Venice. The first licence to operate a printing establishment was granted in Venice in 1469, and by *c.* 1500 some 50 such enterprises were already active. The printing of sheet music with movable lines and notes was also invented here at about this time.

Pal. De Maria (43 Giudecca; near S.Maria della Presentazione, Fondamenta delle Zitelle): Built in 1910–13 for Mario De Maria, the landscape painter, it has one of the few Art Nouveau façades in Venice. Its Venetian character combines typical Gothic motifs, especially from the Doges' Palace (rhombi, decorative battlements), with contemporary ideas of decorative surface composition and window design.

Casa di Otello: See *Scuola Grande dei Carmini* (cf. Schools).

Pal. Patriarcale (Piazzetta dei Leoncini): Built by Lorenzo Santi in 1837–50 using existing fragments, after the patriarch's seat had been moved from the so-called bishops' island of S.Pietro in Castello to the Basilica di S.Marco, now elevated to the status of a cathedral.

Pal. Pesaro degli Orfei (3780 Campo S.Beneto; see also *Museo Fortuny,* cf. Museums): Magnificent monumental late-Gothic building (2nd half of 15C). The front on the square is among the city's richest façades, with an abundance of first-rate carving.

Pal. Pisani (S.Stefano; Campo Morosini. the *Conservatory*): A baroque palace of exceptional size, begun in 1615 and completed in the 18C. The façade lacks the articulation required by such large dimensions. The two courtyards are separated by an elegant multi-storeyed loggia. On the piano nobile there is a small *collection of historical instruments,* and also documents and personal objects belonging to important musicians who were natives of Venice or lived here. Opposite this, in the same square: *Pal. Loredan* (q.v.).

Casa di Marco Polo (5845 Cannaregio; Corte Seconda del Milion): 14C Gothic house (with some elements from the previous 13C Veneto-Byzantine building). Finely worked doorways on the side facing the canal and the street, and a window (partly altered) with several arches and five small circular reliefs ('patere') between or beside the extradoses. *Marco*

Palazzo Dandolo

Palazzo Pisani, statue at entrance

Polo (1254–1324), the great medieval traveller, is said to have lived here. The records of his travels governed European ideas of the Far East for a long time, and also inspired later voyages of discovery. **Pal. Priuli** (mouth of Rio di S.Severo/Rio di S.Provolo): For stylistic reasons this splendid late-Gothic palace is believed to have been built in two stages in the 1st half of the 15C. The corner window on the upper piano nobile is here employed for the first time, but was soon copied in other patricians' houses. The excellent articulation of the wall surfaces on all sides of this free-standing building is an impressive monument to Venetian architecture, and so too are the details of the carved ornament. **Pal. Priuli-Ruzzini** (Campo S.Maria Formosa; 5866 Castello): This grand palace (*c.* 1580) by Bartolomeo Manopola already displays baroque elements (cornices and pediments) in its late-Renaissance façade. The division of the ground floor into two half-storeys for shops and offices is a typical feature from the 15C onwards, because the Venetian palazzo was always both a business establishment and a residence. **Pal. Donà** (No. 6126): A Gothic building (*c.* 1460) with an asymmetrical façade and a good doorway (putti bearing a coat-of-arms) which already hints at the Renaissance, probably from the school of Agostino di Duccio. The building (No. 6123) adjoining this on the left is probably from the same period. **Pal. Vitturi** (No. 5246): Capitals, window arches, and the patere, are well-preserved examples of Byzantine architecture in the 2nd half of the 13C. The building, which forms a harmonious whole, had an extra storey added in the 17C.

Pal. Malipiero (on the Rio di S.Maria Formosa): Renaissance (*c.* 1540), with a 2nd piano nobile added at a later date and a separate entrance to the bridge.

Pal. Soranzo (2169 Campo S.Polo): An imposing Gothic double structure from the 14C (left) and 15C (right). The front façade is best seen from one side, since its pronounced rhythm is emphasized by the foreshortening. It also has a wealth of fine ornament and it will amply repay detailed study. The descendants of the original owners still live here. The massive late-baroque **Pal. Tiepolo-Maffetti** (No. 1957), probably to a design by Giorgio Massari (*c.* 1760), also stands on this square. The *Pal. Corner-Mocenigo* (q.v.). **Pal. Sanudo-Van Axel** (mouth of Rio

Palazzo Pisani, statue at entrance

Palazzo Priuli

Palazzo Priuli-Ruzzini

della Panada/Rio di S.Canciano, near S.Maria dei Miracoli): A Gothic palace built in 1473–9, with an irregular ground plan dictated by its site. There are two buildings, each with their own entrances, courtyards, staircases and fountains. *Ermanno Wolf-Ferrari* (1876–1948), the composer and director of the conservatory, lived in this homogeneous, well-preserved complex.

Casa di Tintoretto (3399 Cannaregio; Rio della Sensa, Fondamenta dei Mori): Domenico Robusti, the Venetian painter known as Tintoretto after the dyer's trade practised by his father, lived in this Gothic house (2nd half of 15C) with its asymmetrical façade. A tablet above the plain entrance commemorates him. Apart from the numerous individual paintings by him in Venice, including portraits and altarpieces, he also produced some large-scale cycles in the Doges' Palace (q.v.), the Scuola Grande di S.Rocco (q.v.; cf. Schools) and elsewhere in Venice.

Pal. Zenobio (2593 Dorsoduro; Rio dei Carmini): A strikingly broad building (1680–5) by Antonio Gaspari, with a baroque façade which is notable for its sober, almost neoclassical, articulation. Gaspari was also involved in the building of the Pal. Pesaro and Ca' Rezzonico (on the Grand Canal, Nos. 22 and 72). Traditional Venetian features (tripartite division, although with a much-extended central section, round arches on the piano nobile) are combined with new elements (accentuated longitudinal axis, loggia reduced to a projecting balcony) to form an impressive, coolly elegant façade. Diagonally opposite this, towards the Canale della Giudecca, is the Gothic *Pal. Ariani-Cicogna* (q.v.) on the Rio Angelo Raffaele.

Pal. Zorzi-Bon (4907 Castello; on the corner of Rio di S.Severo and Salizzada Zorzi): Late-14C Gothic; its façade displays a number of features which were not to become widespread until the 15C: contrasting stone dressings at the corners and around the windows, and pointed arches with a chequer frieze. The colourful loggia (five arches) on the piano ·nobile has columns of grey and red limestone, and white capitals and arches. But the simple water gates, the rectangular windows of the half-storey (mezzà), and the patere above the points of the arches, are typical of the period when the palazzo was built.

VII. The Schools

The Venetian *scuola* (literally 'school') was not an educational institution, but fulfilled social and charitable functions on a broad scale (hospital, caring for orphans, widows' pensions, social services for the members). These institutions grew out of the medieval lay brotherhoods, but the organization of each of them was later precisely laid down and they came to resemble guilds, although they had no real political power. The members either all practised the same trade or belonged to a common ethnic group and from 1539 onwards all craftsmen and workers had to belong to such an association. From the earliest days, the headquarters, likewise known as 'scuola', of each institution stood near the church dedicated to the institu-

Palazzo Loredan degli Ambasciatori

Casa di Tintoretto

tion's patron saint, and the wealthy organizations commissioned major architects and artists to design and decorate their buildings.

Scuola Grande della Carità (Dorsoduro, Campo della Carità; since 1806 it has housed the *Gallerie dell'Accademia;* cf. Museums): Stands at right angles to the Gothic church of S.Maria della Carità, built at about the same time (*c.* 15C). The present neoclassical façade dates from 1820, having previously been altered several times.

Scuola Grande dei Carmini (Dorsoduro, Campo Carmini): A neoclassical building (3rd quarter of 17C) standing outside the large Gothic Carmelite church of S.Maria del Carmelo. This Scuola has preserved most of its original decoration, and so have the Scuole di S.Giorgio and S.Rocco. Monochrome scenes from the life of the Virgin Mary by Nicolò Bambini on the ground floor. The ceiling paintings (1739–44) in the large assembly hall are by Giovanni Battista Tiepolo, who was thereupon elected a member of the Scuola. In the central painting: 'Scapular of the Order being presented to St.Simon Stock' (he was superior-general of the Carmelite order in the 13C). Early-18C wall paintings by Gregorio Lazzarini ('Scenes from the life of Christ') and Antonio Zanchi ('Miracle of the Virgin Mary'). 'Judith and Holofernes' by Giovanni Battista Piazzetta (between Sala dell'Albergo and Archivio) is among the contemporary paintings on this floor. Next to this is the **Casa Otello** (No. 2815): the statue of an armour-bearer (2nd half of 15C) stands on the façade facing the Rio di S.Margherita. Othello, who was a member of the ancient noble Venetian family of Moro and murdered his wife Desdemona out of jealousy, is said to have lived here. In Shakespeare's treatment of this story, he is represented as a Moor, due to an Italian pun on his surname.

Scuola dei Mercanti (Campo Madonna

dell'Orto): Rebuilt in the Renaissance by Andrea Palladio (1570–2); housed the merchants' association.

Scuola Vecchia della Misericordia (Campo della Misericordia): This Gothic building (*c.* 1441–51) for the brotherhood founded in the early 14C stands at right angles to the church of S.Maria della Misericordia (also known as S.Maria Valverde). The well-proportioned façade has been largely stripped of its rich ornament, the work of Bartolomeo Bon. Some of Bon's carving does survive and includes the windows with pendant capitals, and the free-standing columns at the front of the flat niches in the walls. **Scuola Nuova della Misericordia** (Fondamenta della Misericordia): This annexe of the Scuola stands opposite it on the Rio della Sensa and is by Sansovino (2nd quarter of 16C). This monumental Renaissance structure, a conspicuous feature of Venice, remained unfinished. Notwithstanding this, and despite the poor state of repair, the walls, which are without the splendid carved facing planned for them, impress the onlooker by their powerful articulation.

Scuola di S.Fantin (Campo S.Fantin; houses the *adult education department* and the *Ateneo Veneto*). Built by Antonino Contin and Alessandro Vittoria in 1592–1600. There is a small collection of paintings and sculptures in the former assembly room (ground floor) and in the Sala dell'Albergo (rest-house) with its fine original decoration.

Scuola di S.Giorgio degli Schiavoni (3259 Castello; Calle Furlani): The Dalmatian community in Venice commissioned Vittore Carpaccio to decorate the interior of their rebuilt Renaissance school (*c.* 1500). In 1501–11 he painted the famous cycle 'Scenes from the Life of the Dalmatian patron Saints George, Tryphon and Jerome', as well as some 'Scenes from the Life of Christ'. This cycle is among Carpaccio's most splendid works, and is an outstanding example of Venetian narrative painting. Originally intended for the Great Hall (1st floor), the paintings were moved to the ground floor in 1551 when the building was altered by Giovanni de Zan (the façade is also by him).

Scuola Grande di S.Giovanni Ev. (2454 S.Polo; Calle dell'Olio): Seat of one of the city's richest associations. It was reconstituted after Austria had ordered in 1806 that it be dissolved. A large building with a fine early-Renaissance forecourt (*c.* 1490) and, inside, a splendid staircase

Scuola Grande di San Marco

by Mauro Coducci (1498) leading into the now baroque Great Hall (Giovanni Massari, 1727). The cycle 'Miracle of the Relic of the Cross' (1494–1501), which Gentile Bellini, Carpaccio and others painted for the prayer room, has been in Room 20 of the Accademia (q.v.; cf. Museums) since being seized by Napoleon.

Scuola Grande di S.Marco (now a *hospital*; Campo SS.Giovanni e Paolo): Rebuilt, probably by Pietro Lombardo (1485–95), it is a masterpiece of the Venetian early Renaissance. The double façade with its polychrome marble inlay, trompe-l'oeil on the ground floor and carved decoration reflects the division into assembly hall and chapel (left) and albergo/resthouse (right). The left entrance hall is open to the public, and has exhibits showing how the city cared for the sick from the Middle Ages until the early 20C. Public access to the other rooms, which are not an integral part of the hospital, is limited. The staircase by Mauro Coducci (*c.* 1488) has been rebuilt.

Scuola Grande di S.Rocco (S.Polo; Campo S.Rocco): A monumental building probably begun by Bartolomeo Bon Bergamasco in 1515 and completed by 1565 by Scarpagnino and Giangiacomo dei Grigi. A rich marble façade. The Scuola is famous for Tintoretto's extensive series of paintings, which survive intact (over 30 works). Tintoretto was a member and later a director of this Scuola, which still exists today. In the hall on the ground floor are eight large paintings with 'Scenes from the Life of the Virgin Mary' (from the Annunciation to the Assumption). The elegant staircase has baroque paintings (2nd half of 17C) depicting the terrible 'Plague Epidemics in Venice' (St.Roch is the patron saint of plague-sufferers). The left-hand painting (by Pietro Negri, 1673) on the upper flight of stairs is interesting because it shows S.Maria della Salute, which was under construction from 1632 onwards and was consecrated in 1687. The Senate vowed to build this church in 1630, during the plague. The paintings on the walls and ceiling of the Great Hall on the first floor are also by Tintoretto. Old Testament subjects (1577–81) are depicted on the splendid ceiling. In the middle is the 'Brazen Serpent'. Themes from the 'Life of Christ' (from Nativity to Temptation) are seen on the walls. Altar of St.Roch with an altarpiece by Tintoretto. Statues by Girolamo Campagna. The presbytery, which is panelled with wood, has 24

San Rocco, façade detail

scenes in relief by Giovanni Marchiori (1743) from the life of St.Roch. Four individual easel paintings: 'Annunciation' (1526) by Titian on the left. On the right: 'Visitation' (*c.* 1588) by Tintoretto. In front of the balustrade (its railing dates from 1756): 'Abraham' on the right and 'Hagar' on the left, two early works by Giovanni Battista Tiepolo. The adjoining Sala dell'Albergo (rest-house) has a cycle of the 'Passion' as a thematic continuation of the Life of Christ cycle (this is, however, the earliest work painted by Tintoretto in the Scuola, dating from 1564–7). On entering the room, one's attention is immediately drawn to Tintoretto's 'Crucifixion'. The ceiling paintings are dedicated to St.Roch. A 'Christ bearing the Cross', probably painted by Giorgione (*c.* 1508–10), stands in this room.

The Tesoro (treasure) of the Scuola includes sumptuous 15–18C gold pieces. When the brotherhoods were forced to close and their goods were confiscated, the church utensils were moved to the mint and thus escaped being pilfered.

Scuola Grande Tedesca (houses the *Museo Ebraico;* 2902 Cannaregio; Campo del Ghetto Nuovo): The German Scuola was the oldest association to be founded on the basis of nationality or rite (the buildings of what are in all five national synagogues form the largest surviving complex of Jewish religious buildings in Europe). This building (1529) houses the *Israelite Museum:* A interesting collection of exhibits dealing with religious and everyday life, and a survey of the Jewish-Venetian artistic tradition of the 16–19C.

VIII. Arsenale

The Arsenal in the E. of the city was once the largest dockyard in the world. Tradition relates that it was laid out on two islands in 1104, subsequently being enlarged in 1303, 1325 and 1475, and surrounded with walls and towers as if it were a city of its own. There are only two entrances to the Arsenal, which formerly set the standard for Europe's dockyards, but which is now of little importance. The 'Ingresso di Terra', the entrance from the land, was built as a triumphal arch flanked by columns in 1460. A Renaissance relief of the lion of St.Mark surmounts the gate. The statue of St.Justina is by Girolamo Campagna (1578). The eight statues on the bridge are from 1682. The Arsenal is guarded by two famous large and two

Scuola Grande di San Rocco, Christ bearing the Cross, by Giorgione

small lions. They were set up here in 1692 and were originally from Greece (the left-hand small lion dates from *c.* 600 BC). Behind the portal is a Virgin Mary by Jacopo Sansovino (1533). The second entrance to the Arsenal, the 'Ingresso all'Acqua', is a lock between two towers (1570) and connects the dockyard to the open sea.

Vaporetto Line 5 passes directly through the Arsenal. The visitor on foot can go no further than the 'Ingresso di Terra'. The Darsena delle Galeazze was built in the Arsenal in 1539, and in 1544–7 an enormous building to plans by M.Sanmicheli was erected to house the Doge's splendid barge, the 'Bucentoro', on which he journeyed out to the open sea every year from 1000 onwards, accompanied by a large entourage, and there threw a ring into the water in order to solemnize his 'marriage to the sea'. Napoleon ordered the 'Bucentoro' to be destroyed.

Museo Storico Navale: This three-storeyed museum, with exhibits relating to the history of the Venetian and Italian navies, is by the Arsenal, near the 'Ingresso di Terra'. It is reached via the bridge. Here there is also a whole room of Chinese junks, a reconstruction of the last Bucentoro which belonged to the Doge L.Manin, and a monument to Admiral Emo by Canova (1795). (Opening times: Mon.-Fri.: 9 a.m.–1 p.m. Sat.: 9 a.m.–12 noon. Closed on Sundays and holidays.)

IX. Ghetto

Jewish Ghetto (located away from the centre, in the NW district of Cannaregio): Jews settled on the island of Spinalunga (later: Giudecca = Jews' island) in *c.* 1000. They were wealthy merchants and doctors, and therefore aroused the Venetians' envy and were expelled from the city. In 1516 the Jews were once again granted permission to reside in the city, because Venice was dependent on the Jews' financial resources in times of war and emergency (see also Shakespeare's play 'The Merchant of Venice').

The 'infidels' were required to reside in a special district, the *Ghetto Vecchio* and, from 1541 onwards, also in the adjoining *Ghetto Nuovo*. This district took its name from the cannon foundry which once stood here (gettare = to cast metal). The Jews and Christians were separated by the canals and the ghetto gate which was

Lion outside the Arsenal

closed at sunset. Signs in Hebrew and Italian, marking the site of the ghetto gate, can still be seen in a small alleyway (turn left at the Ponte delle Guglie, and immediately turn into the first alleyway on the right). Jews were released from the requirement to live in the ghetto by Napoleon in 1797. The tall six and eight storey houses are a striking feature and indicate that space was once at a premium. All five synagogues (three of them can still be visited) are from the 16C, and are among the finest medieval synagogues still in existence. 16C building regulations forbad any external indication of their religious function and they are simply accommodated in the tall houses of the district. The prayer room could be reached by all the nearby families via the staircase, in order not to attract attention.

Two of the five synagogues are still used for services. They have been partially restored.

Scuola Tedesca: The oldest synagogue, founded in 1528 in the Ghetto Nuovo and built on a trapezoidal ground plan. In the 17C the women's gallery was carved and the synagogue was partly redecorated.

Scuola Levantina: Built in 1538. The Oriental Jews assembled here. The ceiling, and the pulpit lavishly decorated with columns and a curving staircase, are both by Andrea Brustolon (1st half of 18C).

Scuola Espagnol: Built in 1555 for Jews of Spanish and Portuguese origin. Still used for worship. The hall was designed by Baldassare Longhena, who rebuilt it in 1654.

Museo Vittorio Fano: The exhibits include: religious treasures, finely worked Torah shrines (where the prayer scrolls were kept), seven-armed candlesticks, valuable cult implements, copies of the Old Testament printed in Hebrew, tapestries, brocades, embroideries, and shofar horns (used to call the Jews to prayer).

X. Bridges

Bridges: Three bridges span the Grand Canal, which is just over two and a quarter miles long with a width varying between 100 ft. and 230 ft. They are the Istrian

stone *Ponte degli Scalzi* (1934, by the railway station); the *Ponte dell'Accademia* of 1854 and 1930; and, finally, the world-famous *Rialto Bridge*, the only bridge across the Grand Canal before the 19C. There is said to have been a pontoon bridge here in 1181, replaced in the 13C by a wooden toll bridge. In the 15C this bridge gave way to one with shops and a section that could be raised. Then in 1588–91 A.da Ponte and his nephew A.Contin constructed today's stone bridge, which takes the form of a street of shops arching over the canal to allow the ships to pass underneath. The bridge is dedicated to St.Theodore and St.Mark, who are depicted in relief on the face of the bridge, together with an image of the Annunciation.

Over 150 bridges, large and small, span the canals of Venice. The most celebrated of these is the *Bridge of Sighs* (Ponte dei Sospiri), which linked the Doges' Palace to the former State prison. It too was built to plans by Antonio Contin. It was completed in 1603 and is carved in relief. The *Ponte dei tre Archi* over the Canale di Cannaregio near S.Giobbe is a baroque three-arched bridge.

XI. Museums and collections

Gallerie dell'Accademia (Dorsoduro, Campo della Carità): The galleries are housed in the former Gothic church of *S.Maria della Carità*, the former *Scuola Grande della Carità* (both mid 15C), and the former *monastery* of the Lateran Canons, built by Andrea Palladio from 1560 and later rebuilt several times. After the secularization of these buildings, the Accademia, originally founded in 1750, was moved here from the Fontego della Farina (see Palaces on the Canal Grande, No. 113) and re-opened in 1807. When the Republic collapsed the churches, monasteries, public offices, and other institutions were dissolved by order of the French and Austrian occupiers and their works of art (mainly paintings) were assembled here. Endowments, private donations, purchases, and the return of

Arsenal, entrance ▌

works to Venice, expanded the original collection into a comprehensive, internationally renowned display of Venetian painting from the 14–19C.

The collection is well labelled throughout, and is clearly arranged in 24 rooms. The main features are as follows: *Room I:* Late Gothic (14–early 15C). 'Winged altar' by Paolo Veneziano. *Room II:* Early Renaissance. 'Pala S.Giobbe' by Giovanni Bellini. *Room III:* Followers of Giorgione (1st quarter of 16C). *Room IV:* Renaissance (15C). Andrea Mantegna, Piero della Francesca. *Room V:* Renaissance (mid 15C–early 16C): 'Tempesta' by Giorgione. 'Pietà' by Giovanni Bellini. *Room VI:* Renaissance (1st half of 16C): 'Presentation of the Ring' by Paris Bordone (this painting produced for the rest-house in the Scuola Grande di S.Marco relates the last episode of the Venetian legend in which the fisherman presents the Doge with St.Mark's ring which the Saint had given him on 25 February 1340 as a symbol of his assistance in sinking a ship full of demons which had menaced the city). There are also works by Bonifacio de' Pitati, Titian and Tintoretto. *Room VII:* 1st half of 16C. Portrait by Lorenzo Lotto. *Room VIII:* Painters from Bergamo and Brescia (1st half of 16C). 'Sacra Conversazione' by Palma Vecchio. *Room IX:* 1st half of 16C. 'Symbols of Evangelists' by Titian. 'God the Father blessing' (with a view of St.Mark's Square) by Bonifacio de' Pitati. *Room X:* Architecturally speaking, this is among the finest rooms in Venice from the 1st half of the 19C. Leading Renaissance and Mannerist works: 'Pietà', a late work by Titian, completed by Palma Giovane. In a small panel painting: 'Titian and his son Orazio at prayer'. 'The Miracles of St.Mark' and other works by Tintoretto. 'Feast in the House of Levi' by Paolo Veronese. *Room XI, 1st section:* Further 16C masterpieces. Scenes from 'Genesis' by Tintoretto. 'Mystic marriage of St.Catherine' and 'Battle of Lepanto' by Paolo Veronese. 'Raising of Lazarus' by Leandro Bassano. *2nd section:* Mannerism and baroque (late 16–18C). 'Crucifixion of St.Peter' by Luca Giordano. 'Feast in the house of Simon by Bernardo Strozzi. 'St.Helena finding the True Cross' by Giovanni Battista Tiepolo. Paintings by Pietro da Cortona. *Room XII:* 18C landscape paintings. *Room XIII:* Various portraits by Tintoretto, Palma Giovane; 'St.Jerome' by Jacopo Bassano. *Room XIV:* Mannerism and baroque

Rialto

(17C). *Room XV:* Late baroque and rococo (18C). Giovanni Battista Tiepolo, Giovanni Antonio Pellegrini, Gian Domenico Tiepolo. *Room XVI:* Baroque. Portraits. Early works by Giovanni Battista Tiepolo. *Room XVIa:* Rococo. 'Soothsayer' by Giovanni Battista Piazzetta. *Room XVII:* 18C. Various portraits by Rosalba Carriera. Numerous 'Venetian genre scenes' by Pietro Longhi. *Room XVIII:* 18C. Various 'Views of the city', especially by members of the Accademia. Some sketches and sculptures by Antonio Canova. *Room XIX:* 15&16C. 'Vision of Francesco Ottoboni' by Vittore Carpaccio (with an interior view of the church of S.Antonio di Castello, later destroyed). *Room XX:* 'Miracles of the Relic of the Cross' (1494–1501) a cycle of paintings from the Scuola S.Giovanni Ev. (cf. under Schools) by Gentile Bellini, Vittore Carpaccio, Giovanni Mansueti (with views of the city). *Room XXI:* The 'Legend of St.Ursula', a cycle of paintings by Vittore Carpaccio (1490–*c.* 1502) from the Scuola di S.Orsola near SS.Giovanni e Paolo. *Room XXII:* Neoclassical ante-room with scenes fromb the 'Iliad' (19C). *Room XXIII* (former church of S.Maria della Carità): Renaissance (15C). Various triptychs by Giovanni Bellini, polyptych by Bartolomeo Vivarini. *Room XXIV:* (former Sala dell'Albergo): Original ceiling (*c.* 1496). Triptych by Antonio Vivarini and Giovanni d'Alemagna (1446). 'Presentation in the Temple' by Titian (*c.* 1553). 'Portrait of Cardinal Bessarione', a copy (1540) of an original probably by Gentile Bellini. The copy shows the Byzantine reliquary (14C, painted 15C frame) which the Cardinal donated to the Scuola in 1463 when he became a member of the brotherhood. As a Papal legate, he attempted to persuade the republic to take part in the Crusade proclaimed by Pope Pius II.

Museo Archeologico/Archaeological Museum (Piazza S.Marco, entrance on the Piazzetta): The basis of this valuable collection (taken all in all, it is one of the oldest collections in Italy, except for those in the Vatican) was created by rich bequests and by the private collections of Venice's widely travelled merchants. Some of these various collections were brought together after the Republic came to an end. Sculptures from all periods of classical Greece and Rome. Roman frescos (1C BC–3C AD). Greek and Etruscan cer-

Ponte dei tre Archi

118 **Venice**

amics. Small sculptures. Roman coins and cut stones. Egyptian mummies.

Raccolta dei Padri Armeni Mechitaristi (island of S.Lazzaro degli Armeni between S.Giorgio and the Lido): In 1717 the island was granted to an Armenian monk from Sebaste Monug, who had fled from the Turks and was known as Mechitar (comforter). Before this a hospital for incurables had stood here. An educational centre for young Armenians soon developed and by means of numerous translations they propagated Christian writings in their home country. The church and monastery house many fine paintings, mostly Venetian, from the 18C and early 19C. The corridors of the monastery have works by 19C and early-20C Armenian painters. An extensive collection of printing types. Illuminated Armenian manuscripts and printed works from the 10–18C in the library.

Galleria Internazionale d'Arte Moderna (Ca' Pesaro, cf. Palaces on the Grand Canal, No. 22; S.Staè): This collection, founded in 1897 after the first biennial festival, has always been housed in this splendid baroque palace, which the Duchess Felicita Bevilacqua La Masa bequeathed to the city, stipulating that it should be used to promote young artists and organize exhibitions. The stock of works is constantly being added to. It comprises paintings, drawings and sculptures from nearly all the periods and styles of the 19&20C (mostly pre-1945), and also gives the foreign visitor an idea of modern Italian art.

Museo d'Arte Orientale (Ca' Pesaro, 3rd storey; S.Staè): A rich collection of Asian art of all kinds, furniture, musical instruments, utensils, applied arts, coats of mail, and weapons.

Raccolte d'Arte Orientale e di Porcellane (3052 S.Samuele; Ca' del Duca, cf. Palaces on the Grand Canal, No. 79): Two smaller, high-quality collections of Far Eastern art, and 18C and early-19C porcelain from Italian and European factories.

Museo Diocesano di Arte Sacra/Diocesan Museum (4312 Castello; Fondamenta S.Apollonia): Since 1976, this museum of religious art has been housed in the former monastery of S.Apollonia. It has works by the best Italian and Venetian painters of the Renaissance (16–18C), lace from the 17&18C, liturgical utensils, sumptuous examples of metal work, paraments, illuminated manuscripts and early printed works. The collection of 13-15C religious art is unique to Venice.

Collezione Vittorio Cini (864 Dorsoduro; S.Vio): Collection of 13–16C Tuscan art, comprising furniture, other items of interior decoration, and enamel and ivory. The paintings include works by Lorenzo di Niccolò, Beato Angelico, Filippo Lippi, Piero della Francesca and Piero di Cosimo. There is also the famous 'Judgement of Paris' by Botticelli (partly by his workshop), and the 'Double Portrait' by Jacopo da Pontormo.

Raccolta della Fondazione Giorgio Cini (island of S.Giorgio Maggiore; visits by prior arrangement, Tel. 89900): A foundation established by Count Vittorio Cini in 1951 in memory of his son Giorgio. It contains institutions providing social aid, educational establishments, and famous institutes dealing with the history of Venetian culture, art, music, theatre and politics. Special exhibitions from its rich collections of miniatures, early printed works, paintings, drawings and furniture are also organized. The outstanding *Biblioteca d'Arte e di Storia* is also housed here.

Museo del Conservatorio (Campo Morosini): see Palazzo Pisani (cf. Other important palaces).

Museo Correr (Piazza S.Marco, Procuratie Nuove): Teodoro Correr's extensive collections, bequeathed to the city in 1830, form the basis of this museum. Subsequent donations and purchases mean that it now houses an outstanding assembly of works dealing with

Bridge of Sighs

Portrait of a nobleman by Lorenzo Lotto, Accademia

Venetian history, culture and economics and with life in the city. The exhibits include: views and plans of the city of Venice, and a complete collection of Venetian coins until the end of the republic. Doges' portraits and vestments. Decorative arts (lace and fabrics, ceramics, ivory carvings). Works and sketches by Antonio Canova, the neoclassical sculptor. Musical instruments. Uniforms and weapons. The building also houses the *Pinacoteca*, which is largely devoted to Venetian paintings from the 14–19C. Adjoined by the *Biblioteca Correr d'Arte e di Storia* (52 Piazzetta di S.Marco).

Museo dell'Opera: see Palazzo Ducale (M).

Museo Ebraico della Comunità Israelitica: see Scuola Grande Tedesca (cf. 'Scuole').

Museo Fortuny (Palazzo Pesaro degli Orfei; 3780 Campo S.Beneto; cf. also Other important palaces): Henriette Fortuny bequeathed this impressive late-Gothic building to the city in 1956 in memory of her husband Mariano Fortuny. The piano nobile has a collection of textiles, photographs, furniture and paintings by this Spanish artist who worked as a stage and fashion designer and engineer.

Galleria Giorgio Franchetti (Ca' d'Oro; 3932 Cannaregio; cf. also Palaces on the Grand Canal, No. 25): This museum was reopened to the public in 1984, after being extensively and well restored. The splendid collection of choice, mainly Renaissance works of art (15&16C) was bequeathed to the State by Baron Giorgio Franchetti during his lifetime. Other works were added to it from the State's possessions. Paintings by Andrea Mantegna, Vittore Carpaccio, Giovanni Bellini and Titian. Sculptures, bronzes and ceramics.

Pietà by Girolamo Romanino, Accademia

Museo Goldoni (containing the *Istituto di Studi Teatrali):* See Palazzo Centani-Goldoni (2798 S.Polo; Calle Nomboli; cf. Other important palaces).

Collezione Peggy Guggenheim (Palazzo Venier dei Leoni; 701 Dorsoduro; cf. also Palaces on the Grand Canal, No. 104): Open from April to October. A good collection of 20C works of art. This influential patroness of modern art assembled the collection from the 1930s until her death in December 1979, and left it to the city in her will. Two chapters of her memoirs 'I have lived it all' describe the part she played in Venetian cultural life and the way in which this impressive spectrum of modern and contemporary art, displaying a systematic approach unique in Europe, was built up. She was once married to Max Ernst, and later continued to be interested in Surrealist art, which is documented by many major works. The sculptures include master-

pieces by Alexander Archipenko, Hans Arp, Constantin Brancusi, Alexander Calder and Henry Moore. There are also a number of glass sculptures cast in Murano to designs by Arp, Ernst, Oskar Kokoschka, Le Corbusier, Jean Lurçat, and Pegeen who was Peggy Guggenheim's daughter.

Museo di Icone dell'Istituto Ellenico di Studi Bizantini (3412 Castello; near S.Giorgio dei Greci): This institute of the Greek community was founded in 1951 and is housed in the Scuola di S.Nicolò. It contains a collection of Byzantine and more recent icons (from the mid-15C onwards), liturgical utensils and medieval Greek manuscripts.

Pinacoteca Manfrediniana: See *Raccolta del Seminario Patriarcale.*

Pinacoteca Querini Stampalia (4778 Castello; on the Rio di S.Maria Formosa):

The collection of paintings belonging to Count Giovanni Querini Stampalia, framed by the atmospheric setting of the original 18C interior, is on the 2nd storey of this Renaissance building (1st half of 16C), which was bequeathed to the State in 1869. 14–19C frescos and paintings. Some works by Venetian Renaissance artists, and 'Scenes of business and everyday life in Venice' (mid-18C) by Gabriel Bella. On the 1st floor is a fine, very extensive *library* collected by the family over several centuries: manuscripts, maps and early printed books. Literary works, and works on art history and the history of the city; some of these are precious rarities.

Museo del Risorgimento e dell' Ottocento Veneziano (Piazza S.Marco, in the Museo Correr): An extensive collection devoted to the city's history in the period from the end of the republic until the integration of Venice into the Kingdom of Italy (1797–1866). 19C Venetian life is illustrated by historical paintings and portraits of well-known figures, and also by printed works, utensils, uniforms, clothing etc.

Raccolte del Seminario Patriarcale (1 Dorsoduro; Campo della Salute): 14–18C paintings and sculptures. Funerary monuments, tombstones and inscriptions rescued from deconsecrated or destroyed churches in Venice. Roman excavations found in the lagoon. The *Pinacoteca Manfrediniana*, named after its founder Marchese Federico Manfredini, was established in 1829 and later enlarged. It has works (13–19C) by such renowned sculptors as Tullio Lombardo, Gian Lorenzo Bernini and Antonio Canova. Terracotta busts by Alessandro Vittoria (2nd half of 16C) enable the onlooker to draw instructive comparisons on the conception and execution of portraits. There are also examples of paintings by the finest Gothic

◁ *Crucifixion by Giulio Carpioni, Accademia*

Madonna and Child by G.B.Cima da Conegliano Accademia

Feast in the house of Simon (detail) by Bernardo Strozzi, Accademia

and Renaissance schools and artists, such as the school of Leonardo da Vinci, and the painters Filippo Lippi, Antonio Vivarini, Giorgione and Paolo Veronese.

Museo del Settecento Veneziano (Ca' Rezzonico; 3136 S.Barnaba; cf. also Palaces on the Grand Canal, No. 72): This elegant baroque building is of interest in several respects. Its original decoration (1750–60) forms the ideal setting for this unique display of 18C Venetian art, supplemented by other contemporary works, furniture and utensils of all kinds which were imported into Venice. Charming 18C paintings of city life by Pietro Longhi (2nd storey).
Piano nobile/Room 1/Sala del Ballo: The largest room in a Venetian private building. The ceiling paintings by Giovanni Battista Crosato are an allegory of the four continents known at that time. Trompe l'oeil, probably by Pietro Visconti. Furniture by Andrea Brustolon (1700–23).

Room 2/Sala dell'Allegoria Nuziale: Ceiling fresco by Giovanni Battista Tiepolo of the 'Marriage of Ludovico Rezzonico to Faustina Savorgnan'. 'Portrait of Francesco Falier' by Bernardo Castello (*c.* 1787). *Room 3:* On the right is the entrance to the private chapel with an altarpiece by Francesco Zugno. Room 2 leads to the *Mezzanino Falier:* The *Appartamento del Papa* (Papal apartment) has outstanding examples of Venetian decorative art and exhibits relating to Carlo Rezzonico, Pope Clement XIII (1758–69), and also—in the *Saletta Browning*—to the English poet Robert Browning, who died here. The *Salotto Verde* and *Salotto Giallo* have fine furniture. Portraits and scenes from Venetian life. *Room 4/Sala dei Pastelli* with ceiling painting by Crosato ('Apotheosis of Poetry'). Portraits, some by the famous portrait artist Rosalba Carriera, whose self-portrait reveals the beginning of her tragic blindness and later derangement. *Room 5/Sala degli Arazzi:*

Landscape with horsemen by Marco Ricci, Accademia

Ceiling fresco by Jacopo Guarana ('Allegory of Virtue'). Good furniture. 17C Flemish tapestries depicting the contest of wisdom between Solomon and the Queen of Sheba. *Room 6/Sala del Trono:* Ceiling painting by Giovanni Battista Tiepolo ('Allegory of Merit', between 'Nobility' and 'Virtue'). Papal throne. Gorgeously framed portrait of 'Pietro Barbarigo' by Castello. *Room 8/Sala dei Tiepolo:* Ceiling painting of 'Strength and Wisdom' (moved). Wall paintings by Gian Domenico Tiepolo and Giuseppe Angeli. 'Portrait of Bartolomeo Ferracina the architect' by Alessandro Longhi. *Room 10/Library* with ceiling paintings (also moved) by Francesco Maffei. The baroque bookcases contain splendid contemporary editions from Venetian presses. *Room 11/Sala del Lazzarini:* Mythological scenes ('Hercules and Omphale'; 'Orpheus killed by the Bacchantes') by Gregorio Lazzarini. 'Battle of the Centaurs', probably by Antonio Molinari. *Room 12/Sala del*

Brustolon, with splendid furniture and paintings on Biblical and mythological subjects.
2nd floor/Room 13/Portego dei Dipinti: The paintings include an expressive historical painting of 'The Death of Darius' by Giovanni Battista Piazzetta. *Room 14/Sala del Longhi:* Ceiling painting of 'Zephyr and Flora' by Giovanni Battista Tiepolo. The 'Scenes from Venetian life' by Pietro Longhi are well worth seeing: these brilliantly composed paintings are not merely of historical interest, but still captivate the onlooker by their satirical precision in the depiction of persons and individual situations. *Room 15/Sala delle Lacche Verdi:* Ceiling painting by Francesco Guardi ('Diana'), who also painted the frescos ('Minerva, Apollo, Venezia') in the next room. *Rooms 16–20:* Utensils and decorative objects. *Rooms 21–26/Villa dei Tiepolo:* Fresco cycle by Gian Domenico Tiepolo from a villa which his family once owned: carnival scenes and mythological creatures,

Judgement of Midas by Schiavone, Accademia

half human, half animal (fauns, satyrs etc.). *Room 29/Sala del Ridotto:* 'Carnival Party' and 'Parlatory of the Nuns of S.Zaccaria' are two well-known works by F.Guardi. *3rd floor:* Paintings (some of them copies) by Guardi and Tiepolo. Furniture. Masks. Ceramics. The complete contents of a pharmacy have been moved here. A collection of designs by Giovanni Maria Morlaiter, the sculptor.

Museo di Storia Naturale (1730 S.Croce; Fondaco dei Turchi; cf. also Palaces on the Grand Canal, No. 10): Extensive collection of stuffed animals. The *Sala della Laguna* has a graphic display of the flora and fauna to be found in the lagoon. 19C models of ships and fishing nets. The museum's most valuable exhibit is the complete skeleton of a dinosaur, excavated in Africa.

Museo Storico Navale (2418 Castello; Riva S.Biagio): See Arsenal, p.113.

XII. Theatres

More than almost any other city in the world, Venice is a city of music and theatre. The 'Commedia dell'arte', the famous Italian form which originated here, caused a theatrical revival after the age of classical theatre had passed. It formed a basis for writers like Goldoni, who used his comedies to attack the Commedia, and Gozzi, who defended it with his fairytale theatre. Palestrina, the successor to the composers of the Low Countries, continued the development of the Gregorian chant and created a new kind of church music in Rome. The first edition of his works appeared in Venice in 1582. Venice is the birthplace of Monteverdi, who took up the genre of musical theatre initiated by Peri in Florence, and developed it into the 'Coronation of Poppea', the first operatic masterpiece. Vivaldi, the composer and priest of genius, lived, conducted and played the violin here. But it was not only

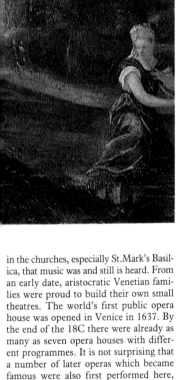

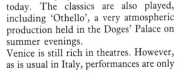

Teatro la Fenice

in the churches, especially St.Mark's Basilica, that music was and still is heard. From an early date, aristocratic Venetian families were proud to build their own small theatres. The world's first public opera house was opened in Venice in 1637. By the end of the 18C there were already as many as seven opera houses with different programmes. It is not surprising that a number of later operas which became famous were also first performed here, including five operas by Giuseppe Verdi, and works by Puccini, Boito, Mascagni, Giordano, Stravinsky, Britten, Prokofiev, Nono and Busoni. Innovations and experiments which are the subject of intense discussion, whether they be operas, concerts or plays, are still attempted here today. The classics are also played, including 'Othello', a very atmospheric production held in the Doges' Palace on summer evenings.

Venice is still rich in theatres. However, as is usual in Italy, performances are only held in the 'stagione' (that is to say, in the season, and with guest actors, as the theatre has no company of its own). Examples are: the 17C *Teatro Goldoni* (Calle Goldoni, San Marco), with the very fine Corte del Teatro, used for open-air performances, which is surrounded by Gothic and Renaissance buildings. The neo-Gothic *Teatro Italia* (Calle dell'Anconeta). The *Teatro Malibran* (Campo S.Giovanni Crisostomo, Cannaregio; opened under Giovanni Grimani in 1678 and restored in 1920). The *Teatro Rossini* (Rio de S.Lucca), rebuilt by F.Costa in 1756 after a fire and restored in 1875. The *Teatro Verde* (on the Isola di S.Giorgio Maggiore) in the middle of a fine garden, designed by L.Viotti and A.Scattolin after the manner of the Greek open-air theatres.

But the most famous of all is the *Teatro la Fenice* (Campo San Fantin, San Marco), the largest theatre in Venice and the best-known in all Italy after La Scala in Milan. Built by A.Selva (1790–2). A theatre and opera house. The great auditorium has 1500 seats. Burned down in 1836, it was rebuilt to Selva's plans by the architects Battista and Meduna. The famous and typically Venetian interior in shades of blue, gold and honey, with red seats and curtains and the large Venetian chandelier, has an inimitable charm when concerts, operas and plays are being performed. Richard Wagner, who died in Venice, refused to have these decorations on display when his operas were being performed. But the decorations provide a framework which enhances the effect produced by the works of Goldoni, Rossini and Verdi, as well as those of Bertolt Brecht and, particularly, Stravinsky.

XIII. Festivals in Venice

Visiting Venice is a festival in itself. It is not surprising that the backdrop created by their fairytale buildings stimulates the Venetians into holding special celebrations. This has always been so. The pomp with which the Doges, together with all their retinue dressed according to special regulations (cf. Bellini's paintings in the Accademia), crossed the festively decorated Piazza S.Marco, the solemn rite in which the Doge sailed out to sea on the 'Bucentoro', the Commedia, the theatrical, operatic and musical performances which have been held in Venice since time immemorial, and, not least, the famous *carnival,* are all witness that Venice, clearly and with unmistakable charm, a charm which is not merely frivolous but often very profound, and not infrequently conceals a cruel and morbid background, is a city of festivals: exuberant, voluptuous, inventive festivals which are without parallel in the world.

The Venetian carnival originated in the Roman Saturnalia, and was always associated with masquerade. It began on 26 December and ended on Ash Wednesday. The disguise was the mask, which was always home-made and ever-changing, spawning hosts of variants. It was often abused for deception and abductions and,

The Carnival in Venice
fascinates young and old alike ▷

in the most serious cases, crimes. Masks were forbidden in the 14C, but always reappeared despite repeated bans. Today the mask is a symbol of Venice, sold in all parts of the city. In the early 18C, the carnival assumed such proportions in Venice that it began in October. Casanova has described the colourful, turbulent and often very secretive hustle and bustle. The carnival fell into oblivion in Venice in the 19C. But in 1979, two actors dressed as the Devil and an Archangel passed through the city with trumpet and fiddle and once again ignited a spark which has since then kindled a flaming fire. Every year the carnival in Venice, attended by thousands, throbs in all corners of the city, particularly the Piazza, but also in all the larger campi and in the ghetto. Commedia dell'arte is the main feature: improvised theatre, musical performances, dancing in the streets and squares, festively decorated gondolas, imaginative costumes, masks and more masks. Puppet theatres, balloons, stilt-walkers, people dressed as priests, skeletons with death's heads, painted beauties, fritelle which are the typical carnival pastry, booths and taverns everywhere selling wine, and an unimaginable throng of humanity. The uproar throbs through Venice, beginning ten days before Ash Wednesday, reaching its climax on 'Fat Thursday' (giovedi grasso), and ending on Ash Wednesday. Then all is quiet again until the Easter holidays.

The *Festa della Liberazione,* the day of liberation, is celebrated on *25 April.* There is almost no shipping on *1 May,* Labour Day *(Festa del lavoro).* The *Festa della Repubblica* is celebrated on *2 June.* The feast of St.Peter and St.Paul, the patron Saints of the church, is observed on *29 June.* The Feast of the Redeemer *(Festa del Redentore)* is celebrated on the *third Sunday in July* in memory of the city's liberation from the plague in 1576. The evening of this holiday is marked by a procession of boats to the Giudecca, a pontoon bridge over the Giudecca Canal to the Redentore, and a large firework display.

The international *film festival* is held on the Lido in late August and early September of every year. The Biennale d'arte is an exhibiton of contemporary art in the Giardini Pubblici. Started in 1895, it is held once every two years, between June and September. It has caused scandals and has been widely discussed. It was banned in 1942–7. The famous *Ferragosta,* Assumption Day, is on 15 August. On the 1st Sunday after Assumption, *Vogalonga* is celebrated, when half the inhabitants of Venice take a rowing boat and row from the Giudecca to Burano and back to S.Marco. The famous *Regata Storica* is held on the Grand Canal on the first Sunday in September. People wearing historical costumes, depicting the Doge and other dignitaries, ride in festively decorated ships, boats and gondolas. There follows the *Regata Sportiva,* with a race between the gondolieri, cheered on by all the spectators. On *1 September,* All Saints' Day *(Ognissanti)* is held, and *4 November* is *Anniversario della Vittoria,* victory day. Since 1670 the *Festa della Salute* has been held on *21 November,* when some shops are closed for half the day and others for the entire day. A procession in memory of the end of the second plague epidemic in 1630 leads from S.Marco over a pontoon bridge, especially built for this purpose across the Grand Canal, to the church of Santa Maria della Salute, whose main portal is only opened on this day. As is the case all over Italy, Christmas is not celebrated in Venice to quite the same extent as in the English-speaking world, but 6 January is observed as *Epifania* or the day of the witch 'Befana' who distributes the presents. The festival of modern music, with operatic performances, is during the winter. Concerts are mainly held in the Teatro La Fenice, in the Malibran theatre and in churches and palaces in spring and autumn, but also on summer evenings. The *Purificazione della Vergine* is celebrated in S.Maria Formosa on *2 February.* This festival, commemorating an event in 942, is held especially for brides and bridegrooms and in veneration of the Virgin Mary.

'Madonna and Child' by Giovanni Bellini in the Galleria dell'Accademia

Environs: Mestre: An industrial town which is part of the city of Venice. Originally a Roman settlement, it was destroyed during the Barbarian Invasions and resettled in the Middle Ages. The early-19C church of *S.Lorenzo* was originally a Romanesque campanile. The clock tower (1108, restored in 1878) is the sole remnant of the medieval castle. Biblioteca Civile.

Marghera: A part of Greater Venice. Its importance as an industrial town increased between 1920 and 1935.

Islands in the lagoon: The sea has washed away countless islands over the centuries. Many islands, numbering perhaps 30 or 40, still survive.

Lido: This island just outside the city is principally a bathing resort, with modern hotels, villas, a casino and the Palazzo del Cinema (a film festival is held each August). The baroque church of *San Nicolò di Lido* (1044) was rebuilt by the Benedictines in the 17C. The Crusaders gathered here in 1202 before embarking for the Orient. The romantic Jewish cemetery, now semi-derelict, has stood near the Catholic cemetery on the Lido since the 16C. It was destroyed by Napoleon's soldiers. The word lido derives from here. It originally signified the sandy strip between the lagoons and the open sea, but has now taken on the general meaning of 'beach'. The S. part of the Lido, with its charming countryside, is known today as Malamocco. The island that originally bore this name disappeared beneath the waves long ago.

Malamocco: The former Castello S.Zaccaria now houses an excellent restaurant. The 15C *chiesa dell'Assunta* has a very fine campanile.

Alberoni: An island still further to the S.

San Michele: This island lies half a mile N. of the Fondamenta Nuove and is of interest to art historians. A monastery stood here from the 13C onwards. Since 1873 it has been regarded as the cemetery island of Venice. It is cared for by reformed fathers. The monastery church built by Mauro Codussi from 1469 onwards is the first early-Renaissance work in Venice. The campanile dates from 1456–69, while the atmospheric cloister is mid 15C. The domed hexagonal *Cappella Emiliana*, to plans by Gugliemo Grigi, stands beside the church and is the last early-Renaissance work in Venice.

Vignole: Market gardening is the main activity on this group of islands NE of Venice (Forte di Sant'Andrea, 16C).

San Erasmo: This large island is further to the N. in the lagoon, lying off Treporti and the Lido di Jesolo.

S.Lazzaro degli Armeni: Between Venice and the Lido, it was once a leper colony. Mechitarists live here now (a good library and a small museum).

S.Clemente: S. of S.Lazzaro degli Armeni, formerly contained a lunatic asylum, today much more humanitarian in character. 17C church of S.Clemente.

The islands of *Murano, Burano* with *Mazzorbo* and *S.Francesco,* and *Torcello* have separate entries in the main text.

The Veneto

45011 Adria

Rovigo   p.322☐G 7

This little town with its canals and alleyways is now 15 miles inland. It dates back to a settlement originally founded by the Veneti. Under the leadership of Dionysios I of Syracuse, the lagoon town of *Adrias*, built on piles, became the Venice of classical times as a result of its trade with the Etruscans. The town gave the Adriatic Sea its name. The *municipium Atria* continued to flourish under the Romans, but later declined in importance as the Po delta silted up.

Cattedrale (piazza Garibaldi): The 19C *Cattedrale Nuova* has a nave, two aisles, and a campanile (1688) to one side. The excellent Coptic *bas relief* (Virgin Mary between the Archangels Michael and Gabriel, Council of Ephesus, 5C) on the third pillar on the left is the oldest testimony to the adoration of the Virgin Mary in the Veneto. The Creto-Byzantine *crucifix* in the sacristy at the end of the right aisle is from Candia (Iraklion). The sacristy also has cupboards (1683) by Jacopo Piazzetta, with half and whole caryatids. The altars were formerly in the *old cathedral*, which is reached through the left aisle. The excavated crypt has remains of 8C Byzantine frescos.

Museo Archeologico (piazzale Ospedale): This museum founded by Francesco Bocchi in 1780 has finds from the environs of Adria dating from prehistoric and Roman times, and also Adria's heyday in the 6–4C BC. *Ceramics* from the Iron Age and Etrusco-Campanian period. Numerous black and red figure Attic vases (6–4C BC). The 'biga del lucumone' is a *bronze two-horse carriage* (4C BC) from a Gallic warrior's tomb. Small Greek and Etruscan bronzes and *gold jewellery*.

S.Maria Assunta delle Tomba (via Angeli): Spoils from the Roman baths were used in building the church, which has been rebuilt several times (most recently in 1718). One such fragment is the 1C stone bearing inscriptions relating to Adriatic seamen on the lower storey of the elegant *brick campanile* to the right of the eclectic façade. Inside the church, on the left, are an early-8C octagonal *piscina* (font and wash basin) and a medieval holy-water stoup of Pentelic marble.

Adria, Museo Archeologico, Roman tombstones

Also worth seeing: The 16C church of *S.Andrea*, and the large *town theatre* by Giovan Battista Scarpari, both stand beside the central, almost Venetian *Canalbianco*.

Environs: Crespino (20 km. SW): Inside the parish church of *SS.Martino e Severo* are a font (1577), fine 17C choir stalls, a Pala of the Virgin Mary and Saints (signed by Garofalo in 1525) at the third altar on the left, and a 15C tablet of Pax in the sacristy.

Loreo (11 km. E.): The parish church of *S.Maria Assunta* was built in 1675 to plans by Baldassare Longhena on the site of an earlier church. The campanile was completed in 1702. The two marble statues (St.Peter and St.Paul, 1714) at the high altar are attributed to Antonio Tarsia. A fine 14C tabernacle at the 3rd altar on the right. The 18C altarpiece of Joseph's Death at the 1st altar on the left is by Giovan Battista Piazzetta.

32021 Agordo

Belluno   p.320□G 2

This small market town is the centre of the Cordévole valley. Holidaymakers frequently use it as a starting point for walks in the wooded hills of the Agordino or climbing expeditions to the nearby Dolomite peaks of *Monte Agner* (9,425 ft.) or *Monte Framont* (7,525 ft.).

Palazzo Manzoni: An old fountain with a lion of St.Mark stands in the central *Piazza della Libertà*. The Piazza is dominated by the façade of the recently restored palazzo (the former *Villa Crotta*), which is among the finest villas in Belluno province. This eclectic structure combines architectural styles ranging from the early 17C to the late 18C. In the 19C, Pietro Paoletti from Belluno painted *frescos* in some of the richly stuccoed rooms inside.

Crespino (Adria), SS.Martino e Severo (left), Loreo (Adria), S.Maria Assunta (right)

Also worth seeing: The *parish church* (1836–52) with its two campaniles contains frescos (*c.* 1840) in the apse by Giovanni De Min, two panel paintings by Palma Giovane, and two 16C paintings attributed to Paris Bordone. The *Istituto Minerario A.Follador* houses a *mineral museum.*

Environs: Cencenighe (10 km. NW): The *parish church* with two winged lions of St.Mark on its façade has an altarpiece by Tizianello depicting St.Antony Abbot with St.Sebastian and St.Roch.
S.Simon di Vallada (14 km. NW): The Romanesque church of *S.Simon* (*c.* 1190), restored in 1966 after severe weather damage, stands with its campanile in a picturesque site on a hill (3,745 ft.) above *Sacchet-Vallada Agordina.* The best of the four fresco cycles (Last Supper, *c.* 1550) inside is by Paris Bordone of Treviso. High altar (16C) by an unknown German artist, and a fine 19C wooden statue from

the school of Valentino Panciera (known as Besarel).

36071 Arzignano
Vicenza   p.322□D 5

This small industrial town in the *Valle del Chiampo* began as a Lombard settlement and was first mentioned in 983.

Castello: The castle, which has a medieval core, occupies a dominant position high above the modern town. The Scaligers built it in the 14C on the site of an older building belonging to the Counts of Arzignano. It took its present form when it became a Venetian fortress in the 17C. The outer wall, which is still in good condition, originally had 14 towers and two gates. It encloses not merely the picturesque medley of houses and the castle, but also the church of *S.Maria in Castello,* rebuilt in 1836–50, with a campanile to one side. In the choir of this enormous building, on the left, is a polyptych (Virgin Mary, Twelve Saints, Crucifixion; *c.* 1450) which has a Gothic frame and is of Paduan provenance; on the right is a painting of the Visitation by Francesco Maffei from Vicenza (1645).

Environs: Castelgomberto (12 km. NE): The parish church of *S.Martino* adjoining the central free-standing campanile of 1630 has a 15C carved stone tabernacle, thought to be by Niccolò da Cornedo. On the road running N. out of the town are the *Villa Trissino-Barbaran* (1710), which has a Gothic loggia, and the *Villa da Schio* (originally Villa Piovene-Da Porto) which was built in 1666, probably to plans by Antonio Pizzocaro. It has a splendid garden front, with a colonnaded portico (*c.* 1750) and marble sculptures which are from the Marinali workshop, as are those in the garden. The rooms of

the villa, which is in a good condition, have fine furniture and paintings, including three early works by Giambattista Tiepolo.

Chiampo (5 km. NW): The neoclassical parish church of *S.Martino* (1828) in this little town known for its marble bridge contains a marble tabernacle (1438) by Niccolò da Cornedo, and several 17C paintings by the Paduan artist Pietro Liberi.

Cornedo Vicentino (14 km. N.): The new *parish church* is worth visiting for the panel painting of the Immaculate Conception, signed by Giovanni Buonconsiglio, 1497, and a 15C tabernacle by Niccolò da Cornedo. The nearby *Villa Trissino* (early-16C) has an elegant arcade.

Montecchio Maggiore (6 km. E.): The neo-Gothic cathedral of *S.Vitale* (1892) has a 17C high altar from the Marinali workshop, and a 15C marble triptych (St.Leo I, St.Vitalis, St.Catherine of Alexandria) in the left side chapel. The church of

Arzignano, S.Maria in Castello (left), Montecchio Maggiore, Castello della Villa

S.Pietro, rebuilt in the 16–18C, houses three 16C statues by Niccolò da Cornedo, and the painting of the Virgin Mary as Mater Sapientiae, signed by Giovanni Buonconsiglio, 1519, at the 2nd side altar on the right. Two castles with a fine view of the town were razed by the Venetians in 1514. They commanded the point where the river Agno flows into the valley. The *Castello della Villa* (1354), built by Cangrande, is popularly also known as 'Castello di Romeo'. The upper castle—the *Castello di Bellaguardia* (c. 1350–60) rebuilt this century—is also known as the 'Castello di Giulia'. The *Villa Cordellino-Lombardi*, built by Giorgio Massari in Palladian style in 1735–60, is on the E. edge of the town. The visitor ascends a flight of steps and enters through a colonnaded portico. Inside there are frescos (1743) by Giovanni Battista Tiepolo on the ceiling (Nobility and Virtue) and walls (Family of Darius before Alexander the Great, Continence of Scipio) in the hall.

Trissino (7.5 km. NE): The *Villa Marzotto* (formerly the Villa Trisino da Porto) is a typical example of an 18C Vicenza villa. The upper Casino, built on the remains of a 16C castle and restored in the 18&19C, has a Doric portal (1593), while the lower Casino (1746; restored in 1843) is frescoed inside by Andrea Porta (1765). Both Casinos are surrounded by an extensive park with nymphaea, terraces, staircases and avenues. The 17C statues are by Orazio Marinali, while those from the 18C are the work of Giacomo Cassetti.

36012 Asiago

Vicenza   p.322☐D/E 4

This, the main town of the *plateau of the Sette Comuni* (seven communities), is a popular summer and ski resort. Here, and also in nearly 20 other towns in the environs, an Old High German Bavarian

Montecchio Maggiore (Arzignano), Villa Cordellino-Lombardi

Montecchio Maggiore, Villa Cordellino-Lombardi (left), Asolo, Museo Civico, Ceres (right)

dialect, which has survived here since the time of the Nibelungenlied, is still spoken.

Parish church of S.Matteo: The choir of this 20C church with a nave, two aisles, and a monumental red marble façade has a sumptuous *panel painting* (Francesco Bassano the elder, early-16C) of the Virgin Mary with saints and angels.

Sacrario Militare: The imposing *war memorial* (1934) to 33,000 Italian and 18,000 Austro-Hungarian soldiers, most of whom died in the bitter battle for the plateau in 1915–18, is approached along a broad avenue.

Environs: Calà del Sasso (15 km. E.): The **Mulattiera** (mule path), which is said to have 4,444 steps of natural stone, leads steeply down from the plateau of the seven communities into the wooded gorge of the *Valle Frenzela.*

Rotzo (11 km. W.): Another of the seven communities. In *Bostell*, which has been part of Rotzo since 1311, a prehistoric Veneto-Gallic settlement with rectangular stone huts was discovered in 1781 and systematically excavated in 1912. Interesting *ara sacrificale di Rotzo* (sacrificial altar).

31011 Asolo

Treviso   p.322☐F 4

This picturesque little town in the Alpine foothills nestles amidst the *Asolanian Hills (Colle Asolani)* which were settled in prehistoric and Roman times. Their gentle outlines inspired the backgrounds in paintings by Venetian artists, especially Giorgone and his school. Asolo became known outside Italy as the adopted home of the ex-Queen of Cyprus, *Caterina Cornaro* (1454–1510) and her illustrious court, and

Asolo, S.Maria di Breda

later as the summer residence of the English poet *Robert Browning* (1812–89) and the American landscape painter *Eugene Benson*.

S.Maria di Breda (piazza Maggiore): The present 'cathedral', completed in 1889 when the neo-Gothic façade was built, was erected by Giorgio Massari in 1747 on the site of the medieval cathedral, which stood above the remains of a Roman thermal bath. The portico with its round pillars, and the *portal* (*c.* 1470) on the S. side, both survive from the previous building. In the interior (one nave, two aisles) there are a *painting* of the Assunta signed by Lorenzo Lotto, 1506, and a Mannerist copy of it (*c.* 1565) by Jacopo Bassano. The altarpiece (1840) in the choir by Lattanzio Querena is a copy of Titian's Assunta in the Frari in Venice (q.v.).

Museo Civico (piazza Maggiore): The *Loggia del Capitano* (15C) is the distinguishing feature of the *former town hall,* which has a severe façade decorated with frescos (1560) by Antonio Contarini. Today it houses the *Municipal Museum,* which has exhibits from prehistoric, early historical, and Roman times, as well as the Middle Ages. The drawing-room has famous classical *marble statues* (Paris, weeping angel) by Antonio Canova, a 17C painting of St.Antony by the Genoese artist Bernardo Strozzi, and a painting of St.Girolamo by Luca Giordano. On the upper floor, there is a wealth of exhibits documenting the life and work of *Eleonora Duse* (1859–1924), who is buried in the cemetery here.

Also worth seeing: The fountain (1516) in the piazza Maggiore has a column crowned by a winged lion (19C) by Antonio dal Zotto. The *Villa Pasini* (formerly Villa Scotti, 17C) in Palladian style to the SE of the piazza was formerly lived in by Robert Browning, and to the NW is the Gothic *Palazzo Marcello* with 15C frescos on its façade and a good Gothic portico (*c.* 1300). All that survives of the *Castello della Regina*, the former residence (pulled down in 1820) of Caterina Cornaro, is the massive clock tower (Via Regina Cornaro). The *Rocca*, a fortress from pre-Roman times standing on a height, has cyclopean walls about 50 ft. high and 13 ft. thick. Ezzelino da Romano ordered a Gothic portal to be built in the walls in 1220. The *Villa Falier* by Giorgio Massari is the best of the numerous 18C villas on the edge of the town.

Environs: Montebelluna (13 km. E.): The upper town, the *Mercato Vecchio* with the column of the Ducali (1593), was built above *Mons Belluni*, a Palaeo-Venetian and Roman settlement. From the centre of this upper town there is a view down to the new town and its eclectic *cathedral* (1908), which has a large 16&17C tapestry depicting manna falling in the desert. The *priory church* (Duomo Vecchio, 1613), which is lower down, has a free-standing campanile 235 ft. high and contains a fine 18C ceiling painting of the Assunta by Jacopo Guarana from Verona.

45021 Badia Polésine
Rovigo   p.322☐D/E 7

In about the mid 10C, Marchese Almerico of Mantua ordered a castle and the church of S.Maria sull'Adige to be built at the confluence of the Adige and the Adigetto. The church was enlarged into an abbey in 994 by Marchese Ugo di Toscana. Badia Polésine had grown into a fortified settlement in the 13C, when it fell to Padua. The Este of Ferrara took it over

Asolo, Castello della Regina

Badia Polésine, Abbazia della Vangadizza

in 1355, but in 1482 it came under Venetian rule.

Abbazia della Vangadizza: This Benedictine monastery founded in the 10C was occupied by Camaldolese monks from 1213 onwards before being dissolved in 1810 under Napoleon.
The *Palazzo d'Espagnac* includes some parts of the former abbey. The picturesque remains of the abbey also include fragments of the *church*, destroyed in 1835, with the chapel of the Virgin Mary (*c.* 1490) probably decorated by Filippo Zaniberti, and a slightly leaning 12C campanile, with a Hellenistic bas relief adorning its lower storey. The *cloister* (1233) includes a loggia. On the left is the refectory (1466) with a decorative frieze. In the centre of the courtyard there is a Venetian-Gothic marble fountain.

Also worth seeing: The 15C Venetian-Gothic *Palazzo degli Estensi* (13 Via S.Alberto). The *sarcophagus* of Azzo II of Este (d. 1097) and his wife Unnigunde of Bavaria (d. 1060). The gorgeous sarcophagus of Azzo VI of Este (d. 1212) on the Piazza Vangadizza. The 17C oratory of *S.Maria della Salute* with its carved marble altarpieces (1715) by Pietro Baratta. The spacious *Villa Pellegrini* (fraz. Salvaterra), and the 17C *Palazzo Bassi*.

Environs: Canda (8 km. S.): The *Villa Nani Mocenigo* (1580–4), probably by Vincenzo Scamozzi, is among the earliest villas in the Polésine. The centre of the façade is accentuated by a loggia with Corinthian columns and by the flight of steps leading up to it. 18C outbuildings. The interior, which was damaged by fire in 1944 (now restored), has 18C frescos by Girolamo Mengozzi-Colonna, and is open to visitors, although it is advisable to make an appointment.
Ficarolo (21 km. S.): The 16C *Villa Schiati* has an elegant brick façade, and corner towers which survive from the previous building. Today it is the *town hall* of this picturesque little town.
Lendinara (8 km. E.): The council chamber of the central *Palazzo Comunale* (1801) has a fine 15C inlaid wooden screen by Lorenzo and Cristoforo Canozzi. Across the Piazza Risorgimento from this Palazzo is the battlemented *gatehouse tower* of the old Este castle and this leads to the cathedral of *S.Sofia*, rebuilt in 1767–86, with the tall free-standing campanile

Canda (Badia Polésine), Villa Nani Mocenigo

Badia Polésine, sarcophagus of Azzo II of Este (left), Lendinara, S.Sofia cathedral

(1797–1857). In the sacristy there is a painting of the Virgin Mary and angels making music, signed by Domenico Mancini in 1511, and also one of the Virgin Mary Enthroned with St.Antony of Padua and St.Lawrence by Francesco Bissolo. The most splendid of the paintings in the *Santuario della Madonna del Pilastrello* (16–19C) is the Ascension on the 2nd altar on the left, which depicts a donor and is by the school of Paolo Veronese (*c.* 1581). The outstanding painting in *S.Biagio* (16–19C) is the Pala depicting the Visitation, signed by Sebastiano Filippi da Lendinara, 1525, at the 3rd altar on the right. There are numerous *Renaissance* and *baroque palazzi*.

Melara (34 km. W.): Pre-Roman and Roman archaeological exhibits are to be found in the *Museo Archeologico* (Municipio).

Sariano (14 km. SW): The 16C *Castello* at the entrance to this little village founded in Roman times was later turned into a baroque villa (today used as a farm), but it still has its massive old fortified tower. Remains of 14C frescos in Ferrarese style were discovered in the choir of the *parish church* in 1953.

36061 Bassano del Grappa

Vicenza   p.322□E 4

This town on the Brenta, below the plateau of the seven communities and Monte Grappa, was mentioned in 901 and it was inhabited in prehistoric and Roman times. In the 13C, under the Ezzelini, Bassano was fortified by defensive walls and a castle, and was elevated to the status of capital of the Vicentino. Thereafter it was a free town for a short period, fell to Padua in 1268, and later to the Scaligers, Carrara and Visconti, before voluntarily submitting to the supremacy of Venice in 1402 and subsequently developing into a

Bassano del Grappa with Ponte degli Alpini

centre of trade and art. The picturesque *old quarter* of the town is characterized by its little winding alleyways with painted house fronts, arcades, and many Renaissance and Venetian baroque palazzi.

Piazza Libertà: This central piazza (formerly known as dei Signori) has a 17C *statue* on a pedestal of S.Bassiano, the town's patron saint, by Orazio Marinali. But the piazza is dominated by the monumental façade of the church of *S.Giovanni Battista* (1308), rebuilt by Giovanni Mazzi in 1747–82 in Palladian style; and also by the *town hall* (1582) with its clock tower (1746), the 16C fresco of St.Christopher on its façade, and its 15C Loggia del Comune.

S.Francesco: This early-Gothic monastery church with its slender campanile surmounted by a spire stands in the nearby Piazza Garibaldi, which is overlooked by the 13C *Torre di Ezzelino*, a medieval fortified tower. An elegant *canopied portico* (1306) leads to the wide main doorway, whose tympanum has 17C frescos by Luca Martinelli depicting the Virgin Mary, St.Antony of Padua and St.Francis of Assisi. To the right of this is a 14C fresco of the Annunciation by Guariento di Arpo. In the sober Franciscan interior, a monument to Francesco da Ponte (d. 1592), a painter who worked here, is to the left of the entrance. The *crucifix* (c. 1360) painted on the wall of the choir is thought to be a late work by Guariento.

Duomo S.Maria in Colle: In the portico of 52 Via Matteotti (a house on the left-hand side), which leads off the Piazza Libertà, there is a fresco of the Virgin Mary Enthroned (1523) by Bassano the elder. On the right of this street is the rustic 14/15C *Palazzo Pretorio* whose right-hand portal has a lozenge design and is adorned by a lion of St.Mark. The Via

Matteotti leads to the small cathedral square high above the Brenta. The *Castello Superiore,* built by the bishops of Vicenza in *c.* 900–950, originally stood here. The defences were strengthened under the town's later rulers, and remains of their walls survive. These remains have been incorporated in the houses in the square. A massive tower that was once part of the castle is now the cathedral's campanile. The interior of this single-aisled 11–15C church, which was rebuilt in the 16&18C, has a flat-roofed nave with a ceiling painting of the Assumption by Giambattista Volpato and a tunnel-vaulted choir with side apses. The painting at the side altar depicts the Martyrdom of St.Stephen below and the Glorification of St.Lucy above, and is signed by Leandro Bassano, who was also responsible for the Virgin Mary in Glory at the S. *altar of the rosary* (18C). The marble figures of the Virgin Mary, St.Dominic and St.Theresa at this last altar are by Orazio Marinali, 1704. The Nativity at the left side altar is attributed to Jacopo Bassano and captivates the onlooker by its interesting treatment of light. A late-12C Romanesque *wooden crucifix* is to be found at the altar to the right of the organ gallery. The outstanding item in the church treasure in the sacristy is the *silver crucifix* signed by Filarete (Antonio Averlino), 1449.

Ponte degli Alpini: This wooden bridge (*Ponte Vecchio,* 1209) has been rebuilt several times. It takes its present name from the mountain infantry who, in 1948, rebuilt it after it had been burnt down in the war. The model created by Palladio in 1569 for this town landmark was used as the basis for later rebuilding work on the bridge. The *Museo del Ponte degli Alpini,* with exhibits relating to the history of the bridge, stands near the *Taverna al Ponte* to the NW. The spacious early-

Piazza Libertà (left), portico of S.Francesco with Torre di Ezzelino in the background (right)

{}

17C *Palazzo Bonaguro* stands on the Via Angarano W. of the bridge. Exhibitions of decorative art are held in this palazzo during the summer.

Museo Civico (piazza Garibaldi): The entrance to the *former Franciscan monastery*, now the Town Museum, is to the right of the portico of S.Francesco. A collection of Roman architectural fragments and statues is housed in the plain 17C monastery *cloister*. The *ground floor* of the S. wing is devoted to the town's political and artistic history, collections of ceramics and majolica (14–19C) from the factories in Nove and Bassano, and prints, woodcuts and printing blocks from this area. The library (90,000 volumes, 46,000 manuscripts and early printed books) also has 23 volumes of letters by Canova. The frescos (15C) in the chapterhouse are by Battista da Vicenza. The Corpus canovianum (with 2,000 drawings by Canova), the Riva collection with drawings by Carpac-

cio, Lotto, Bernini, Tiepolo and Guardi, a set of 20,000 prints by the Remondini press in the Piazza Libertà, a coin cabinet, and a *picture gallery*, are all to be found on the *upper floor*. The collection contains regional art and outstanding items from the 12–16C are the Romanesque frescos from the church of S.Bartolomeo, the large crucifix signed by Guariento di Arpo, and the works of Jacopo Bassano (including Exodus, Baptism of St.Lucilla, 1568), Bartolomeo Vivarini (Christ blessing), and Michele Giambono (Virgin Mary). Veneto art in the 17/18C is represented by paintings by Francesco Maffei (Virgin Mary), Giovanni Battista Tiepolo (Manger and Virgin Mary), Pietro Longhi (Four Shepherd Boys) and Alessandro Magnasco (Monk's Burial, Refectory). 19C art works, including sketches, paintings and plaster models by Canova, are to be found in the left wing.

Also worth seeing: A fine view of the

Bassano del Grappa, S.Francesco, Annunciation (left), Cartigliano (Bassano), fresco

Cartigliano (Bassano), parish church, fresco by J.Bassano (left)

Maròstica (Bassano), Castello Inferiore

Ponte degli Alpini is to be had from the 18C *Palazzo Sturm* on the E. bank of the Brenta. Art exhibitions of different works from the Museo Civico are held in the rooms of this palazzo, which were stuccoed and frescoed by Antonio Bellucci. A painting by Francesco Bassano the elder, depicting the Virgin Mary, S.Bassiano, the Archangel Michael, and donors, is to be found behind the high altar of the church of *S.Donato* (Vicolo S.Donato). The 17C *Ca' Rezzonico* at the edge of the town is thought to be an early work by Baldassare Longhena, the architect. In the hall there are rococo stuccoes, and paintings by Canova, Domenico Pellegrini and Giovanni Busato. The *Villa Biachi-Michiel*, built in the early 18C in the manner of Longhena, stands amidst a garden with statues by Giacomo Cassetti.

Environs: Cartigliano (7 km. S.): The chapel of the Virgin Mary (12C) of the

17C *parish church* which was rebuilt in the 19C has an altarpiece (Virgin Mary with God the Father, saints and angels; *c.* 1500) by Bartolomeo Montagna, and also the only fresco cycle (restored) by Jacopo Bassano and his son Francesco to have survived in its entirety, depicting St.Peter and St.Paul, Sacrifice of Isaac, Moses receiving the tablets of the Law, Crucifixion, and the Expulsion from Paradise (all from 1575). Francesco Zamberlan, a pupil of Palladio, is thought to be the architect of the nearby *Villa Cappello* (*c.* 1590). The distinguishing features of the villa are its arcaded ground floor, and the loggie, with their Ionic columns, along all the sides of the upper storey.

Maròstica (7 km. SW): This town, first mentioned in 753, retains much of its late-medieval appearance. The 14C *town wall* is defended by towers, the battlemented 14C *Castello Inferiore* is now the town hall, and the *piazza* with its chessboard paving

is decorated by a tall flagpole and a pillar bearing the lion of St.Mark. The medieval impression is intensified by the battlemented silhouette of the 14C *Castello Superiore*, which stands 2 km. away on a height. St.Paul's Sermon in Athens, a masterpiece by Jacopo and Francesco Bassano (1577), is in the parish church of *S.Antonio Abate* (12/18C). Every other September (1988 will be the next occasion), a game of chess with live pieces is played in 15C historical costumes in the town square in memory of the legendary chess match held between two noblemen for the hand of Lionara, daughter of Taddco Parisio, who was lord of the castle and rector at that time.

Monte Grappa (31 km. NE): In 1935, a massive *monument to the fallen*, dedicated to some 12,600 Italian and 10,000 Austro-Hungarian dead, was built under the supervision of the architect Giovanni Greppi, to plans by the sculptor Giannino Castiglione, on the *Cima Grappa* (5,825 ft.), which was hotly contested in 1917/18. The semicircular staircase-shaped *ossuary* is surmounted by the *Santuario della Madonna del Grappa*, from which the Via Eroica leads to the *Sala storica*, which has pictorial records of the battle for Monte Grappa.

Mussolente (5 km. E.): The majestic *Villa Negri-Piovene* was built in 1769 to plans by Antonio Gaidon on the summit of a hill. A long flight of steps flanked by hedges accentuates the intended link between landscape and architecture, and leads to the three-storeyed Casino with its small portico and arcades connecting it to lower wings on either side.

Rosà (5 km. S.): The *Ca' Dolfin-Boldù* (2nd half of 18C) on the road to Cartigliano is said to have been built by Antonio Gaidon. The central section of this splendid four-storeyed villa is emphasized by a curved pediment. Arcades on both sides of the building link it with wings to form a U.

Maròstica (Bassano), Palazzo del Doglione

Belluno, city gate

Schiavòn (13 km. SW): The *Villa Chiericarti-Lambert* (fraz. Longo), built in about the mid 16C, was rebuilt in neoclassical style by Caregaro Negrin in the 2nd half of the 19C. Jacopo Cabianco laid out the extensive English garden around the villa at the same time. In a small room of the original building are 16C frescos by Lodewik Toeput, the Flemish artist known as Pozzoserrato (landscapes), and Paolo Veronese (page with dog).

Valstagna: (13 km. N.): In the parish church of *S.Antonio* (1783, restored) there are two fine paintings: a Deposition by Palma Giovane above the right-hand door, and a Nativity and a Descent of the Holy Ghost by Francesco Bassano the elder at the 3rd altar on the left. This same Francesco Bassano also painted works in the *parish church* (14–18C) in fraz. Oliero, including the Descent of the Holy Ghost (1523) at the high altar, St.Peter in Cathedra (damaged in 1966) at the left side

altar, and the Ascension at the right side altar. The altarpiece (Pietà with St.Roch and St.Sebastian) at the 2nd altar on the left is believed to be by Francesco Bassano the younger.

32100 Belluno

Belluno   p.320☐G 3

Bellodunum, founded in ancient times, was part of the Roman Empire from 180 BC onwards. In the early Middle Ages it was Lombard and in the 10C it was a Frankish county, being ruled by bishops whose office was granted them by the German Emperors. Johannes I, the warlike soldier and bishop who armed the town and its citizens, managed to extend its area of rule as far as Montebelluna (q.v.), and to conclude an alliance with Doge Orseolo in 996. Belluno joined the Lombard League

Belluno, panorama with Duomo

as a free city in the 12C. After a period of rule by the Carrara, Scaligers and Visconti in the 13&14C, Belluno became part of the republic of Venice in 1404. The town's heyday as a centre of trade and art was from the 15–18C. The fame of *Andrea Brustolon*, the local sculptor and carver, spread beyond the Veneto. Belluno was in Austrian hands from 1797–1866 and in 1917&18, apart from some brief interruptions.

The picturesque *old quarter*, with numerous late-Gothic and Renaissance buildings, stands on the spur of a hill above the confluence of the Ardo and the Piave. Under the Venetians, the plan of the medieval town was altered and the *Piazza del Duomo* was laid out in the 15&16C as a separate administrative centre away from the middle-class commercial bustle of the *Via Mezzaterra*, which was a business street, and the *Piazza del Mercato*.

Duomo S.Maria Assunta (piazza del Duomo): The present structure was built in the 16C to plans by the Venetian architect Tullio Lombardo on the site of an earlier church (15C). After suffering earthquake damage (to the choir in 1873, and to the dome in 1936), it was partly rebuilt. Its *campanile* (225 ft. high), regarded as one of the best Italian baroque campaniles, was built of ashlars in 1732–43 to a design by the Sicilian artist Filippo Juvarra. The Duomo is oriented westwards. Its N. *nave wall* is decorated with stone coats-of-arms and inscriptions, and also with carved torsos (including a 15C Crucifixion). The octagonal *fountain* (by Vera da Pozzo, 1532) outside the Duomo displays the coats-of-arms of the Gradenigo (a Venetian patrician family) and of the town of Belluno. As can be seen from the two Gothic windows to the sides of the main portal (*c.* 1560), parts of the previous building were incorporated in the incomplete E. façade built of brick.

Inside, the basilican structure has tall

arcades of pillars to form a nave and two aisles. There are some superb *altarpieces.* In the choir, which is crowned by a dome, octagonal on the outside and supported by pendentives, there are a monumental painting (Coronation of the Virgin Mary, saints, and donor, 1670) by Pietro della Vecchia, and a 17C Adoration of the Magi to the left of and behind the high altar. The 1st of the baroque marble altars in the right aisle has a mid-16C Pala (St.Bernardino of Siena, St.Jerome, St.John the Baptist) by Andrea Meldolla (known as Schiavone), and at the next altar is a 16C altarpiece by Cesare Vecellio depicting St.Sebastian, St.Gregory the Great, the Virgin Mary in Glory, and the Podestà Giovanni Loredan in the piazza del Duomo with the rector's palace. The 3rd altar has an oil painting (Martyrdom of St.Lawrence, 1571) by Jacopo Bassano, and at the last altar is a Deposition by Palma Giovane. The two marble niche statuettes of the patron Saints of Belluno

Belluno, Duomo S.Maria Assunta

on either side of the 1st altar in the left aisle are attributed to an unknown follower of Tullio Lombardi. The *crypt* (now the sacristy) below the choir has two aisles and a groin vault, and in it is the alabaster sarcophagus of the Avosan family, used as an altar table. This sarcophagus is decorated at the front with reliefs (Virgin Mary Enthroned, Annunciation; *c.* 1330). Above this is an early-15C polyptych (Life of St.Martin), and just to the left is the bishop's coat-of-arms carved in wood by Andrea Brustolon.

Opposite the E. façade of the Duomo is the baptistery of *S.Maria delle Grazie* (1520), rebuilt in 1895.

S.Stefano (piazza S.Stefano): Late-Gothic 15C monastery church, its S. wall is pierced by pointed double windows and has a richly carved *portal* (*c.* 1440) taken from the deconsecrated church of *S.Maria dei Battuti* and incorporated in 1899. The portal has a tympanum relief (Virgin Mary of the Protecting Cloak) and a carved wooden door. To the right of the portal a *late-Roman sarcophagus* rests on six columns, and has reliefs of Gaius Flavius Ostilius with his wife Domitilla, as well as hunting scenes. It bears a Greek inscription which may be roughly translated as 'Greetings to you! Continue to delight in these mountains which you loved so much!' This sarcophagus was discovered in 1480 when the choir was being built. The massive campanile with its spire towers above the choir's polygonal apse. Arcades of round pillars and pointed arches divide the groin-vaulted interior into a nave and two aisles. The tabernacle, set with figures, on the altar in the choir was carved by Francesco della Dia, the Capuchin monk who was a pupil of Brustolon. On the choir walls are 16C paintings by a pupil of Titian (the Adoration of the Magi, on the left) and Nicola de Stefani (Virgin Mary Enthroned with Saints). The chapel to the right of the choir was painted by Jacopo da Montagnana (the subjects include the Conversion of St.Paul), and is dominated by the *retable* (Virgin Mary Enthroned with six saints and angels making music, *c.* 1500) by Andrea di Foro, in a gold and polychrome frame. The *Cappella dell' Addolorata*, enlarged in 1730, has a gilded altarpiece and paintings by Francesco Frigimelica and Antonio Lazzarini. Andrea Brustolon carved the splendid mounted *wooden crucifix* in the left aisle and also the candelabras and candlestick angels in the chapels to the sides of the choir. The *Servite monastery* (c. 1490) to the left of the church has a fine cloister with pointed arches resting on low round pillars.

Palazzo dei Rettori (piazza del Duomo): The *rector's palace* stands on the N. side of the piazza del Duomo amd was once used by the Venetian governors (rectors) as their residence. It is now the prefecture. The broad *Renaissance façade* of the palace begun in 1491 to plans by Giovanni Candi has features reminiscent of the Procuratie Vecchie in Venice (q.v.): the elegant round arches of the loggia, the two upper storeys with their plethora of windows, and the cube of the *clock tower*, added in 1549 as

an extra storey on the right. The coats-of-arms and busts of the governors on the areas of wall between the double windows of the upper floors have obscured the original clear articulation of the surfaces. To the right of the Palazzo dei Rettori, the *Torre Civica* (1190), the fortified tower rebuilt in the 17C, is all that survives of the medieval bishop's palace. Today the *Museo Civico* (see below), founded in 1876, is housed in the *Palazzo dei Giuristi* (1664) in the E. extension of the square and the *Palazzo del Municipio* in Venetian Gothic style was built on the W. side of the square in 1838.

Museo Civico (16 via Duomo): The collection of stones on the *ground floor* comprises archaeological finds and fragments of medieval carvings from buildings and fountains. Small 17&18C works of art, and paintings by 19C Veneto artists, are on display in the *piano nobile*. The museum's finest exhibits are on the *upper floor:* In

Belluno, Palazzo dei Rettori

Belluno, S.Pietro, cloister

Room I: two 15C triptychs by Matteo Cesa, fragments of frescos by Jacopo da Montagnana (15C) and Pomponio Amalteo (16C), four miniature bronzes (*c.* 1500) by Andrea Briosco, and a terracotta model by Andrea Brustolon for his Crucifixion in the church of S.Pietro (see below). *Room II:* two 15C panel paintings of the Virgin Mary by Bartolomeo Montagna, and other paintings from the 16C, some by the Milanese artist Antonio Solario and an unknown pupil of Perugino. *Room III:* paintings by 17C Italian artists such as Francesco Frigimelica, Palma Giovane, Tiberio Tinelli, Luca Giordano, Agostino Ridolfi, and Fra' Galgario (Vittore Ghislandi). *Room IIIa:* 15/16C forgeries of classical works, and bronze plaques (15–17C). *Room IV* has works by 18C artists from Belluno, such as Andrea Brustolon, Sebastiano and Marco Ricci, and Gaspare Diziani, and the Venetian artist Alessandro Longhi.

Also worth seeing: The via Rialto and the via Mezzaterra, which form the main axis of the town's old quarter, are lined by numerous *Renaissance palazzi*, which used to belong to merchants and whose double and treble windows make a Vene-

Burano

tian impression. These palazzi stand between the 12C *Porta Dioana*, faced in 1553/4, to the N., and the early-baroque *Porta Ruga* (1622) to the S. At the Torre Civico (see above), the street widens into the *Piazza delle Erbe* (market place), which is given a picturesque air by arcades and a beautiful fountain (1410) in front of the coat-of-arms bedecked façade of the *Monte di Pietà*, which was founded in 1501 and was one of the first Italian emergency money-lending institutions. The church of *S.Pietro* (1326), rebuilt in 1750, has two masterpieces by Andrea Brustolon: these are the two carved retables (Death of St.Francis Xavier, 1727; Crucifixion, 1729) at the side altars. This church also has four paintings by Andrea Schiavone (including an Annunciation) and one by Sebastiano Ricci in the choir (Virgin Mary with the Apostles Peter and John). The library in the nearby *Seminario Gregoriano* has a copy of Dante's 'Divine Comedy', made by Francesco di Nardo da Barberino in 1337–45.

Environs: Borsoi: (24 km. E.): This village has remained almost untouched. With its many rustic *farmhouses* along the alleyways built of stones from the river, it is typical of the mountainous Alpago region.
Longarone (18 km. NE): Giovanni Michelucci, the renowned architect from Pistoia, built the imaginatively designed *memorial church* in 1966–77 on the site of the village church which, like all the rest of the old village, was washed away by water overflowing the Vajont reservoir during a landslide on 9 October 1963. The central round oratory of the present church is surrounded by concentric passages and a spiral ramp. These rise up to the roof.
Mel (16 km. SW): Palazzi with elegant late-Renaissance and baroque façades are grouped around the *Piazza Umberto I*. The 18C *parish church* is to the N. of the piazza, with 16C altarpieces by Schiavone (St.Andrew, St.Roch and St.Sebastian), Cesare Vecellio (John the Baptist), and Giovanni da Mel (Virgin Mary Enthroned with saints). The nearby *Chiesa dell' Addolorata* (18C) has some more paintings by Schiavone and a font from 1481.

S.Mamante (6 km. SE): The former small pilgrimage church of *S.Mamante*, rebuilt in the 16C, stands on a spur of Monte Nevegal. Inside are 16C frescos by Pomponio Amalteo, and paintings by Francesco Frigimelica.

Vedana (11 km. NW): The *Certosa di Vedana*, in a secluded position at the end of the Canale di Agordo valley, was built in 1456 on the site of the 12C hospice of S.Marco. The large cloister was added in 1521, and the charterhouse was secularized in 1768. Only male visitors are permitted to enter the church, which has statues on the façade of St.Mark and St.Bruno by Besarel. The interior is richly decorated: the tabernacle at the high altar is attributed to Andrea Brustolon, the large Crucifixion altarpiece is by Francesco Frigimelica, and there are two paintings by Sebastiano Ricci. In the refectory is an oil painting of the Last Supper by Cesare da Conegliano.

Burano

p.322☐H 6

Burano consists of four small islands in

the lagoon some 6 miles to the N. of Venice. Most of the inhabitants are fishermen or skilled lace-makers.

The line 5 vaporetto leaves the Fondamenta Nuove in Venice, and passes the island of S.Michele (q.v.) for Murano, where it first stops at the Fondamenta Vetrai. The line 12 vaporetto leaves from the Faro on the Canale San Giovanni, Murano, and follows the route marked by piles which are driven into the mud and which have for centuries marked the navigable channels in the lagoon. The boat passes islands and islets, most of which are completely uninhabited or have ruined buildings and wild gardens which bear witness to settlement in the past. Such islands include S.Giacomo in Palude, Madonna del Monte, and *Mazzorbo* which has been settled since earliest times and was called Maiurbium in classical times; the 13C church of Santa Caterina stands here. The boat rounds the island and finally reaches Burano, which is linked to Mazzorbo.

Here there are a garden and brightly and picturesquely painted houses on the Campo and on both sides of the canals which are joined by arching bridges. The lace-makers sit working in front of the

Burano, valance for Cardinal de Retz

doors of their houses, while others have their stalls everywhere, selling filet embroidery, crochet and bobbin work, blankets and garments. Excellent, charming fish restaurants, particularly those along the Via Galuppi by the canal, tempt the visitor to stay. The famous sewn lace and bone lace gave the island a certain amount of wealth from the 15C until the late 18C. When lace-makers from Burano were sent to Belgium and France, Burano lost its monopoly of lace-making. The skill was almost forgotten, and the families were reduced to poverty. But in *c.* 1870 a lace-making school was founded and the young women were once again taught this traditional handicraft. The bishopric of Torcello was temporarily moved to Burano in the 18C. Tourism, which is today substantial, made its hesitant start in the late 19C. Painters and writers have always been attracted by the enticing appeal of Burano.

S.Martino: The parish church, whose chapel of St.Barbara houses a Crucifixion by Giambattista Tiepolo, stands in the Piazza Bald. Galuppi at the E. end of the island. The campanile leans noticeably to one side.

Vecchia Scuola Merletti: The old school of lace-making, which operated from about 1870 until 1972, is in the Palazzo del Podestà on the N. side of the Piazza. Since 1970 the old school building has housed a museum of lace with exhibits spanning five centuries, including 16C altar cloths, fans owned by Louis XIV of France, and an embroidered handkerchief for Napoleon Buonaparte.

Environs: The vaporetto departs from Burano and heads northwards, past the lagoon's islands, along the Canale S.Antonio to Torcello. But the small, romantic island of *S.Francesco del Deserto* to the SE of Murano can also be reached in a few minutes by boat. Legend relates that S.Francis founded a small colony on this island to the NW of the large island of San Erasmo. Franciscan monks still live in a small monastery here. They maintain a church and a beautiful garden.

30015 Chioggia

Venezia   p.322☐H 7

This town at the S. end of the Venetian lagoon was founded by the Romans as a harbour on the man-made *Fossa Clodia*. Like Venice, this island town offered the

Chioggia, Oratory of S.Martino

Veneti protection from barbarian invasions in the early Middle Ages and it has had the status of a town since the 9C. Its flourishing trade was destroyed when it was occupied and plundered by the Genoese in 1379.

Today this 'Venice in miniature', linked to the mainland by two bridges, is more picturesque than its great model. The harbour, the shell-fish beds and fish farms, and also the blossoming gardens on the nearby mainland, mean that the economy of Chioggia has remained more lively and natural than has that of Venice, which is dependent on tourism. The decorative *bragozzi* (fishermen's barges), with their painted sails, are a feature of the canals, which are spanned by bridges and lined by Venetian palazzi. Fishermen mending their nets, and old women at work making lace and embroidery, are still to be seen in the narrow calli (alleyways) which intersect the three waterways and the *Corso del Popolo,* which is the main street.

Duomo (Campo del Duomo): This 12C cathedral, rebuilt in 1633–74 to plans by Baldassare Longhena, has a 13C bas relief of the Virgin Mary between saints on the tympanum of its portal. In the basilican interior there are an elegant *marble pulpit* (1677) by Pietro Cavaliere, a marble font (1708), and several sculptures and paintings. The 'Agony of two Martyrs', which is an early work by Giovanni Battista Tiepolo, and other paintings of martyrs by the 16–18C Venetian school, are in the chapel to the left of the choir. The choir itself has a beautifully inlaid *marble altar* with angels (1650). The medieval Campo del Duomo, overlooked by the 14C *campanile* (210 ft. high, fine view), is immediately to the N. of the Duomo and on the N. side of the square is the *Oratorio S.Martino* (1392), with a polyptych (1349) attributed to the school of Paolo Veronese inside. The impressive *Piazza Vescovile,* with a garden surrounded by an 18C balustrade with baroque sculptures,

Chioggia, Duomo

extends along the S. flank of the Duomo.

S.Domenico: The 13C church, rebuilt several times, has a 14C campanile and stands on an islet at the NE tip of Chioggia, reached by the Calle S.Croce. The paintings inside the church include a *Crucifixion* (left) attributed to Jacopo Tintoretto, and a *St.Paul* (1520, right) by Vittore Carpaccio.

Also worth seeing: The *church of S.Andrea*, rebuilt in baroque style in 1743, has a free-standing Romanesque campanile and stands in the area between the Canale della Vena and the Corso del Popolo. The *Gothic granary* (1322, restored), the old fish market, and the church of *S.Giacomo* with an 18C fresco (Beheading of St.James) by Antonio Marinetti in its baroque interior, are also all in this area. The Corso del Popolo was referred to by the novelist Curzio Malaparte as 'Europe's largest café', owing to the many bars here.

Environs: Brugine (29 km. NW): The rooms of the 16C *Villa Roberti*, which was restored in 1946, are decorated through-

out with 16C wall paintings, some of them by Giovanni Battista Zelotti from Verona, one of Paolo Veronese's fellow workers. The house is open on Wednesdays and Fridays.

Piove di Sacco (25 km. NW): The parish church of *S.Martino* has a number of paintings from the Venetian school: the Virgin Mary of Mount Carmel at the 2nd altar on the right and the St.Francis of Paola in the sacristy are both by Giovanni Battista Tiepolo. The sacristy also has a 14C polyptych by Paolo Veneziano (Virgin Mary with saints, Annunciation and Pietà) on a gold ground.

Near the town is the Romanesque *Santuario della Madonna delle Grazie*. It is a matter of dispute as to whether the fine Virgin Mary altarpiece in the single-aisled interior is by Giovanni Bellini.

Pontecasale (33 km. W.): The *Villa Carraretto* (formerly Garzoni), built by Jacopo Tatti (known as Sansovino) after 1537, is regarded as his best work outside Venice. A gently sloping flight of steps ascends to the central loggia on the ground floor. The motif of this loggia is repeated on the upper storey. Two fireplaces by Sansovino survive in the interior (which can be visited only by prior appointment).

Chioggia, Gothic granary and fish market

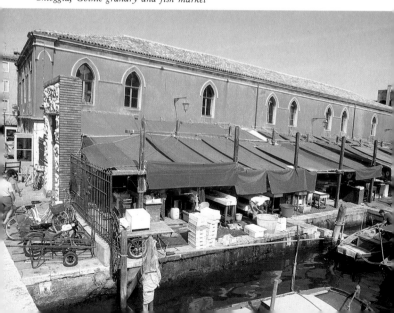

31015 Conegliano

Treviso   p.322☐H 4

This town first mentioned in 1016 was a free community for a while (12&13C). In the 14C it was fought over during the conflicts between the rulers of Treviso, the Ezzelini, the Scaligers and the Carrara. Conegliano voluntarily submitted to the supremacy of Venice in 1388. The town's most famous sons are the two Venetian Renaissance painters Giambattista Cima (known as *Cima da Conegliano*), and *Francesco Beccaruzzi* (who was active in the 1st half of the 16C). Luckily, the damage caused by the two World Wars did not affect the town's picturesque old quarter with its frescoed house façades and loggie along the *Via XX Settembre*, the main street. Conegliano has a viticulture research institute and it is also the starting point for two (signposted) wine routes: the *strada del vino bianco* leading to Voldobiadene (q.v.) and the *strada del vino rosso* going to Oderzo (q.v.).

SS.Maria dei Battuti e Leonardo (via XX Settembre): The complex of buildings (14&15C) belonging to the flagellant brotherhood *Scuola di S.Maria dei Battuti*, founded in 1272, consists of the Scuola and the brotherhood's church (consecrated in 1491) which is popularly known as the 'Duomo'. The campanile was not begun until 1497.

The Scuola has an impressive *street façade*, with a pointed archway in the portico on the ground floor. The façade was frescoed in 1595 by Pozzoserrato. There are sibyls and prophets in the spandrels of the arches and on the areas of wall on the piano nobile there are scenes from the Old Testament. The piano nobile has seven triple windows. The portico, and a portal with an aedicule, lead into the *church* with its nave and two aisles. The alterations carried out here in the 18C were removed in 1956–62. In this process, 15C frescos of St.Stephen and St.Lawrence were uncovered on the arcade pillars. The ornamental paintings on the wall arches are also 15C. The best of the many paintings are: the restored *altarpiece* on the high altar (Sacra Conversazione, 1493) by Cima da Conegliano, and, in the right aisle, a Baptism of St.Catherine by Palma Giovane, and a St.Francis of Assisi receiving the Stigmata (1545) by Francesco Beccaruzzi. In the choir and the adjoining

Conegliano, Museo Civico del Castello

Vittorio Véneto (Conegliano), town gate

rooms there are paintings by followers of Palma Giovane (David, Isaiah), and also from the Venetian school (Moses, Jacob, Abraham and Noah, 16C).

Above the portico is the 14C *Sala dei Battuti*, the room where the flagellants formerly met. Its upper walls are decorated with 16C frescos showing New Testament scenes, some of them by Francesco da Milano (rear wall) and Andrea Previtali (on the wall with the window).

Casa natale di Giambattista Cima (24 via Cima): Thanks to two documents dating from 1516 and 1578, the *birthplace of Giambattista Cima (da Conegliano)* was precisely identified in the late 19C. When the house was restored in the 20C, the later alterations were removed. The archaeological finds made in this process date back to the 12C BC. These excavated objects, together with documents, mementoes and reproductions of famous works by the artist, are on display in the rooms of this three-storeyed house, which is open on Saturday and Sunday afternoons or by prior appointment.

Castelvecchio: The only structures still surviving from the *Piazzale Castelvecchio,*

which was the medieval town centre, are the choir (now the Oratorio di S.Orsola) from the former collegiate church of S.Leonardo (torn down in 1757), the square's fountain (1576), and two fortified towers from the old castle: these are the 14C *Torre Mozza* (a look-out tower, now a restaurant) and the *Torre della Campana* watchtower, which since 1952 has housed the Town Museum (see below).

Villa Gera (viale Ferruccio Benini): This elegant villa (1827/8) built by Giuseppe Japelli on the slope of the castle hill has an Ionic portico with eight columns. The reliefs on the portico by Marco Casagrande, and the frescos inside by Giovanni De Min date from the time when the villa was built.

Museo Civico del Castello (piazzale Castelvecchio): The lower rooms contain some medieval fragments, and also several detached 15/16 frescos, including an apse fresco by Pordenone from the Oratorio S.Antonio Abate which was pulled down. There are also a 15C *wooden crucifix* and paintings by Palma Giovane, Parmigianino and Antonio Bellucci. The upper floors of the tower contain exhibits

S.Pietro di Feletto (Conegliano)

S.Pietro di Feletto (Conegliano), fresco

dealing with the town's history, and collections of coins and weapons. A fine view of the town is obtained from the top storey.

Also worth seeing: The church of *S.Martino* (Via Fenzi), built in 1674–1730, has baroque decorations and a painting of the Last Supper (1615) by Sante Peranda. In the church of *S.Rocco* (Corso Vittorio Emanuele), which was built in 1630 but much altered in the 19&20C, the altarpiece of the high altar (Marriage of St.Catherine) is by Francesco Beccaruzzi. The large ceiling fresco of St.Roch is by Giovanni De Min (1827). Three of the best palazzi along the Via XX Settembre are the *Casa Colussi* (No. 108) with portico frescos by Girolamo da Treviso the elder or the younger, the *Casa Longega* (formerly Montalban, No. 128) with stone ornament on the façade (early-15C), and the former *Monte di Pietà* (No. 133) with a fine lunette in its portal (Pietà, 1524) by Pordenone and its façade (1st half of 16C) which is painted all over.

Environs: Refrontolo (3 km. NW): The *Molinetto della Croda*, a picturesque water mill (18&19C), is set in a quiet river valley between the vine-covered hills of Refrontolo.

S.Fior (5 km. NE): The dismantled triptych (John the Baptist and saints), a late work by Cima da Conegliano, is a surprising feature at the high altar of the parish church in the fraz. *S.Fior di Sopra.* The wooden crucifix to the right of the choir is attributed to Andrea Brustolon. The *Castello di Roganzuolo* was destroyed by the Venetians in 1338. It originally included the campanile and choir of the church of *SS.Pietro e Paolo*. That choir has a fresco cycle (1536) by Pomponio Amalteo. A much-restored triptych (1549) by Titian is to be found behind the high altar.

S.Pietro di Feletto (11 km. NW): The Romanesque parish church of *S.Pietro Vecchio* (10–12C) has a detached campanile, and 13C arcaded porticos attached in the W. and S. It is distinguished by rich frescos (13–15C) on the façade and in the basilican interior. The best of the recently uncovered wall paintings, which are Byzantine in style, is an Annunciation (*c.* 1300).

Vittorio Véneto (13 km. N.): The two districts of *Ceneda* and *Serravalle*, both founded in Roman times, were united in

Vittorio Véneto, Piazza Marc' Antonio Flaminio (left), Cortina d'Ampezzo, parish church (right)

1866 and given the town's present name, which is in honour of the Italian king Vittorio Emanuele II. Points of interest in Ceneda include: the 18C *Cattedrale* with its old 13C campanile and the 15C altarpiece by Jacopo da Valenza. Nearby, the *Loggia Cenedese* (1537/8, today a commemorative museum) with its portico decorated with frescos by Pomponio Amalteo. The church of *S.Maria del Meschio*, with the superb Annunciation (1514) on the high altar by Andrea Previtali. There is a good view from the *Castello di S.Martino*, a castle with battlements and towers standing above the town. It was probably built by the Lombards in *c.* 630. Today it is a bishop's palace. The *Via Martiri della Libertà* in Serravalle is lined with elegant Gothic and Renaissance arcaded houses. It leads into the *Piazza Marc' Antonio Flaminio*. The *Loggia Serravallese* (1462), decorated with coats-of-arms and the lion of St.Mark,

stands in the Piazza, and so too does the 18C *Duomo* with its Romanesque campanile. A painting (1547) by Titian of the Virgin Mary with St.Andrew and St.Peter is to be seen behind the high altar in the Duomo. Since 1938, the Loggia Serravallese has housed the *Museo del Cenedese*, the town museum, with its Roman and medieval archaeological finds, sculptures, detached frescos, and paintings by the Venetian school (mostly 15&16C). The 14C church of *S.Andrea* (fraz. Bigonzo) has an elegant little portico at the side. Four Renaissance aedicules set in the corners lend a special air to the interior, which is decorated with 15&16C frescos.

32043 Cortina d'Ampezzo

Belluno   p.320□G 1

This fashionable tourist resort in the

sunny valley of the river Bóite is surrounded by gently rising meadows and,
behind these, by the ring of Dolomite
peaks climbing steeply to over 9,800 ft.
in the Tofane, Cristallo and Sorapis mas-
sif. The 7th Winter Olympics were held
in Cortina d'Ampezzo in 1956, and the
town has since then developed into a
modern winter sports centre.
There is an active cultural life: art exhibitions are held periodically, and the
Cortina-Ulisse, an international literature
prize, is awarded here.

Corso d'Italia: The main street, which
is mainly closed to traffic, widens into the
two central squares *Piazza Roma* and
Piazza Venezia. Between them is the 18C
parish church with its campanile (250 ft.
high) dating from 1853. The vault of the
nave was frescoed (1773) by Franz Anton
Zeiller. The restored *altarpiece* (Virgin
Mary with St.Philip and St.James, 1679)
on the high altar is by Antonio Zanchi,
while the splendidly carved *tabernacle* at
the 1st side altar on the left is the work
of Andrea Brustolon. The *Casa de Ra
Regoles* (No. 67) houses the *local museum*
with collections dealing with geology,
mineralogy and regional customs. The
Rimoldi collection is also here, with
modern works of art including those by
Carrà, de Chirico, Guttuso and Morandi.
The monument (1958) to *Déodat Gratet
de Dolomieu* commemorates this famous
French geologist and mineralogist
(1750–1801), who investigated the local
stone, which was called dolomite after
him. The Dolomite mountains also take
their name from Dolomieu.

Environs: S.Fosca (30 km. S.): The
Gothic church of *S.Fosca*, rebuilt in the
16C, has an immense fresco of
St.Christopher on its façade, and a campanile surmounted by a baroque onion
dome. A surprising feature of the plain
interior is a carved and gilded baroque
tabernacle thought to be the work of
Andrea Brustolon.
The nearby *former priest's house*, with its
wooden outdoor staircase, has two fine
frescos (Virgin Mary, lion of St.Mark).

*Este, S.Maria delle Consolazioni,
'Madonna'*

35042 Este

Padova   p.322□ E 7

This, the oldest town in the Veneto, developed from an Iron Age settlement to the
S. of the Euganean hills. *Ateste*, the capi-

tal of the Veneti, was a municipium and military colony under the Romans. It lost almost all significance after being raided by the barbarians, and especially after the course of the river Adige was altered in 589. But the remaining village of *Este* regained some importance in the mid 11C, when a castle was built here by a Tuscan or German aristocratic family which was to make history under the assumed name of Este. In the Middle Ages, the town experienced a period of rule by the Scaligers, Carrara, Visconti and Este, before voluntarily submitting to the supremacy of Venice in 1405.

Duomo S.Tecla (piazza S.Tecla): The previous early-medieval structure was destroyed by an earthquake in 1688, and only the 8C lower storey of the tall campanile survived. The present church was built in 1690–1708 to plans by Antonio Gaspari. Its oval interior has Corinthian pilasters and a cornice, and its dome has a painting by Jacopo Amigoni depicting the Martyrdom of St.Thecla (*c.* 1740). The outstanding feature of its rich decoration is the *apse painting* signed by Giovanni Battista Tiepolo, 1759, showing St.Thecla liberating the town of Este from the plague

in 1630. This work is in the choir, above which there is a drum and an oval dome set across the axis of the cathedral. There are 18C marble figures on the right side altar, and also beside the 16C wooden crucifix at the left side altar. The 15C carved Gothic *pulpit* in the middle side chapel on the right is from the previous building.

Castello (via Guido Negri): Albert Azzo II of Este founded a castle in 1050. A large residence, and the surviving *tower*, were built by Ubertino of Carrara in 1339 on the remains of the first castle. The platform of the tower looks down on the massive battlemented *castle walls*, which are reinforced by towers and today surround the town park and the late-16C *Palazzo Mocenigo* which, since 1887, has housed the *Este National Museum*, one of Este's main attractions (see below). Three villas on the gently rising slope of the hill behind the Castello can be seen from the Via Cappuccini. The first of these, on the left, is the *Villa Benvenuti* (formerly Cornaro, 16C) with its fine garden gate (*c.* 1510/20) by Giovanni Maria Falconetto from Verona. To the right is the 17C *Villa Contarini-Gagliardo* with its splendidly

Este, Castello   *Este, Villa Contarini-Gagliardo* ▷

decorated rooms (17&18C). Finally, on the left, the *Villa de Kunkler* (a former Capuchin monastery, 1591), where Lord Byron and his friend Shelley stayed in 1817&18.

Museo Nazionale Atestino (pal. Mocenigo): A tour through this museum begins on the upper floor, which houses one of the best Italian collections dealing with pre-Roman times. The main emphasis is on the exhibits from the Ateste or ancient Veneto culture. They document a separate historical development which was independent of the Etruscans and had its heyday in the 6&5C BC. *Room I:* Prehistoric finds from the region of Este and the Euganean hills. *Rooms II* and *III:* Iron Age finds from ancient burial grounds in the Veneto, including the bronze vases decorated with ornaments and figures and known as Situla Ricovero (8C BC) and Situla Benvenuti (6C BC). *Room IV:* Utensils (5C BC) from ancient Veneto settlements around Este. *Room V:* Votive offerings from shrines, including ex voto objects imitating parts of the body and presented to Reitia, the goddess of health. The Roman department on the ground floor *(Rooms VI–XIII)* comprises collections of Roman inscriptions, architectural

fragments, sculptures, ceramics and glassware. A bronze relief of Medusa's head from the 1C BC, and a mosaic and fragments of frescos from Roman villas which were excavated in the environs of Este. There are medieval exhibits in the entrance hall and staircase, including a detached fresco of the Crucifixion in the manner of Giotto, brought here from Galzignano (q.v.).

Also worth seeing: The *Porta Vecchia*, a battlemented gatehouse rebuilt in 1690, has a floor containing a clock and bells. It stands at the end of the Corso Matteotti, which is lined by 18&19C *arcaded houses*. From the nearby *Ponte Vecchio*, there is a fine view of the simple, brightly coloured backs of the houses reflected in the *Canale d'Este*. The Gothic church of *S.Martino* (Via S.Martino) has a slightly leaning campanile (1293). There are also the churches of *S.Maria delle Grazie* (15–18C; Via Principe Umberto) with a 15C Virgin Mary painted in Byzantine style, and *S.Maria delle Consolazioni* (16C; Via d. Consolazioni) with a Virgin Mary altarpiece (1504) by Cima da Conegliano and a Roman mosaic in the chapel of the Virgin Mary.

Montagnana (Este), cathedral of S.Maria

Environs: Càrceri (6 km. SW): The *abbey of Càrceri* was built in *c.* 1100 by order of the rulers of Este. Next to the remains of the 12C Romanesque cloister is the larger Renaissance cloister with its fine central fountain (1585); the library on the upper storey has a 16C fresco cycle by Giuseppe Porta (known as Salviati). The monastery church was rebuilt in 1643 after a fire (consecrated in 1686), and has a two-storeyed façade. It has an octagonal interior with an oval ground plan.

Eremo di Rua (23 km. NE): Only male visitors are permitted to enter the small *Camaldolensian monastery* standing on Monte Rua (1,365 ft.). It was founded in 1339 and rebuilt in 1537. The small entrance portico has 17C frescos of St.Romuald and St.Benedict. In the 18C interior of the church there are two paintings by Palma Giovane (Crucifixion, St.Romuald).

Montagnana (15 km. W.): The *town wall* is one of the best-preserved examples of medieval military architecture in Italy. It is 2,105 yards long, forms a rectangle, and has a rampart and a fosse, with tall polygonal towers spaced about 250 ft. apart. It was built by the Ezzelini (after 1242) and the rulers of Carrara (after 1260). It is breached by four (originally three) town gates, of which the 14C *Porta Legnago* is the finest, having been built by Francesco da Schicci by order of Francesco V da Carrara. The cathedral of *S.Maria*, rebuilt in 1431–1502, has a richly decorated interior and an outstanding high altarpiece (Transfiguration of Christ, 1555/6) by Paolo Veronese. There is a Pala (Assumption, 1555) by Giovanni Buonconsiglio at the baroque left-hand side altar. To the E. of the Porta Padova is the *Villa Pisáni*, built in *c.* 1560 to plans by Andrea Palladio, with a Doric portico on the ground floor and an Ionic loggia on the piano nobile. The 16C *town hall* in the Via Carrarese was enlarged in the 17&18C. It is based on a design by Michele Sanmicheli of Verona.

Téolo (19 km. N.): This village dates back to the Roman *Titolum*. The archpriest's church of *S.Giustina* (*c.* 1210; rebuilt in the 18C) has a free-standing 15C campanile. Inside there are ceiling frescos

(Assumption, 19C) by Giacomo Manzoni, and a fine 16C high altarpiece (Assumption and Baptism of St.Justina) from the school of Campagnola (Padua). The *Palazzetto dei Vicari* has a clock (1543), a belfry, and a tower with an octagonal upper section, an open-air staircase and a portal.

Valbona (10 km. NW): The coats-of-arms of the Carrara, who were formerly lords of the castle, shine forth resplendently above the entrances to the 13C *Castello*. This castle occupies a strategic site on the road to Vicenza. Its seven towers and battlemented walls survive in good condition.

Valnogaredo (11 km. N.): The hall of the *Villa Piva* (formerly Contarini), built in the 16&18C, is completely covered with 18C frescos by Jacopo Guarana, who is also responsible for the ceiling painting and an altarpiece (Virgin Mary, saints, and the Saved) in the nearby church of *S.Bartolomeo*. This church, rebuilt in 1758, has a rococo façade decorated with statues by Antonio Bonazza.

Vo (13 km. N.): The *Ca' Watlington* (formerly Paruta), built in 1630, with an elegant frescoed loggia in the Palladian manner, the early-17C *Ca' Trevisan* (formerly Lando), and the 16&17C *Villa Benato*

Montagnana (Este), cathedral, fresco

(formerly Mariani), with an oratory from 1692, are all to be found in the fraz. Zovon. The façade of the 17C *Villa* *Contarini-Venier* dominates the beautiful arcaded square of the fraz. Vo Vecchio by the Canale della Nina.

32032 Feltre

Belluno   p.320□F 3

In the 6C BC, the Raeti recognized the strategically favourable location of a hill at the confluence of the rivers Colmeda and Stizzòn and set up a fortress. The Romans conquered the town in 172 BC, and under them *Feltria* developed into an important stopping post on the Via Claudia Augusta. *Feltre* was ruled by bishops until the 12C. After a period of independence the town was ruled by aristocrats and voluntarily submitted to the supremacy of the Serenissima in 1404. As part of the republic of Venice, it was plundered and almost destroyed by the troops of Emperor Maximilian I in 1509/10 in the war against the League of Cambrai. This picturesque town was rapidly rebuilt in the 16C, from which time its almost uniform architectural style dates.

Cattedrale S.Pietro: Near the *Porta Pusterla* on the old town wall. Built in about the mid 16C, using parts of a former church, including lower storeys (1392) of the campanile (height increased in 1690), the Gothic polygonal choir, and the early-medieval *crypt*. On the wall to the left of

Feltre, Cattedrale S.Pietro (left), Chiesa di Ognissanti, Gothic tomb (right)

the campanile there is a relief on the *tomb-stone of Giovanni Tiepone* (d. 1473). Inside (nave and two aisles) the visitor's attention is attracted by the monumental baroque altar and the late-Romanesque red marble *bishop's throne* (13C) in the choir apse. A fine *tomb monument by Tullio Lombardi* (d. 1528) can be seen on the right choir wall. In the right aisle there is a monument (1734) by Giuseppe Torretti to Lucrezio degli Azzoni. The chapel to the left of the choir has five 17C oil paintings by Giovanni Battista Volpato from Bassano del Grappa. Side altars have paintings (16–19C) by the Venetian school, including some by Pietro Marescalchi who was born here. The showpiece of the church treasure is a small Byzantine boxwood cross, with 52 panels showing scenes from the New Testament (*Archivio Capitolare.*)

Battistero di S.Lorenzo (Porta Pusterla): Originally a Gothic baptistery (14C), it has been altered several times. The 17C façade portico and the elegant side portal on the right are both Renaissance. Inside, the altarpiece of the Martyrdom of St.Stephen is by Leandro Bassano. The splendid Gothic *font* (1399), which

has a 17C wooden cover with a carving of John the Baptist, is by Francesco Terilli (*c.* 1620/30).

Chiesa di Ognissanti (Borgo Rua): Inside this 14C church there is an exquisite *altarpiece* (Virgin Mary Enthroned between St. Victor and St.Nicholas of Bari) by Jacopo Tintoretto. A fine *fresco* in the sacristy, depicting Christ appearing to St.Antony and St.Lucy, is regarded as the best work by Lorenzo Luzzo (also known as il Morto da Feltre).

Palazzo del Comune (via Mezzaterra): The massive *loggia* with rusticated pilasters was built in 1557/8 to designs by Palladio. In 1729 the first comedies by Carlo Goldoni (clerk in the local court at the time) were performed on the upper storey. In 1802 Giovanni Antonio Selva, a Venetian, made it into a small theatre which is still there today. The adjoining *Palazzo del Municipio,* built at right angles to the Palazzo del Comune, was formerly the seat of the Venetian administration. Inside there is a large *Renaissance hall* with heavy wooden beams, 16C frescos, and the coats-of-arms of Venetian 'rettori' (governors).

Feltre, Piazza Maggiore

Lentiai (Feltre), S.Maria Assunta

Piazza Maggiore: Feltre's main square, it resembles a stage with three ascending levels linked by open-air staircases. *S.Rocco* (1599), whose campanile has the original top, stands at the N. end of the Piazza. To the right of the latter, the clock tower and the tall fortified tower of the former *Castello Albuino* (destroyed in 1510) dominate the other buildings. Originally, the only things in the piazza were the fountain (1520) by Tommaso da Lombardo, a flagpole and a column with the lion of St. Mark. The layout was then altered by Giuseppe Segusini in 1886, when balustrades were added along with two statues on pedestals by Costantino Corti which depict Vittorino da Feltre and Panfilo Castaldi. Fine Renaissance arcaded houses (16C) stand at the S. end of the Piazza. In the W. extension of the Piazza, the *Piazzetta della Legna*, stands the *Monte di Pietà* which is decorated with sgraffito, and the neo-Gothic *Palazzo Guarnieri* (19C).

Museums: *Museo Civico* (23 via Lorenzo Luzzo): The Municipal Museum is housed in the 16C *Palazzo Villabruna*, which has retained the Venetian-Gothic courtyard façade of the previous medieval building. Archaeological finds from the ancient Venetian and Roman periods are on display on the *ground floor*. They include the altar of Anna Perluna (1C BC), a theatrical mask from the Imperial period, a marble relief of the head and shoulders of a young man from the 2C AD, and fragments of medieval buildings and frescos. The *piano nobile* has coats-of-arms of the Feltre families and Venetian governors, and also furniture and small art works from the 16–18C. Room IV leads into the four rooms of the *Museo Storico Maria Gaggia* with exhibits (16–20C) related to the town's history. The *upper storey* of the Municipal Museum houses the *art gallery*, with Renaissance paintings by Giovanni Bellini (portrait of a prelate, *c.* 1465), Lorenzo Luzzo (Virgin Mary and Saints; early 16C), Cima da Conegliano (Virgin Mary, Christ and Saints; early 16C), and Pietro Marescalchi (16C portraits). Works by 17/18C Venetian artists include paintings by Palma Giovane (Raising of Lazarus, 1599), Francesco Maffei (Virgin Mary and Saints, mid 17C), and Marco Ricci (four 18C landscapes). The *Galleria d'Arte Moderna* (8 via del Paradiso) is housed in the former *Palazzo Cumano* (16C), which the craftsman Carlo Rizzarda (1883–1931) bequeathed to the town along with a valuable collection of wrought iron and a collection of 19/20C sculptures and paintings.

Also worth seeing: In the *Via Mezzaterra* there are fine 16C Renaissance palazzi with frescoed façades, arcades and overhanging roofs (houses Nos. 9, 19, 26, 35 and 41), and the marble Renaissance portal of the 15C *S.Giacomo Maggiore* church. Other good building façades are to be seen in the *Via Lorenzo Luzzo* (houses Nos. 3, 13, 23 and 40).

Environs: Arten (7 km. W.): The *Villa Zampiero* (formerly Tonello) was built in the 2nd half of the 16C. 16C fresco cycle by Pietro Marescalchi on the loggia.

Lentiai (Feltre), S.Maria Assunta, interior view

Lentiai (11 km. E.): The Renaissance church of *S.Maria Assunta* (15/16C) was enlarged in 1558. Round-arched arcades, with frescos (Apostles) by Cesare Vecellio on their spandrels, divide the interior into nave and two aisles. The paintings (Death of the Virgin Mary, Assumption, Martyrs, and Old Testament scenes; 1577–9) on the splendid *coffered ceiling* of the nave are also by Vecellio. On the back wall of the choir there is a polyptych from the workshop of Titian. Baptism of Christ by Palma Giovane in the left side aisle; Deposition by Cesare Vecellio above the left side altar.

Pedavena (2.5 km. NW): The best of the villas in this town at the foot of Monte Avena is the 17C *Villa Luciani* (formerly Berton), built by the Pasoli family and with a fine park in the Italian style. 16C Nativity by Pietro Marescalchi behind the high altar of the 18C *parish church;* on the left wall, a Deposition by Antonio Balestra. Old *brewery* (19C) with beer garden.

SS.Vittore e Corona (6 km. E .): The oldest *pilgrimage church* in the province of Belluno stands on the round top of a hill on Monte Miesna. Founded in 1096, it was built in the Byzantine-Romanesque manner and finished in the 12C. The interior, decorated with impressive 13–15C frescos, is divided by four pillars to form nave and two aisles. The *sarcophagus* containing the relics of the two martyrs St.Victor and St.Corona stands in the square choir. Donated by Emperor Charles IV in 1335, it is surrounded by columns decorated with inlay. Also of interest are the monolithic Romanesque bishop's throne, a charming Gothic tabernacle and, in the 19C sacristy behind the choir, the richly sculpted *tomb* (1096) supported on two Byzantine columns of *John of Vidor*, who founded the church. The adjoining *cloister* (1495) originally had two storeys throughout. The red dome of the Romanesque campanile was added in the 19C and is similar to those found in Sicily.

Zumelle (15 km. E.): Legend relates that the Romans built a fortress to protect the *Via Claudia Augusta*. It is, however, certain that the oldest parts of the *Castello Zumelle*, including the lower storeys of the tall castle keep, date back to the 9C.

37016 Garda

Verona   p.322□A 5

In the Iron Age, the ancient Veneti found the protected bay of Lake Garda at the foot of Monte Baldo such a favourable location that they settled it. This is documented by the burial grounds discovered at the edge of today's town, and by the *drawings* scratched into the rocks. These drawings can be admired on a walk along the panoramic route to Torri del Benaco (q.v.). Garda flourished as a fishing port under the Romans and Lombards. Charlemagne elevated it to the seat of a count in 768, and the town had a law court in 1084. After a period of aristocratic rule under the Scaligeri (13C), Garda came under the rule of Venice.

S.Maria Maggiore: The parish church, it was rebuilt in the 18C incorporating part of the former monastery (15C), namely the *campanile* and the remains of the cloister (in the courtyard on the right). Roman and Lombard decorative slabs can be seen outside. The interior, with its nave and two aisles, has a painting of St.Blasius by Palma Giovane above the entrance and a fine oil painting by Francesco Paglia on the 1st altar on the right. The sacristy has

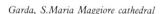

Garda, S.Maria Maggiore cathedral

altar columns from the previous (10C) church and a late-Gothic Virgin Mary fresco from *c.* 1450. The high altar of the neighbouring church of *S.Stefano* has a splendid painting of St.Stephen (1576) by Paolo Farinati from Verona.

Also worth seeing: Despite the brisk tourist business, some picturesque houses have survived along *Lungolago Regina Adelaide,* the tree-lined lakeside promenade, including the 15C Venetian *Palazzo del Capitano,* the seat of the town's former rulers, in the *Piazzetta Catullo.* The English garden of the *Villa Albertini* was laid out in the 19C. There is a wonderful view from the small Camaldolensian monastery (built in 1663–73 on the remains of the medieval Rocca) which stands above the town, at a height of 1015 ft. A fine painting of St.Romuald by Palma Giovane can be seen in a side chapel of *S.Giorgio,* the monastery church.

Environs: Affi (9 km. SE): The 17C *Villa Da Persico* (formerly Poggi) near the parish church was enlarged in the early 19C by Giuseppe Barbieri from Verona. In the garden there are fountains, statues and an 18C oratory.

Bardolino (3 km. S.): This holiday town, known for its light wine, dates back to an Iron Age and Roman settlement. A document dating from 807 records that this fishing village was owned by the S.Zeno monastery in Verona. The little church of *S.Zeno* was built in the 9C on a cruciform ground plan. Elegant Corinthian columns supporting barrel vaults make it among the best Carolingian buildings in Italy. Not far away is the Romanesque church of *S.Severo,* mentioned in 893 and enlarged in the 12C, which has a campanile with a spire. The fresco cycle (Apocalypse, battle scenes, Vita Christi) in the Ottonian *crypt* dates from the 12/13C.

Caprino (8.5 km. NE): The 18C *Villa Carlotti* (now the town hall) stands in the centre of this peasant village. It has a lordly façade and side portico, and is decorated inside with stuccoes and frescos. The hamlet of Platano, with several 15/16C *Renaissance villas,* and the hamlet of Ceredello, with the little Romanesque church of *S.Cristina* dating back to the 13C, lie nearby.

Costermano (4 km. E.): The plain *Villa Rizzardi,* erected in the late 16C and rebuilt in the early 19C, stands in the centre of this peasant village which

Garda, Corso Vittorio Emanuele

Bardolino (Garda), S.Severo

itself lies amidst vineyards and olive groves.

Rivoli Veronese (12 km. E.): Napoleon's victory over the Austrian troops led by Field Marshal Alvinczy in the battle for the valley of Verona on 14 January 1797 is documented by the ruins of the Austrian *fortress*, which stands on a rocky spur high above the town, and also by the small *Museo Napoleonico*.

Spiazzi (17 km. NE): The 16/17C pilgrimage church of *Santuario S.Maria della Corona* stands at a dizzy height on an overhanging rocky precipice of Monte Baldo. It was rebuilt in Romanesque-Gothic style in the 19/20C. Legend has it that the small Madonna della Corona (high altar), which has a multicoloured frame, was stolen in Rhodes by the Turks in 1522 and miraculously reappeared here.

37045 Legnago

Verona   p.322☐D 7

Archaeological finds prove that this part of the E. bank of the Adige was inhabited by the Veneti and Romans. Due to its strategic importance, *Lendinara* was enlarged into a fortified bridgehead under the Lombards and Carolingians, and was repeatedly disputed up to the 20C. Hence only parts of buildings of historical importance have survived in the town.

Piazza della Libertà: The ruined tower of *Torrione* remains of the formerly immense castle which, along with the military bases of Mantua, Peschiera del Garda (q.v.) and Verona (q.v.), formed the square of Austrian fortifications defending the Adige plain. The town hall (1767) by Bernardo Maccaruzzi was destroyed in bombing raids in World War 2. The classical interior of the soberly designed brick

cathedral (rebuilt 1773−1814) has a fine sculptured Pietà (late 14C) in a polychrome frame over the Addolorata altar.

Museo Fondazione Fioroni (39 via Matteoti): On the ground floor there are weapons and household utensils (early and mid medieval); 15/16C Renaissance furniture and ceramics are also on display. The *piano nobile* is devoted to exhibits related to the town's history during the 19/20C. An interesting archaeological collection comprises prehistoric and valuable Roman finds, as well as medieval architectural sculptures (open only on Sunday afternoons).

Also worth seeing: The elegant 15C *Palazzo Bianchi*, in Venetian style, in the via Minghetti. The free-standing *baroque campanile* of the former church of S.Rocco (Piazza S.Rocco). Several 16C *lions of St.Mark*, which have been re-erected in prominent positions in the town (Piazza della Libertà, Piazzale XX Settembre, Palestra).

Environs: Cerea (8 km. W.): At the N. end of the town stand the *Villa Bertelè* (built in 1705 in a large park; sumptuous façade) and the Romanesque *church of S.Zeno* (reputedly founded by Mathilde of Canossa in the 12C; ponderous campanile, nave and two aisles, apses articulated by pilaster strips and 14C frescos).

Cologna Veneta (16 km. N.): Founded by the Romans in 170 BC and called *Colonia*. Theoderic re-named it *Colonia Gotica*, and after 1496 the Venetians changed it to *Cologna Veneta*. S.Maria, the cathedral, was rebuilt in classical style in the 19C. Inside: outstanding ivory sculpture (Crucifix with St.Mary Magdalene) by Andrea Brustolon and fine paintings by Bartolomeo Montagna (Nativity, 1522) and Domenico Ricci (Adoration of the Christ-child). The *Palazzo di Città*, which stands by the massive *Torre Civica*, a fortified tower (1555), was rebuilt in 1870 after a fire and today houses a small *museum* with prehistoric and early historical finds, a splendid carved 15C retable, and a coin collection.

Pressana (15 km. NE): The *Villa de' Grandi* (formerly Grimani) stands in the heart of the village. Built in the 16/17C, it has a large central loggia and towered side façades. The early-16C *Villa Baldisserotto* is worth a short visit for its fine façade frescos, Renaissance fountain, and the 12C Romanesque oratory of *S.Giovanni.*

Villa Bartolomea (6 km. SE): The originally Gothic *parish church* was converted in classical style in 1855. Inside, above the entrance portal, there is a painting (Descent of the Holy Ghost; 16C) attributed to Orazio Farinati. The painting in the apse (Virgin Mary in Glory, Saints) is thought to be by Palma Giovane.

37018 Malcésine
Verona   p.322□B 4

Surrounded by gardens and olive groves, Malcésine lies at the foot of Monte Baldo on the E. shore of Lake Garda. A cable railway leads up to *La Colma* (5850 ft.), the secondary N. peak of the mountain. The town fortifications, probably originally Lombard and Frankish, were enlarged by Berengar in the 10C. In the 13C, the Scaligers took part in building the town's *castle.* When Goethe made a

Malcésine, Scaliger castle

Malcésine, harbour

drawing of the castle in 1786, he was almost captured as a spy, the border between the Veneto and Austria running just N. of Malcésine at that time.

Castello Scaligero: This battlemented castle was built in the 13/14C on a rocky spur projecting into the lake and was enlarged in the 17C. The small *Museo Pariani,* with collections of prehistory, early history and local history, occupies the building below the tall *castle keep.*

Palazzo dei Capitani del Lago: The character of the windows, including double windows, show this 15C Renaissance palazzo (today the town hall) to be typically Venetian, although the crenellation is Moorish in form. A charming *courtyard* faces the sea. The *council chamber* on the upper storey has frescos showing the former governors' coats-of-arms.

Also worth seeing: The parish church of *S.Stefano* (1729–49) has an early work (Deposition) by Girolamo dai Libri above the 1st right side altar. The town's *old quarter* below the Scaligers' castle is delightful and has many picturesque corners.

Environs: Brenzone (9 km. SW): The Romanesque church of *S.Zeno* (12C), whose campanile is breached by double windows, occupies a somewhat secluded spot by the cemetery in the Castelletto district. Remains of 15C frescos (Vita Christi) can be seen in the double-aisled church. *Ruins* of the castle which formerly belonged to the counts of Brenzone stand on higher ground.

31010 Maser
Treviso   p.323☐F 4

Villa Barbaro (now Volpi di Misurata): The *Villa Barbaro* , built on the slope of a hill in *c.* 1560 for Daniele Barbaro, Palladio's friend and patron, is one of the happiest examples in the Veneto of the harmonious relationship between architecture and surrounding countryside. The organization of the symmetrical villa also demonstrates the connection between humanist philosophy and the return to a vision of classical agriculture (Pliny, Vitruvius). The grand central house projects forwards in a gabled Ionic colonnaded façade, with plainer domestic build-

Maser, Villa Barbaro, Heracles

Maser, Villa Barbaro, Bacchus room

ings on both sides. The interior decoration, with the sumptuous allegorical and trompe l'oeil *frescos* (1566–8) by Paolo Veronese and *stuccoes* by Alessandro Vittoria from the same period, harmonizes wonderfully with Palladio's theatrical architectural style. The sculptured decorations of the pediment of the central façade and of the semicircular *nymphaeum* in the garden are thought to be by Vittoria, as are the figures inside the neighbouring *round temple* (1580) (dedicated to Marc Antonio Barbaro) which was begun by Palladio in imitation of the Pantheon in Rome. However, the temple, which has a dome, was not completed until after Palladio's death.

Coach museum: Like the villa, the coach museum on the nearby hill is open to the public on Tuesday, Saturday and Sunday afternoons.

30171-74 Mestre

Venezia   p.322□ G 6

The modern industrial town of Mestre is actually a district of Venice (q.v.), although its population is higher than Venice's.

Founded by the Romans before the lagoon city, it was devastated several times by the Huns, Franks and Hungarians in the 5–10C. After a period of aristocratic rule under Ezzelino da Romano and the Scaligers in the 13/14C, Mestre voluntarily submitted to the domination of Venice in 1337.

Piazza Ferretto: The old town centre has low *houses with arcades*. The massive *clock tower*, said to be the only surviving tower of a medieval castle with eleven towers, dates from 1108; the Romanesque campanile belongs to the parish church of *S.Lorenzo* which was rebuilt in the 18C to the plans of Bernardo Maccaruzzi, a Venetian. The classical interior has 18C statues.

To the right of the church stands a 15C building which formerly belonged to the *Scuoletta dei Battuti,* a flagellant order. The windows of the piano nobile look on to the via Poerio and are particularly fine.

Also worth seeing: The *Palazzo della Provvederia* (restored in 1926; via Palazzo) has a Romanesque portico and Renaissance window design.

Maser, Villa Barbaro, round temple

Malcontenta (Mestre), park statue

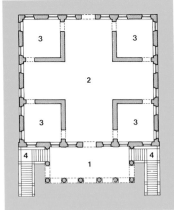

Malcontenta, Villa Foscari 1 Colonnaded portico **2** Drawing room **3** Side rooms **4** Steps at the sides

Environs: Altino (16 km. NE): Collections in the *Museo Archeologico* (Piazza della Chiesa) consist mainly of Roman excavation finds from the ancient town of *Altinum*, built by the Romans where the *Via Claudia-Augusta* branches off from the *Via Annia* (the coastal road). Altinum was devastated by Attila in 452 and by Albuin in 568.

Malcontenta (6.5 km. S.): The temple-like *Villa Foscari* (La Malcontenta) was built by Andrea Palladio for the Venetian patrician Foscari family in 1559/60 on the N. canal at the mouth of the river Brenta near Fusina. It is considered to be one of the most mature of Palladio's designs. Facing the canal, it was built on a raised base, with an Ionic colonnaded portico framed by flights of stairs at the sides. Frescos (allegories, grotesques, Battle of the Giants) in the central drawing room are by Giovanni Battista Zelotti and Giovanni Battista Franco (*c*. 1560).

Martellago (9 km. NW): The 16C *Villa*

◁ *Malcontenta (Mestre), park statue*

Malcontenta (Mestre), Villa Foscari

Grimani-Morosini is also known as the *Ca'della Nave* after Giovanni Battista Zelotti's painting of a ship on the right side of the façade. The splendid park surrounding the house has 18C statues.

Oriago (9 km. SW): Some of the finest examples of Venetian villa architecture can be found here, in one of the mainland possessions of the republic of Venice. 16C *Villa Gradenigo,* has frescos within by Benedetto Caliari from Verona. 18C *Villa Mocenigo* is now a school. 16C *Villa Moro.* 17C *Villa Priuli,* a little way outside the town, has a portico with 3 arches on the splendid rear façade. The Romanesque campanile survives from the former parish church of *S.Pietro.*

Spinea (6 km. W.): The 18C *Villa Bellati* is a country house of modest size, interesting for its rich rococo stucco decorations.

35043 Monsélice

Padova   p.322□F 7

This little town on the SE edge of the Euganean hills was called *mons silicis,* by the Romans after the steep trachyte cone at whose foot it stands. Under Emperor Otto I, *Monsélice* was an important centre of administration and justice. After a period of foreign rule under the Scaligers, Carrara and Visconti, it shared the fate of Venice; the town was severely damaged in the battle against the imperial troops of the League of Cambrai.

Duomo Vecchio (via al Santuario): The former cathedral of *S.Giustina,* it dates from 1256. The *façade* has brick pilaster strips, an early-Gothic rose window and late-Romanesque double windows. The *porch* in front is a 15C addition. The 13C battlemented *campanile* in the S. has Romanesque round-arched friezes, as does the choir. The single-aisled interior, with its open roof truss and three rectangular choir chapels, has 18C decorations and a 15C *high altar polyptych* of St.Justina by the Venetian school.

Santuario delle Sette Chiese and Villa

Duodo: The baroque gate arch on the W. side of the old cathedral leads to the pilgrims' way to the left of which there are seven *chapels.* Paintings by Palma Giovane can be seen in these small centrally planned buildings (modelled on the seven pilgrims' churches in Rome). The chapels were built to plans by Vincenzo Scamozzi, who also designed the plain *Villa Duodo* (1593–1611). At the end of the pilgrims' way there is a picturesque scene, which includes the Villa, the 18C *building with wings* which adjoins the Villa at right angles and which has a façade designed by Andrea Tarili with triumphal arches and serlian motifs, and the centrally planned church of *S.Giorgio* (11–18C) in the W.

Castello (via al Santuario): This battlemented complex of buildings from the 13C is also known as *Ca' Marcello.* Ezzelino da Romano added the great hall in 1249–56, and the complex was enlarged by the Carrara and Marcello families. The interior was restored in 1935–9 by the Cini family who are the present owners, and today the building houses the sumptuous *private collection,* including the best Italian *furniture collection* dating from medieval and Renaissance times, which can be visited on weekdays by permission of the 'Fondazione Cini' (Isola di S.Giorgio, Venezia).

Also worth seeing: The central *Piazza Mazzini* is adjoined in the NW by the surviving section of the medieval *town wall.* Next to this stands the *Torre Civica* (1244), the municipal tower whose height was increased in 1504. The *Monte di Pietà,* a Renaissance palace with an Ionic colonnaded loggia (16C), stands in the S. of the Piazza. The 16/17C *Villa Nani-Mocenigo* (via al Santuario) has a splendid external terraced staircase. The Villa's name comes from the imaginatively designed *'nani'* (dwarf statues) which crown the surrounding walls. The ruined *Rocca,* with its massive residential tower, stands on the peak of the mountain which overlooks the town. Built by Emperor Frederick II, it has an oval ground plan.

Environs: Arquà Petrarca (6.5 km.

NW): This town nestling picturesquely in the Euganean hills has retained much of its medieval appearance and holds very special the memory of *Francesco Petrarca* (1304–74), the poet, who lived in the town from 1370 onwards. The town's name has incorporated that of Petrarch since 1868. In the Piazza Petrarca, Petrarch's red *marble sarcophagus* (restored in the 19C) can be seen. This was placed on pillars by his son-in-law Francesco da Brossano in 1380. *Petrarch's house* dates from the 14/16C (via Valleselle) and here the poet created his last works. Inside there are fine Renaissance decorations and a *museum* devoted to the poet's life and work. *S.Maria*, the parish church (11/17C; altered in 1926) has frescos from the 11–14C, an apse painting (Assumption) signed by Palma Giovane and paintings by Pietro Damini in the right side altar (Baptism of Christ) and in the sacristy (Madonna of the Rosary). The *Piazza S.Marco* has a column with a lion of St.Mark (1612). The *Oratorio della Trinità* (12/14C), which stands in the Piazza, has an altarpiece of the Holy Trinity with Saints (1626) by Palma Giovane at the high altar.

Battaglia Terme (7 km. NE): A staircase with 142 steps leads up the S.Elena hill to the *Villa Emo Capodilista*, which was begun in 1593 and completed *c.* 1650. Heinrich Heine stayed here as a guest. The S. façade is designed in Palladian style; the lead dome between the villa's battlemented turrets is Oriental in style. Frescos in the cruciform drawing-room on the piano nobile are by Luca Ferrari (1650).

Carrara S.Stefano (10 km. NE): The home town of the *Carrara* family, who ruled Padua 1318–1405. *S.Stefano*, the parish church (10–19C), has been redesigned several times and has a Romanesque campanile (1239) with large double windows and a conical roof. In the left of the single-aisled interior stands a splendid marble sarcophagus built by Andriolo de' Santi for Marsilio da Carrara (d. 1338).

Cataio (8 km. NE): *Cataio Castle,* a lordly structure with terraces at the front, was built in 1570–2 by order of Pio Enea I degli Obizzi, who invented the howitzer. The wing on the hill was added in the 19C. Victories won by the Obizzi were glorified by Giovanni Battista Zelotti in

Monsélice, Duomo Vecchio (left), Arquà Petrarca (Monsélice), Petrarch's monument (right)

Murano, cathedral

his frescos on the drawing-room walls. The elephant fountain in the entrance courtyard dates from the villa's most vibrant period in the 17C. Emperor Franz I of Austria stayed here in 1838.
Galzignano Terme (11 km. N.): The *Villa Saggini,* which has a Venetian appearance, is the best of several 17C villas. The *Corsa dei Mussi* (donkeys' procession), a most entertaining celebration, is held annually in the village on the first Sunday in October and commemorates the Venetians' victory at Lepanto on 7 October 1571.
Valsanzibio (8 km. N.): The spacious *park around the Villa Barbarigo* (17C) is a typical example of Italian garden design and is the finest and most lavish park in the Veneto. Laid out in *c.* 1667 for the Venetian procurator Andrea Barbarigo, it has a baroque exedra, fountains with imaginative waterworks, statues and a labyrinth, all of which display Roman inventiveness.

30121 Murano

p.322□H 6

The group of five small islands, which joined to form Murano, lies about 2 km. N. of Venice. The glass furnaces were moved here from Venice in 1291. Aristocrats of the community which lived in Murano until that time were known as 'Uomini di grande spirito e abilità' according to medieval tradition and it was they who founded the church of S.Maria. In 1291, Murano became the island base of a guild of craftsmen, who were some of the most sought-after artists. These were practically kept prisoner here, not infrequently by force, in order to preserve the secret of the glass-blower's art. An early form of the mirror was invented here by Muzi da Murano in 1317. Indigenous families of artists discovered ever new varieties and modes of expression for the fragile material. (In the Middle Ages glass

Murano, cathedral

Murano, palazzo

was cast in small balls resembling coins and these were used for trading and payment.) Pure crystal glass existed in the early 15C. Glass-makers like Angelo Barovier, who created splendid goblets decorated with drawings and incorporating materials in addition to glass, were admired in the 15C. Venetian chandeliers became world-famous. The Vivarini family, following the example of Bellini from Venice, shrugged off the influence of Byzantine art and created a new early-Renaissance style inspired by realism. Local churches still contain many of these works. Rich Venetians had their gardens and summer villas in Murano and at one time the population increased to 30,000. A cruder form of glass manufacture (milk glass) existed in ancient times, but in Murano glass production was refined into an art form which secured a monopoly for Murano over a period of centuries. Hence, when the secrets of glass manufacture were discovered elsewhere in the 17C,

Murano's affluence and significance correspondingly diminished. The island began to fall into decline in the late 18C; churches, palazzi, villas and houses became empty, many buildings fell into ruin and the formerly flourishing town became a meagre settlement with few inhabitants. Towards the mid 19C, an archive and a glass museum were set up in the Palazzo Giustinian, and at the same time a school of drawing was opened. This was the new beginning. The glass industry was stimulated and products of the Venetian glass-blowers from Murano once again found acceptance world-wide. Restoration work began on churches and houses. Tourism extended from Venice as far as Murano-Burano and Torcello and there was a regular shipping service linking the islands with Venice. Today the islands have much to offer the visitor. In contrast to the rather monotonous workers' village, there are streets with countless and often tiny shops offering glassware for sale;

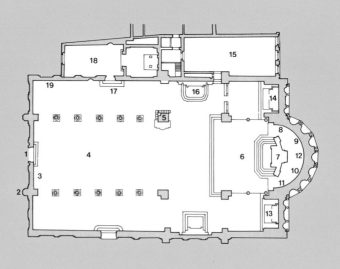

Murano, SS.Maria e Donato 1 Marble relief with St.Donatus and praying woman above the entrance portal **2** Immured pilaster fragment from the 2C AD **3** Holy water stoup on pillar from the 7C or 8C **4** Finest part of floor mosaics **5** Byzantine pulpit **6** 9C sarcophagus **7** 17C altar with relics of St.Donatus **8, 9, 10, 11** Remains of late-14C frescos depicting the Evangelists, probably by Niccolò di Pietro **12** Apse mosaic with 12C Virgin Mary praying **13** Gradine altar, baroque **14** Baroque altar with Byzantine icon of the Virgin Mary (Madonna delle Grazie) **15** Sacristy, sales and exhibition room **16** Altar retable with Death of the Virgin Mary by a pupil of Paolo Veneziano (13C), above which there is a 14C Byzantine icon of the Virgin Mary, the 'Madonna delle Stelle' **17** Painting by Bastiani (Adoration of the Virgin Mary, 1484) above the door to the baptistery **18** 19C baptistery (Cappella di Santa Filomena) with ancient and medieval marble sculptures including a 4C sarcophagus **19** St.Donatus with founder figures (1310)

popular consumer goods and innumerable charming little glass products alongside some items of undoubted trash. The large factories have splendid exhibition rooms displaying for sale wonderful glassware designed on the medieval model. Anyone wishing to see more of old

Murano should visit the Museo Vetrario and the three restored churches.

SS. Maria e Donato: This basilica, probably originally founded in the 7C, stands in the Campo di San Donato, the ancient and inspiring main square of Murano. Beside the basilica is the Palazzo della Ragione, where the town's mayor resided in the Middle Ages. Legend relates that Otto I the Great, the Roman-German Emperor, founded the basilica in 950 after the town had been spared from a tidal wave thanks to the assistance of the Virgin Mary. According to the legend, the basilica was consecrated by the Pope himself and by 25 bishops. However, works of art which have been found (including sarcophagi from the 4–9C and an early font), and also medieval chronicles, indicate that the first church on this site was considerably older. It can be shown for certain that the first church of the Virgin Mary was built in the 7C (with the aid of

Murano, glass museum

donations from the aristocracy) and rebuilt in the 9C. The relics of St.Donato were brought to Murano on 7 August 1125 and interred in the church of the Virgin Mary. A new, richly-decorated and elegant basilica was built in the 12C above the old basilica. The new structure was given the name 'Basilica dei SS.Maria e Donato' and its decoration and embellishment, particularly with mosaics, continued apace. There is an annual holiday on 7 August, with processions in memory of the arrival of the Saint's relics. The church was held in honour until the 15C, its decline beginning in the 16C. The church was redesigned in baroque style under Bishop Marco Giustinian (d. 1735), whose tomb slab is let into the cathedral floor. All the baroque additions later disappeared. The baptistery had been knocked down by 1719, although the walls of the present baptistery include remnants of the original structure. It also houses the late-classical sarcophagus of a Roman family,

which was used as a Romanesque font. The campanile is 12C.

The 12C church is a cruciform brick basilica with a tripartite sanctuary. The façade is simple, the side walls plain, but the choir consists of a two-storeyed arcaded wall interrupted by a frieze of terracotta slabs. The upper storey was built as an ambulatory; the two-storeyed colonnaded arcades are reminiscent of the outer wall of the choir of S.Marco.

Inside, the church has an early-15C Venetian keel vault and a fine polychrome mosaic floor (1140) richly decorated with figures. Despite the beautiful marble columns with Romanesque capitals, this church interior makes a bare impression today.

Decorations: Wooden Venetian altar retable, Byzantine images of the Virgin Mary, 12C Virgin Mary Praying in the apse, a votive painting (1484) by Lazzaro Bastiani above the door to the baptistery, a gilded and painted relief of St.Donatus

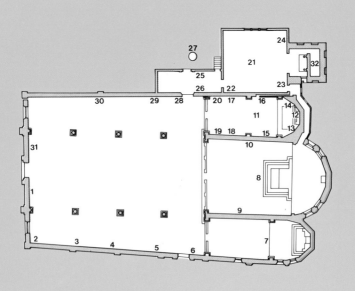

Murano, S.Pietro Martire 1 Altarpiece of St.Antony by Antonio Zanchi (1631-1722) **2** Altarpiece by Giacomo Palma il Giovane (1544-1622) **3** Giovanni Bellini (1430-1516), altarpiece of eight Saints looking upon the Virgin Mary **4** Giovanni Bellini painting of the Virgin Mary Enthroned between St.Mark the Evangelist, who is presenting the Doge Agostino Barbarigo, and St.Augustine **5** Jacopo Tintoretto (1518-94), altarpiece depicting the Baptism of Christ **6** Altarpiece of John the Baptist from the school of Titian **7** Cappella Ballarin **8** Sanctuary **9** Enormous painting by Bartolomeo Letterini (1669-1745) depicting the Marriage at Cana **10** Enormous painting of the Feeding of the Five Thousand by B.Letterini **11** Cappella SS.Sacramento **12** Gilded marble altar in Lombard style (1495) **13** Painting of St.Augustine by Gregorio Lazzarini (1655-1730) **14** Painting of St.Mark by Tintoretto (1560-1635) **15** Two angels praying, by Nicolò Rondinelli (1460-1502) **16** Two

angels making music, by Piermaria Pennachi (1464-1514) **17** Altarpiece (1507) from the church of S.M. degli Angeli in Murano **18** Deposition altarpiece by Marco Angelo da Moro (1537-1586) **19** Altarpiece of the Virgin Mary Enthroned, by Bernardino Licinio (1490-1565) **20** Altarpiece of the Virgin Mary Enthroned, by Giovanni Agostino di Lodi (Boccaccino) (c. 1500) **21** Sacristy **22, 23, 24** Wooden altar casings (17C) by P.Morando **25** Painting of Christ's Entry into Jerusalem by Gaspare Diziani (Belluno) (1689-1767) **26** Virgin Mary by Gregorio Lazzarini (1655-1730) **27** Pozzo (fountain enclosure built of Istrian stone, 1348) **28** Altarpiece of St.Jerome by Paolo Veronese (1528-88) **29** 'St.Agatha in prison' by Veronese **30** Deposition altarpiece by Giuseppe Porta (Salviati) (1520-73) **31** Altarpiece with St.Vincenzo Ferreri, St.Antony Abbot and St.Luigi Gonzaga **32** Campanile (1498-1502)

(1310) in the left aisle, fragmentary late-14C frescos, and a pillar with a holy-water stoup (7C or 8C).

S.Maria degli Angeli (NW of Murano's main island, opposite the point where the ship operating the service between here and Venice berths): This convent and church were founded in the 12C, rebuilt in the 16C and deconsecrated during the period of secularization. The church interior was built in c. 1500, but in the 19C it was completely altered in poor style. Good features which have survived include the coffered ceiling by Nicolò Rondinelli (c. 1500), showing the

Coronation of the Virgin Mary, Saints and Prophets, and some baroque altars with their scagliola inlay work, a late-16C altarpiece (Glorification of the Virgin Mary) by Jacopo Palma Giovane the younger and a monument to Senator G.Batt. Perandas by A.Vittoria (1586/7).

S.Pietro Martire: The E. side of the church of S.Pietro Martire, which has a N. orientation, is to be found not far from the Canal Grande di Murano, at the point where the canal joins the Rio dei Vetrai and where a small bridge links the Campo S.Stefano to the Fondamenta S.Pietro. This colonnaded basilica (nave, two aisles) dates from 1348 and was originally the Dominicans' monastery church. After a fire in 1474 it was rebuilt in Venetian Renaissance style. The portal, round-arched windows, and the campanile (modern roof), were built at that time. In the much-restored arcaded courtyard there is a fountain with a surrounding frame of Istrian marble (1348), restored in 1748. Inside, there are interesting paintings. A large panel painting of the Assumption (*c.* 1510) by G.Bellini's workshop is in the right aisle. To the left of this, there is a fine painting by Bellini (*c.* 1488), but sadly when it was restored, insufficient attention was paid to the colouring. In the right aisle there is a painting by Jacopo Tintoretto depicting the Baptism of Christ. In the left aisle there are two paintings by Paolo Veronese (St.Agatha in prison, and St.Jerome in the desert), both *c.* 1566, and a Deposition by G.Porta (16C). In the sanctuary there are enormous 18C paintings by Bart. Letterini. The altar (1495) in the Cappella del Sacramento is in Lombard style and comes from the church of S.Stefano, which no longer exists.

Museo Civico dell'Arte Vetraria (S. side of the campo on the Canale di San Donato): This museum documents the glass-blower's art in Murano. Set up in 1861, the museum occupies the Palazzo Giustinian, which was built in 1689 and was the palace of the Bishop of Torcello until 1805. Glass manufactured in Murano was much sought after in the 13C, but the earliest surviving examples

date from the 2nd half of the 15C. Coloured vessels decorated with many figures, and glass treated together with other materials, are shown here in manifold designs. The famous 'marriage bowl', probably the work of Andrea Barovier, is in Room X of the museum. The mirrors for which Murano held the monopoly in the 15–17C are also on display. There are also exhibits from the history of Murano, including a manuscript dating from 1500.

Also worth seeing: The *Fondamenta Novagero* lies opposite SS.Maria e Donato. The *Palazzo da Mula* (on the Fondamenta Vetrai, opposite the Ponte Vivarini): The house and garden are the only example of a Venetian Renaissance summer villa surviving in Murano. The 15C palazzo was rebuilt in the 16C; 12&13C relief fragments in Veneto-Byzantine style were built into the late-Gothic façade at that time. The *Palazzo Trevisan* (No. 34 on the Fondamenta Novagero) is a 16C Venetian structure.

36025 Noventa Vicentina

Vicenza   p.322☐E 6

This little country town to the W. of the Euganean hills was first mentioned in *c.* 1000. It suffered in the battles between Padua and Verona in the 14C and consequently buildings around the central *Piazza* date from after that time.

Duomo: The *cathedral* (1856), with campanile and spire, stands to the left of the *town hall*. In the spacious interior, the baroque *high altar* by Bonazza stands out. However, more significant from the art history point of view is the 2nd *altar* on the left, which has a painting of St.Roch and St.Sebastian signed by Giovanni Battista Tiepolo, along with 15C bas-reliefs at the sides depicting the two Saints who provided relief from the plague.

Villa Barbarigo-Rezzonico: This palazzo (today the town hall) with its elegant colonnaded loggia also stands in the main square. Dating from *c.* 1600, it is the work of a Venetian architect. The rooms inside are painted throughout with *frescos* by Antonio Foller and Antonio Vassilacchi (known as Aliense) from Milos. The loggia, with its Doric columns, is echoed

in the arcaded *houses* on the other sides of the square.

Environs: Agugliaro (6 km. NE): The two late-Gothic *villas of Pigafetto* and *Da Verme* (15C), with fine triple windows on the upper storey. The 17C *Villa Trolio.* Two more country houses in the district of Finale: The *Palazzo delle Trombe* (16C) is attributed to Michele Sanmicheli, while the small *Villa Saraceno* (*c.* 1545), with its three-arched pedimented portico, is an unfinished work by Palladio (fresco decorations in the portico vault).

Barbarano Vicentina (16 km. N.): The parish church of *S.Maria Assunta*, rebuilt in 1747, has retained the 13C campanile which belonged to the previous building. Inside there are a high altarpiece (Assumption) by Palma Giovane, and sculptures from the 13−16C. The *castle* on the hill above the town was converted into a classical villa in the 17C, and is known for its orangery.

Lonigo (Noventa Vicentina), Santuario della Madonna dei Miracoli, portal figures

Lonigo (17 km. NW): The typically Venetian *Piazza Garibaldi* is dominated by the *Palazzo Comunale* (1557) with its elegant external staircase. The parish church of *SS. Quirico e Giulitta* (nave and two aisles; rebuilt in 1615), has a fine campanile (1573) and a high altarpiece (Virgin Mary and Saints, 16C) by Benedetto Montagna. The *Villa Pisani* (1578) by Vincenzo Scamozzi, which stands above the town, imitates Palladio's 'Rotonda' near Vicenza (q.v.). The *Santuario della Madonna dei Miracoli*, on the road to S.Bonifacio (q.v.), originally a Chapel of the Virgin Mary, was enlarged into an Olivetan monastery, with a Gothic church with a Lombard-Gothic façade, after a miraculous event. Inside the Santuario there are ex voto paintings (15/16C) and large-scale baroque frescos. The *Villa Pisani* in the district of Bagnolo was built by Andrea Palladio in 1542 and 1545, and has a pedimented rusticated façade with three tall arcades.
Poiana Maggiore (3 km. W.): Two *villas*

stand at the edge of the town. One dates from the 14C and has a tall residential tower. The other, the *Villa Poiana,* has features reminiscent of Bramante, but was in fact designed by Andrea Palladio, who built it for Bonifazio Pogliana in 1548/9, making use of his entire repertoire of architectural forms. This country house fits harmoniously into the surrounding countryside. Inside the building there are stuccoes by Bartolomeo Ridolfi and frescos by Bernardino Ludia and Anselmo Canera. *Grotesque paintings* are here seen for the first time in a Palladian building. The statues (1658) on the parapets of the external staircase outside the Serlian main portal are by Girolamo Albanese from Vicenza.

31046 Oderzo

Treviso   p.320☐H 4

The Romans built the town of *Opitergium* on the site of a former settlement of the ancient Veneti. Destroyed by Pompey in 49 BC, this strategically important town on the *via Postumia* was rebuilt five years later by order of Julius Caesar. Although *Oderzo* was devastated several times in the Middle Ages, its inhabitants never abandoned the town.

Duomo S.Giovanni Battista: This late-Gothic cathedral (14/15C) was built on the site of a 10C church. Side chapels were added in the 17C; later additions were

Motta di Livenza (Oderzo), Santuario

removed in the 20C. *Outside* the building boasts a Renaissance portal in a plain Gothic façade articulated by pilasters, a Gothic side portal on the right, an unfaced dome and a tall *campanile* with a spire. The lower part of the campanile is a medieval fortified tower which was part of the former town wall. 14–16C frescos, including some by Jacopo Veneziano (Saint Bishops of Oderzo, 1606), survive on the inner entrance wall of the *nave*, which has no side aisles. The elevated *choir* has ancient floor mosaics. Interesting *features* include paintings by Palma Giovane (Descent of the Holy Ghost) in the choir, by Pomponio Amalteo (Life of John the Baptist, *c.* 1550) in the chapel of St.Francis to the left of the choir and by Andrea Bellunello (Madonna and Child, 1477) in the chapel to the right. Three more paintings (Vita Christi, 1549) by

◁ *Oderzo, cathedral, altar of St.Antony*

of S.Maria Mater Domini in Venice (q.v.).
Within, there are fine choir stalls (*c.* 1600)
and altarpieces, including one of the Virgin Mary and Saints (1556) by *Pomponio
Amalteo*, who was born here in 1505, as
well as one by Leandro Bassano (Virgin
Mary with St.Nicholas, St.Roch and
St.Sebastian; 1589). The *Santuario della
Madonna dei Miracoli* (1510–13) has a
façade with curving gable and portico.
Inside the building (nave, two aisles) there
are paintings from the Venetian school,
some by Palma Giovane (Assumption) and
a marble retable in relief (*c.* 1590) at the
high altar. The adjoining *monastery building* has two 16C cloisters with lunette
frescos (1674).

Padua, Gattamelata statue

Pomponio Amalteo can be seen on the S.
nave wall.

Museo Civico: Apart from medieval
architectural fragments and a *collection of
medals,* the Municipal Museum is devoted
to the archaeological finds from the
Roman town of Opitergium. Multicoloured *floor mosaics* (early 4C), showing scenes from hunting and everyday life,
come from an excavated Roman villa and
are extremely fine.

Environs: Méolo: (23 km. S.): The
Palazzi Malipiero and *Cappello* (today the
town hall) are both 15C. The sacristy of
the *parish church* has fine ceiling frescos
(1758) by Giovanni Battista Tiepolo.
Motta di Livenza (8.5 km. E.): This little
town on the W. bank of the Livenza is
known for its first-class wines and two
Renaissance churches. The façade of the
16/17C cathedral of *S.Niccolo* has pilasters
and volutes and is modelled on the façade

35100 Padova/Padua

Padova   p.322☐F 6

This old episcopal seat and university city
lies to the W. of Venice on both sides of
the *Bacchiglione,* which is joined by canals
to the rivers Brenta, Adige and Po.
Situated at the intersection of the main
lines of communication in the NE plain
of the Po, the city has become of increasing importance as a centre of trade and
industry and also of regional culture.

History: According to Virgil, Antenor the
Trojan fled here along with his retinue.
The first proven *prehistoric settlement* dates
back to 10C BC and the site was also
occupied by the ancient Veneti (4C BC).

The city was attacked by Kleonymos of Sparta in 301 BC. *Patavium* was allied to Rome from 225 BC onwards due to constant battles with the Gauls, and it became a Roman municipium in 49 BC. *Titus Livy,* the eminent Roman historian (59 BC–AD 17), lived and wrote here and the city became the wealthiest and most important centre of trade in Northern Italy in the Augustan period because of its favourable location on the communication routes. The Lombards devastated the city in 601, but remains of the ancient grid of streets, the Roman harbour on the river and the amphitheatre still survive. Thanks to the privileges granted by Charlemagne and Otto I, *Padua* was rebuilt in the 8–11C, and became independent in the early 12C. Operating as part of the Lombard League, Padua won a victory against Frederick Barbarossa and thereby increased its political power, gaining control of the territories of Bassano (q.v.), Belluno (q.v.), Conegliano (q.v.) and Feltre (q.v.). The university, later to become world-famous, was founded in Padua in 1222. The Franciscan monk *Antony of Lisbon* (1195–1231) held his penitential sermons in Padua and attracted considerable attention. The Hohenstaufen ruled here in 1237–56 under the governor Ezzelino III da Romano. Emperor Frederick II spent two years in Padua, learning of his excommunication here in 1239. In the 14C, under the rule of the Carraresi, Padua experienced great activity in the fields of trade, science and art and this success continued into the period of Venetian supremacy (1405–1797). Under Austrian rule from 1813 onwards, Padua became part of the Kingdom of Italy in 1866. Famous artists such as Dante, Giotto, Donatello, Filippo Lippi, Andrea Mantegna and Paolo Uccello worked in Padua. *Sperone Speroni* the humanist (1500–85), *Andrea Palladio* the architect, *Tiziano Aspetti* the sculptor and *Bartolomeo Cristofori* (1653–1731) who invented the pianoforte, were all born here.

The city's appearance: The layout of the city, which has a modern wall surrounding it, is based on a roughly equilateral triangle whose W. side runs from N. to S. The city walls run mainly along the bank of or near to the river Bacchiglione, which formerly flowed S. in a great arc by *Largo Europa* and along the roads *Riviera dei Ponti Romani* and *Riviera Tito Livio.* This natural loop in the river gave protection to both the Roman and the medieval settlement. The *core of the city's old quarter* now stands in the area enclosed by the loop, and its numerous medieval and modern buildings are grouped around the following nine squares: The two central market squares *Piazza delle Erbe* and *Piazza delle Frutta.* The *Piazza dei Signori, Piazza Capitaniato* and *Piazza Duomo* which all adjoin the central squares in the W. *Piazzetta Pedrocchi* and *Piazza Cavour,* and two squares to the NE. *Piazza Insurrezione* and *Piazza Garibaldi,* both to the N. The old river course appears at the *Riviera Ruzzante,* curving in a broad loop around the *S.Antonio* quarter, which contains the Saint's basilica, and flowing eastwards. To the S. of this second loop in the river is the *S.Giustina* quarter, with two municipal gardens, *Prato della Valle* and *Orto Botanico.* The buildings in this area are more recent, like those in the *S.Sofia* quarter in the E. The central line of streets (the Corso del Popolo, Corso Garibaldi, Via VIII Settembre, Via Roma and Via Umberto I) lead from the railway station in the N. (where there is a car park) to the Prato della Valle in the S. This main axis helps the visitor find his way about Padua's irregularly arranged streets; forays to either side will take in all the main sights.

Religious buildings

Basilica di S.Antonio (piazza del Santo): Antony of Lisbon, the Franciscan monk, was canonized in 1232 and made patron Saint of Padua. The *church containing his tomb* was erected 1232–1307. This pillared basilica was built on the site of the previous church, *S.Maria Mater Domini* (12/13C), of which one section (Chapel of the Black Madonna, see below) survives. The present church has a cruciform ground plan, an ambulatory and a ring of

Padua, S.Antonio

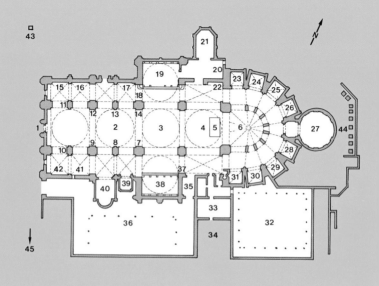

Padua, S.Antonio 1 Main portal **2** Nave (13C) **3** Transept with crossing (13/14C) **4** Sanctuary (14C) **5** High altar (1895) with Donatello bronzes (1446-50) **6** Choir with baroque choir stalls **7** Late-Gothic pulpit **8** Virgin Mary fresco (14C) attributed to Guariento **9** Monument to P.Bembo and, to the E., painting of St.Agatha (1736) by Tiepolo **10** Pillar with holy water stoup; opposite Lamentation fresco (15C) by Jacopo Parisati **11** Pillar with holy water stoup and, to the W., fresco (Madonna of the Blind, c. 1390) **12** Mausoleum of A.Contarini **13** Painting of St.Roch and St.Liberalis (17C) by Giovanni Battista Pelizzari **14** Monument to G.Michiel **15** Altar of Stanislaus with Pala (St.Stanislaus, 1607) by Pietro Malombra **16** Altar of Our Lady of Sorrows (1662) with Pietà painting (1652) by Luca Ferrari **17** Monument (1464-7) to Judge Antonio Rosselli by Pietro Lombardo **18** Baroque monument to the Venetian general Caterino Cornaro (d. 1669) by Giusto Le Court **19** Tomb chapel of St.Antony **20** Capella della Madonna Mora **21** Cappella dei Conti **22** Ecce Homo fresco (15C) by Pietro Calzetta **23** Chapel of St. Joseph **24** Chapel of St.Francis with modern frescos (20C) **25** Austro-Hungarian chapel **26** Polish chapel **27** Treasure chapel (18C) **28** Chapel of St.Stephen with frescos (1907/08) by Ludwig Seitz and bronze statue (St.Stephen, 1905) by Ludovico Pogliaghi **29** German chapel **30** American chapel **31** Chapel of St.Catherine with frescos (8 Saints) attributed to Giotto **32** Novices' cloister **33** Sacristy with vault fresco (St.Antony in Glory, 1665) by Pietro Liberi, and intarsia cupboards (1474-7) **34** Chapterhouse **35**
Passage with monuments (14C) **36** Chapter Cloister **37** Holy water stoup with bronze figure (St.Catherine, 1564) by Francesco Segala **38** Chapel of St.Felix or St.James **39** Chapel of the Sacred Heart (17/20C) **40** Chapel of the Sacrament (1456; restored) with the sarcophagus of Erasmo Gattamelata by Gregorio Allegretto (1458) **41** Poor Souls' altar (1648) by Tomaso and Matteo Allio **42** Altar of St.Charles Borromeo with pala (1758) by Francesco Zannoni **43** Equestrian monument to Gattamelata **44** Chiostro del Paradiso, the former monks' graveyard (1229) **45** Oratorio di S.Giorgio and Scuola del Santo

chapels and is 360 ft. long by 180 ft. wide. Its construction was begun in the W. on the model of Italian churches belonging to mendicant orders, and completed in the E. on the pattern of French cathedrals. The Belludi chapel (1382) is attached to the right transept. The treasure chapel (1690–1739) adjoining the apse is by Filippo Parodi. The church is a conglomerate of different architectural styles: the façade is Romanesque, the choir

S.Antonio

Gothic, the domes Byzantine and the campaniles Islamic.

The colours of the *exterior* are captivating: the red of the brick walls joins with their white marble decorations and the greyish-white leaden slabs of the roof to form a harmonious whole. The exemplary design of S.Marco in Venice (q.v.), with its five domes, is here added to in the shape of a dome at each end of the longitudinal axis (excluding the dome of the treasure chapel which is later). The present church also differs from S.Marco in that the dome (220 ft. high) over the crossing takes the form of a cone crowned by a lantern. Other features peculiar to the building can be seen most clearly in the exterior of the *choir section*, where the dwarf gallery, the graduated roofs, and the hemispherical calotte, are surmounted by two slender octangular *campaniles* which, with the multicoloured arches of the bell chambers, white marble parapets, and conical spires, are reminiscent of Oriental minarets. The *W. façade*, 90 ft. high, unites Romanesque forms (portals, capitals of the dwarf gallery, round-arched frieze) with Lombard-Gothic forms (pointed-arched blind arcades and the tracery of the rose window in the triangular gable). The fresco on the tympanum of the main portal (depicting the monogram of Christ, with St.Antony of Padua and St.Bernardino of Siena) is a copy of the original (1452) by Andrea Mantegna, which is today in the Museo Antoniano (see below). The bronze doors are the work of Camillo Boito (1895).

Arcades of pointed arches articulate the spacious *interior* to form a nave and two aisles. By means of these arcades, the load of the nave walls—which, in the clerestory, are shortened by the length of the galleries—is concentrated on to massive pillars. These pillars, acting through broad wall arches, also bear the load of the four tall pendentive domes which raise the height of the nave. The dome of the E. choir is reinforced by means of ribs, and is the only dome whose height is lower.

◁ *S.Antonio, portal detail*

S.Antonio

The choir and the slightly elevated sanctuary are separated from the nave by a *marble balustrade* (1651) with Mannerist bronze statues (Four Virtues, 1593) by Tiziano Aspetti.

Fine decorations include numerous captivating 15&16C works of art. The famous *bronze sculptures* and *reliefs* (crucifix, Virgin Mary Enthroned with Saints and Bishops, miracle of St.Antony, angels making music, all 1446–50) at the *high altar* (rebuilt by Camillo Boito in 1895) are the work of Donatello and his pupils. Behind the altar there is an expressive Entombment relief carved in soft Paduan stone and known as 'pietra di Nanto'. The splendid *bronze candelabrum* (1515) to the left of the altar is among the tallest of all Easter chandeliers (17 ft. 7 in. tall), and is the work of the Paduan artist Andrea Briosco, who also added two images (David dancing; Judith and Holofernes) to the ten bronze *bas reliefs* of Old Testament scenes (1484–8) by Bartolomeo Bellano on the sanctuary walls. The *walnut choir stalls* (1753) of Giorgio Massari replaced the former choir stalls by Lorenzo Canozzi (1462–9) which were destroyed in the fire in 1749. There is a large 15C fresco (Virgin Mary with the two Saints John) above the multicoloured *late-Gothic marble pulpit*. On the arcade pillar opposite this is the severe Doric *monument* to the Venetian patrician Girolamo Michiel (d. 1557) with the expressive *bronze bust* of the deceased by Francesco Segala. On the left, by the next pair of pillars but one there is a *monument* commemorating Alessandro Contarini (Venetian general and admiral, d. 1553), which was built in splendid style by Michele Sanmicheli and Alessandro Vittoria in 1555–8. On the right, opposite, there is a monument to Cardinal Pietro Bembo (d. 1547). Also by Sanmicheli, it takes the form of a Corinthian aedicule; the *bust* of the Cardinal is the work of Danese Cattaneo. The next pair of pillars each have a holy-water stoup decorated with figures by Giovanni Minello. Above them the following two works are to be seen: on the left, a statue of the Baptism of Christ signed by Tizi-

◁ *S.Antonio, epitaph*

no Aspetti (1599) and, on the right, an
early-16C figure of John the Baptist by
Tullio Lombardo. The following are the
most interesting of the church's 15
chapels: The *Cappella dell' Arca del Santo*
tomb chapel of St.Antony, 1500–33),
whose altar, the work of Tiziano Aspetti
1593/4), contains the Saint's relics. The
chapel is decorated with high reliefs (Life
and Miracles of St.Antony, 16C), some of
which are by Antonio and Tullio Lombardo, Antonio Minello and Jacopo Sansovino. In the adjoining *chapel of the Black
Madonna,* which survives from the previous church of S.Maria Mater Domini,
there are 14/15C tomb monuments, and
a marble Virgin Mary (1396) by Rinaldino
di Francia in a polychrome frame. The
adjacent *Cappella dei Conti* (chapel of the
beatified Lucas Belludi, 1382) has the last
great *fresco cycle* (Virgin Mary Enthroned
with Saints, Life of the Beatified, 1382)
by Giusto de' Menabuoi. Ubaldo Oppi
painted the frescos of the life of St.Francis
of Assisi in the *Cappella di S.Francesco*
known as the Austro-Hungarian chapel)
in 1932, while the frescos of the Life of
St.Stanislaus (1899) in the adjoining *Cappella di S.Stanislao* (known as the Polish
chapel) were painted by Taddeusz Popiel.
In the *Cappella delle Reliquie* (known as
the Treasury chapel), a special visitor's
permit must be obtained in order to view
the following: balustrade sculptures by
Filippo Parodi who was a pupil of Bernini; the silver-gilt reliquaries (13–15C)
containing the jawbone, tongue and scalp
of St.Antony; fragments of Christ's Cross
and Crown of Thorns. Modern frescos
20C) are to be found in the *Cappella di
S.Bonifazio* (known as the German chapel)
and in the *Cappella della S.Rosa di Lima*
known as the American chapel). At the
beginning of the ambulatory, a passage on
the right leads to the *sacristy* and to the
novices' cloister (15C), while another passage runs to the more attractive *chapter
cloister* (1290) where there are two 6C
Byzantine sarcophagi. The excellent *fresco
cycle* (Crucifixion, Life of St.James,
1377–9) in the *Chapel of St.Felix* (1372–7)
in the right transept is the work of

Cappella degli Scrovegni, Giotto fresco ▷

Padua, Cappella degli Scrovegni, frescos 1 God the Father and choirs of angels* **2** Joachim cast out of the Temple **3** Joachim with his shepherds **4** The annunciation to Anne **5** Joachim's sacrifice **6** Joachim's dream **7** Joachim and Anne meeting at the Golden Gate **8** Nativity of the Virgin Mary **9** Virgin Mary in the Temple* **10** The suitors' rods being presented* **11** Suitors' prayer that the rods should bloom* **12** Marriage of the Virgin Mary* **13** Marriage procession* **14** Annunciation (Archangel Gabriel on left, Virgin Mary on right) **15** Visitation **16** Nativity **17** Adoration of the Magi **18** Presentation in the Temple* **19** Flight into Egypt **20** Massacre of the Innocents* **21** Jesus among the Doctors **22** Baptism of Jesus **23** Marriage at Cana **24** Raising of Lazarus **25** Entry into Jerusalem **26** Cleansing of the Temple **27** Betrayal by Judas **28** Last Supper **29** Washing of the Feet **30** Kiss of Judas **31** Jesus before Caiaphas **32** Crown of Thorns, and Flagellation **33** Christ Bearing the Cross **34** Crucifixion **35** Lamentation **36** Resurrection of Christ **37** Ascension** **38** Descent of the Holy Ghost** (* = participation by other artists; ** = considerable participation by other artists; no asterisk = frescos genuinely by Giotto)

Altichiero Altichieri. The monument to the Condottiere Erasmo Gattamelata (d. 1443) is in the *sacrament chapel* (1456–9). The *monastery buildings* to the S. of the church include the *Biblioteca Antoniana*

with a rich collection of medieval manuscripts and early printed books, and also the *Museo Antoniano* which is being altered. The *Oratorio di S.Giorgio* (1377) with its plain exterior, is the burial chapel of the Dukes of Soranzo. This chapel, which adjoins the monastery in the W., contains another *fresco cycle* (Life of Christ, Lives of St.George, St.Catherine of Alexandria, St.Lucy, Saints and Prophets) by Altichiero Altichieri.

The neighbouring *Scuola del Santo* (1427) was enlarged in 1504/05 by the addition of the upper storey with a fine wooden coffered ceiling and here the chapterhouse of the brotherhood was established. The walls have a fine *fresco cycle* by 16C artists, including Titian (the miracles of St.Antony, all 1511). There are also paintings by Girolamo de' Santo (Death of St.Antony; miracles worked by the Saint, 1511–13), and Gian Antonio Corona (sermon and meeting with Ezzelino da Romano, 1509–11). The *Piazza del Santo*, with its many pigeons, is surrounded by souvenir stalls. To the left of the church façade, the monumental *equestrian statue of Gattamelata* stands. Erasmo Narni, the Venetian condottiere (d. 1443), was called Gattamelata (= honeyed cat) because of his military cunning. The statue was commissioned from the Florentine sculptor by his widow. Donatello placed the bronze statue (1447–53) of the mounted Gattamelata above a cenotaph base (*c.* 25 ft. high) where it could be seen from five different streets. In this first Renaissance equestrian statue, Donatello chose to employ a classical pose full of dignity, as opposed to rendering motion pent with energy which was Verrochio's choice 40 years later in the Colleoni monument in Venice (q.v.).

Cappella degli Scrovegni/Arena chapel (giardini dell'Arena): Enrico Scrovegni, one of the richest merchants in Padua in the early 14C, built the small brick church of *S.Maria della Carità (dell' Arena)* with polygonal apse in 1303–05 in the area of the *Roman amphitheatre* (arena), whose foundation walls are still

Cappella degli Scrovegni

Cappella degli Scrovegni, Giotto fresco

visible. Six lancet windows in the S. let light into the simple tunnel-vaulted interior, which is completely covered by a *fresco cycle* (1304/05) by Giotto and his pupils. The lowest level of paintings are *grisaille* and depict Vices (left) and Virtues (right). Above these Giotto illustrated the Lives of the Virgin Mary and Christ in 37 panels (see diagram). Thanks to their very good state of preservation, they are among Giotto's finest surviving work, possibly surpassing even the fresco cycles of S.Francesco in Assisi and S.Croce in Florence. Giotto's innovations consist of the introduction of a three-dimensional quality in the figures and a naturalism which replaced the 'maniera greca' of 13C Italian painting.

The decorative strips in the frames, and the large *Last Judgement fresco* on the W. wall, were painted by Giotto in collaboration with his pupils, while the ceiling medallions were produced exclusively by his workshop; the frescos (Death, Assump-

tion and Coronation of the Virgin Mary) in the choir are by one of Giotto's pupils. Behind the altar, with its splendid *statues* (Virgin Mary and two angels) by Giovanni Pisano, is the marble tomb of Enrico Scrovegni, the chapel's founder (d. 1336). Frescos of 'Mater lactans' (Madonna suckling the Child) in the two side niches are by Giusto de'Menabuoi.

Duomo S.Maria Assunta (piazza Duomo): Except for the 17C enlargements (dome with drum, side chapels), the *cathedral* (9/12C) appears today in the sober Renaissance form given to it by the architects Andrea da Valle and Agostino Righetti in 1552, whose work was very loosely based on plans by Michelangelo. A brick structure rebuilt above a cruciform ground plan, it has three apses divided by pilasters at the end of the choir section which faces west. At each end of the transept there is a single apse. The height of the plain *interior* (nave and two aisles) is

Cappella degli Scrovegni, Giotto fresco

raised by the drum (octagonal exterior) and by the dome over the crossing. Drum and dome articulate the tunnel vault of the nave to form alternate bays. *Furnishings* include: *Holy-water stoup* decorated with sculptures (Baptism of Christ, Ascension) by Andrea Bonazza. 14–16C *wall tombs* in the transepts, including the Gothic monument (1427) to Cardinal Zabarella in the N., with fine statues of the Virgin Mary and Saints, and in the S., the *Renaissance monument* to Bishop Pietro Barozzi (d. 1507), attributed to Tullio Lombardo. Opposite this is the late-Gothic wall tomb of Bishop Pileo da Prata beneath a baldachin. This tomb is decorated with reliefs of saints. There is a bronze relief of the Martyrdom of St.Daniel (1592) on the rear side of the ancient sarcophagus (used as an altar) in the *crypt* below the sanctuary. In the *Sagrestia dei Canonici* to the S. of the sanctuary there are paintings by Nicoletto Semitecolo (Life of St.Sebastian, 1367), Giorgio Schiavone (St.Antony of

Padua, St.Louis, St.Francis of Assisi, St.Antony Abbot), Francesco Bassano (Flight into Egypt), Jacopo da Montagnana (Deposition), Paris Bordone (Ecce Homo), and Giovanni Domenico Tiepolo (two paintings of the Virgin Mary with Saints). The sacristy is also the home of the *church treasure*, which is kept in a carved walnut cabinet (1563) and consists of ornate silver utensils, 14/15C reliquaries, a beautiful processional Cross of 1228 and two illuminated manuscripts (Evangelistary, 1170; Epistolary, 1229). To the right of the cathedral façade is the *baptistery*, a brick structure articulated by pilaster strips and round-arched friezes. It was mentioned in 1170 and rebuilt in 1260. The graceful round-arched portico leads into the square interior which, like the small choir chapel, is topped by a *pendentive dome*, an architectural rarity in 13C Italy. A font (1260) stands in the middle. The immense *fresco cycle* (c. 1374–8), the work of the Florentine artist Giusto

Cappella degli Scrovegni, Giotto fresco

de'Menabuoi, is Tuscan in style. (Menabuoi is interesting for he introduced the forms and colours of trecento Tuscan painting to the Veneto.) Some 100 sections extend over the dome (Christ the Pantocrator, with saints and choirs of angels), drum (Old Testament scenes), pendentives (Evangelists and Prophets) and walls (New Testament scenes), and also over the small dome (Descent of the Holy Ghost) and walls of the choir (Apocalypse). The *altar polyptych* (Virgin Mary Enthroned, Fathers of the Church, Life of John the Baptist) is also by Menabuoi.

Buildings grouped around the rectangular *Piazza Duomo* include the *bishops' palace* (14–18C) in the S. which has two chapels frescoed by Jacopo da Montagna, and also the *Biblioteca Capitolare* (ornate medieval manuscripts and early printed works). In the E. of the Piazza is the *Casa Bonafori* (*c.* 1300) with a three-storeyed loggia (14C) in the courtyard, and in the N. is the 13C *Monte di Pietà*, which has

a loggia and a fine Renaissance façade (1531–5) and was designed by Giovanni Maria Falconetto; the *Arco Valaresso*, a triumphal arch (1632), adjoins the façade in the W.

SS. Filippo e Giacomo/Eremitani (piazza Eremitani): The Augustinian hermits built this early-Gothic structure (1276–1306) as a monastery church. It was seriously damaged in a bombing raid in 1944, but was rebuilt in accordance with the original in 1946–50. Next to this is the new *Museo Archéologico* (see below), standing on the site of the *monastery*, which was visited by Martin Luther in 1510 and was secularized in 1806. The church's two-storeyed *façade* has two tall niches in blind arches to the sides of its main portal, and so too does the façade of the Basilica di S.Antonio. The gabled upper storey is articulated by pilaster strips and contains a rose window. On the S. side is an elegant *Renaissance portal* (1442); its

Duomo

portico, and the reliefs in the frame, are by Nicolò Baroncelli. In the single-aisled interior, the visitor is initially struck by the unusual *wooden vault* (restored) with its crosscut pointed arches. Attention is then drawn to the two *Gothic monuments* of Ubertino and Jacopo II de Carrara and Andriolo de Sanctis. In front of the left wall of the nave is the *Renaissance monument* (1546) to Marco Mantoa Benavides (d. 1582). It was built in the manner of Michelangelo by Bartolomeo Ammannati from Florence. Gothic fresco fragments, some by Giusto de'Menabuoi, and the Gothic sarcophagus of Ilario Sanguinacci (d. 1381), are to be found in the *Cappella Sanguinacci* to the left of the choir. The groin-vaulted polygonal choir has remains of frescos (Saviour and Evangelists, Coronation of the Virgin Mary) and a 14C crucifix by Guarento di Arpo. The *Cappella Ovetari* to the right of the choir has the scanty remains of a fresco cycle (most of which was destroyed in 1944) by Andrea

Mantegna, Ansuino da Forli and Bono da Ferrara.

S.Francesco (via S.Francesco): The *Gothic portico* of the Franciscan church (1416) is unusual in that it forms part of a row of arcaded houses. A large *Ascension painting*, attributed to Paolo Veronese, hangs above the entrance to the Gothic interior, which has a nave, two aisles, and columns alternating with pillars. The 2nd chapel on the right has frescos (including the Life of the Virgin Mary, 1523) thought to be by Girolamo de'Santo. Large *bronze reliefs* by Bartolomeo Bellano (Pietro Roccabonella, Virgin Mary with St.Francis of Assisi and St.Peter the Martyr; 1498) are to be found to one side of the sanctuary which, like the transept, was rebuilt in the early 16C. A fine view of the exterior and campanile is obtained from the *cloister* (c. 1490) on the left. On the upper storey of the *Capitolo di S.Maria della Carità* (1420) opposite the church there are frescos by

Duomo, Battistero, 'Baptism of Christ' by Giusto de' Menabuoi (left), Duomo (right

Dario Varotari (Life of the Virgin Mary, 1579).

S.Giustina (prato della Valle): This, the largest Renaissance church in the Veneto, was built in the 16C under the supervision of Alessandro Leopardi, Andrea Moroni and Andrea da Valle on the site of previous buildings from the 5–12C. The *exterior* has extensive brick walls with round and thermal windows. The eight *domes,* which have drums and were built with the assistance of Vincenzo Scamozzi, are over-looked by the tall *campanile* which has an octagonal roof. The two red marble gryphons outside the sober W. façade were taken from the Romanesque Benedictine church.

The bright *interior,* 400 ft. long, is divided into a nave and two aisles by massive pillars with Ionic capitals. Six chapels on each side open into the aisles. The E. choir (lengthened by the addition of a monks' choir), and the transepts, are all flanked by side chapels, which also have apses at their ends. From the ground plan, it can be seen that the church is a combination of the present cruciform domed basilica (see the drawing) and, at right angles to this an earlier building. Behind the baroque *high altar* (1640) is one of the church's finest possessions, a large oil painting (*c.* 1575) signed by Paolo Veronese and depicting the martyrdom of St.Justina, the Paduan woman in whose honour the previous church (5C) was built. Richly carved choir stalls date from 1558–66. The *sarcophagus of St.Luke* (1316; restored 1562) has Pisan alabaster sculptures in the left transept. A painting by Luca Giordano of the Death of St.Scholastica (1673–5) can be seen in the 4th chapel of the right aisle. The 5C *shrine of St.Prosdocimus,* with 6C marble altar rails, is reached through the apse portal of the right transept. The *old choir* (1462), with inlaid choir stalls (1467–77) and the tomb of Lodovico Barbo (d. 1443), is

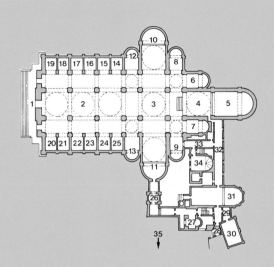

reached via the so-called *great corridor*, as is the adjoining *room preceding the sacristy*. Housed here are a sculpted portal architrave (Life of the Virgin Mary, early 13C) taken from the previous Romanesque church, fresco fragments and a terracotta Virgin Mary (*c.* 1490). To the S. of the church lie the *painted cloister* (15C), with fresco fragments by Bernardo Parentino (1489–94) and Girolamo de' Santo

Padua, S.Giustina 1 Main portal **2** Nave with domed bays **3** Crossing **4** Raised sanctuary, beneath which lies the crypt ending in an apse **5** Choir with painting (Martyrdom of St.Justina) by Paolo Veronese **6** Chapel of the Sacrament with sumptuous 17C baroque altar and vault paintings (Adoration of the Shepherds) by Sebastiano Ricci **7** Pietà chapel with marble sculptures (Lamentation, 1689) by Filippo Parodi **8** Chapel of St.Arnoldus with baroque tomb urn (1682) of St.Arnoldus by Bernardo Falcone **9** Chapel of St.Bartholomew with urn of Bishop Maximus Vitalianus by B.Falcone **10** Sarcophagus of St.Luke (1316) with his relics **11** Sarcophagus of St.Matthew (1561/2) by Francesco de'Sordi **12** Chapel of St.Felicitas with baroque tomb urn (1682) of St.Felicitas by B.Falcone **13** Chapel of St.Uriel

with urn (1682) of St.Uriel by B.Falcone **14** Chapel of St.Giuliano with urn (1680) of the Paduan martyr St.Giuliano by B.Falcone **15** Chapel of St.Maurus with altarpiece (Apparition of St.Bishop Maurontus, c. 1671/2) by Valentin Lefèbvre **16** Chapel of St.Placidus with altarpiece (Martyrdom of St.Placidus, c. 1675) by Luca Giordano **17** Chapel of St Daniel chapel with altarpiece (St.Deacon Daniel, 17C) by Antonio Zanchi **18** Chapel of Pope Gregory with altarpiece (Virgin Mary with Pope Gregory the Great, c. 1700) by Sebastiano Ricci **19** Chapel of St.James with altarpiece (Martyrdom of St.James the Less, 16C) by a pupil of Veronese **20** Chapel of St.Paul with a painting (Conversion of St.Paul, 16C) attributed to Benedetto Caliari **21** Chapel of St.Gertrude with altarpiece (St.Gertrude, 1678) by Pietro Liberi **22** Chapel of St.Gerard with altarpiece (Martyrdom of St.Gerard Sagredo, 17C) by the Munich artist Karl Loth **23** Chapel of St.Scholastica with altarpiece (Death of St.Scholastica, 1673-5) by Luca Giordano **24** Chapel of St.Benedict with altarpiece (St.Benedict, 1618) by Palma Giovane **25** Chapel of the Poor Souls with baroque altar (1679) by Giovanni Comino **26** Martyrs' fountain (1565/6), and terracotta statues of Saints by Tiziano Aspetti **27** Prosdocimus shrine (5C) **28** Entrance to monastery **29** Anteroom of sacristy **30** Sacristy **31** Old choir (former monks' choir of the previous Romanesque church) **32** Great corridor with early-13C reliefs of figures, and mosaic fragments (5/6C) **33** Little corridor **34** Chapel of St.Luke with frescos (Life of St.Luke, 1437/8) by Giovanni Storlato **35** Monastery cloisters

S. Giustina

(1542–6), the *novices' cloister* (16C), and the *chapter cloister* (c. 1595) with a fountain by Pietro Lombardo (1494/5).

S.Lucia (via S.Lucia): Documented in the 10C, it was given its present form by the Paduan architect Sante Benato in 1740. Semi-columns and pilasters articulate the classical *façade*, which is crowned by a pediment. The single-aisled *interior* is articulated by three-quarter columns and carved beams. Side niches contain statues (Apostles and Saints) by Giovanni Bonazza and his pupils; above there are *chiaroscuro paintings* of Saints' busts on a golden ground by Jacopo Ceruti and Giovanni Battista Tiepolo (St.Luke). The nave walls have 17/18C paintings by Domenico Campagnola (Presentation in the Temple), Jacopo Ceruti (Virgin Mary and Saints), Antonio de'Pieri (St.Joseph and Saints), and Giovanni Bonazza (Doubting Thomas). The adjoining *Scuola di S.Rocco* (1480), enlarged in 1525, has a two-

storeyed Renaissance façade with a triangular pediment. The walls of the single-aisled oratory (key obtainable from the sacristan of the church of S.Lucia) are painted with 16C *frescos* (Life of St.Roch) by Domenico and Gualtiero Campagnola. The 16C altarpiece of the Virgin Mary with St.Roch and St.Lucy is by Alessandro Maganza.

S.Maria del Carmine (piazza Petrarca): The façade of the Romanesque *I Carmini* church, founded in 1212 and redesigned by Lorenzo da Bologna in the 16C, was given its present (incomplete) form in the 18C. The copper covering of the dome is 20C. Three stone *Virtues* (1736) above the pediment of the portal are by Tommaso Bonazza, as are the *statues of Prophets* beside the 3rd altar on the right of the single-aisled interior. The *tomb of Tiberio Deciani* (d. 1582) has sculptures by Francesco Segala. The *sacristy* was designed by Lorenzo da Bologna in Renaissance style. A fine niche figure of St.James (c. 1400) can be seen on the S. wall. The *Petrarch monument* (1874) by Luigi Ceccon stands in the middle of the lawn in the *Piazza Petrarca*, which extends in front of the façade. To the right of the façade is the 14C *Scuola del Carmine*, which has been altered and restored several times. The oratory walls are decorated with a fresco cycle (Life of the Virgin Mary) by various 16C Veneto artists, including Giulio Campagnola who painted his friend Albrecht Dürer wearing a black biretta and cloak (to the left of the entrance) in the scene showing the marriage of the Virgin Mary.

S.Maria dei Servi (via Roma): The tall Gothic brick church of the Servites (1372–92) stands in the city's busiest street and is oriented towards the S. The E. wall faces the street and its Gothic windows are partly concealed by the *round-arched portico* built in front of them in 1510. The portico has fine Byzantine-style medieval *capitals*, which originally decorated the old chapel of St.Antony of the 'Santo'. The portico above the Gothic E. portal extends in baldachin-like fashion. The *portal surround* of the N. façade is early Renais-

Eremitani, fresco details in the right side chapel

sance. Frescos in the single-aisled interior include a Pietà by Jacopo da Montagnana in a niche of the W. wall. Next to this is the immense *baroque altar of Our Lady of Sorrows* (1710–30) by Giovanni Bonazza.

S.Maria del Torresino (via Torresino): This church built by Girolamo Frigimelica in 1726 above a circular ground plan has 18C statues (St.John the Evangelist, St.Mary Magdalene, Virtues) by the Bonazza, a family of sculptors from Padua.

S.Maria in Vanzo (via del Seminario): Buildings from the 17–20C of the *episcopal seminary* (founded in 1571) stand diagonally opposite the temple-like façade of S.Maria del Torresino to the SW. These buildings include the single-aisled church of *S.Maria* which was built by Domenico Campolongo in 1436 and enlarged in 1525 (key obtainable from seminary). *Frescos* (Fathers of the Church, Virtues; *c.* 1530) by Domenico Campag-

nola can be seen at the front of the choir loft above the entrance. Altarpieces of the right side chapels are by Giovanni de Mio (Adoration of the Shepherds) and Francesco Bassano (Entombment, 1574). The choir apse has paintings by Bartolomeo Montagna (Virgin Mary, Angels and Saints, *c.* 1510) and a fresco in the calotte (Coronation of the Virgin Mary) by Girolamo de' Santo. The large *Crucifixion* (1505) in the sanctuary (right) is by Michele da Verona.

S.Michele (Riviera Tiso da Camposampiero): The *oratory* (key obtainable from the pastor of S.Maria del Torresino) is all that remains of a former Ottonian church (970). Inside the oratory, Jacopo da Verona's frescos (Epiphany, Descent of the Holy Ghost, Death of the Virgin Mary, *c.* 1397) have figures with the features of historical personages (several Counts of Carrara on the left, Boccaccio, Dante, Petrarch and Pietro d'Abano on the right).

The city's former castle stands on the other side of the canal and was enlarged by Ezzelino III da Romano in 1242. The *keep* dates from the 9C; in 1767–7, Domenico Cerato added an extra storey and this houses the university's *astronomical observatory* (fine view of the city's old quarter).

S.Nicolò (via S.Nicolò): The Romanesque church of *S.Nicolò* (1090), which has been altered several times, stands near the *Teatro Verdi* with its curving façade (1847) by Giuseppe Japelli. The *Renaissance portal* in the church's brick façade has Lombard relief work. The church's interior (14/17C; nave and two aisles) has a painting by Giandomenico Tiepolo (Virgin Mary and Saints, 1777) at the baroque *high altar* (1682); the 2nd chapel on the right has four carved reliefs (Franciscan Saints and John the Evangelist, *c.* 1608) thought to be by the Flemish artist Alexander Colen.

SS.Simone, Giuda e Bartolomeo (via Altinate): This church is popularly also known as *S.Gaetano*. Built by Vincenzo Scamozzi in 1586, it has a magnificent Renaissance façade. The rectangular interior, with rounded corners, has *colossal pilasters* and a projecting cornice. The *dome fresco* (Paradise, *c.* 1725) in the choir, and the altarpiece (Flagellation of Christ) in the *Cappella del Sepolcro*, are both by the Parisian artist Guy Louis de Vernansal the younger.

S.Sofia (via Altinate): This basilica with a nave and two aisles was built in the 12–14C on the remains of a previous early-medieval church (9C). It was restored in 1959/60. The 11C lower section of the façade was rebuilt in the 14C; the *choir apse* with flying buttresses and blind arcades is evocative of 11C Byzantine Venetian buildings. The groin-vaulted interior has a row of columns with *Byzantine capitals* which divide the broad choir apse into two, a choir and a kind of ambulatory.

Secular buildings

1. Public buildings
Palazzo della Ragione (piazza delle Erbe/piazza delle Frutta): A medieval town hall built 1218/19, it is also known as *the Salone*. The two-storeyed *loggia* looking on to the two market squares, and also the

Piazza delle Erbe

Piazza delle Erbe, Palazzo della Ragione

characteristic *keel-shaped roof,* were built under the supervision of the Augustinian monk Giovanni degli Eremiti. The roof, along with the former Giotto frescos on the upper storey, was destroyed by fire in 1420. Further damaged by strong winds in 1756, the roof was rebuilt in 1756–9. The low arcaded passages are 15C. From the entrance at the SE corner, a flight of stairs leads up to the spacious Salone (some 260 ft. long, 90 ft. wide and high), which has open roof beams. The walls are covered with a large *fresco cycle,* the lower part of which is mainly by Giusto de'Menabuoi (late 14C); the upper frescos were restored by Giovanni and Niccolò Miretto and others some time after 1420. Frescos depict the calendar year in *paintings of the months,* with about 26 other subordinate pictures (Apostles, signs of the zodiac, planets, seasonal activities, etc.) for each month. On the W. wall there are Renaissance monuments to Padua's most important personalities (Titus Livy, Sperone Speroni and Lucrezia Dondi). In front of these is a large *wooden copy* (restored in 1446) of the horse of the Gattamelata monument (see above). Outside the E. wall, on the left, there is a 13C medieval pillory stone.

Palazzo Municipale (via VIII Febbraio): The complex of buildings making up the town hall, whose E. section was rebuilt in 1929/30, comprises the following: The *Palazzo del Podestà* in the W. dates from the 13/16C and has a partly rusticated façade by Andrea Moroni on the side facing the Piazza delle Erbe. The *Palazzo del Consiglio* (1238) in the NW has three round-arched double windows in the W. façade, which overlooks the Piazza delle Frutta. In the N. stands the *Palazzo degli Anziani* (1285) with the slightly leaning medieval *city tower* of the same name. The 16C *courtyard* by Moroni is surrounded by colonnaded passages on two levels. Inside, the *Sala dei Matrimoni* (wedding room) is worth seeing for its frescos and paintings by Domenico Campagnola and Gaspare Giona.

Piazza dei Signori/Piazza Capitaniato: The picturesque *Piazza dei Signori,* to the W. of the Piazza delle Frutta, is surrounded by houses with loggias and is dominated by the façades of the *church of S.Clemente* (16/17C) in the E., the *Loggia della Gran Guardia* (1496–1523) in the S.(an elegant Renaissance building modelled on the Loggia del

Piazza della Erbe, Arco dell'Orologio

Consiglio in Verona) and the *Palazzo del Capitaniato* in the W. This latter palazzo was built in 1599–1605 on the site once occupied by the city residence (14C) of the Counts of Carrara and today all that has survived is the *Arco dell'Orologio* (1344), a gatehouse tower with one of the oldest tower clocks (1427–37) in Italy (the fine Renaissance arch of 1533 is by Giovanni Maria Falconetto and leads to the palazzo courtyard which opens into the *Piazza Capitaniato*). The mid-16C *Loggia del Capitanio* occupies the S. side of this Piazza. At the W. end is the *Liviano* (1939), which includes parts of the Carrara residence. Of interest in the latter are the *Sala dei Giganti* with frescos of kings and heroes (14C) by Stefano dall'Arzere, Domenico and Gualtiero Campagnola, and the delicate *Loggia Carrarese* (1343) in the courtyard. The *Museo di Scienze Archeologiche e d'Arte* (see Museums) occupies the upper storey.

University (via VIII Febbraio): The university, founded in 1222, with its faculties of law, literature, medicine and philosophy, is the second oldest university in Italy after Bologna. Albertus Magnus and Galileo Galilei were among those to teach there. In 1493 it was housed in a building named *Il Bo'* (The Ox) after a former inn. The square *courtyard* surrounded by two-arched loggias (1546–87) with Doric and Ionic columns, and the *anatomy theatre* (1594; the first academic dissecting room) with its wooden rows of seats for the medical students, are both of greater interest than the façade, which was rebuilt in 1938–43.

2. Patrician and bourgeois architecture

Caffè Pedrocchi (piazzetta Pedrocchi): The café, built in 1826–31 to the designs of Giuseppe Japelli, stands near the Palazzo Municipale and the University (see above). It became famous as the starting place of the abortive students' insurrection held on 8 February 1848 against the Austrian occupation, and also as the 'coffee-house without doors' which remained open day and night. Its classical exterior has remained unaltered, as has the *Saletta Verde* inside. The *Pedrocchino*, a neo-Gothic building by Japelli (1837), stands beside the S. portico which has Gothic columns.

Casa di Ezzelino il Balbo (19 via S.Lucia): In the 15C, this large 12C brick building was given richly decorated Gothic *triple windows* on the 1st storey, and double windows on the 2nd.

Casa dei Mocenigo (piazzetta Ippolito Nievo): *Ippolito Nievo*, the writer (1831–61), was born here in 1831. A 16C building, it is partly the work of Andrea Palladio.

Casa degli Specchi (31 via Vescovado): Maggi da Bassano, the architect, built this palazzo for himself in 1502. Its name derives from the multicoloured *round marble sculptures*, a Lombard feature.

Palazzo Priuli-Pesaro (69 via Altinate):

The S. section of this two-winged patricians' palazzo (*c.* 1590) by Vincenzo Scamozzi borders on the Piazza Ippolito on which the church of S.Sofia and the Casa dei Mocenigo (see above) also stand. The palazzo's distinguishing feature is its long *façade* facing the street.

Palazzo Trento-Papafava (31 via Marsala): This palazzo by Giovan Battista Novello (1763) has an elegant late-baroque façade. Its interior (visits by prior appointment) was redesigned in classical style in 1805. The *Sala Neoclassica* has large alto-relievo scenes from the Odyssey (1st half of the 19C). Giovanni De Min frescoed the *small drawing-room* with scenes from the Iliad in the 19C. Decorations in the dining-room, bedroom and dressing-room are also his work. There are interesting decorations from the 1st quarter of 18C in the drawing-room on the upper storey including a bas-relief of the Sacrifice of Isaac by Giovanni Bonazza, a marble group (Fall of the Rebel Angels) by Agostino Fasolato and frescos of the Four Seasons by Francesco Zugno.

Via S.Francesco: Several of the city's sights can be seen in the course of a walk along this street: The *Palazzo Capodivacca* (house No. 3) attached to the University (see above) has a Renaissance façade (1530). The wide arch of an imperial *Roman bridge* is to be seen in the pedestrian subway at the Riviera dei Ponti Romani. The Gothic *Palazzo Romanin-Jacur* (No. 9), where Dante stayed in 1306, stands on the left. Then, on the right comes the *Antenor monument* below an aedicule (1233) with four columns. The 15C *Palazzo Sala* (No.11) has frames around the portals and windows divided into diamond shapes. The battlemented *Palazzo degli Zabarella* (13/15C, No. 19), built by the Counts of Carrara, is crowned by corner towers. The early-16C *Palazzo Papafava* (No. 27) has Renaissance windows and fresco decorations.

Via Umberto I: This street leading from the old quarter to the Prato della Valle (see below) is lined by arcades in the W. The beautiful *Casa Olzignano* (No. 4), with a

Piazza Antenore

low façade in early-Renaissance style, is by Pietro Lombardo (1466). The residential tower and battlemented walls of the *Palazzo Capodilista* (No. 30) reveal that it dates from the 13C. In the drawing-room there are 18C frescos by Francesco Zugno.

3. Gates and fortifications

Porta Altinate (via Altinate): This, the oldest surviving city gate, stands in the E. of the old city centre. Originally 13C, it has been altered more than once.

Porta di Ponte Molino (via Dante): This gate at the end of the Via Dante has a massive tower. There were originally 14 gates in the city walls (14C) built by the Carrarese, but this, together with the adjoining *Ponte Molino* bridge, is the only one to have survived.

City wall: This fortification, some 10 km.

long, was built by the Venetians in the 1st half of the 16C after the siege of the city by Emperor Maximilian I in 1509. The city wall survives in good condition, and with its 20 bastions in the corners and along the sides it is one of the finest city walls in Europe. The two best gates are the *Porta S.Giovanni* in the W., which was built by Giovanni Maria Falconetto in 1528–30, and the Renaissance-style *Porta Venezia* (1519), another structure with a triumphal arch, on the *Ponte Portello*, a bridge over a canal in the NE of the city.

4. Public gardens

Giardini Pubblici: The Via Giotto divides the municipal park into a S. section containing the Cappella degli Scrovegni (see above) and a N. zone which includes the *monument* (1916) to *Giuseppe Mazzini* and a fragment of the 16C *Bastione della Gatta* (from which in 1509 the Paduans successfully fought off the attempts of Emperor Maximilian to capture the city with battering engines and scaling equipment).

Orto Botanico: The *Botanical Garden,* laid out with concentric paths in 1545–54 to the designs of Andrea Moroni, is the oldest in Europe. The Mediterranean and exotic plants include some very old examples, such as the *Goethe palm* in the NE (surrounded by a greenhouse and studied by Goethe, poet and natural scientist, in 1788), an ancient *agnus castus* (1550), and a *Ginko* which is 65 ft. high, stands in the NW and dates from 1750.

Prato della Valle: In the Middle Ages, tournaments and fairs were held on the site of the devastated Roman Zairo theatre, which occupied almost 22 acres. In 1775/6, the Venetian governor Andrea Memmo gave orders that the square be symmetrically designed and the oval *Isola Memmia* be laid out. This tree-rimmed island park is surrounded by a canal lined on both sides by 78 *statues* (1775–1838) of famous people from Padua University, including a statue (1779) by Antonio Canova of the mathematician Giovanni Poleni.

5. Museums

Museo Civico/Pinacoteca (12 piazza del Santo): The *picture collection* in the upper storey of this building by Camillo Boito (1880) comprises 14–18C works (mostly Venetian artists), the best of which are: *Room I:* Giotto crucifix from the Cappella degli Scrovegni (*c.* 1317) and polyptychs by Francesco dei Franceschi and Francesco Squarcione. *Room II:* Venetian paintings (15/16C), some by Jacopo da Montagnana (triptych), Jacopo (Hermit Saint, Limbo) and Giovanni Bellini (Young Senator), Palma Vecchio (poetess), Giovanni Mansueti (Adoration of the Magi), Francesco Torbido (shepherd), Garofalo (Sacra Conversazione), works attributed to Giorgione (Leda with the swan, scene with shepherds), and a wall tapestry (15C equestrian scene) by Jourdain de Blaye from Arras. *Room III:* Renaissance paintings by Francesco Bassano (St.Jerome, Mocking of Christ) and Paolo Veronese (Last Supper). *Rooms IV* and *V:* 17C Veneto paintings, including some by Padovanino (Judith, Virgin Mary and Saints), Daniel Van Dyck (Martyrdom of St.Catherine), Pietro Vecchia (Holy Family) and Pietro Liberi (self-portrait). *Room VI:* Renaissance terracottas by Andrea Briosco (Virgin Mary weeping) and Guido Mazzoni (Pietà). *Room VII:* 16C Veneto paintings, including works by Domenico (Senator) and Jacopo Tintoretto (Crucifixion, Supper in the Pharisee's house), Paolo Veronese (Martyrdom of St.Primus and St.Felician) and Tiziano Aspetti (a satyr drinking). *Rooms VIII–X:* 18C Veneto paintings, some by Giovan Battista Piazzetta (Supper in Emmaus), Giuseppe Zais (landscapes), Antonio Diziani (four seasons) and Giovanni Battista Tiepolo (St.Paul minor healing a man possessed). Room VIII leads into the *Salette Rosse* with some more splendid paintings, including those by Albrecht Altdorfer (Beheading of John the Baptist), Jacopo Tintoretto (Descent of the Holy Ghost), Palma Giovane (Crucifixion), Francesco Maffei (Temptation of a Carthusian), Nicolò Grassi (Holy Family, Descent of the Holy Ghost), Francesco

S.Antonio, 'Miracle of the foot' by Titian

Guardi (Virgin Mary), Giovanni Battista (Christ on the Mount of Olives) and Giandomenico Tiepolo (Virgin Mary, St.Christopher), as well as valuable Venetian and Paduan *sculptures* (14–16C). Room X gives access to the *Collezione Emo-Capodilista* with its 14–18C paintings, including those by Leandro Bassano (Portrait of a Captain), Palma Giovane (Virgin Mary and Saints), Luca Giordano (Job) and Guido Reni (John the Evangelist).

Museo Civico/Sezione Archeologica (8 piazza Eremitani): The collections of the *Municipal Museum*, which date from the prehistoric and early historical periods, were recently moved to the (restored) buildings of the former Eremitani monastery of SS.Filippo e Giacomo (see above). They have been re-arranged and can now be viewed. There are Iron Age finds in the *New Cloister*. The *Sala Preromana* on the upper storey, near the old Chiostro Maggiore, has pre-Roman finds, including a terracotta vase (animal figures) and a bas relief (Veneto tribesman fighting a Gaul). Roman objects, including fine statues and a mosaic, are already on display in the *Sala Romana,* and the famous *tomb of the Volumnia family,* restored in Florence in 1985, is also to be housed there.

Museo di Scienze Archeologiche e d'Arte (7 piazza Capitaniato): A collection, clearly and instructively laid out, is to be found on the upper storey of the Liviano (see above). Apart from Greek and Roman bronzes, glasses, ceramics and terracottas, there are also *sculptures,* including a classical torso of Athena (4C BC), Attic stele fragments (4C BC), and busts from the Roman imperial period. Renaissance items include a wax model by Donatello and statues in stucco by Bartolomeo Ammannati.

Customs and public events
The *Festa di S.Antonio* is attended by thousands of pilgrims on 13 June every year. In the two preceding weeks, an international *fair* is held on the grounds of the 'Fiera dei Campioni' (via Nicolò Tom-

maseo). The *festival weeks* (September/October) of the Teatro Verdi, and the *Biennial Art Festival of the Three Veneti,* should also be mentioned.

Also worth seeing: The modern *Santuario S.Antonio* (in the Arcella district) includes the medieval monk's cell where St.Antony died on 13 June 1321.

Environs: Camposampiero (19 km. N.): The medieval *Santuario del Noce* was built on the site of a walnut tree under which St.Antony used to preach. Inside there are wall frescos (Life of St.Antony of Padua and Franciscan Saints, 16C) and an apse painting (St.Antony's sermon). Stairs lead from the right aisle of the modern *church of SS.Giovanni e Antonio* (1922) up to the cell where St.Antony lay ill before he was taken to Arcella (see above). To the left of the altar is a painting of St.Antony of Padua signed by Andrea da Murano (1486).

Cittadella (29 km. N.): This little town built on an elliptical ground plan stands in a dominating position on a strategically important crossroads. Hence its medieval *town wall,* which is 41 ft. high and some 1.5 km. long and has 32 well-preserved rectangular fortified towers, a Romanesque round-arched frieze under the former battlements, and four three-arched early-Gothic town gates. The *Torre di Malta,* a massive tower (1251/2), was built here under Ezzelino III da Romano. In the sacristy of the late-18C classical *parish church* by Ottavio Bertotti Scamozzi there are paintings by Jacopo Bassano (Supper in Emmaus) and Palma Giovane (Flagellation of Christ).

Noventa Padovana (8 km. E.): This collection of villas is today to be found near the triangle of autostrade called Padova Est. It formerly enjoyed a quiet location not far from the Brenta.

Piazzola sul Brenta (17 km. NW): The *Villa Contarini-Simes* was probably built by Palladio in 1545/6. Its grand central section was redesigned in baroque style in the 17C and the two wings were added at the same time (wings are decorated with

S.Antonio, St.Antony by Donatello

Cittadella (Padua), town walls

balustrades and statues). Some of the 25 rooms have frescos in the manner of Giulio Romano and Paolo Veronese. The library, the art gallery and the two concert halls bear witness to the client's artistic tastes.

Piombino Dese (27 km. NE): The distinguishing feature of the *Villa Cornaro* by Palladio (1553) is its two-storeyed portico, with Ionic columns in the lower loggia and Corinthian columns in the upper. Inside there are 18C frescos and stuccoes.

S.Pelagio (11 km. S.): The massive battlemented fortified tower of the *Villa Zaborra* (1775) is from the previous structure, a medieval castle of *c.* 1300.

37025 Parona di Valpolicella

Verona   p.322☐B 6

S.Dionigi: This small 11C Romanesque church (restored) was rebuilt in the 14C and decorated with a *fresco* (Virgin Mary Enthroned with Saints, 1390). Jacopo and Paolo Ligozzi added other Mannerist wall paintings about a year later.

Villa Erbisti-Rossi: The villa and its large park occupy a hill near the church of S.Dionigi. Built in 1834, the villa is a large and lordly structure with a classical façade by Jacopo Mutinelli.

Also worth seeing: *S.Crescenziano* (12C–18C) with its Romanesque campanile. Nearby stands the 18C *Villa Zorzi* with a fine central colonnaded portico.

Environs: Arbizzano (2.5 km. N.): *Parish church* with Romanesque portal and 14C Gothic arch. Inside the church: octagonal 14C font, a 14C Pietà triptych in the sacristy and a marble slab with an 11C Crucifixion. The *Villa Zamboni* dates from the 2nd half of the 16C.

Negrar (7 km. N.): The *parish church* was rebuilt in classical style in 1807. The campanile, with its massive friezes of round arches and double windows, derives from the previous Romanesque baptismal church. Outside, an inscription cut in stone is dated 1166.

Pedemonte (4.5 km. NW): The *Villa Sarego-Boccoli* (*c.* 1569), built to plans by Palladio, has a portico with three wings, two storeys, and colossal rusticated Ionic columns in rustic style. The Romanesque *chapel of S.Sofia* has Gothic frescos (Crucifixion, Virgin Mary and Saints, 14C).

S.Anna d'Alfaedo (23 km. N.): The *town hall* contains a small *prehistoric museum* with numerous Stone Age tools, earthen vessels and weapons discovered in the caves near the *Ponte di Veia* (a natural rock bridge to the S).

37019 Peschiera del Garda

Verona   p.322□A 6

This area occupies that part of the S. shore of Lake Garda where the Mincio flows out of the lake. Pile dwellers lived here in prehistoric times. The Roman town of *Arilica* was enlarged into a naval port by Gaius Marius in the 1C BC. In contrast to the fortifications built by Berengar, the Scaligers and Ezzelino III da Romano, the Venetian *fortification* survives in good condition. The Austrians enlarged it into a town fortification after 1859. Today Peschiera del Garda is the southernmost of the tourist resorts on what is known as the *Riviera degli Olivi.*

Old quarter: The old quarter of the town is surrounded by canals and a *double ring of walls* 2 km. long and pentagonal in shape. Near the harbour stands the spacious *Piazza Betteloni.* The many military buildings call to mind the town's strategic importance. *S.Martino*, the parish church (piazza Ferdinando di Savoia), is documented since 1008. Redesigned in the 18C, it has a 16C Renaissance painting

Pieve di Cadore, Titian monument ▷

of the Deposition. Memorabilia of the Risorgimento and World War 1 are on display in the *Palazzina del Commando del Presidio*.

Environs: Castelnuovo del Garda (5 km. E.): The *parish church* has an octagonal ground plan and was rebuilt by Luigi Trezza in 1793–1830. Its 15C campanile survives from the previous medieval church. Four fine classical altars can be seen inside the church. The adjoining *fortified tower*, with its battlements, is all that survives of the medieval castle.

Cisano (11 km. N.): The classical baptismal church of *S.Maria* originates in previous buildings from the 8C, 11/12C and 14/15C. Campanile, choir, and the façade with 16C frescos of the Virgin Mary in its colonnaded portico, all come from the previous Romanesque structure.

Lazise (8 km. N.): The former *customs building* (16C) is in the tiny harbour square, along with the Romanesque *S.Nicolò*, which has 14C frescos inside and choir dating from 1595. The 14C *Scaligers' castle* (Villa Bernini-Buri) has five fortified towers and a tall keep with crenellations. A little way outside the town to the N. is the 19C *Villa Pergolana*.

Madonna del Fràssino (3 km. SW): The 16C pilgrimage church of the *Santuario della Madonna del Fràssino* (restored in 1910) has a portico with 17C frescos. The single-aisled interior is enhanced by 10 side chapels with Renaissance altarpieces (some by Paolo Farinati). The choir has choir stalls dating from 1652 and frescos of the eucharistic miracles (2nd half of 17C) by Bernardino Muttoni the younger. The high altar dates from 1781. The ornately stuccoed chapel of the Virgin Mary has paintings by Farinati of the Franciscan Saints interceding (1560). 24 lunette frescos (17C) of the Life of St.Francis of Assisi can be seen in the monastery *cloister*.

Pieve di Cadore, parish church, painting by Titian

32044 Pieve di Cadore

Belluno   p.320☐H 2

The main town of the Cadore district, it was formerly a Roman settlement. In the Middle Ages it gradually developed into a small town and was ruled by the patriarchs of Aquileia (11C–14C). Its first constitution dates from 1388. It voluntarily submitted to the supremacy of Venice in 1420, and supplied that maritime republic with long beams for building houses and ships. The Vecellio family of artists came from here. *Titian*, their most famous son, had a decisive influence on the development of Venetian painting. The town lies in charming countryside near the *Lago di Pieve di Cadore*, a dammed reservoir, and is surrounded by wooded slopes and the southern Dolomite peaks. It is a popular resort both for summer holidays and winter sports.

Parish church: Built in neoclassical style in 1814–19 to the plans of Domenico Schiavi. The eclectic façade was added by Giovanni Miglioranza in 1876. The single-aisled interior is amply decorated with paintings. The best of these, in the chapel on the left, is the only *painting by Titian* (Madonna suckling the Child between Saints, *c.* 1561) to be found in Pieve di Cadore. The adjoining chapel of the rosary has a 16C painting (Virgin Mary of the Rosary) attributed to Giovan Battista Maganza the elder.

Town hall: This structure, built in 1447 and rebuilt in 1525, bears the self-adulatory name of *Palazzo della Magnifica Comunità Cadorina*. Standing in the central *Piazza di Tiziano*, with its bronze statue of Titian by Antonio dal Zotto (1880), it is overlooked by the battlemented municipal tower. A double staircase leads to the upper storey, which houses the *Municipal Museum* with its col-

Pieve di Cadore, Titian's birthplace

Vigo di Cadore (Pieve d.C.), S.Orsola

lection (ancient Veneti finds from the environs), and a small *picture gallery* (paintings by the Vecellio family).

Titian's birthplace: A modest 15C house (much restored), with a projecting roof, outdoor staircase and wooden balcony. There is some dispute as to whether his date of birth was 1477, 1487 or 1490. Today the building houses a small *museum* with letters in Titian's handwriting and the patent of nobility which Emperor Charles V presented to him on 13 May 1533.

Environs: Auronzo di Cadore (20 km. NE): The skiing resort of Auronzo lies on another dammed reservoir, the *Lago di S.Caterina*. *S.Giustina*, the single-aisled parish church in the Villagrande quarter was given its present neoclassical shape in 1772. The campanile (1436, restored in the 18C and 20C), which stands to one side, comes from the previous medieval

church, as do the panel and wall paintings by Giovanni De Min from Belluno (Coronation of the Virgin Mary, 19C).
Cibiana (14 km. SW): This beautifully located summer resort is known for its 'murale', the modern *wall paintings* on the houses. The rather isolated *parish church* (1852) is by Giuseppe Segusini from Feltre.
S.Nicola di Comélico (26 km. NE): This *parish church* (14–18C) has been altered several times. Inside, by the apse, there is a fresco cycle (Annunciation, Nativity, Adoration of the Shepherds, Adoration of the Magi, Saints, Prophets, and Symbols of the Evangelists; all 1492) by Giovanni Francesco da Tolmezzo.
Vigo di Cadore (16 km. NE): The *church of S.Orsola* (1344/5) is decorated with frescos from *c.* 1400 both on the outside (Virgin Mary and St.Christopher) and inside (Life of St.Ursula). The small *Oratorio S.Maria della Difesa* (1512), with frescos from the 16C and 18C, stands beside *S.Martino*, the parish church (1559), which has three paintings (Purification of the Temple, Jesus with the children, Holy Family with Saints who brought relief from the plague; all 1894) by Tommaso da Rin from Laggio. The medieval church of *S.Margherita* (*c.* 1300), surrounded by meadows, stands about 1 km. to the S. of the Laggio district of the town and provides a fine view of the surrounding countryside. Inside there is a 14/15C fresco cycle showing the life of the church's patron Saint.

30026 Portogruaro
Venezia   p.320□K 4

From the early Christian period onwards, the former port area of the nearby Roman town of *Concordia Julia* was within the area ruled by the patriarchs of Aquileia. It then joined Venice in 1420. Portogruaro assisted Venice in the struggle against imperial troops of the League of Cambrai. As a reward, the Serenissima awarded Portogruaro certain trading privileges which led to a period of economic prosperity in the town in the 16&17C. The old quarter

Portogruaro, Palazzo Comunale

of the town, with its numerous *houses with loggias* (15/16C), extends along both sides of the little river Lémene. Three *town gates* from the 13C/16C, and also the moats, still survive from the former town fortifications.

Duomo: This early-18C episcopal church stands on the site of a previous Romanesque structure. The slender *campanile*, with its triple windows, octagonal superstructure and spire, dates from the earlier period. A fine 14C *marble relief* of the Virgin Mary can be seen on the outer wall of the apse. Inside (nave and two aisles) there are *altarpieces* by the Renaissance painters Giovanni di Martino (Presentation in the Temple, 1515) and Pomponio Amalteo (Sacra Conversazione, 1583), and also by the baroque artists Palma Giovane (Resurrection) and Gregorio Lazzarini (Last Supper).

Palazzo Comunale: The originally Gothic *town hall* (restored 1890) was enlarged in the 16C. It has a battlemented brick façade of two storeys, fine windows and an external staircase built at an angle. Five marble blocks with large sculpted busts, which were part of a former bridge across the Lémene, decorate the façade. A *Renaissance fountain* (1494) with bronze cranes stands on the left of the façade.

Museo Concordiese (22 via del Seminario): This museum was founded in 1887 and concentrates on ancient and early medieval finds from *Concordia Sagittaria* (see Environs). *Entrance hall:* Tomb stele of Marcus Acutius Noetus, fragments of architectural sculpture from the 1C AD, and a classical *altar tomb substructure* with a medieval relief (Virgin Mary Enthroned with half figures of Saints, 1314). *Main room:* More tomb urns, tomb stele, tomb aedicules, and altar tombs, from the Roman imperial period. Fragments of sculptures (1/2C AD). A mosaic discovered in 1958 (Three Graces, 2/3C AD). The *antiquarium* is on the upper storey. *Room I:* Roman coins, weights and sculptures (1/2C AD), including a head of Flora. *Room II:* Glass cases with more sculpture fragments and small art objects, including a fine bronze group (Diana the hunter, 3C AD), and a very fine and historically important *early-Christian glass bowl* (Daniel in the Lions' Den, 4C).

Also worth seeing: The best of the Renaissance palazzi in the Via Seminario is the *Casa Fabrici* (No. 10), although much of the structure is actually Romanesque. Fine wall frescos (Prometheus stealing fire, Apollo and Muses, shepherds and putti; 16C) on the upper storey.

In the same street is the church of *S.Cristoforo* with choir frescos (Virgin Mary with St.Christopher and St.Roch, 1532) by Pomponio Amalteo.

Environs: Caorle (26 km. S.): This former port on the N. Adriatic coast was an episcopal seat after 1000. Today it is only a fishing village and seaside resort. The *brick cathedral,* begun in 1038, is built in a style very like that seen in the churches in Ravenna. Byzantine bas reliefs (St.William of Toulouse and St.Agathonicus, 12C) flank the main portal. The round Romanesque campanile, which has a little loggia half way up, also betrays Byzantine influence. Inside, the basilica has a nave and two aisles.

Cessalto (16 km. SW): After the shell of the *Villa Giacomini* (formerly known as Emo Capodilista) had been completed in the 3rd quarter of the 16C, Giovanni Antonio Fasolo and Giovanni Battista Zelotti, two pupils of Veronese, painted frescos (Roman legend) inside the building. The *Villa Zeno* (Donegal), built to plans by Palladio, is in need of restoration.

Concordia Sagittaria (2.5 km. S.): This military colony founded by Julius Caesar

Concordia Sagittaria (Portogruaro), brick basilica

flourished until the 4C AD. The visitor is reminded of this colony by the three-arched *Roman bridge* near the cemetery, which was built by order of Marcus Acilius Eudamus in the 2C AD, and also by the *early Christian tombs* near the Gothic *brick basilica* (rebuilt in 1466). Work on uncovering the tombs began in 1950. A fragment of a fresco of Christ between Angels survives in the portico of the Romanesque *baptistery*, which is built on a Greek cross and has 11–14C frescos. This baptistery and the Romanesque campanile both survive from the building which preceded the basilica.

Summaga (3 km. W.): The 13C parish church of *S.Maria Assunta* has apse frescos of the Virgin Mary in a mandorla, Angels and Prophets, Christ with the Apostles, Wise and Foolish Virgins (all *c*. 1210–20). The early-Romanesque *chapel of the martyrs*, decorated with 11C frescos, stands at the end of the right aisle. Beside the church are the uncovered remains of a former Benedictine monastery (10/11C).

31054 Possagno

Treviso   p.323☐F 4

Birthplace of Antonio Canova, the famous sculptor (1757–1822).

Tempio Canoviano (S.Trinità church): Built by G.A. Selva and A.Diedo in 1819–32 as a gift from Canova to his native town. The exterior is a combination of the Pantheon in Rome and the Parthenon in Athens, the main structure being circular with a portico with two rows of Doric columns. The frieze has seven metopes with reliefs by Canova (the remaining 20 panels are empty). The height of the interior is equal to the diameter of the dome (about 90 ft.). The dome is coffered like the Pantheon, and the chapel niches have been cut out of the

Concordia Sagittaria (Portogruaro), baptistery (left), Possagno, Tempio Canoviano (right)

Possagno, Canova's house

walls which are about 13 ft. thick. The *1st chapel* on the right has a painting by Luca Giordano and beside this are Canova's plaster models for the metope reliefs (see above). The *3rd chapel* has a 17C altarpiece by Palma Giovane. There is a *Lamentation* (1797–9) by Canova in the main chapel. In the chapel to the left of this is the *artist's tomb* (the sarcophagus is his own work) and underneath, on the right, there is a self-portrait by Canova (1812).

Canova Museum (next to the house in which he was born): Built in 1834–6. The exhibits include: models (mostly clay and plaster) for the marble originals, plaster casts of originals and some original sculptures. Some individual objects include the plaster model of *Daedalus and Icarus*, designs for *Amor and Psyche* and an original model for the recumbent figure of Pauline Bonaparte.

His work tools and his death mask are in the house where he was born.

35100 Praglia

Padova   p.322□E 6

The Benedictine abbey stands in charming countryside on the N. fringe of the Euganean hills. It was founded in 1080 under its former name of *Pratalia*, and its status as an abbey was confirmed in 1232 by Emperor Frederick II, who presented it with lands. From 1448 onwards the monastery was part of the Cassinese Congregation of S. Giustina in Padua. It was completely redesigned in Renaissance style in *c.* 1460–1520. Secularized under Napoleon in 1810, it returned to the Benedictines in 1904. 'The Small World of Our Time', the realistic, humorous novel by Antonio Fogazzaro, a writer from Vicenza (1842–1911), made Praglia known to the European public around 1900. The abbey is internationally significant today because of its *book restoration workshops* where precious manuscripts,

Possagno, Canova's house

early printed works and valuable books are carefully repaired and restored.

Monastery church of S.Maria dell' Assunta: An external staircase leads up to a rusticated platform at a height of 20 ft., on which the monastery church was built in Venetian Renaissance style in 1490–1548 to plans by Tullio Lombardi. The *façade* has round windows, three portals with Ionic aedicule frames, and a curving gable above. The *campanile* (1300), which has survived from the previous medieval structure, is articulated by pilaster strips and friezes of round arches. There are double arches around the bell chamber. The crenellation is 19C.
The *interior* was restored in 1963. Walls are white, while the architectural elements are light grey. Ionic pilasters on tall pedestals articulate the area to form a nave and two aisles, and side chapels complement the scene. Above the crossing of the barrel-vaulted nave there is a tall dome

(1550) with drum and *frescos* (Instruments of the Passion, Christ's Nativity and Childhood, Evangelists) by Giovanni Battista Zelotti from Verona. The choir has further frescos by Zelotti (Fathers of the Church) and Domenico Campagnola (Ascension), and good *choir stalls* (1564) by Giovanni Fiorentino. A 14C painted altar crucifix in the manner of Giotto is to be seen in the sanctuary. The first side chapel on the left leads into the sacristy anteroom with paintings (monastery benefactors, 1572) by Palma Giovane. This adjoins the *sacristy* (c. 1500), with paintings by Dario Varotari (Nativity of the Virgin Mary), Pietro Liberi (St.Scholastica, St.Mary Magdalene; both 17C), and a pupil of Jacopo Bassano (Entombment, late 16C).

Monastery buildings: This extensive complex can be visited in the afternoons in the company of a monk. Its buildings are grouped around three cloisters:

◁ *Praglia, monastery cloister*

Praglia, Benedictine abbey 1 Main portal **2** Nave **3** Crossing **4** Choir and sanctuary **5** Altarpiece (Holy Family, 1648) by Alessandro Varotari **6** Anteroom to sacristy **7** Sacristy **8** Altarpiece (Keys delivered to St.Peter, 16C) by Giovanni Battista Zelotti **9** Altarpiece (Virgin Mary, John the Baptist and Saints, 1560) by Antonio Badile **10** Chapel of St.Benedict with altarpiece (St.Benedict of Nursia) by Palma Giovane **11** Chapel of St.Laurence with altarpiece (St.Laurence, 1574) by Camillo Ballini **12** Chapel of the Holy Cross with Flemish wooden crucifix (18C) by Michael Bertens **13** Chapel of St.Cajetan with altarpiece (St.Cajetan and Saints, 1717) by Francesco Zanella **14** Chapel of St.Antony with altarpiece (St.Antony Abbot, 16C) by Dario Varotari **15** Chapel of St.Justina with altarpiece (St.Justina, 1632) by Luca Longhi **16** Chapel of St.Sebastian with altarpiece (St.Sebastian, 1575) by D.Varotari **17** Chapel of the Rosary with paintings by Luca Longhi (Presentation in the Temple) and Giovan Battista Bissoni (Mysteries of the Rosary, 1634) **18** Chapel of St.Stephen with altarpiece (St.Stephen, 1572) by D.Varotari **19** Chapel of St.Nicholas with altarpiece (St.Nicholas of Bari, 16C) by Domenico Campagnola **20** Monastery porch **21** Botanical garden **22** Colonnaded courtyard **23** Library (former calidarium) **24** Double cloister with enclosure buildings **25** Monks' refectory **26** Lay brothers' refectory **27** Cells **28** Farmyard and baroque fountain with colonnaded aedicule (1726)

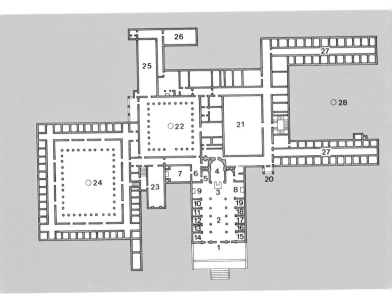

Praglia, S.Maria dell'Assunta

Chiostro Botanico (former herb garden, 15C), *Chiostro Pensile* and *Chiostro Doppio* (two storeys, with portico and loggia, 1460). To the W. is the *Chiostro Rustico*, a farmyard. The Chiostro Pensile (1495), with its fine colonnaded ambulatory and a fountain in the middle of the courtyard, is adjoined in the N. by the *library*, which has a relief of the Virgin Mary (c. 1600), in the W. by the *chapterhouse with 16C frescos* by Girolamo de' Santo (Entombment), Domenico Campagnola and Luca Longhi (Saints), and in the S. by the early-Renaissance *monks' refectory*. The portal of the latter building has splendid reliefs and inlay work, and 16C Lombard wash basins at the sides. The tunnel-vaulted interior of the refectory has carved baroque benches (1726–30) by Bartolomeo Biasi, a Crucifixion fresco (c. 1495) by Bartolomeo Montagna above the abbot's chair, and nine paintings (Old and New Testament scenes) by Giovanni Battista Zelotti. From the Chiostro Botanico,

where there are *book restoration workshops,* a monumental double staircase (1712) leads to the upper storey. In the S. of the latter is the *abbot's dwelling* (with frescos by Pozzoserrato and Dario Varotari), adjoined by the Sala degli Stucchi, which has a small *picture collection* (works by Lorenzo Lotto and Palma Giovane).

Environs: Abano Terme (4 km.E.): The *Aquae Patavinae* thermal springs were prized by the ancient Romans for their curative powers. The chief spring is the *Sorgente Montirone*, with a temperature of 87°C (mud treatments). The springs indicate the Euganean hills are volcanic in origin. The archpriests' church of *S.Lorenzo*, founded in 971 and altered several times, has a fine campanile with a Romanesque lower storey and brick upper storeys (1314) decorated with pilaster strips, arched friezes, double arches in the bell chamber, and a spire.
Bresseo (3 km. SE): The 17C *Villa*

Cavalli-Lugli, a building on a grand scale, had a church added to it in 1740. Inside there are paintings by Faustino Bocchi (known as Bamboccio) from Brescia.

Montecchio di Selvazzano (6 km. NE): The *Villa Emo Capodilista* (2nd half of 16C) by Dario Varotari, the painter and architect from Verona, is one of the most originally designed villas in the Veneto. This square building has four façades identically articulated. The two upper storeys of the façades have five-arched loggias with imaginative pediments.

Despite some radical alterations, the 11C *Castello,* with its tall keep and four corner towers, has retained many of its medieval fortifications.

Montegrotto Terme (8.5 km. SE): This much-frequented spa derives its name from the Latin *Mons Aegrotorum,* which may be roughly translated 'Mountain of the Sick'. The *Parco Archeologico* contains the remains of a small theatre, and thermal baths from the Roman imperial period. The archpriests' church of *S.Pietro* was rebuilt in 1724. Its Romanesque campanile, which has rows of three arches in its bell chamber, survives from the previous medieval church.

Monteortone (3.5 km. E.): The pilgrimage church of *Santuario della Madonna della Salute* (1435–97) has a fine campanile. The church interior is partly Gothic and partly early Renaissance in style. In the sacristy there are some splendid frescos by Jacopo da Montagnana (Assumption, Fathers of the Church, Discovery of the Miraculous Image by the soldier Pietro Falco, Meeting at the Golden Gate, Nativity of the Virgin Mary; all 1497). The elegant Renaissance high altar houses a miraculous image of the Virgin Mary and has a superstructure in the form of a small temple.

Torreglia (5 km. S.): A village with a distillery, it is worth visiting to see the 18C *Virgin Mary column* by Francesco Rizzi, the *Trattoria Ballotta* (1605) which is the oldest surviving inn in the Euganean hills, and the nearby 16C *Villa dei Vescovi-Olcese* (fraz. Luvigliano) which has an elegant staircase and three façades with Doric columns in their loggias.

45100 Rovigo

Rovigo, first mentioned in 838, is the main town of *Polesine,* the fertile alluvial territory between the Adige and the Po. *Rhodigo* was fortified in the 10C because

Rovigo, Torre Mozza

of Magyar invasions. At the same time the episcopal seat was transferred from Adria (q.v.). The town was chiefly under the rule of the Este from Ferrara from 1002 until it came under the supremacy of the republic of Venice in favourable contractual conditions in 1482.

Religious buildings

Duomo S.Stefano (piazza del Duomo): Occupies the site of previous medieval structures from the 10/15C. Rebuilt in baroque style to the plans of Girolamo Frigimelica in 1696; the façade is unfinished. The single-aisled *interior* is enhanced by three interconnected chapels on each side, concluded with a polygonal choir in the SE. Decorations include an ornate 16C bronze *Easter candlestick* probably by Desiderio da Firenze, decorated with putti, fauns, goats' heads, masks, Sirens and Harpies. Small figures (1718) of the risen Christ, and of the Virtues

(Fides and Spes) are by Antonio Corradini. On the altar in the left transept there is a painting of the risen Christ and Saints by Palma Giovane. The large apse painting of Pope Stephen baptizing St.Lucilla (1794) is by the Sicilian artist Tommaso Sciacca.

Beata Vergine del Soccorso (piazza XX Settembre): The church of the Vergine del Soccorso is better known as 'La Rotunda'. Built 1594–1602 to plans by Francesco Zamberlan, it has an octagonal ground plan. Outside, it is without ornament, but is surrounded by a Doric colonnaded passage. The *brick campanile* (1655 and 185 ft. high) was built to the designs of Baldassare Longhena and has a domed octagonal lantern. The *church interior* is surprisingly richly decorated. The high altar, designed by Zamberlan, has a tempietto, a miraculous image of the Madonna del Soccorso and elegant statues (Crucifixion, Angels and Saints; 1607). The walls are completely covered with large paint-

Arquà Polesine, Rovigo, castle (left), Rovigo, Beata Vergine del Soccorso

Victor Emmanuel monument

ings, such as those by Francesco Maffei (Coronation of the Virgin Mary, Virgin Mary with Benedetto Civran, Presentation of the Virgin Mary in the Temple, Virgin Mary with Sante Moro; all mid-17C), Antonio Zanchi (Virgin Mary with Pietro Loredan, 1673; Virgin Mary with Almorà Dolfin, 1683), and Tiberio Tinelli (Virgin Mary with Luigi Morosini, 1636).

S.Francesco (via Silvestri): Parts of the right transept have survived from this originally Gothic church (14/15C) which was rebuilt in the 19C. The *campanile* dates from 1520. Eight interconnected side chapels in the single-aisled interior have altarpieces by Domenico Panetti (Virgin Mary between the Apostles Peter and Andrew), Pietro Antonio Novelli (Presentation of Jesus in the Temple, 1759) and Girolamo da Carpi (St.Francis of Assisi). The 3rd chapel on the left has *Renaissance sculptures* (Pietà and Saints) thought to be by Tullio Lombardo from Tessin.

Secular buildings

Castello (piazza Matteotti): The grounds of the 10C medieval castle today form the *Giardino Pubblico* municipal park. Apart from parts of walls, all that survives of the castle is two defensive towers. The S. tower, the *Torre Donà* is among the highest medieval towers in Italy and leans slightly, as does the N. *Torre Mozza* which is joined to a fragment of the old castle wall which has a round-arched frieze.

Municipio (piazza Victor Emmanuel II): The trapezoidal *Piazza Vittorio Emanuele II* has a monument (1881) to the king and a column (1519) of Istrian marble crowned by the lion of St.Mark (1881). The piazza's NW side is dominated by the clock tower (1763) and by the façade of the *Palazzo del Municipio*, the town hall, which dates from the 16/18C. This façade has a two-arched portico, known as the *Loggia dei Notai*, on the ground floor, with a nine-arched 10C loggia in the piano nobile. A central niche in the latter loggia has a statue of the Virgin Mary by Giulio Mauro (1590). There is a Pietà by Francesco Maffei inside the town hall.

Palazzo Angeli (28 via Angeli): Emperor Franz I of Austria and Giusepe Garibaldi both stayed in this patrician's house by Francesco Schiavi (1780). Giovanni Battista Canal painted mythical and symbolic frescos (Apollo and Muses, Orpheus and Eurydice, Ixion and Hera) in the drawing-room.

Palazzo Roncalli (piazza Vittorio Emanuele II): This patricians' palace (1555), a scarcely-known late work by Michele Sanmicheli, is part of the row of houses which includes the town hall (see above). The *façade* is splendid, with a rusticated portico on the ground floor where the patrician family conducted business, and tall round-arched windows, fluted Ionic pilasters and balustrade parapets, on the upper storeys.

Palazzo Roverella (piazza Vittorio Emanuele II): Probably built to the plans of Biagio Rossetti. The façade of this tall

Pinacoteca dei Concordi, 'Joseph and Potiphar's Wife' by Gerolamo Forabosco

palazzo (15/16C) has a loggia, and clearly indicates the interior divisions: ground floor, upper storey and two mezzanines. Parts of the courtyard, the columns and pilasters of the round-arched portico, survive unaltered from the 15C.

Porta S.Bartolo (piazza Merlin): The S. *town gate,* built in 1482–6 after Rovigo joined Venice, is the only good remnant of the former pentagonal town walls. This single-arched brick structure is reinforced with a double crenellation. A richly decorated 16C *coat-of-arms* of the Donà delle Rose family can be seen on the right side.

Museums

Pinacoteca dei Concordi (piazza Vittorio Emanuele II): The *Palazzo dell'-Accademia dei Concordi* (1814) by Sante Baseggio houses a library on the ground floor and, on the upper storeys, an art

gallery with works by members of the artists' and scholars' association, which was founded by Gaspare Campo and bears his name. Donations by Casilini, Campanari, Gobbetti and Silvestri made the *picture gallery* one of the finest in the Veneto; today only about a quarter of its rich collection is on display. *Room I:* 15C Venetian artists, including Giovanni Bellini (Virgin Mary, *c.* 1480) and Quirizio da Murano (St.Lucy and six legends, 1462). *Room II:* 16C Venetian artists, including Palma Vecchio (Sacra Conversazione, *c.* 1520), Domenico Capriolo (scholar's portrait) and Palma Giovane (Passover feast). *Room III:* 15/16C artists from Verona and Ferrara, including Sebastiano Filippi (St.Paul), Dosso and Battista Dossi (Virgin Mary and Saints), Girolamo da Carpi (St.Lucy, St.Agatha, Benedict of Nursia and Bartholomew) and Mabuse (Venus with the looking-glass). *Room IV:* 17C Venetian artists, among them Sebastiano Mazzoni (Death of Cleopatra, Lot and his daughters, Finding of Moses) and Luca Giordano (Odysseus and Calypso). *Room V:* 18C Venetian artists, including Giovan Battista Pittoni (St.Joseph with the Christ Child, Nativity, Visitation) and Giovanni Battista Piazzetta (St.Francis of Paola). *Room VI:* Portraits of well-known members of the Accademia dei Concordi by 18C Venetian artists including Pittoni (Cardinal Roverella) and Piazzetta (Gaspare Campo, Celio Rodigino), Giovanni Battista Tiepolo (Antonio Riccoboni), Alessandro Longhi (Giulio Contarini da Mula) and Rosalba Carriera (self-portrait). Other rooms: The *Sala degli Arazzi,* with four Flemish tapestries (Petrarch's Triumphs of Time, Death, Love and Fame; all early 17C). The *Sala di Archeologica* has exhibits of Egyptian and Roman art and a collection of coins and medals. The splendid *library* with over 140,000 volumes has sumptuous manuscripts and early printed works,

including the paupers' bible, the *Libro di Ruth* (c. 1390), which is written in Paduan dialect and has 344 miniatures painted in the manner of Jacopo Avanzo and Giusto de'Menabuoi.

Museo Silvestriano (89 viale Tre Martiri): The modern Episcopal Seminary is on the road to Adria (q.v.). It houses the *Pinacoteca del Seminario* with the Camillo Silvestri collection (prior application required), which is composed mainly of paintings by 17/18C Veneto painters, including Palma Giovane (Christ's Passion), Bernardo Strozzi (Tribute to Caesar), Luca Giordano (Venus and Psyche, Fortuna), Sebastiano Bombelli (portraits of three advocates), Giovan Battista Piazzetta (John the Baptist), Gaspare Diziani (Triumph of Diana), Pietro Longhi (Shepherd Boy) and Giuseppe Zais (Landscapes). Pre-Roman and Romano-Veneti finds from the excavations at Bor-

Rovigo, Torre Donà

Fiesso Umbertiano (Rovigo), parish church

sea and Adria (q.v.) are to be seen in the small archaeological department.

Also worth seeing: The church of *S.Bartolomeo* (piazza S.Bartolo) lies S. of the old town. A 15C brick building with a fine 16C campanile, it is part of the Olivetan monastery (founded 1255), whose Renaissance cloister was probably built to a design by Biagio Rossetti, an architect from Ferrara. The *Teatro Sociale* (piazza Garibaldi), with a classical façade (1818/19) by Sante Baseggio, was redesigned inside after a fire in 1904.

Environs: Arquà Polésine (9.45 km. SW): This town existed in Roman times under the name of *Arquatum.* The 13C *Este castle* fortifications have been altered several times. The 19C *parish church* has a portal and frieze fragments on the right which have survived from the previous 16/17C building. Inside, the apse painting

of St.Andrew (1789) is by Giovanni Battista Canal. 15C font.

Fiesso Umbertiano (26 km. SW): The *Palazzo Vendramin* (today the town hall) was built in the 18C to plans by Andrea Tirali and has a double external staircase and the original octagonal superstructure. Frescos attributed to Matia Bortoloni are found inside. Paintings by the Ferraran school decorate the inside of the *parish church* (1620), including the coffered ceiling (1691). To the left of the choir the gilded Renaissance altar retable has a painting of the Adoration of the Christ Child attributed to Garofalo.

Fratta Polésine (16 km. W.): This little town was founded anew in the Middle Ages on the site of a prehistoric village. In the 18C interior of the 16/17C *SS.Pietro e Paolo* parish church there are ceiling frescos by Francesco Zugno and late-baroque sculptures of saints by Pietro Baratta, Marino Groppelli, Tommaso

Polesella (Rovigo), Ca' Morosini

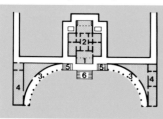

Fratta Polésine, Villa Badoer 1 Colonnaded portico **2** Drawing room **3** Colonnades **4** Domestic buildings **5** Steps at the sides **6** Central external staircase

Pietro Liberi (St.Anthony of Padua, *c.* 1670). The *Villa Badoer* (1556), with its Ionic portico, grand staircase and two domestic wings obscured by the colonnade, is by Andrea Palladio. His Villa Foscari in Malcontenta (q.v.) may be the model for the adjoining late-16C *Villa Bragadin.* **Polesella** (12 km.S.): The late-16C *Ca'Morosini* has an external staircase with frescos of putti in the manner of Giulio Romano, as well as other splendidly stuccoed rooms.
Raccano (13 km. S.): Like the larger neighbouring town of Polesella, this village is situated on the N. bank of the Po. Its small *parish church* houses quite a rarity in the form of a terracotta altar polyptych of the Virgin Mary and Saints (15C) with a multicoloured frame.

Bonazza, Giovanni Marchiori and Giovanni Maria Morlaiter. The transept has altarpieces by Mattia Bortoloni (Adoration of the Christ-child, 1734/5) and

37010 S.Ambrogio di Valpolicella
Verona p.322☐B 5

This little town in the *Valpolicella Classico* area is famous both for its 'Recioto della Valpolicella', a red wine pressed from partly dried grapes, and for its 'Rosso di Verona', a red marble whose qualities are celebrated in the *marble fair* held in the Villa Bassani in September of each year. The *Pieve di S.Giorgio* was important under the Lombard period up until the high Middle Ages and occupies a site on a hill, 1,230 ft. up, just N. of S.Ambrogio and near the S.Giorgio di Valpolicella

district of the town. The hill has been inhabited since pre-Roman times.

S.Giorgio: This late-11C basilica of light-coloured stone has an E. choir with three apses, and another choir apse in the W. (now breached by the neo-Gothic portal) and hence is one of the few examples in Italy of those churches with two choirs which were common in Germany in the Carolingian and Ottonian periods. The low aisles and clerestory walls apparent from outside suggest the basilican form of the interior. The 13C Romanesque *campanile* is massive. The interior has round-arched arcades, Romanesque *frescos* (Christ in Judgement in a mandorla, the four beasts of the Apocalypse, and Saints; early 12C) in the W. apse, and a *ciborium* dating from 712 at the high altar. The latter, which was reconstructed in 1923 from fragments found in the 12C *cloister* adjoining the church in the S., is decorated with early Christian and Lombard motifs. The altar, which is supported on columns, bears an inscription stating that a Master Ursus and his pupils Juvinatinus and Juvianus made it.

Environs: Fumane (8 km. E.): This village lying amidst vine-covered slopes flourished under the Scaligers in the 14C.

The restored *Villa della Torre* (c. 1558) is thought to be by Michele Sanmicheli or Giulio Romano. The square courtyard with arcades is entered through two round-arched portals in the S. and N. The house includes parts of a previous building, as can be seen from the remains of Romanesque frescos inside. Rooms have imaginatively designed baroque fireplaces. The octagonal private chapel (16C) is by Sanmicheli. The park surrounding the villa is enlivened by steps, bridges and fountains. The *Pieve S.Maria di Degnano,* mentioned in 801, stands in charming countryside near to Fumane (Vaio district). It has a squat Romanesque campanile and, inside, early-18C frescos by Paolo Lozzi. The 15C *Villa Selle,* enlarged in the 18C, is also near Fumane (Volta district). 18C attic, portico and a loggia extending the entire width of the façade.

Gargagnago (3 km. E.): The *village school* is housed in a rustic 14C palazzo which looks to be Romanesque; it has a portico and loggia. The *Villa Serego Alighieri* (altered several times), which Dante's son Pietro Alighieri built for himself shortly before 1300, stands in a park a little way outside the town. The chapel is a 17C addition.

Ponton (2.5 km. W.): The little-known *Villa Nichesola* (16C) has good decorations by Paolo Farinati, architect, wood-carver and painter from Verona.

S.Floriano (6.5 km. E.): The tufa façade of the 12C *Pieve di S.Floriano* includes some structural elements from the previous Carolingian church which was itself built above the remains of a heathen temple. More such spoils are to be found on the campanile which is decorated with multicoloured layers of limestone, brick and tufa, with double arches around the bell chamber. An elegant Renaissance portico graces the right side of the church. Inside there are a nave, two aisles, a rebuilt choir section, and ponderous baroque decorations dating from 1743.

S.Pietro in Cariano (4.5 km. E.): The *Piazza del Municipio* in this picturesque little town is dominated by the façade of the town hall, which is decorated with the coats-of-arms of the 'Vicari' who formerly resided here. The park of the *Villa Acquistapace-Dettoni* (1562) adjoins the Piazza S.Giuseppe lying to the SW. The design for this park may be based on a design by Palladio. The *Villa Buri-Forapan* (c. 1490) outside the little town has an elegant portico in front of its charming two-storeyed façade. Decorative frescos are early 16C. There are classical statues in the interior of the *Villa Saibante-Monga* (1630), and also in the garden. The drawing-room has frescos by Jacopo Ligozzi.

Volargne (5 km. NW): In this little village stands the 15C *Villa del Bene*—one of the best Renaissance villas in the province of Verona—enlarged by Michele Sanmicheli in 1551. A splendid entrance portal opens into the small courtyard; the façade has a portico and loggia (15C). 16C frescos by Domenico Brusasorci and Giovanni Caroto decorate the loggia and the rooms which are open to the public.

36015 Schio

Vicenza   p.322□D 5

This small town lies at the S. edge of the *Little Dolomites,* which consist of *Monte Pasubio* (7,335 ft.), *Monte Novegno* (5,080 ft.) and *Monte Summano* (4,120 ft.). It was first mentioned in 975 under the name of *Schledum.* The textile industry, which is still of importance today, developed in the 12–14C under the rule of the Scaligers and Visconti. The town joined Venice in 1406. The only parts of the old town centre to have survived 19&20C modernization are to be found near the cathedral and castle.

Duomo S.Pietro (piazza Rossi): This cathedral (1740–2) by Giovanni Miazzi is built on a high platform. Its impressive Corinthian *portico* was added in 1805–19. The building was completed when Antonio Negrin converted the former side chapels into aisles in 1877–9. The imposing appearance created by the cathedral as a whole is further enhanced by the monumental *double staircase* outside the church. The severely classical *interior* has a nave, two aisles and 19C frescos by Valentino Puppin. In the sacristy there is

Schio, Duomo S.Pietro

a painting by Palma Vecchio (Virgin Mary between St.Catherine of Siena and John the Baptist, 1520).

S.Francesco (via Leonardo da Vinci): This late-Gothic church (1436) by Fra Vincenzo da Cori belonged to a mendicant order. Along with its slender 16C *campanile*, it stands near to the *Grumi dei Frati* park where there are two geologically interesting sink-holes. The light round-arched portico in the sober façade leads into the tunnel-vaulted interior which has two aisles. Between the roof beams there are *frescos* (Life of St.Francis of Assisi) by Francesco Verla. The *sgraffito* (St.Catherine of Siena) above the sacristy portal and the paintings (Life of St.Catherine, 1512) at the 3rd altar in the side aisle, are also by Verla. The side aisle was formed in 1520–2 by joining the former side chapels. The choir has good monks' choir stalls (1509) by Bernardinus de Ronchius from Vicenza, and two paintings (Virgin

Mary and Saints, Franciscan martyrs, 17C) by Francesco Maffei.

Environs: Caldogno (17 km. SE): The *Villa Caldogno Pagello* (1570) is attributed to Palladio. It has a wide façade with a slight central projection topped by a pediment with a lozenge-shaped window of original design. Three rusticated round arches lead into the entrance hall. The rooms are decorated with 16C frescos by Giovanni Antonio Fasolo, Giovanni Battista Zelotti and Giulio Carpioni. Wall paintings in the drawing room show groups of people wearing the dress of the time.

Dueville (22 km. SE): The *Villa Monza* (now the town hall) in the tree-lined Piazza was built in 1715 to plans by Francesco Muttoni. It is decorated with statues from Marinali's workshop. The *Villa da Porto da Schio* in Palladian style stands in the S. of the town. The imposing external staircase and the tall portico with its colossal Ionic columns and pediment topped by a statue have been untouched by 19C conversions.

Lugo di Vicenza (18 km. E.): The *Villa Godi-Malinverni* (1537) is the first work by Palladio. The loggia and the ten rooms have frescos by Giovanni Battista Zelotti, Gualtiero Campagnola and Bergognone. The rooms also contain period furniture, bronzes by Vincenzo Gemito, and paintings on canvas by Bergognone, Alessandro Maganza and Titian. The *Museo Preistorico Piovene*, with fossil finds from the Oligocene, is on the ground floor. The villa also houses the *Malinverni collection* of 19C Italian painting, with works by Boldini, Cremona, de Nittis, Faruffini, Fattori, Favretto, Fontanesi, Induno, Lega, Mancini, Morelli, Piccio, Previati, Ranzoni, Segantini and others. The well stocked library and the 17C private chapel are two further features. The well tended park in the Italian garden has 17/18C statues by Girolamo Albanese and Orazio Marinali. The main body of the nearby *Villa Piovene-Porto Godi* is another early work by Andrea Palladio, but its Ionic portico (1587), the external staircase and the large portal (18C) are later additions.

Thiene (10 km. E.): The Venetian-Gothic

Thiene (Schio), S.Maria church attached to Palazzo da Porto (left), cathedral (right)

Palazzo da Porto Colleoni-Thiene, surrounded by a fenced garden, was built in the 2nd half of the 15C above the remains of a medieval castle. The main façade has a portico, a five-arched window and unusual corner towers with battlements. The 18C stables are by Francesco Muttoni. The interior is open to the public and has 16C frescos by Giovanni Antonio Fasolo and Giovanni Battista Zelotti, as well as fine old furniture. The drawing room has a splendid fireplace and historical frescos (Cleopatra's banquet; Provinces paying homage to Xerxes; 15C) by Giangiorgio Trissino. The *cathedral* was rebuilt in 1625–30; the slender campanile (1540–50) by Sebastiano Serlio survives from the previous structure. Classical interior, with nave and two aisles, paintings in the choir by Giulio Carpioni, Alessandro Maganza, Giovan Battista Pittoni and Sebastiano Ricci.

Velo d'Astico (16 km. N.): The best of the frescos in the church of *S.Giorgio* are those in the choir by Giovanni Speranza (Virgin Mary and Saints).

37038 Soave

Verona   p.322☐D 6

This little town, first mentioned in 568, lies at the S. edge of the *Lessini mountains* amidst gently rising slopes covered with vines which produce the light, white wine for which *Soave* is famous. Fortified by the Scaligers, the historical *centre* of the town has retained many features of its medieval appearance.

Castello: This *castle* was built in irregular fashion in the 12/13C and was enlarged by the Scaligers and Venetians in the 14/15C. The later alterations were removed in 1892. A *drawbridge* leads into the 1st courtyard, with traces of a former church, across a 2nd courtyard with the

Soave, city wall

former stables, and into the 3rd courtyard which is at a higher level. The *castle keep* and *great hall* are here. The piano nobile of the main building contains drawing room with a fine fireplace, dining-room, a bedroom with a fresco (Crucifixion, *c.* 1300), and a study. From the wall passage and castle keep, there is a fine panoramic view of the town and the well-preserved *town wall* (1369) with its 24 fortified towers. Cansignorio della Scala ordered the building of this wall as far as the castle.

Piazza dell'Antenna: This picturesque main square is named after the Venetian *flagpole* which was set up here again in 1940. The *Palazzo della Giustizia* (1375), with a Gothic arched portico, marble external staircase and battlemented façade, stands in the Piazza, along with the Venetian-Gothic *Palazzo Cavalli* (1411), whose façade has 16C fresco fragments.

Also worth seeing: The 18C *parish church,* enlarged in 1884, has altarpieces by Francesco Morone (Sacra Conversazione, 1529) and Paolo Farinati (Saints, 1592). The *Palazzi Pieropan* (15C), *Moscardo* (17C) and *Scaligero* (14C) all stand in the Via Camuzzoni.

Environs: Caldiero (7 km. SW): The *parish church* (1831–63) by Giuseppe Barbieri has an incomplete campanile. The other small campanile (15C), and the altarpiece (Delivery of the Keys to Peter, 16C) by Felice Brusasorci, both survive from the previous structure. The *Casa Campostrini-Fortini* has a 13C Gothic portal and a fine courtyard. The *Terme Giunone*, where the water temperature of the hot Brentella springs is 30C, was known to the Romans, who called the town *Calidarium*.

Illasi (10 km. NW): Here there is a generous park extending uphill as far as the 13/14C *Castello* which was destroyed by Ezzelino da Romano in 1239 and rebuilt

Soave, Palazzo della Giustizia, detail

by the Scaligers. In the park stands the imposing *Villa Sagramoso-Perez Pompei*, with a splendid central section, wings and domestic buildings. It was built in 1737 to a design by Giovanni Battista Pozzo from Cesarea and buildings from the 16/17C were incorporated in the design. The drawing room has a ceiling painting (Triumph of Apollo) by Francesco Lorenzi and other 18C frescos by Giambettino Gignaroli and Francesco Mela. The imposing *Villa Carlotti* (1735–7) by the brothers Alberto and Alessandro Pompei is built in Palladian style with a tall portico. The 18C balustrade statues are by Giuseppe Antonio Schiavi. Some of the fresco decorations inside are by Antonio Balestra (1738) and others are by Andrea and Tommaso Porta (1756).

Montecchia di Crosara (11 km. N.): The Romanesque church of *S.Salvatore* (11/12C) in the graveyard of the Castello district formerly belonged to the 10C castle of the Maltraverso, an aristocratic

family. Inside the church there are 14C frescos and a crypt whose columns with Roman capitals divide it into nave and two aisles.

Monteforte d'Alpone (6 km. E.): The *parish church* (1805–16) by Bartolomeo Giuliari stands in the central Piazza. It has a tall campanile (1894–7) by Raimondo Zampini; the high altarpiece (Visitation, 19C) is by Giovanni Caliari. Another building in the Piazza, the *bishops' palace* (1453–71) by Ermolao Barbaro, has an arcaded passage at the side and a fine courtyard surrounded by two-storeyed arcades with red marble columns.

S.Bonifacio (4 km. SE): The Parco della Rimembranza contains the remains of the *Castello di S.Bonifacio*, destroyed by Ezzelino da Romano in 1243. Near the park is the picturesque little Romanesque church of *S.Abbondio*, which has a campanile with a spire. The church façade is built of layers of yellowish-grey tufa stone and red brick with a fine colonnaded pas-

S.Bonifacio (Soave), S.Pietro Apostolo, crypt

sage in front. There are 15C frescos of votive images inside the church. The abbey church of *S.Pietro Apostolo* (8C, restored several times), which stands near the autostrada, is one of the finest churches in the province of Verona. Its immense campanile (1139) has triple Gothic arches around the bell chamber, and a 15C spire. The choir, with three apses and a round-arched frieze, is very well preserved. Pillars and columns with Roman, Byzantine and Romanesque capitals articulate the Romanesque interior to form a nave and two aisles. The choir section has a raised sanctuary above the crypt, which itself has a nave, four aisles, Byzantine-style capitals and 14C fresco fragments. Frescos after Giotto in the right aisle (Life of St.Benedict of Nursia, *c.* 1380/90) survive in better condition, as do the frescos on the left choir wall (Archangel Michael, Coronation of the Virgin Mary with Saints, *c.* 1510) which are probably the work of a Greek icon artist from Venice.

The late-Gothic sandstone ancona (*c.* 1450/60) in the choir is sculpted in the manner of Bartolomeo Giolfino (St.Peter Enthroned with St.Paul, St.Benedict of Nursia, St.Andrew and St.Nicholas of Bari). The *monastery* chapterhouse and refectory are interesting.

S.Giovanni Ilarione (19 km. N.): The *parish church* (1806), which stands on the remains of the medieval *Castello dei Maltraverso,* has a Greek cross ground plan and provides fine views. The painting (Virgin Mary with St.Antony of Padua and St.John the Evangelist, *c.* 1500) to the right of the choir is by Bartolomeo Montagna. The originally Romanesque *Chiesetta di Scandolaro* houses a good statue of St.Zeno (*c.* 1442).

S.Mauro di Saline (24 km. NW): The little mountain church of *S.Leonardo* (1388) is also known as 'San Moro'. The interior has a nave and two aisles, and ends in a choir with three apses. There is a fresco of the Virgin Mary and Believers,

S.Bonifacio (Soave), S.Pietro Apostolo

Stra, Villa Pisani

c. 1390, above the entrance portal and a carved 14C polyptych on the high altar.

30039 Stra

Venezia   p.322☐ G 6

This little town lies at the point where the canal, the *Naviglio di Brenta*, branches away from the S.-flowing river Brenta. Numerous villas stand in the town's environs, and in Noventa Padovana (q.v.) on the opposite river bank.

Villa Pisani (Villa Nazionale di Stra): This villa was built by order of the Pisani family of Doges to the plans of Girolamo Frigimelica from Padua. Francesco Maria Preti from Castelfranco Veneto, who completed the building in 1736–56, gave it its castle-like appearance. A typically 18C mixture of courtly impressiveness and high-class playfulness characterizes not only the villa itself, but also the very extensive *park* with its boundary walls, splendid gateways, radiating avenues, maze, orangery, statues, urns, fish-pond and pavilions. The grand central section of the villa has a tall *main façade* whose rusticated lower storey is decorated with Atlantes. Above this comes a double-storeyed pseudo-loggia with colossal Corinthian semi-columns, an attic adorned with putti and garlands, and a pediment topped with statues and the family coat-of-arms in the middle. The central portal in the piano nobile is decorated with serlian motifs and opens on to a narrow terrace with parapet and balustrade. The wings are articulated by pairs of Ionic pilaster strips and rectangular windows above which there are alternately triangular and curved pediments. Similar motifs are seen on the façades of the domestic buildings at the side.

The 32 rooms inside were decorated by well-known 18C Venetian artists, among

Previous pages:
Stra, Villa Pisani

them Jacopo Amigoni, Jacopo Guarana, Pietro Longhi, Pietro Antonio Novelli and Francesco Simonini. The central building stands between two courtyards. The *ballroom* extends through two storeys and has a gallery. The splendid frescos (Fame of the Pisani family, with allegorical figures, 1761/2) on the ballroom ceiling are the last work of Giovanni Battista Tiepolo before his journey to Spain, from which he never returned.

Numerous crowned political leaders stayed in the villa, including Gustav III of Sweden, Napoleon I, Alexander I of Russia, Ferdinand I and Marianne of Habsburg, and Victor Emmanuel II of Savoy.

Also worth seeing: More Venetian patrician villas: *Villa Badoer-Draghi* (15C) with its three-arched portico. *Villa Moschini-Briani* (17C), whose façade is decorated with statues. *Villas Valier* and *Foscarini-Nerelli*, which are both 18C. The gorgeous 19C *Villa Cocchini-Zoldan* with a large colonnaded veranda and a fine park.

Environs: Dolo (6 km. E.): The Brenta canal has a small 16C *shipyard* and some old *floodgates* which Canaletto (in *c.* 1730) recorded for posterity in his famous Dolo painting (now in the Staatsgalerie in Stuttgart, Germany). The *Villa Mocenigo-Spica* (18C), and the *Villa Ferretti-Angeli* (1596–1608) by Vincenzo Scamozzi, stand opposite one another further downriver.
Fiesso d'Artico (2.5 km. E.): Interesting stucco inside the early-18C *Villa Contarini Basegio-Medail,* whose private chapel has a painting in the style of Tiepolo. The façade of the 16C *Villa Soranza-Favaro,* with frescos by Benedetto Caliari, is visible from the canal. Opposite it is the broad rear façade of the *Villa Lazara Pisani* (18C), built on a grand scale with lavish decorations (stuccoes, chinoiserie) and furnishings from the same period.
Mira (10 km. E.): The core structure of the *Villa Foscarini-Dei Carmini* dates back to the 15C; 19C conversion. The picturesque *Piazza Municipio* and the 18C *Villa Bon-Tessier,* are located on the far

Torcello, S.Maria Assunta

side of the 'Taglio Nuovissimo', a subsidiary canal.
Mirano (16 km. NE): The *Villa Contarini* (1558) is also known as 'Villa dei Leoni', after the two sculptures of lions on the steps. Originally the villa had frescos by Tiepolo, but these are now in the Louvre in Paris. The *Villa Widmann-Foscari* (1719), with its sweeping gable, was decorated in the 18C in French baroque style. 18C statues from various villas stand in the garden.
Noale (18 km. N.): The town's *graveyard* is surrounded by the ivy-clad remains of the medieval castle walls. Nearby is the *parish church,* which has a Renaissance altar attributed to Jacopo Sansovino in the choir and a painting of the Assumption by Palma Giovane on the right side altar. *The Oratorio dell'Assunta* (restored), not far away, has three sumptuous 15C marble altars. The 17C *Casa Rossi* is built in an individual style, with a turret and a small loggia.

Torcello

p.322☐H 5

This island in the very N. of the Venetian lagoon can be reached by boat via Burano. A powerful maritime and trading power for a period of centuries, it played a vital part in the emergence of Venice, the capital of the Veneto. Before Venice came into existence after the downfall of Malamocco, Torcello was the main town of the archipelago, only decreasing in importance with the development and increasing power of Venice. Excavations carried out in 1961/2 show that Torcello was settled by the Romans in the 1&2C AD. The island seems to have been swamped by disastrous floods in the 5&6C and settled anew in the course of the 6C. Tradition relates that in 638 Bishop Paolo and his followers, fleeing from the Lombards, came here from Altinum. A stone inscription, which can still be seen in the basilica, states that Bishop Mauro ordered a church to be built on the island in 639 in honour of the Virgin Mary. Torcello became the seat of an archpriest after 1100. The town flourished in the Middle Ages, when it had eight churches, villas, gardens and palazzi—today the visitor (if he should not happen to arrive at the height of the

Torcello, throne of Attila (left), basilica. Last Judgement, detail

tourist season) is greeted by a wilderness. The island declined in importance from the 14C onwards and epidemics (malaria and later the plague) brought sickness and disease in their wake. Churches fell into ruin and canals became silted up. The bishopric ceased in 1818 when Torcello joined the patriarchate of Venice. Gradually nearly all the inhabitants moved away and the island fell into oblivion. Today, the route leading from the ship's landing place is not a road, but an overgrown path which, after running for about 1,300 ft. along a canal and passing a few semi-ruined houses, comes to a square, so overgrown as to have become a meadow. Only occasionally is the tranquillity interrupted by the call of a bird or the chirping of a cricket. Amid this rural setting stand two quite marvellous churches, a reminder of another world and another time: the monumental basilica of Santa Maria and Santa Fosca, a rotunda. Entry into the basilica brings even greater delights for the

inside is adorned with glittering and colourful 12&13C Byzantine mosaics depicting the Last Judgement.

Cathedral of S.Maria Assunta, and Baptistery: This church was founded by Bishop Mauro in 639. A baptistery was built immediately outside the church at the same time. Remains of this formerly circular baptistery can still be found in the square, now overgrown with grass, near the basilica's portal.

The church was structurally altered in the 9C and early 10C, when the crypt, which still survives, and the two lateral apses were added. In the 11C, Bishop Orso Orseolo ordered a new structure to be added to the cathedral, which has a nave and two aisles, but no transept. The resulting colonnaded basilica has a raised nave, an open roof truss and marble columns with particularly fine capitals (the 2nd and 6th capitals from the right are 6C). The lower part of the iconostasis (probably

Torcello, basilica, Last Judgement, detail

11C) has large, splendidly carved Byzantine reliefs (that showing a pair of peacocks is particularly lovely). The row of panel paintings in the upper section (half pictures of the Apostles and the Virgin Mary) was added in the 15C. The geometric inlaid floor is 11C. However, undoubtedly the church's main attraction lies in its mosaics. The central apse shows the Madonna and Child (early 13C) above the Apostles (12C). In the S. part of the choir is a mosaic which derives from those in the church of San Vitale in Ravenna, and which was reworked in the 12C. The W. wall is decorated with a mosaic of six rows of images of Christ in Judgement. This was created in two phases in the 12&13C, and shows the Last Judgement on an enormous showpiece wall. In 1929, the altar was stripped of all the baroque accretions and restored to its original 7C state. The priests' seats are built up like an amphitheatre, with the bishop's throne in the centre. The pulpit from the 11&12C

can be seen on the left of the cathedral. An 11C wooden crucifix hangs above the iconostasis. The holy-water stoup by the main portal is probably *c.* 1100. The majestic campanile was built shortly after 1000. Outside the basilica runs the 9C colonnaded passage, which was altered in the 14&15C.

S.Fosca: This centrally planned cruciform brick building of charming design was built in *c.* 1100 as a church in memory of St.Fosca who was martyred in Ravenna in 1011. The 12C portico outside the church is supported on columns. In the sparse but well-designed interior, the main area, although actually square, appears circular due to architectural features. This area, which has a flat ceiling, is delimited by eight columns with fine capitals, and there are niches behind the columns. The sanctuary expands into three apses in the E. The altar is modern, dating from 1935. The recumbent figure of the Saint on the

248   Torri del Benaco

church's S. side dates from 1407. S.Fosca
is linked to the basilica by a 16C colonnaded passage. A 15C relief, showing
monks venerating St.Fosca, can be seen
in the outer wall of the church. The
sacristy, with its small campanile, was
built at a much later date and contains the
remains of 9C arcades and a 14C wooden
crucifix.

Museo dell'Estuario: This museum has
monuments, some of which are important,
dating from classical times to the 16C. It
is housed in the Palazzi dell'Archivio and
del Consiglio, which are mostly 13&14C.
Initially a collection of excavations finds
from ancient Torcello was set up in 1870
in the 14C Palazzo del Consiglio. Roman
finds, weapons from the 3C BC onwards,
seals, writings, paintings, mosaics (7C
onwards), reliefs, and architectural fragments (6C onwards), all bear witness to
Torcello's history, coming as they do from
Roman settlements, from Altinum (pre-
Christian art), and from the islands own
early churches and villas which housed
Byzantine and medieval art works. The
Palazzo dell'Archivio was restored in
1877. Beneath its portico there are Roman
tomb monuments, sculptures and architectural fragments from Altinum and the
lagoon. The palazzo's upper storey contains early vessels and sculptures, pre-
Christian monuments in glass cases, and
medieval wooden reliefs and sculptures
from the former churches.
The upper storey of the Palazzo del Consiglio houses silver-gilt reliefs, including
a very fine Virgin Mary icon (part of the
cathedral's original Pala d'Argento from
the 1st half of the 13C). The paintings,
which are from the Veronese school and
show scenes from the life of St.Christina,
come from the former church of S.Anto-
nio, which stood on a small island joined
to Torcello and located to the SE of the
cathedral. The same church also housed
the oil paintings 'Annunciation' and 'Adoration of the Shepherds' to be found in the
next room. These two works were
produced in Veronese's workshop and
were intended to be organ panels.

Also worth seeing: The square outside

the basilica, where the remains of the baptistery survive, has an ancient stone seat
traditionally referred to as *Attila's throne.*
However, no legend relates any particular event which is supposed to have
occurred here during the Barbarian Invasions. Despite the knowledge of archaeol-
ogists and art historians, it seems the
history of Torcello still has some hidden
secrets. Housed in an old ruined farm-
house close to the cathedral there is a
famous restaurant in which the visitor can
rest, and await the next boat, and dream
of the splendour and glory of this island
which fell into oblivion 500 years ago.

37010 Torri del Benaco
Verona   p.322□A 5

Known as *Castrum Turrium* in the Roman
period, the town gained importance during the 9C when the 'Concilium bena-
cense' was held here. This assembly,
attended by deputies from the 18 leading
communities on Lake Garda, was presided
over by the head man of Verona. 'Benaco',
a name for Lake Garda, derives from its
Latin name 'Lacus Benacus'. Today Torri
del Benaco is very popular as a holiday
resort.

Castello: This *castle*, fortified with tall
battlements and three towers, was built in
1383 by the Scaligers. The buildings
grouped around the *harbour* at the foot of
the castle include medieval houses with
loggias and the small church of *SS. Trinità*
with 15C frescos.

Also worth seeing: The 18C *parish
church* near the *Torre di Berengario* from
the high Middle Ages has an 18C painting by Giambettino Cignaroli from
Verona.

Environs: S.Vigilio (4 km. S.): Some of
the most charming countryside on Lake
Garda is to be found on the *Punta di
S.Vigilio* peninsula. The park of the 16C
Villa Guarienti is laid out in the Italian

Torcella, Museo, Pala d'Argento

manner and is surrounded by olive groves and cypresses. The villa is thought to be by Michele Sanmicheli. From the tiny harbour, the little medieval church of *S. Vigilio* can be seen through the cypresses.
S.Zeno di Montagna (10 km. NE): This holiday village in the mountains gives a good view of Lake Garda, reaching as far as the Adamello mountain range to the NW. The steep winding road leading up to it passes by two *quarries*. Two types of marble quarried here, the yellow 'Giallo di Torri' and the red-veined 'Mandorlato', were used in numerous churches in the province of Verona.

31100 Treviso

Treviso   p.322 □ G 5

The Roman *Tarvisium* became a bishopric as early as 396. The city was spared by Attila. The Carolingians gave it the right of coinage. It was destroyed by the Hungarians in 911. Frederick Barbarossa confirmed the city's privileges in 1164, but it turned against the Emperor in the same year. In doing so, Treviso sided first with Verona and later with the Lombard League. The city subsequently flourished before falling to Ezzelino and Alberico da Romano in 1237. Weakened by internal struggles the city came under the supremacy of Venice in 1344. During World War 2 Treviso was subjected to more air raids than any other Italian town, and it is therefore surprising that there are still so many houses with loggias and frescos. Together with the Sile and Botteniga rivers, which converge here, these houses lend a peculiar charm to the city's old quarter which is surrounded by a wall.

Religious buildings

Cathedral of S.Pietro (piazza del Duomo): This Romanesque structure built

Treviso, cathedral, 'Adoration of the Magi' by Pordenone (left), S.Francesco (right)

in 1141 stands on the site of a 9C church. A new choir was added in 1481–8 by Pietro Lombardo, the architect from Ticino. New chapels were added to the N. and S. of this choir in the early 16C. The nave was rebuilt in the 18/19C to the plans of Giordano Riccati. Bomb damage inflicted in World War 2 was repaired when the cathedral was thoroughly restored in 1951–5. Of interest *outside* are the marble-faced choir, Romanesque wall fragments, with pilaster strips and round-arched friezes and the seven lead and copper domes, which are of different heights; the façade has Romanesque sculptures of lions on the steps up to the classical portico (1836).

Arcades with massive pilasters divide the *interior* into nave and two aisles. The system of domes, with the central one elevated by a drum, is reminiscent of a cruciform domed basilica. The marble *reliquary sarcophagus* (1506) at the high altar has relief busts of the martyrs Tabra, Tabrata and Theonestus. The tomb (1485/6) on the left wall of the raised sanctuary is that of Bishop Giovanni and this also has relief figures. Modern frescos of the Life of Pius X in the choir are by Biagio Biagetti. To the side of the choir steps, other steps lead down to the low pre-Romanesque *crypt*, whose groin vault is supported on circular and rectangular pillars with capitals from the 9/10C, from which time the mosaic fragments on the floor also date. Three chapels each end in an apse. On the altar of the central chapel is the late-Gothic reliquary sarcophagus of St.Liberalis, the town's patron Saint. The former *chapel of the sacrament* (1506–13) by Antonio Maria da Milano to the N. of the choir has a dome and is faced with multicoloured marble. Sculptures at the altar (Angels) and in the wall niches (St.Peter, Redeemer and two Angels, St. Paul) are by Lorenzo Bregno (1509–13). An oblong painting (Finding of Christ's Shroud) by Francesco Bassano can be seen on the S. wall of the long anteroom outside the chapel. Opposite this is the tomb (1501) of Bishop Niccolò Franco. The splendid *chapel of the Annun-*

Treviso, S.Maria Maggiore ▷

ciation (1519/20) designed by Martino Lombardo is to the S. of the choir and has the famous *altarpiece* of the Annunciation (*c.* 1520–3) by Titian and frescos (1520) by Pordenone and his workshop on the left wall (Annunciation, Adoration of the Magi) and in the apse (Sibylla Tiburtina and Augustus, St.Peter and St.Andrew). The Gothic wall tomb of the brothers Castellano and Francesco Salomone is on the S. side of the anteroom, along with Romanesque reliefs (Life of the Virgin Mary, late 12C). On the opposite wall there are three good paintings: by Domenico Capriolo (Ascension, 1520), Girolamo da Treviso the elder (Virgin Mary with St.Roch and St.Sebastian, 1487) and Paris Bordone (St.Laurence and Saints). The two interesting *sacristies* are also reached from the chapel anteroom. These house a carved and gilded former antependium (Last Judgement, 14C), paintings by Girolamo Treviso the elder (Virgin Mary and Saints), by Francesco Domenici (Procession on the cathedral square, 1571) and by Paris Bordone (Sacred Mysteries) along with the *church treasure* (manuscripts with sumptuous bindings, 13C). The semicircular chapel in the S. aisle is decorated with another painting by Paris Bordone (Adoration of the Shepherds). The pillar outside the chapel has a statue of John the Baptist by Alessandro Vittoria (*c.* 1560). On the next pillar there is a marble bas-relief of the Visitation by Lorenzo Bregno, who also carved the partially gilded statue of St.Sebastian opposite. A marble tabernacle (1629/30) decorated with bronze sculptures (1630) stands in the middle chapel of the N. aisle.

The early-Romanesque *campanile* and *S.Giovanni*, the baptistery (11/12C), are both on the N. side of the cathedral. The interior of the baptistery is rectangular and has 12–14C frescos and a fine red marble font. Another feature of the *piazza del Duomo* is *house No. 7,* with 15C façade paintings.

S.Caterina dei Servi (via S.Caterina): The interior of this Servite church (1346) was redesigned in baroque style in 1690. On the right is the *Cappella degli Innocenti,*

which is frescoed throughout (Life of the Virgin Mary, Crucifixion and Saints; *c.* 1410–20). Frescos by Tomaso da Modena from the secularized church of S.Margherita were detached and brought here in 1979 (Life of St.Ursula, 14C). The fresco of the Virgin Mary and Saints (*c.* 1400) above the entrance are by a follower of the same artist. Numerous 15/16C houses with well-preserved 16C frescos line the nearby *Via S.Agostino;* house *No. 61* shows the Judgement of Paris and *No. 65* the Justice of Emperor Trajan.

S.Francesco (piazza S.Francesco): This 13C church (restored 1926–8) belonging to a mendicants' order contains some good frescos, including those on the choir vault (St.Francis of Assisi between the Virgin Mary and Adam, 14C) and *monuments* to Petrarch's daughter *Francesca* (d. 1384) and Dante's son *Pietro Alighieri* (d. 1364). The fresco of the Virgin Mary with Saints in the 1st chapel to the left of the choir is a mature work by Tomaso da Modena. Some fine 16C façade paintings are to be found on houses 8–10 in the *Via S.Francesco* behind the modern campanile.

S.Leonardo (piazza S.Leonardo): This church, modernized in the 19/20C, has a ceiling fresco of the Apotheosis of St.Leonard by Giovanni Battista Canal. The *main altar tabernacle,* which is made of rock crystal and resembles a tempietto, is something of a rarity; its bronze sculptures (1768) are by Giovanni Marchiori. The altarpiece of St.Leonard and Saints (16C) is thought to be by Pozzoserrato. The triptych of the Virgin Mary with St.Bartholomew and St.Prosdocimus on the 1st side altar on the right is from the workshop of Cima da Conegliano. Another building in the *Piazza Leonardo* is the *Ca'Spineda* (No. 1, today the seat of the 'Cassa di Risparmio'), a palazzo built in the 16C and redesigned in the 18C, with fine staircase and banqueting halls decorated with frescos by Gaspare Diziani and Basilio Lasinio. The *Via*

S.Nicolò, fresco by Tomaso da Modena

Palestra, with a fine palazzo (No. 33–35) dating from *c.* 1300, starts at the W. corner of the piazza.

S.Lucia/S.Vito (piazza S.Vito): The two small churches of S.Lucia (14C; restored 1919–24) and S.Vito (12/16C; restored 1925/6) adjoin one another and are connected by a portal within. *S.Lucia,* the more easterly church, has Gothic arches which divide it into nave and two aisles. The *Cappella della Crocifissione* on the right has a damaged fresco cycle of Christ's Passion (14C) by pupils of Tomaso da Modena. The altar fresco (Madonna delle Carceri), partly painted over in the 15C, is by da Modena himself. Busts of Saints on the choir parapet are 15C additions, as are the late-Gothic bas-reliefs on the walls. The interior of *S.Vito* also has a nave and two aisles, but this time there are massive Doric columns. The main altarpiece of the Virgin Mary and Saints is by Titian's nephew Marco Vecellio. To the left of this there is a Gothic tabernacle (1363). The ceiling painting of the Coronation of the Virgin is by Antonio Zanchi. The fresco (Christ and Apostles; 12/13C) in the calotte of the S. apse is Byzantine in inspiration, and was uncovered in 1926.

Piazza dei Signori

A few steps further on, the *Canale dei Buranelli* with its old houses with loggias beside the water reminds the visitor that Venice is nearby.

S.Maria Maggiore (via Carlo Alberto). Rebuilt in Gothic style in 1473 the church goes back to a previous structure (S.Fosca) from the 9C. The unfinished brick campanile was added in 1516. The *façade,* with its round windows framed in terracotta, is enlivened by a curving gable of original design. In the 16C, the transept and choir chapels, Lombard Renaissance in style, were built on to the E. of the Gothic nave and two aisles. The high altarpiece (Assumption) is thought to be by Sante Peranda. The highly-regarded fresco of the miraculous image in the *Tempietto della Madonna,* a chapel (1492) in the N. transept, was reworked by Tomaso da Modena in *c.* 1352. Behind this chapel is the *baptistery,* frescoed throughout by Francesco Beccaruzzi and Gian Pietro Silvio (Christological scenes, evangelists, prophets and sibyls; *c.* 1540). The sacristy, with a fine alto relievo above the portal (Virgin Mary, *c.* 1500), leads into the Lateran canons' *cloister* (1474), only part of which survives in the original. The *Via Carlo Alberti* is lined with houses with loggias, including the Romanesque *Casa Carrarese* (No. 22), a small Gothic house (No. 72) and a row of classical buildings (Nos. 41–43) by Francesco Maria Preti.

S.Nicolò (via S.Nicolò): This massive brick Dominican basilica (*c.* 1282–1389) was built in Italian Gothic style and is tall and well-proportioned. The *exterior* is articulated by buttresses and pilaster strips. The three apses of the choir section have tall lancet windows and post-Romanesque round-arched friezes. Marble columns are inserted into the round arches around the bell chamber on the top storey of the tall *campanile.*
The nave is over 110 ft. tall and has a restored Venetian-Gothic wooden vault. Arches on round pillars divide the area to form a nave and two aisles. In the E. is the transept with immediately adjoining chapels. The three central chapels are polygonal. The white and red marble

screens in front of the rib-vaulted choir chapel date from 1666. The *main altar*, also 1666, is inlaid with semi-precious stones and mother-of-pearl, the work of Marcantonio Burini. On the left stands the sumptuous tomb (1490–1502) of Agostino d'Onigo, a patrician from Treviso who was appointed a Roman senator. The sculptures on the tomb are probably from the Lombardo workshop. The *Cappella degli Apostoli* to the right of the choir has 14C frescos of possibly Sienese origin, and an altarpiece (Doubting Thomas, 1506) which is most probably by Lorenzo Lotto. The oldest frescos (Crucifixion with the Virgin Mary and John the Evangelist, Pope Benedict XI; *c.* 1303/04) are to be found in the next chapel to the right. The front wall of the S. transept has a late-Gothic South Tyrolean *Pietà* (*c.* 1420) framed by an altarpiece (Holy Trinity, 1669) by Antonio Zanchi, who also painted the Pietà with Albertus Magnus, Saints and founder on the adjoining W. wall. In the nave there are paintings by Palma Giovane (St.Augustine) and Francesco Bassano (Christ and the Virgin Mary, with St.Francis of Assisi and St.Dominic as intercessors) in the 2nd bay of the right aisle. There are excellent

frescos (St.Agnes, St.Jerome, St.John the Baptist and St.Romuald) by Tomaso da Modena by the 2nd round pillar on the left. Two large paintings, Christ's Passion and Holy Mysteries (both 1623), by Sante Peranda are to the side of the entrance portal.

The *Seminario Vescovile* which adjoins the church in the S. is the former Dominican monastery. Its cloister leads into the Dominican chapterhouse (13/14C), whose walls are covered with *frescos* (Dominicans at their desks, 1352) by Tomaso da Modena which are particularly of interest. In the *Via S.Nicolò* there are façade frescos dating from 1525 (house No. 18–20) and 1530 (Holy Bishop Enthroned, house No. 78).

Secular buildings

Palazzo dei Trecento (piazza dei Signori): The restored Romanesque *town hall*, built of brick, stands in the central piazza. It was built in *c.* 1217 for the Great State Assembly of 150 nobles and 150 citizens. Its battlemented façade with pediment has three arches in the portico on the ground floor, and three triple-arched windows in the piano nobile. The windows have small

Piazza dei Signori

S.Nicolò

S.Nicolò, frescos by Tomaso da Modena

marble columns and the whole window is contained within a decorative blind arch. The ground floor was partly converted into a three-aisled hall in 1553. Above it is the gigantic 'Assembly Hall of the Three Hundred', which was hit by a bomb in World War 2 but rebuilt in exemplary fashion by Ferdinando Forlati from Verona. On its walls, and also on the exterior of the building, are the restored coats-of-arms of Venetian governors. Adjoining this building at right angles is the *Palazzo del Podestà*, which was rebuilt in 1874–7 in accordance with the original. Its *clock tower* (155 ft. high) has notched battlements. The *Palazzo Pretorio* (1491) stands at the W. end of the piazza. Upper sections of the façade facing the piazza are rather odd and the result of 17C rustication and 19C alterations; the façade towards the Calmaggiore passageway, however, still has its original appearance.

Loggia dei Cavalieri (piazza Crispi):

This almost square Romanesque structure (1276/7) is open on three sides, which have shallow arcades of round arches on slender pillars. The roof is tent-shaped. Sources record that it was formerly a *tavern* for the nobles ('Cavalieri') who met here for conversation and to play at chess and dice. The Loggia was the only place of its kind, and its medieval wall paintings of the Trojan War made it a rarity. After severe bomb damage in 1944, the building was restored using the original materials but sadly only scant remnants of the frescos survived.

Monte di Pietà (piazzetta Monte di Pietà): The charming *Saletta dei Reggitori* (14C), a chapel with a painted timber ceiling and apse, is to be found on the upper storey of this medieval pawnbroker's shop (entrance at house No. 2). Gilded Venetian leather tapestries (17C) cover the walls, above which there is a frieze of panel paintings of the Christian Virtues (16C)

S.Nicolò, chapterhouse, frescos by Tomaso da Modena

by Pozzoserrato. Lodovico Fiumicelli painted the fresco of the Feeding of the Five Thousand (16C) on the calotte of the apse, which also has a copy of a Pietà, a painting attributed to Francesco Vecellio (the original is in the Ca' Spineda, 1 Piazza S.Leonardo).

Pescheria (isoletta sul Botteniga): The 'banchi' (counters) of the old fish market stand in the shadow of plane-trees on this island in the river. A market is still held here, just as in the Middle Ages. The market was originally located here due to health regulations laid down by the city fathers. (This was also true of the Pescheria on the Canale Grande in Venice.)

Palazzi and houses: The houses of Treviso, with their *ground-floor loggias* and *frescoed façades,* reveal a design which has been passed on through the centuries. Despite bomb damage in the last World War, many of the painted façades have survived. Frescos in the main *Colmaggiore* passageway are attributed to Pozzoserrato (houses Nos. 4–6). In the *Via Canova,* the extension of the Calmaggiore, is the *Casa da Noal* (No. 38, cf. Museums) and the *Casa Robegan* (No. 40), which has splendid ornamental frescos with figures (1528). The *Ca'dei Ricchi* (Nos. 22–24) in the *Via Barberia* near the Piazza dei Signori has a fresco of the Virgin Mary (*c.* 1490) attributed to Girolamo da Treviso the elder. A palazzo in Venetian-Gothic style can be found in the neighbouring *Vicolo S.Gregorio* passageway (Nos. 4–8). *Via Riccati,* which runs parallel to the Via Canova, is lined by houses in Gothic style, with trompe l'oeil (No. 15a) and historical frescos (Judith and Holofernes, Justice of Trajan; house No. 15b) from the mid-15C; there are also terracotta decorations (No. 36).

City fortifications: The *city wall* has survived well in places. Most of it was built in 1511–18 under the architects Fra Giovanni Giocondo and Alessandro Leopardi, working for the Condottiere Bartolommeo d'Alviano. The *Porta dei SS.Quaranta* (1517) is the W. gate of the city. The *Porta di S.Tomaso* (1518), the elegant Renaissance city gate in the NE, was designed by Giuglielmo Bergamaseso.

Museums

Museo Civico (22 borgo Cavour): 'Luigi Bailo', the city museum, is housed in the 16C buildings of the former Carmelite monastery. The *Archaeological Department* (ground floor) has prehistoric finds (interesting swords), Roman architectural fragments, portrait busts, sculptures, bronze statuettes, and early-Christian and medieval sculptures. The *picture gallery* (upper storey) has paintings, sculptures and small art objects extending through 30 rooms. The collection focuses mainly on painting from the Veneto, particularly from Treviso. *Room I:* Monumental fresco of scenes from the 'Entrée de Spagne', a 14C medieval novel. *Room II:* 12C Romanesque capitals and a crucifix (1352) from the Guariento workshop. *Rooms IV and V:* Early-15C statue of the Virgin Mary and frescos (Virgin Mary, Journey to Emmaus, Christ, Inferno) from the Tomaso da Modena circle of artists. *Room VI:* Frescos by Gentile da Fabriano (Virgin Mary) and Girolamo da Treviso the elder (Crucifixion, Virgin Mary and Saints). *Room VII:* 15C sculptures. *Room VIII:* Paintings by Girolamo da Treviso the elder (St.Antony Abbot, Resurrection), Giovanni Bellini (Virgin Mary), Girolamo da Treviso the younger (Adoration of the Magi) and Cima da Conegliano (Virgin Mary). *Room IX:* Portraits by Lorenzo Lotto (Dominican monk, 1526) and Titian (Sperone Speroni, 1544). *Room X:* Paintings by Paris Bordone. *Room XI:* Paintings by Jacopo Bassano. *Room XII:* Paintings by Francesco da Milano (Virgin Mary with Angels) and Pordenone (St.Antony Abbot). *Room XIII:* Paintings from the Paolo Veronese circle of artists. *Room XIV* and *XV:* 16/17C Venetian paintings. *Room XVI:* Landscape paint-

ings by Pozzoserrato. *Room XVII:* 17/18C Venetian paintings. *Rooms XVIII* and *XIX:* 16–18C German and Dutch paintings. *Room XX:* 17C Italian paintings. *Room XXI:* Works by Pietro Longhi (Young Nobleman) and Giandomenico Tiepolo (Prophecy of John the Baptist, and Madonna and Child), landscape paintings by Francesco Guardi and Giuseppe Zais, and portraits by Rosalba Carriera. *Room XXII:* 18C Venetian paintings, including some by Alessandro Longhi (portrait, 1786; Capuchin monk). *Room XXIII:* Small Venetian sculptures (18C). *Room XXIV:* Portraits (18/19C) and a bust (M.Angeli Pascoli) by Antonio Canova. *Room XXV:* 18/19C vedutas. *Room XXVI:* Sculptures (Lilian Gish, Pisan woman) by Arturo Martini from Treviso. *Rooms XXVII–XXX:* Works by 19/20C Venetian artists including Alberto Martini, the surrealist artist from Oderzo. Nearby, at 18 Borgo Cavour, is the well-stocked *Biblioteca Comunale* with 200,000 volumes, over 1500 manuscripts, and 750 early printed books, including Dante's 'Divina Commedia' in an early edition (15C) and an edition of 1481 illustrated by Botticelli.

Opposite the museum is the church of *S.Agnese in SS.Quaranta* (1616), built by Andrea Pagnossin in Palladian manner, with a baroque interior. The *Renaissance house* at No. 38 has frescos from *c.* 1525/30 on the portico lunettes.

Museo della Casa Trevigiana (38 via Canova): The 15C Gothic *Casa da Noal*, with its tall portico, has an extensive collection devoted to the history of the city and to the applied arts of the province (including wrought iron, sculptures and furniture).

Environs: Castelfranco Veneto (26 km. W.): The cathedral of *S.Liberale* (1723–45), built by Francesco Maria Preti in the Palladian manner, has a campanile remodelled from a fortified tower which formerly belonged to the city fortifications. The single-aisled interior has Ionic columns; the chapel to the right of the sanctuary houses a famous early work by *Giorgione* (Virgin Mary Enthroned with

Castelfranco Veneto (Treviso), cathedral, painting by Giorgione (left), gatehouse tower (right)

St.Francis of Assisi and St.Liberalis, 1504). *Casa Pellizzari,* where Giorgione was born, is house No. 15 in the nearby alleyway, the Vicolo della Chiesa. The interesting grisaille paintings (Free Arts) on the upper storey are attributed to Giorgione. The square *Castello* (1199–1202) was built by Treviso. Well-preserved walls and five tall fortified towers surround the town's old quarter.

Fanzolo (23 km. W.): The *Villa Emo* (*c.* 1564), built by Andrea Palladio for Leonardo Emo, consists of a plain central structure with a fine colonnaded portico and wings breached by round arches. Low wings and the long path, which runs in front of the ramp leading up to the central building, blend in harmoniously with the flat surrounding countryside. The baroque pediment reliefs (angels with a coat-of-arms in a cartouche) are the only feature in any conspicuous contrast to the clear, sober overall design. Mythological frescos in the portico and inside rooms are by Giovanni Battista Zelotti, who also painted an interesting historical painting of Scipio liberating an enslaved Punic princess in the central drawing room.

Preganziol (7.5 km. S.): Numerous liberal artists and men of letters active in the time of Napoleon stayed at the 18C *Villa Albrizzi-Franchetti,* invited by Isabella Teotochi Albrizzi, a lover of the arts. These included Napoleon's opponent Ugo Foscolo, Ippolito Pindemonti who translated the Odyssey, Vincenzo Monti who translated the Iliad, and Antonio Canova, the artist whose four *low reliefs* of the life of Socrates can be seen inside the villa.

Vedelago (19 km. W.): The *parish church* in the Fossalunga district has frescos by Giovanni Battista Canal. The whole façade of the small *Villa Sernagiotto* (16C) in the same district is decorated with frescos by the Venetian school.

31049 Valdobbiàdene

Treviso   p.322☐F 4

A wine-growing town, known for its 'Cartizze Superiore' a sparkling prosecco, it stands at the end of the *Strada del Vino Bianco*, a wine route, beginning at Coneglíano (q.v.). A fair devoted to sparkling wine, the 'Mostra degli Spumanti Veneti', is held here each September. This old town's most famous son, *Venantius Fortunatus* (530–606), later became Bishop of Poitiers; a Christian man of letters (his

Valdobbiàdene, archpriest's church

works include the four books of 'De Virtutibus S.Martini'), he was also a pioneer of early medieval poetry ('Pangue Lingua').

Archpriest's church: A 14C church rebuilt in the 17/18C, when the Doric portico by Bernardo Salomoni was added. The 1st altarpiece on the right (John the Baptist with St.Jerome and St.Antony Abbot) is by Palma Giovane; the 2nd altar on the right (Virgin Mary Enthroned and Saints who gave relief from the Plague) is by Paris Bordone. A fine 14C *ciborium*, with bronze fittings, stands on the altar opposite. The choir has a painting of the Assumption by Francesco Beccaruzzi. The *campanile* (245 ft. high) was built by Francesco Maria Preti (1775). A splendid silver cross (14C) and a pastel portrait of the Blessed Gregorio Barbarigo by Rosalba Carriera can be seen in the nearby *priest's house*.

S.Gregorio: *Paintings* by Rosa Bortolan (St.Venantius Fortunatus, 19C) and Brusasorci (Virgin Mary of the Rosary, 16C) are to be found to the sides of the high altar in this church of 1482 which stands among tall cypresses at the edge of the town.

Environs: Follina (14 km. NE): The *Cistercian abbey of Follina* was founded in 1146 by Humiliati who later adopted the monastic discipline of St.Bernard. The *basilica* (*c.* 1200) was altered in 1305–35 and restored in 1919–22. There is a 14C tympanum fresco of the Virgin Mary and Saints above the large central portal in the façade. The interior consists of three roughly square Romanesque choir chapels and a Gothic nave and two aisles with pointed arches on round pillars. The tall clerestory is articulated by pilaster strips and there is an open roof truss above the nave. An unusual feature for a Cistercian church is the *painting*, which appears on the ribs of the vault in the choir chapels, on the front faces of the arches in the nave (ornamental plant motifs, 14C) and in the

Follina (Valdobbiàdene), Cistercian abbey

clerestory (decoration including figures from the 13C; frieze of climbing plants from the 17C). A 14C sandstone statue of the *Virgin Mary* in a gilded ancona (15C, restored) stands at the high altar. There is a fresco of the Virgin Mary with Saints (1507) in the right aisle. This aisle leads into the monastery *cloister* (1170–1268) which has pairs of late-Romanesque columns of richly varied design. The arcades (1535) of the former *pilgrims' house* can be seen on the left of the 2nd courtyard, in the centre of which there is a pretty fountain.

37100 Verona

Verona   p.322□C 6

The most important city in the Veneto after Venice, it occupies both sides of a great loop in the river Adige, on the edge of the last lower Alpine spurs in the N. and along the broad plain of the Po in the S. Further, the city is situated at a crossroads on the major road link between Italy and the N., and also on the road from Turin to Trieste. Hence its importance as

an industrial and trading city (it is the venue of an industrial fair). Today Verona also possesses one of the largest cooling stations in Europe. Cultural life reaches its peak in the *opera festival* held in the Arena, which entices an international audience to the city every summer.

History: This area, protected by the loop in the river, was settled by the Euganeans and Rhaeti and later by the Etruscans and Gauls. A Roman colony from 89 BC onwards, it was granted the status of town in 49 BC. Its key position at the crossing point of the *Via Claudia Augusta, Via Galliena* and *Via Postumia*, three Roman roads, meant that Verona was the leading administrative and trading centre in Northern Italy. The surviving Roman buildings (see below) bear witness to this flourishing in the Imperial period. A second heyday followed under the Ostrogoth king Theoderic, who extended the classical town walls and ruled that Verona should be his seat of government along with Ravenna. During Lombard rule, King Albuin liked to use Verona as his residence. It fell to Charlemagne in 774. From the 10C onwards the Verona

Follina (Valdobbiàdene), Cistercian church

Verona, Arena

March belonged to the Duchy of Bavaria. A *free town* from 1107, Verona fought on the side of the Lombard League against Emperor Frederick Barbarossa in the 12C. After the tyrannical rule (1227–59) of Ezzelino III da Romano, the elected captain of the city militia, Mastino I della Scala, began one of the best-known Italian aristocratic rules. The most important Scaliger was Cangrande I, who was appointed imperial deputy by Emperor Henry VII in 1311, and elected to be the most senior captain of the Lombard Ghibelline League in 1318. He was famous for his lack of political scruples as well as for his artistic sense, and Dante was among those to enjoy his protection. Overthrown by Giangaleazzo Visconti in 1387, the Scaligers fled N. and were assimilated into the Bavarian landed aristocracy. Verona was under the rule of Venice from 1405–1796. In 1859–66, during the Austrian occupation which lasted from 1814 onwards, the city was a key strategic point in the square of fortified towns consisting of *Verona—Peschiera del Garda—Mantua—Legnano*. The city finally joined the Kingdom of Italy in 1866. The city's most famous sons were the Roman poet *Gaius Valerius Catullus*

(*c.* 87–54 BC), the architect *Michele Sanmicheli* and the painter *Paolo Caliari*, better known as Veronese.

The city: The grid pattern of the city's old quarter, around which the Adige flows, still indicates the basic pattern of the former Roman *camp* whose central *forum* (today the Piazza delle Erbe) is the point where the two main streets—the *Decumanus* (Corso Porta Borsari/Corso S.Anastasia) and the *Cardo* (Via Cappello/Via Leoni)—intersect one another. Scaliger walls, later reinforced by the Venetians, include the medieval enlargements to the S. of the city's old quarter and on the left bank of the Adige. A visitor to the city is assisted in finding his way about by the succession of streets running from the Porta Palio in the SW to the church of S.Anastasia in the NE (namely, Stradone Porta Palio—Corso Castelvecchio—Corso Cavour—Corso Porta Borsari—Corso S.Anastasia). Many of the sights of Verona are to be found along these streets. The Via Mazzini which runs parallel to them joins the Piazza Brà (Arena) to the SE end of the Piazza delle Erbe. The Roman theatre is reached by crossing the Ponte Pietra bridge in the N. of the old quarter. The

Porta dei Borsari

Duomo S.Maria Matricolare

line of streets which begins here (Via Redentore—Via S.Chiara —Via S.Maria in Organo—Via Giardini Giusti—Via Muri Padri—Via S.Nazaro) gives access to the sights on the left bank of the Adige.

Religious buildings

Arena (piazza Brà): The *amphitheatre*, probably built in AD *c*. 60/70, is the third largest of all amphitheatres, coming after the Colosseum in Rome and the amphitheatre in Capua. Originally erected outside the city walls, it was incorporated into the city area in AD 265 when the Roman Emperor Gallienus enlarged the city walls. Classical authors (including Pliny the younger) mention the Arena as having been the scene of fights between gladiators and the baiting of African beasts, but they do not report that persecuted Christians were executed here. On the other hand, 166 alleged heretics from Sirmione were burned to death here on 13

February 1278 at a public mock trial. In the 15/16C the Arena was used as a knights' tiltyard. Comedies and concerts began to be performed here in the 18/19C. The open-air performances of the *opera festival* have now become a tradition. They began in 1913 with a production of Verdi's 'Aida'.

In classical times, the amphitheatre took the shape of an immense three-storeyed building, 500 ft. long and 405 ft. wide, above an elliptical ground plan. The 'Cavea' provided seats for some 25,000 spectators in 44 rows, which was thus half the capacity of the Colosseum in Rome. The outer surrounding wall was destroyed by earthquakes in 1183 and 1221 and the dimensions of the Arena, which now only had two storeys, were reduced to a length of 455 ft. and a width of 360 ft. The N. remains of the former surrounding wall are known to the Veronese as 'Ala', and still give an impression of the building's original height. Rows of seats inside were

Duomo, portal detail

Duomo, portal detail

formerly divided into three horizontal tiers. When they were rebuilt in the late 16C they were redivided, this time into sectors. Almost all the marble slabs were removed in the Middle Ages because they provided a cheap building material. In 1688, balustrades were attached above the portals leading on to the stage. In the 19C the later additions were removed from the outside of the Arena, where the former internal structure now stands revealed. In the 20C the arcade wall, which was leaning at a dangerous angle, was made vertical as part of a thorough restoration of the entire complex. The opera performances held on summer nights are traditionally begun by the assembled audience lighting thousands upon thousands of little candles. On these occasions, in contrast to performances held in bright daylight, the Arena gives an impression of technical perfection in areas other than acoustic.

A remnant of the Roman city wall built under Emperor Gallienus survives on the Piazza Mura Gallieno behind the amphitheatre.

Arco dei Gavi (piazzetta Castelvecchio): The Roman architect Lucius Vitruvius Cerdore built the *triumphal arch* (c. mid-1C AD) in honour of the Gavius family in the Via Postumia (Corso Cavour) outside the ancient city walls. It was used as a city gate from the 12–14C, when it was known as 'Porta S.Zeno'. The tall central opening, between two low side openings which also have round arches, is framed by pairs of Corinthian columns. French occupying troops pulled it down in 1805. The present structure was reconstructed E. of the Castelvecchio in 1933 from architectural remains rediscovered in the Arena in 1932. This arch often served as a model for altars and tombs in Venice and the surrounding area, because its architect was confused with Marcus Vitruvius Pollio, the author of 'De Architectura', the famous treatise on architecture.

Ponte Pietra: This *bridge over the Adige* has been partly rebuilt several times but dates back to a Roman structure from the pre-Imperial period. Two of the original total of four arches survived until the bridge was blown up by the Germans in 1945. After the war the bridge was rebuilt in accordance with the original, using the Roman marble blocks.

Porta dei Borsari (corso Porta Borsari): The Roman *city gate* (AD 80) at the W. end of the former Decumanus Maximus was built in AD 265. Its three-storeyed front wall of white Veronese stone is still standing, the lower storey is breached by two wide gate arches between Corinthian semi-columns. This gate was known as 'Porta di S.Zeno' before the Arco dei Gavi (see above) was re-named in the 12C. After the city walls had been enlarged at that time, the gatehouse was used as a customs post. The gate is now named after the 'Bursarii', the customs officials of those days.

Porta dei Leoni (via Leoni): Another Roman *city gate*, built at about the same time as the Porta Borsari on the site of an earlier gate in the Doric style; remains of the latter can be seen in the basement of the building on the corner. Remains of the Roman gate, on the wall of the building on the corner of Via Leoni and Corticella Leoni, give an idea of the gate's former splendour.

Teatro Romano (rigaste Redentore): Surrounded by tall cypresses and Roman terraces, the *Roman theatre* was built into the slope of the hill of S.Pietro during the lifetime of Christ. The part with the stage was originally on the side towards the Adige. Some sections of the entrance portals at the sides still survive. A double-storeyed arcaded passage rises above the (restored) semicircular rows of seats. The ruined theatre was given a thorough restoration in the 20C, and between 1830 and today the structures which had been built above the theatre were removed, with the exception of the small church of *SS.Siro*

◁ *Duomo, side portal, detail*

S.Anastasia

S.Anastasia

e Libera (10/17C). *Shakespeare festival performances* are held every summer in the theatre.

Roman buildings

Duomo S.Maria Matricolare (piazza del Duomo): The *cathedral* (1139–87) built on the site of previous structures (4–10C) was radically altered in the 15/16C. In the 15C the nave was increased in height and a rib vault installed. An extra storey was added to the façade in 1565–1606. The incomplete *campanile*, whose Romanesque lower storey was decorated with *sgraffiti* in the 12/13C, was increased in height in the 16C to plans by Michele Sanmicheli; the octagonal bell chamber was finally added in 1926. The *E. section*, built in blocks of tufa, is a fine example of Veronese Romanesque. The main apse has fine carving on the capitals of its graceful pilasters and a foliate frieze under the eaves. Lion statues in front of

the façade support the turned columns of the 15C polychrome *portal baldacchino* which was given an upper storey in the 15C. The reliefs (hunting frieze, the two Saints John, and symbols of the Evangelists; 1139) are among the most mature works of the craftsman Master Nicolao named in an inscription. He also carved *reliefs* on the frame of the portal (Prophets, paladins of Charlemagne) and in the tympanum (Virgin Mary Enthroned, seen between an Angel appearing to the Shepherds and the Wise Men).

The Gothic arches in the hall-like *interior* rest on red marble bundles of columns with late-Gothic foliate capitals. These arches divide the structure into five bays, nave and two aisles. Trompe l'oeil *architectural paintings* (1503) by Giovanni Maria Falconetto in the side chapels of the first three bays were uncovered in 1870. A superb *Assumption* (1532) by Titian in a marble frame by Jacopo Sansovino can be seen on the 1st altar on the left. The triptych of the Virgin Mary with St.George and St.Jerome is signed by Antonio Brenzoni (1533). An Epiphany altarpiece by Liberale da Verona on the 2nd altar in the right aisle is surrounded by three paintings by Niccolò Giolfino (Lamentation, Saints, 1529). The white marble Romanesque *font* by the pillar is supported by three small caryatids. The *Cappella del Sacramento* (1435), the 4th chapel on the right, was redesigned and domed in 1759–62 in a style partly baroque and partly already neoclassical. The organ galleries (16C) are in the 5th bay. Behind the altar of the *Cappella Mazzanti* (1508) at the end of the right aisle is the sumptuous Gothic *tomb* (1353) of the martyred St.Agatha of Verona; a statue of the Saint surmounts the urn which is decorated with a bas-relief (Pietà) and the whole stands beneath a Gothic baldacchino. It was probably the wish of Bishop Pietro della Scala, who discovered the relics, that the monument should be similar to the Scaliger tombs (see p.283). The elegant marble *choir screens* by Michele Sanmicheli in 1534 on the site of a former late-Gothic rood screen, have Ionic columns, plain architrave beams and a central triumphal arch. The frescos (1534) on the choir arch (Annunciation with Prophets Isaiah and Ezekiel), choir vault (Nativity, Coronation of the Virgin Mary) and apse calotte (Ascension) were painted by Francesco Torbido to cartoons by Giulio Romano. The large Resurrection fresco in the *Cappella Maffei* on the left of the church, with lavish Renaissance decorations, is also by Torbido.

To the N. of the cathedral is the Romanesque *cloister*, with narrow arcades on delicate pairs of columns (*c.* 1140), and the remnants of former floor mosaics (late 4C) from the early-Christian basilica. The cloister leads to two further buildings. The first of these is the small 12C church of *S.Elena*, which was founded in 813 by Pacificus, a famous architect, mathematician and arch-deacon, and this church has a stone triptych (Virgin Mary with Saints; 15C) in a polychrome frame. The second building is the baptistery of *S.Giovanni in Fonte* (1122–35), whose low basilican interior has a superb *font* (*c.*

1200). This splendid example of local Romanesque sculpture consists of an octagonal marble monolith with a hollowed out clover-leaf shape; the outer sides have reliefs showing scenes from the life and sufferings of Christ.

The outer walls of the baptistery are built of layers of red and white stone and may be best appreciated from the *Piazza Vescovado* (N. of the cathedral choir apse) with the *bishops' palace*. The latter's façade (1502) has Venetian battlements and an *early-Renaissance portal* in Venetian style, with good sculptures (Virgin Mary Enthroned between St.Peter, St.Paul and the Archangel Michael). The small *courtyard* with its Romanesque colonnaded portico is overlooked by the *tower* (1172) of the former bishops' palace. In front of this, on a tall pedestal, stands a monumental *figure of David* (16C) by Alessandro Vittoria. The *Palazzo Malaspina*, crowned by a tall loggia, is in the *Piazza Duomo;* in the adjoining *Via Duomo* there are three houses *(Nos. 1, 6, 10)* with fine Renaissance portals.

S.Anastasia (piazza S.Anastasia): In *c.* 1290 the Dominicans began building this Gothic brick church in honour of *Peter the Martyr* (Peter of Verona), their brother and inquisitor who was murdered in 1252. The church, which takes its name from the previous Arian church of Theoderic, was completed in the 15C and restored in the 19/20C. The unfaced *façade* has a double portal (*c.* 1335) with splendid architrave reliefs of New Testament scenes, above which there is a *rose window*. The tall *campanile* (1423–81) has a conical roof with white marble ribs. Arcades on gigantic round pillars divide the spacious, groin-vaulted *interior* into nave and two aisles; a broad transept immediately adjoined by five choir chapels to the E., follows the scheme of Italian churches of the mendicant orders. Polygonal apses replacing the flat part usually at the back of the choir, are a typically Veneto variation on this scheme. The interior houses several sumptuous items from the 14–16C, including a 16C *holy water stoup* supported on

Scaligers' tomb

S.Fermo Maggiore, fresco above the entrance

hunchbacked caryatids at the first pair of pillars. The 4th chapel in the left aisle has a polychrome *marble Renaissance altar* of the Miniscalchi family, with fine sculptures (*c.* 1490) on both sides of the altarpiece (Descent of the Holy Spirit, 1518) by Niccolò Giolfino. At the beginning of the right aisle is the *tomb* of Condottiere Giano Fregoso, designed by Michele Sanmicheli and decorated with outstanding statues (1565) by Danese Cattaneo. The *tomb monument* (1424–9) of Condottiere Cortesia Serego, whose *equestrian statue* surmounts the sarcophagus, is especially interesting. Opposite the latter, on the right of the choir, is a large *fresco of the Last Judgement* from the 14C, discovered in 1942. To the right of the main chapel is the *Cappella Pellegrini* with two Gothic wall tombs of the Pellegrini and Bevilacqua families and 24 terracotta alto-relievos of the Life of Christ (1435) by Michele da Firenze. Also to the right is the *Cappella Cavalli* with well-known frescos by Altichiero Altichieri (St.George, St.Martin and St.James recommending three knights of the Cavalli family to the Enthroned Virgin Mary; St.Eligius curing a horse; *c.* 1395). The domed *chapel of the rosary,* which opens towards the 5th bay of the left aisle, was added in 1586–96 and has 17C sculptures and paintings.

The wide gateway arch of the former Dominican monastery to the left of the church façade is surmounted by the Gothic *baldacchino monument* to Count Guglielmo da Castelbarco (d. 1320). Also in the *Piazza S.Anastasia,* on the W. side, is the Gothic brick church of *S.Giorgetto,* also known as S.Pietro Martire.

S.Bernardino (vicolo Lungo S.Bernardino): This *Franciscan church* lies in an obscure location to the W. of the Castelvecchio (see below). It was built in 1452–75 in honour of Bernardino of Siena, who was canonized in 1450. A *cloister* with small red marble columns extends—in the manner of Romanesque paradises (projections in front of portals)—outside the brick façade. The latter has a marble Renaissance portal (1474/5) with statues. On the right of the tall single-aisled *interior* there are five chapels with frescos and other paintings by numerous artists: Niccolò Giolfino (Arrest of Christ, Christ before Pilate, Crucifixion, all 1500; Lives of St.John and St.Francis, 1522), Francesco Bonsignori (Virgin Mary Enthroned between Angels, St.George and St.Jerome, 1488), Domenico and Francesco Morone (Crucifixion, 1498) and Antonio Badile (Raising of Lazarus, 1546). The *triptych at the high altar* (Virgin Mary with Angels and Saints; 1462) was painted by Francesco Benaglio in the manner of Mantegna (cf. S.Zeno Maggiore, below). The old *library* on the upper storey of the monastery can be visited in the company of a Franciscan monk. It is also known as 'Sala Morone', owing to its lavish frescos by Domenico and Francesco Morone and their pupils (St.Francis of Assisi and St.Clare commending the Sagramosi, the married couple who founded the building, to the Virgin Mary's intercession; Franciscan Saints, martyrs and scholars; 1503).

S.Eufemia (via Francesco Emilei): Gothic church with a brick façade built by an order of hermits in 1275–1331. A Renaissance monument (1550) to the Lavagnoli family, designed by Michele Sanmicheli, and a Romanesque monument (1279) to Cavalcan Cavalcani, are to be found to the left and right respectively of the late-Gothic *portal* (1486). The single-aisled *interior* was redesigned in baroque style in 1739 and given a vault. Behind the 19C high altar is the cenotaph (*c.* 1400) of the Dal Verme family. Fresco fragments of a Last Judgement (*c.* 1400) by Martino da Verona can be seen on the right choir wall. The rib-vaulted *Cappella Dal Verme* (1390) has retained its Gothic appearance; the left wall has frescos of the life of Tobias (early 15C) by Francesco Caroto. The nave also contains some good altarpieces by Giambettino Cignaroli (Virgin Mary and St.Thomas of Villanova, 18C), Domenico Brusasorci (Virgin Mary with St.Augustine, St.Monica, St.Roch,

S.Fermo Maggiore

St.Sebastian and two founders, 16C) and Moretto da Brescia (Virgin Mary in Glory with St.Antony Abbot and St.Onofrius, 16C).

S.Fermo Maggiore (stradone S.Fermo): This church consists of an early-Christian *lower church* (*c.* 490) rebuilt by the Benedictines in 1065–1138, and a 12C *upper church* redesigned in Gothic style by the Minorites in *c.* 1313. The *exterior* has a correspondingly inconsistent appearance. The fine E. section has Romanesque side apses and a polygonal main apse rebuilt in Gothic style. The Romanesque *cloister* lies to the left of the 13C Romanesque *campanile*, which is built mostly of tufa and has a 14C Gothic conical roof. External steps (1592) outside the *W. façade* lead to the stepped main portal. The tomb (1385) of Avertino Fracastoro, the Scaligers' personal physician, is let into the façade wall to the left of the steps. Blind arches which articulate the pedestal

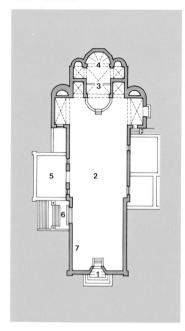

Verona, S.Fermo, upper church 1 Main portal with steps (1592) **2** Nave with keel vault (1314) **3** Sanctuary with frescos (14C) **4** Polygonal choir apse with late-Gothic choir stalls (15C) **5** Cappella del Santissimo with altarpiece (1528) by Francesco Caroto **6** Double portal (1363) with portal baldacchino (c. 1400) **7** Monument (1427-39) to Niccolò Brenzoni by Nanni di Bartolo

area of the façade are interrupted on the N. side by the two portals of the lower church. A wide portal baldacchino (c. 1400) covers the *double portal* (1363) leading into the upper church.

The single-aisled upper church is distinguished by its stepped wooden *keel vault* (1314), the oldest one surviving in the Veneto. The rich decorations are of varying artistic quality, and include numerous frescos (14/15C) and sculptures (15/16C). The monument of Niccolò Brenzoni (1427/39) by Nanni di Bartolo (known as Rosso Fiorentino) on the N. wall is framed by the earliest surviving *fresco* (Annunciation) by Antonio Pisano (known as Pisanello). There is an excellent painting of St.Nicholas by Battista dal Moro on the

altar next to this. The *Cappella del Santissimo*, with an altarpiece by Giovanni Francesco Caroto (St.Anne with the Madonna and Child and Saints, 1528) is in the middle of the N. wall. The *screens* outside the choir (with 14C frescos) were built in 1573 in imitation of the choir screens in the cathedral (see above). 15C late-Gothic *choir stalls* of original design stand behind the baroque altar (1759). The *lower church*, which can be entered from the sacristy, may be visited in the company of the sacristan. Three rows of columns and pillars divide it into four aisles with groin vaults. Among the 13/14C frescos on the pillars, that of the *Trinity* on the 2nd pillar on the right in the nave may be mentioned as an iconographic rarity. A late-14C wooden crucifix stands behind the high altar (1758).

S.Giorgio in Braida (via S.Alessio): This church (1477–1536) stands on the left bank of the Adige opposite the cathedral and has a white early-baroque *marble façade*, and a dome (completed 1604) with a drum designed by Michele Sanmicheli. The rather severe single-aisled *interior* boasts an abundance of *High Renaissance paintings* by Northern Italian artists. The four side chapels on the left have altarpieces by Francesco Caroto (St.Ursula with virgins, c. 1545; St.Joseph with the Saints who provided relief from the plague), Sigismondo de' Stefani (Martyrdom of St.Laurence, 1564) and Girolamo dai Libri (Sacra Conversazione, 1526). Paintings in the four chapels on the right are by Francesco Montemezzano (Noli me tangere, 1580), Pasquale Ottino (Virgin Mary in Glory and Saints), Domenico Tintoretto (Descent of the Holy Ghost) and Felice Brusasorci (Virgin Mary in Glory and three Archangels, c. 1590). Paintings of the Annunciation (16C) on both sides of the choir opening are by Giovanni Caroto. Two enormous paintings are by Felice Brusasorci (Miracle of Manna; completed by his pupils) and Paolo Farinati (Feeding of the Five Thousand, 1603).

S.Giovanni in Foro (corso Porta Borsari): A small Romanesque church with

S.Zeno Maggiore, portal

conspicuous masonry consisting of alternating layers of ashlars and brick.

S.Giovanni in Valle (vicolo Pozzo): This little church mentioned in the 8C stands to the E. of the Roman theatre (see above). Rebuilt in Romanesque style after earthquake damage (1117), it was consecrated in 1164. The three apses in the E. section have a round-arched frieze under the eaves, with bas-reliefs. The *N. apse* also has polychrome masonry (layers of tufa and brick) and projections which articulate the wall. The decorations in the basilican *interior* were destroyed in a bombing raid in 1944. The *crypt* below the raised sanctuary also has a nave and two aisles, and in its W. pre-Romanesque section there are 9C columns; the E. section is 12C. On the right there is a late-Romanesque sarcophagus and, opposite it on the left, an *early-Christian sarcophagus*

S.Zeno Maggiore, portal detail ▷

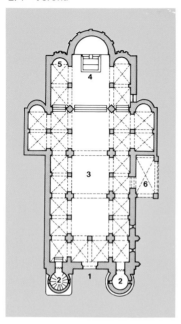

Verona, S.Lorenzo **1** W. portal **2** Cylindrical façade towers **3** Nave **4** Choir with painting (1566) by Domenico Brusasorci **5** Fresco of St.Francis of Assisi (1st half of 15C) **6** Main entrance with Renaissance portico

(4C) carved from a single block of Parian marble and bearing interesting reliefs (bearded Christ above the four rivers of Paradise with the Apostle princes, three miraculous scenes, the kiss of Judas with a beardless Christ, and Old Testament scenes).

S.Lorenzo (corso Cavour): Documented in the late 8C, this church—like S.Giovanni in Valle—was restored in Romanesque style after the earthquake of 1117. Later decorations were removed in the 19/20C. Polychrome outer walls show that initially the church was built with alternating layers of tufa, brick and pebbles (c. 1100); a second phase of building shows alternating layers of tufa and brick—a characteristic feature of the city's architecture (c. 1120–90). The Romanesque form of the two round *corner towers* (c. 1190)

on the façade is unusual in the Veneto, as is that of the two side chapels which resemble transepts and have apses in the E. The S. portal has a *Renaissance colonnaded portico* (later than 1477).

Much inside the church was destroyed in World War 2, but the *interior*, which is built in alternating layers of yellow and red stone, is still worth visiting. Round arches with alternating columns and pillars divide the area into a nave with an open roof truss (restored) and groin-vaulted aisles with galleries, which are interconnected by a *narthex* in the W. The tall main apse has a good painting by Domenico Brusasorci (Virgin Mary appearing to St.Laurence, St.Augustine and St.John the Baptist). There are two 16C Renaissance tomb monuments in the left aisle.

S.Maria in Organo (interrato dell' Acqua Morta): This late-Romanesque *Olivetan church* is most attractive architecturally and received its present form in 1481. The *façade* is surmounted by Gothic decorations; the lower part has a splendid 16C marble facing by Michele Sanmicheli. The *campanile* (1495–1533) was built to designs by Fra Giovanni da Verona. The *interior* has nave, two aisles, transept, crossing with dome, sanctuary with side chapels, and a monks' choir. The *crypt* (nave and two aisles) has remains of the previous structure (7/8C) and parts of Roman walls. There are fine *Renaissance decorations*. The nave walls have frescos of scenes from the Old Testament by Giovanni Francesco Caroto (left) and Niccolò Giolfino (right), who also painted the frescos both outside and inside the right side chapel (Ascension, Collecting the Manna, Passover Feast, Instruments of the Passion, and Saints). The corresponding frescos of New Testament scenes in the left side chapel are by Domenico Brusasorci, to whom the landscape paintings on the two groups of three seats in the sanctuary and on the wooden facing of the right sacristy wall are also attributed. The monks' choir, with *choir stalls* with charming inlay work (1491–9)

S.Zeno Maggiore

◁ *S.Zeno Maggiore*

by Fra Giovanni (architectural views and still lifes), extends behind the colonnaded *baroque altar* (1714) in the sanctuary. Fra Giovanni also did the inlays on the rear walls (1519) of the stalls and on the cupboards in the *sacristy* (1504) which itself has frescos by Francesco Morone (Olivetan brethren, Popes, Fathers of the Church, Christ the Saviour). Vasari described the sacristy as the finest in Italy.

S.Pietro Incarnario (stradone di S.Fermo): Built in 955 on the remains of a Roman building, this church is overlooked by its 14C *campanile* which has a spire. The 3rd altar on the left has a painting of the Virgin Mary and Saints by Felice Brusasorci.
Remains of Roman buildings and a 12C *fresco of the Crucifixion* in the Carolingian tradition can be seen in an underground passage (if accompanied by the sacristan).

S.Stefano (via S.Alessio): This building (now restored) is one of the oldest churches in Verona. It stands on the left bank of the Adige to the N. of the Ponte Pietra bridge (see above) and was built as a single-aisled structure in the 5C and 8C, and rebuilt in Romanesque style in the 12C, when a tower with a Lombard appearance was added to the choir. The façade which is built of layers of tufa and brick has a massive *portal baldacchino* supported on columns. 6C fragments of the outer wall of the pre-Romanesque structure are still discernible under the crossing. The interior is rather plain and sombre and consists of nave and two aisles. The transversely aligned rectangular *crypt* (10C) with groin vault has a row of columns with good capitals (8/9C) and extends below the raised sanctuary which has a 10C *ambulatory* and an 8C stone bishop's throne in the apse. The *vault paintings* (Mysteries of the Passion, *c.* 1550) are by Domenico Brusasorci, and the altarpiece of the Massacre of the Innocents and ceiling frescos in the *Cappella degli Innocenti* (1618/19) in the right aisle, are by Pasquale Ottino.

S.Tommaso Cantuariense (via

Carducci): This former *Carmelite church* (1484–1504) was dedicated to St.Thomas à Becket. In 1518, its late-Gothic façade facing the river was provided with a splendid *portal* (1493) adorned with statues, and a *rose window* (1493), both of which were taken from the disused church of S.Maria Mater Domini. The single-aisled interior is adjoined by eight Renaissance chapels (four on each side) in which there are altarpieces (right side) by Alessandro Turchi (Mary Magdalene, 1604), Antonio Balestra (Annunciation, *c.* 1700), and Girolamo dai Libri (Job, Saints who provided relief from the plague, 16C). The 13-year-old Mozart played the *baroque altar* in the choir. The apse painting of the Virgin Mary and Saints (1579) by Felice Brusasorci is in the manner of Veronese.

S.Zeno Maggiore (piazza S.Zeno): This church is among the finest Romanesque religious edifices in Northern Italy, and is certainly the best building in Verona after the Arena (see above). It was founded in the 5C above the tomb of Zeno (d. 380), the first bishop of Verona who was later canonized and became the city's patron saint. Enlarged under King Pipin in the 9/10C, it was rebuilt in its present form in 1118–38 after the earthquake of 1117. The *façade* of yellowish tufa ashlars is articulated into three sections by two massive pilaster strips which have polygonal cross-sections; in between there are more delicate pilaster strips, with round-arched friezes under the eaves. The strong vertical lines in the façade are counteracted in the lower section by a horizontal succession of round-arched pairs of windows with small red marble columns, and in the upper section by the large twelve-spoke *rose window* (*c.* 1200) by Master Brioloto. This window is the first monumental rose window in Italy; two sculptures (a man falling and a man rising) around its edge suggest it may be interpreted as a wheel of fortune, to which the Last Judgement relief (*c.* 1290), previously discernible in the gable panel above, was symbolically related. A few steps lead up to the *portal* (*c.* 1138) which is by Master Nicolao and

S.Zeno Maggiore, portal detail ▷

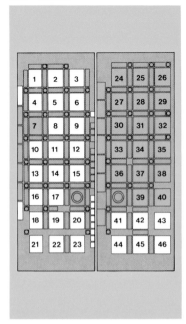

Castelvecchio

Verona, S.Zeno, bronze door panels 1 Annunciation 2 Nativity, Angel appearing to the Shepherds, and Adoration of the Magi 3 Flight into Egypt 4 Cleansing of the Temple 5 Baptism of Christ, Christ and the Adulteress 6 Dispute with the Doctors 7 Entry into Jerusalem 8 Washing the Feet 9 Last Supper 10 Arrest of Christ 11 Christ bearing the Cross 12 Christ before Pilate 13 Flagellation 14 Deposition 15 Women at Christ's tomb 16 Christ in Limbo 17 Christ in Judgement 18 Beheading of John the Baptist 19 Dance of Salome 20 Herod receiving John the Baptist's head 21 Personifications of the earth (Terra) and the primeval sea (Mare) 22 Expulsion from Paradise 23 Toiling in the fields, and Cain's killing of his brother Abel 24 Creation of Eve, Temptation by the Serpent 25 Adam and Eve before God the Father 26 Expulsion from Paradise 27 Cain's and Abel's offerings to God, the killing of Abel 28 Noah's dove with the olive twig 29 Drunkenness of Noah, Shem and Japheth accusing Ham 30 God's promise to Abraham 31 Abraham greeting the Angels, Disownment of Hagar 32 Sacrifice of Isaac 33 Moses on Mount Sinai, Aaron's flowering rod 34 Egyptian plagues, Moses before Pharaoh 35 Brazen serpent 36 Prophet Bileam 37 Rod of Jesse 38 King Solomon? 39 Messengers of Galienus encountering St.Zeno 40 St.Zeno healing Galienus' daughter 41 King Nebuchadnezzar 42 Miracle of Zeno 43 Galienus offering St.Zeno the crown 44 Sacrifice of Isaac 45 Noah's Ark 46 Archangel Michael slaying the dragon. The brass panels on the left door date from c. 1100, except for panel 7 (c. 1200); panels on the right door are c. 1200, except panels 41, 44, 45 and 46 (c. 1100).

his assistants. A large *projecting baldacchino* is supported on slender marble columns with red marble Romanesque lions at their bases. Figures of the two Saints John by 'Maestro Nicolao', as he is named in inscriptions, are seen on the portal baldacchinos of the cathedrals both in Verona (see above) and Ferrara, as well as in this particular example. The gable panel has a tondo with the hand of God by Nicolao. Other *reliefs*, mainly from Nicolao's workshop, include the architraves of the baldacchino (Cycle of the Months), the sides, the tympanum (St.Zeno presenting the banner of the free city community to knights and soldiers, Miracle of St.Zeno), and wall panels beside the portal (Life of Christ on the left, Story of Creation on the right). The bronze reliefs (of which there were originally 48) on the two wings of the famous 12C medieval *bronze door* (see drawing) depict scenes from the Old

and New Testaments, and the Miracle of St.Zeno. Two structures contributing to the harmony of the façade are the massive 13/14C *tower,* with grooved battlements, which belonged to the former Benedictine abbey (left of the church) and the tall 11/12C *campanile* with spire which stands on a white pedestal just to the side of the attractive *E. end.*

As is often the case in churches in Verona, a few steps lead down from the portal to the *interior,* which has a nave and two aisles and columns alternating with compound piers.

The nave has a late-Gothic wooden *keel vault* (1386), whose cross section is like the top half of a clover leaf. The polygonal Gothic choir (late 14C) stands on a raised platform above the *crypt* which has nave, eight aisles, ancient columns, and sculptures on the capitals and in the archivolts (*c.* 1225). A 14C crucifix by Lorenzo Veneziano hangs on the inside of the façade wall. An octagonal Romanesque

marble font (late 14C) stands at the beginning of the right aisle. In the same aisle there are 13/14C frescos, including a 13C *St.Christopher* popularly known as King Pipin. 13C *statues* (Christ and six Apostles) stand on the modern choir parapet. The finest of the decorations, however, is the splendid and celebrated *triptych* dating from 1456–9 by Andrea Mantegna. The central panel shows the Virgin Mary Enthroned between Angels making music; St.Peter, St.Paul, St.John the Evangelist and St.Zeno (left); St.John the Baptist, St.Augustine, St.Laurence, and St.Benedict of Nursia (right); the predella has the Mount of Olives, Crucifixion, and Resurrection. This triptych has occupied this, its original, place on the high altar since 1935. The choir has 14/15C frescos and 15C Gothic *choir stalls.* The polychrome *statue of Zeno* (14C) in the left side apse is known as 'San Zeno che ride', because of its smile.

The left aisle leads into the Romanesque

cloister with round arches (1123) and pointed arches (14C) supported on red marble double columns. In the ambulatory there are numerous tombs (14/15C) and the entrance (SE) to the 12C *Oratorio di S.Benedetto,* which houses beautifully worked capitals, some of which are from the 6C.

SS. Apostoli (piazzetta SS.Apostoli): This Romanesque church consecrated in 1194 has an originally free-standing *campanile* with Gothic tomb monuments built into its lower storey. In the single-aisled interior there is a baroque *high altar* (18C) by Stefano Tomezzoli. A door on the right of the choir leads to the former Romanesque *cloister,* whose small red marble double columns appear again in the two-storeyed loggia (18C) of the priest's house on the N. side of the church. The sacristy leads down to the church of *SS.Tosca e Teuteria* (consecrated in 751), which is among the oldest churches in the Veneto and was built in the 5C as a heathen temple above the remains of a 2C Roman shrine (mosaic fragments) on a Greek cross ground plan; rebuilt in 1160.

SS.Nazaro e Celso (via Muro Padri): This church was built 1464–83 by the Benedictines on a Latin cruciform ground plan and stands on the site of a former Romanesque church; late-Gothic *brick façade* and *Renaissance campanile* (c. 1550). Inside there are nave and four aisles, frescos and altarpieces by Venetian Renaissance artists, including Paolo Farinati, Girolamo Mocetto, Girolamo dai Libri, Bartolomeo Montagna and Palma Giovane. The 2nd chapel on the left has an interesting *altarpiece* of the Virgin Mary appearing to St.Antony Abbot, St.John the Baptist, St.Benedict of Nursia and St.Blasius (1544), signed by Veronese's teacher Antonio Badile. Above the high altar there is a painted processional crucifix (late 14C).

Secular buildings

1. Public buildings

Castel S.Pietro (colle S.Pietro): The *Scalone Castel S.Pietro* is an attractively wind-ing flight of steps lined by cypresses, which leads from the Ponte Pietra bridge (see above) upwards past gardens to the fortress built by the Austrians in 1854 as a barracks (originally the site of the *Castello Visconteo* which was destroyed by the French in 1801). Imposing remnants of the Castello still survive. There is a fine view of the city from this vantage point.

Castelvecchio (corso Castelvecchio): The finest secular medieval building in Verona, it was built on the orders of Cangrande II della Scala by Francesco Bevilacqua in 1354–6 and formed an extension of the city wall at the time. Bevilacqua wanted it both for his personal protection in the event of unrest within the city, and as a defence against outside enemies. The complex includes the *Ponte Scaligero* bridge (1355–75) in the N., which is 395 ft. long. Blown up by the retreating Germans on 25 April 1945, it was later rebuilt in accordance with the original. The bridge's three arches over the Adige are supported in the river by pentagonal pillars built as bastions with wall passages. The walls of the bridge have *grooved battlements* with the swallowtail shape typical of Scaliger buildings. Protection provided by these walls meant that the bridge provided a safe transport route and escape to the left bank of the Adige. Both bridgeheads were secured by gatehouse towers of which the *castle keep* (1375), the tallest of the seven towers in the Castelvecchio, still survives. The access road leading to the Scaliger bridge divides the castle into two courtyards surrounded by high brick walls with grooved battlements. The W. *palace courtyard* is adjoined in the N. by the buildings housing the court household and bodyguard, and the larger E. *barrack square* has an N. wing which also adjoins the Adige, and an E. wing with quarters for the soldiers manning the fortifications. After the Scaligers had been expelled, the city fortifications were used by the Venetians as a depot for weapons and ammunition, and also as a prison. The Austrians later employed it as a barracks. The building was thoroughly restored in 1923–6,

Juliet's balcony ▶

and since then the *Civico Museo d'Arte*, the city art museum (see below), has been housed in the rooms inside.

Piazza Brà: This Piazza, named after the broad tract of land (Braida) between the Roman and medieval city walls, lies to the SW of the Arena (see above), and has been Verona's *city centre* since the *Liston* (1770), the pedestrian promenade to the NW, was built. The *Gran Guardia* (1610–1821, now the bourse) on its S. side has a splendid staircase and rusticated arcades with a Palladian appearance. The *tower* adjoining in the W., and the *Portoni della Brà* (1389), the two-arched city gate altered in *c*. 1495, were both part of the medieval fortifications, which included a covered passage leading from the Castelvecchio (see above) to the former citadel (near today's Piazza Cittadella). The 18C *Accademia Filarmonica* by Andrea Cristofali in the W. corner of the Piazza Brà houses a *theatre* of the same name, and also the *Museo Lapidario Maffeiano* (see below). The *Palazzo Municipale* (1838, 1947–50), built on the E. side of the Piazza to plans by Giuseppe Barbieri, has large *paintings of the history of Verona* by Felice Brusasorci (Victory of Verona over the troops of Torri del Benaco in 849), Paolo (Victory over Barbarossa at Vaccaldo in 1164) and Orazio Farinati (Victory over Mantua at Ponte Molino in 1199) and Pasquale Ottino (Battle at Ponte delle Navi in 1354).

Piazza delle Erbe: This, the most picturesque square in Verona, is still used as a *market place* (it was the former Roman forum) and is surrounded by medieval buildings. Along the central axis of the square there stand a Gothic *market column* (1401), the so-called *Berlina* (14C, a marble baldacchino for the city's ruler), the *market fountain* (1368) with a Romanesque statue of the Virgin Mary, the 'Madonna Verona', and a *column of St.Mark* (1523). The narrow N. side of the square is taken up by the baroque façade of the *Palazzo Maffei* (1668), which has statues (Hercules, Zeus, Venus, Mercury, Apollo and Minerva) on its balustrade. This façade is overlooked by the tall *Torre Gardello* (1370) to its left. Remnants of 16C frescos can still be seen on the 14–16C *Case Mazzanti* (houses with loggias) in the NE. The battlemented *Casa dei Mercanti* (14C) in the SW has fine pairs of windows. The rear façades of the *Palazzo Giudici* and

Victor Emmanuel's monument

Piazza delle Erbe

Palazzo del Comune on the E. side of the square are linked by the *Arco della Costa*, through which lies the adjoining Piazza dei Signori.

Piazza dei Signori: The closed appearance of the city's former main square makes it resemble a large courtyard. A *monument to Dante* (1865) by Ugo Zannoni stands in its centre. The *Palazzo del Comune* (12–16C) in the SW corner has walls of layers of yellowish tufa and red brick. The upper section has triple windows with inserted pairs of small white marble columns, and a round-arched frieze under the eaves. Its picturesque Romanesque *courtyard*, the so-called 'Mercato Vecchio', has an elegant 15C *external staircase* known as 'Scala della Ragione', and is overlooked by the 12C *Torre dei Lamberti*, an observation tower 275 ft. high, whose fine octagonal roof dates from 1448–64. After the Palazzo del Comune come the following buildings, in a clockwise direction. The *Palazzo dei Tribunali* has a massive Scaliger tower (14C) and a splendid Renaissance portal (1532) by Michele Sanmicheli. Next comes a Renaissance house containing the old *Caffè Dante* and then there is a *triumphal arch* with a statue of Girolamo Fracastoro (1559) by Danese Cattaneo. The *Loggia del Consiglio*, built for the city council in 1476–93, is the outstanding example of Verona's early-Renaissance architecture. A round-arched loggia on the ground floor is surmounted by an upper storey with four pairs of windows, mounted by segments; above the cornice there are statues of Catullus, Pliny, Aemilius Macer, Vitruvius and Cornelius Nepos (all 15C) by Alberto da Milano. The E. side of the Piazza ends with the *Palazzo del Governo*, the Scaligers' residence (*c.* 1300), which the Venetians used as the residence of the governor (Podestà) of Verona. The *Renaissance portal* by Michele Sanmicheli on the façade (1533) facing the Piazza resembles a triumphal arch. The medieval main façade, whose gateway arch leads to a fine courtyard, looks upon the *Piazzetta S.Maria*. On the charming little square outside the 12C Romanesque basilica of *S.Maria Antica*, the Scaligers ordered architects from Ticino and sculptors from Campione to build them lavish Gothic *baldacchino tombs*, whose flattened pyramidal roofs are surmounted by equestrian statues of the deceased. The monument to Cangrande

Piazza delle Erbe

Piazza dei Signori, Dante monument

Piazza delle Erbe

I (1304–29), the greatest Scaliger, stands out above the N. portal of the church.

2. Houses and palazzi
Casa di Giulietta (21–23 via Cappello): A well-preserved medieval house (*c.* 1300) with a fine (restored) *balcony* looking onto a little courtyard, it is held in the popular imagination to have been Juliet's house and to have provided the setting for scenes from Shakespeare's play 'Romeo and Juliet' (1597).

Casa di Romeo (2–4 arche Scaligere): A 14C house, with grooved battlements, fine windows, and a courtyard lined with arcades, it is regarded as Romeo's home, although the first known version of the tragedy, the work of Masuccio Salernitano ('Il novellino', 1476), is set in Siena. Luigi da Porto moved the scene to Verona in 'Giulietta e Romeo' (1524).

Corso Cavour: This street which runs

above the Roman Decumanus Maximus contains many of the best palazzi in the city. The *Palazzo Carlotti* (No. 2) by Prospero Schiavi has a slightly convex façade (1665). *Palazzo Carnesali* (Nos. 5–9) is early 16C. *Palazzo Pozzani* (No. 10) is Gothic. The Renaissance palazzo of the *Scannagatti* family (No. 11) has elegantly sculptured casings around the portal and windows. The *Palazzo Bevilacqua* (No. 19) was built using ancient forms by Michele Sanmicheli in 1530. The classical *Palazzo Portalupi* (No. 38, 1802–04) is the work of Gaetano Pinter. The impressive *Palazzo Canossa* (No. 44) is by Sanmicheli (1530–7). The classical *Palazzo Balladoro* (No. 41) is by Luigi Trezza.

Palazzo e Giardino Giusti (2 via Giardino Giusti): Behind the *Villa Giusti* (1580), with its elegant portico, there is an 18C *garden*, laid out on a hill with terraces, belvedere and shady paths.

S.Anastasia, 'St.George and the Princess', fresco by Pisanello

Palazzo Malfatti (16 piazza Brà): Of all the houses along the Liston (see Piazza Brà, above), this palazzo is especially striking. Built by Michele Sanmicheli in 1555, it has a rusticated portico and Doric pillars. It was formerly the Palazzo Guastaverza.

Palazzo Pompei (9 lungadige Porta Vittoria): Today the *Museum of Natural Science* is housed in this palazzo, which was built by Sanmicheli in imitation of the Palazzo Bevilacqua (also 1530; see Corso Cavour, above). The museum is devoted to cultural finds (Rooms XVIII and XIX), including Bronze Age objects from the region around Lake Garda.

Tomba di Giulietta (via del Pontiere): The pretty *Capuchin cloister* with the former church of *S.Francesco al Corso* leads past a bust of Shakespeare (1910) to a small staircase descending to two underground rooms, the smaller of which contains a pink *marble sarcophagus*. Although 'unfeeling connoisseurs assert that it was formerly probably used as a horse-trough' (H.V. Morton), the loving couples who make the pilgrimage here take it to be Juliet's tomb, and it is here that they swear to be eternally true to one another.

Via Sottoriva: Charming medieval *houses with loggias* survive in the picturesque street S. of the church of S.Anastasia (see above). The 14C *Casa Azzini* has two large Romanesque double windows and 15C Gothic windows.

3. Gates and city fortifications

The *city walls*, extended by the Scaligers in *c.* 1300, were reinforced under the Venetians in the 16C after the war against the League of Cambrai. New city gates were also begun at that time; these included the (restored) *Porta Vescovo* (1520) in the SE, and the *Porta S.Giorgio* (1525), the white marble Renaissance gate in the N. of the city. The other gates, built under the supervision of and to plans by Michele Sanmicheli, are the imposing *Porta Nuova* (1533–40) in the S., the *Porta S.Zeno* (1541/2) in the W., and the rusticated *Porta Palio* (1542–57) in the S., which has Doric semi-columns and a triglyph frieze, and was described by G.Vasari as the 'miracolo del Sanmicheli'.

4. Libraries

Biblioteca Capitolare (13 piazza Duomo): This *library* was founded in the 5C by the 'Schola Sacerdotum Sanctae Veronensis Ecclesiae', then a seminary. It is among the oldest and best collections of ecclesiastical manuscripts and books in the Western world. The best of its treasures are a 5C *Evangelistary* written entirely in silver and gold, a *palimpsest* ('Institutions of Gaius', 5C), a copy of *St.Augustine's work* 'De Civitate Dei' (5C), the *Codex Justiniani* (6C) and a *manuscript by Ursicinus* (Sulpicius Severus) dating from 517.

Biblioteca Civica (43 via Cappello): The well-stocked *city library* (over 400,000 volumes) was founded in 1792 and has over 3,700 manuscripts and 1,200 early

Verona, Piazza dei Signori

printed books, including ecclesiastical manuscripts from the 9–14C and the *statutes of the city of Verona* in several editions (13/14C), some of which are illuminated; it also has a copy of the first book printed in Italy to bear the date of printing (an edition of Lactantius, 1465).

5. Museums

Galleria d'Arte Moderna (1 via Forti): The *Museo del Risorgimento,* dealing with 19/20C Italian history, and the *State Gallery of Modern Art,* with 19/20C paintings and sculptures by renowned local and Italian artists, are housed in the 18C *Palazzo Forti-Emilei,* where a section of the previous Romanesque building can be seen in the courtyard. The recently rearranged collections give a good combined view of neoclassical, Romanesque and contemporary art in Verona.

Museo Archeologico (formerly the Convento di S.Girolamo): The *Archaeological Museum* is housed in a former monastery building above the Roman theatre (see above). It is a surprisingly good collection arranged in exemplary fashion in the rooms around the cloister and includes Etruscan finds, Greek and Roman small bronzes, terracottas and vases, and fragments of Roman architecture, sculpture and mosaics. Two particularly interesting items are a marble head (the youthful Augustus) and another portrait sculpture (the Pestrino portrait) from the 1C BC. On the far side of the *monastery church* (which has ceiling frescos by Caroto) there are well-preserved Roman *terraces,* from which there is a view over the tops of the cypresses by the Roman theatre down to the Adige and the city's old quarter.

Museo d'Arte (Castelvecchio): This, the best art collection in Verona, has been housed in the former residential rooms (restored) of the Castelvecchio (see above) since 1933. The entrance is in the NE corner of the large barrack square. *Room I:* Romanesque sculptures and gold items from the early Middle Ages. *Room II:* 14C Local figures of saints carved in tufa. *Rooms III* and *IV:* Fragments of 14C Veronese sculptures and reliefs. *Room V:*

Early-15C Veronese sculptures. *Room VI:* 14C Veronese bells. *Room VII:* Weapons from the Middle Ages and the early modern period. *Room VIII:* 14C Venetian gold work. *Room IX:* 14C fresco fragments. *Room X:* 14C paintings, including some by Tomaso da Modena (Apostles James and Thomas). *Room XI:* Late-Gothic Veronese and Venetian artists, including: Stefano da Verona, Jacopo Bellini, Michele Giambono, and Pisanello (Virgin Mary of the Quail). *Room XII* (cabinet): 15C Flemish paintings. *Room XIII:* Crucifixes and altar paintings from the 14/15C. *Room XIV:* Renaissance frescos and panel paintings by 15C Veronese artists: Niccolò Giolfino, Domenico Morone, Giovanni Maria Falconetto and Girolamo Mocetto. *Room XV:* Venetian Renaissance paintings from *c.* 1500, by Gentile and Giovanni Bellini (two Virgin Mary paintings), Vittore Carpaccio, Bartolomeo Montagna and Marco Basaiti. *Rooms XVI* and *XVII:* Veronese Renaissance paintings by Francesco Morone, Francesco dai Libri, Domenico Morone, Francesco Bonsignori and Antonio Vivarini (St.Christopher). *Room XVIII:* Renaissance paintings by Liberale da Verona. *Room XIX:* (cabinet in a tower): Fine Renaissance paintings by Andrea Mantegna (Virgin Mary with St.Juliana, Holy Family, Christ carrying the Cross), Carlo Crivelli (Lady of Sorrows), Girolamo dai Libri (Virgin Mary) and Francesco Francia (Sacra Conversazione). *Room XX:* (upper storey of tower): Weapons and Oriental fabrics from the tomb of Cangrande I (opened in 1921). *Rooms XXI* and *XXII:* Renaissance paintings by Giovanni and Giovanni Francesco Caroto (boy with drawing, young monk, Pietà, Virgin Mary with St.Joseph, St.Francis and St.Clare of Assisi, and St.John as a boy). *Room XXIII:* 16C Venetian paintings by Lorenzo Lotto (portrait of a man), Jacopo Tintoretto (Virgin Mary suckling the infant Christ, Concert of Muses, Presentation in the Temple) and Paolo Veronese (two Depositions, Pala Bevilacqua). *Room XXIV:* 16/17C Veneto artists influenced by Tintoretto and Veronese, and a life-sized portrait (Pase Guarienti, 1556) by Paolo Veronese. *Rooms XXV* and *XXVI:* Veronese and Venetian paintings from the 17/18C by: Francesco Maffei, Pasquale Ottino (Body of Christ), Marcantonio Bassetti, Pietro Longhi (Venetian family), Giovanni Battista Tiepolo (three Camaldolensian Saints

Verona, performance of La Traviata in the Arena

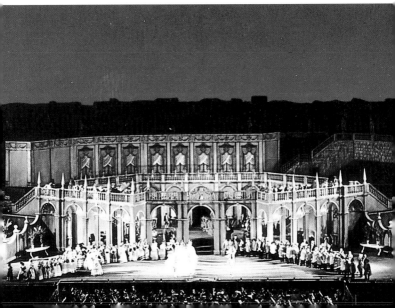

with St.Theresa), Francesco Guardi (Landscapes) and Bernardo Strozzi (Expulsion from Paradise).

Museo Lapidario Maffeiano (28 piazza Brà): The first European collection of stone monuments was set up in the forecourt of the Accademia Filarmonica (see Piazza Brà, above) in 1714 by *Scipione Maffei*, antiquarian and linguist (1675–1755). This important collection includes Etruscan, Greek, Roman, early-Christian and Medieval marble monuments and architectural fragments from Italy and former Venetian colonies in the Greek world. There are *Greek tombstone stelae* and *reliefs* from the 4C BC, and the Imperial Roman tomb sculptures which so moved Goethe when he visited the museum on 16 September 1786.

Museo Miniscalchi Erizzo (2 via S.Mammaso): The late-Gothic *Palazzo Miniscalchi*, enlarged in the 16C, houses a valuable *art collection* (open to the public), consisting of ancient ceramics, sculptures, bronzes, glassware and small art objects, along with paintings by Palma Giovane, Pordenone, Tintoretto and Alessandro Longhi (portrait of Nicolò Erizzo).

Customs and public events: The *'Baccanale del Gnocco'*, a traditional procession with festive carriages, is held on the last Friday of the carnival. It proceeds from the Piazza S.Zeno to the Piazza dei Signori and back. The *spring opera season* at the Philharmonic Theatre runs from March to June. The *festival opera performances* are held in the Arena from mid-July to mid-August. The *Shakespeare festival performances* can be seen in the Roman theatre in July and August. The *autumn symphony season* at the Philharmonic Theatre lasts from October to December.

Environs: Grezzana (11 km. N.): The Romanesque parish church of *S.Maria*, which has been altered several times, has a fine Romanesque campanile (restored 1950). Of interest inside the church are a Romanesque font, 15C Gothic choir stalls, and a 16C altarpiece by Felice Brusasorci. The 17C *Villa Allegri-Arvedi*

(Cuzzana district), built to the plans of Giovan Battista Bianchi, has towers at the sides, and steps leading up to the rear façade. Ceiling frescos by Louis Dorigny in the central drawing room. Fine *park* in the Italian garden style.

Lavagno-S.Pietro (13 km. E.): Near the neo-Gothic Villa Milano is the early-Gothic Olivetan church of *S.Giacomo del Grigiano* (late 14C). Its E. section is based on the designs of Giovanni and Niccolò da Ferrara. The choir chapel and the right side chapel have early-15C frescos by pupils of Altichieri.

Montòrio Veronese (7 km. NE): Only ruins survive from the 14C *Castello di Montorio*, a Scaliger castle with four tall fortified towers, which was built as a military outpost to guard the N. and E. access roads to Verona.

S.Maria in Stelle (8.5 km. N.): The *Pantheon di S.Maria in Stelle* (key obtainable from the parish priest) stands near this pre-Romanesque parish church which has been altered several times. The underground Roman nymphaeum was founded by Pomponius Cornelianus, as an inscription declares. From the atrium a low passage leads into a square fountain room. The side room on the left has good frescos of New Testament scenes (5C), fragments of Roman floor mosaics, and a Roman tomb altar reworked in the late 15C.

S.Michele Extra (4 km. E.): The *Madonna di Campagna* is a 16C pilgrimage church attributed to Sanmicheli. A circular building, it has a Tuscan colonnaded ambulatory. The interior is octagonal and has fine altarpieces by Felice Brusasorci (Flagellation of Christ, 16C) and Carlo Ridolfi (Assumption, 17C).

Zevio (16 km. SE): In the central Piazza stand the medieval *Castello*, rebuilt in the 18C, and the 19C *parish church* by Bartolomeo Giuliari, with a 15C campanile with spire. There are paintings by Domenico Brusasorci (Virgin Mary with Apostle Princes and two Bishops) in the right aisle and by Pasquale Ottino (Coronation of the Virgin Mary, with Saints who provided relief from the plague) in the choir. The nearby priest's *house* has an elegant Renaissance portal of red Veronese marble.

36100 Vicenza

Vicenza   p.322☐E 5

This city stands at the foot of the *Monti Bérici,* at the confluence of the *Retrone* and *Bacchiglione* rivers. Thanks to the well-preserved architecture in its old quarter, Vicenza is among the most artistically interesting towns not only in the Veneto but in the whole of Italy. The Roman town of *Vicetia* (first mentioned in 135 BC) on the *Via Postumia* was granted the status of a town in 49 BC. The grid pattern of the roads in the ancient camp with its central forum (Piazza dei Signori) is still evident in the city's appearance today. Vicenza was devastated in the Barbarian Invasions. After a period of Lombard, and later episcopal rule, the city became a free community in the 12C, and fought on the side of the Lombard League in 1146 against Emperor Frederick Barbarossa. Frederick II laid Vicenza waste in 1236. A period of Scaliger rule (1311–87) was followed by the domination of the Visconti, until the city voluntarily submitted to the rule of Venice in 1404. Among the famous sons of Vicenza were: *Antonio Pigafetta* (1491–1534), the seafarer who sailed round the world at Magellan's side; the architect *Vincenzo Scamozzi* who, in his textbook entitled 'Idea dell'Architettura Universale' (1615), propagated throughout Europe the classicism which he had imbibed from Palladio and Sansovino; *Francesco Maffei,* the main representative of the Vicenza school of painting which flourished in the 17C; and above all *Andrea Palladio,* the Paduan architect who lived and worked in Vicenza (the city is often referred to as the 'Città del Palladio').

Sacred buildings

Duomo S.Maria Maggiore (piazza del Duomo): The Gothic cathedral was begun in *c.* 1400 on the site of a previous Romanesque building. It was only completed in the 16C when the dome, to which Palladio contributed, was added. The damage sustained in World War 2

Vicenza, Loggia del P.del Capitano ▷

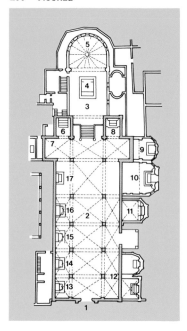

S. Corona

Vicenza, S.Corona 1 Main portal, with rose window 2 Gothic nave 3 Renaissance sanctuary 4 High altar (1669) with two altar tables and a marble tabernacle 5 Choir apse with intarsia pews (architectural scenes and landscapes) 6 Cappella della S.Spina with Gothic thorn reliquary 7 Altarpiece (St.Raymund with Christ in Glory) by Alessandro Maganza 8 Cappella Thiene with monuments (14/15C) to the Thiene family, and an altarpiece (1723) by Giovan Battista Pittoni 9 Cappella Barbaran 10 Chapel of the Rosary with statues (17C) by Giovanni Battista Albanese 11 Altarpiece (Adoration of the Magi, 1573) by Paolo Veronese 12 Painted marble slab (Blessed Carriero) by Francesco Maffei 13 Alto relievo (Holy Trinity with Angels) by Giovanni Battista Krone 14 Lombard Renaissance altar (1530) with paintings (Life of St.Mary Magdalene) by Bartolomeo Montagna 15 Altar (1598) attributed to Francesco Albanese, with painting (St.Antony of Padua distributing alms) by Leandro Bassano 16 Altarpiece (Virgin Mary with Angels) by an unknown High Renaissance artist 17 Altar by Rocco da Vicenza, with painting (Baptism of Christ) by Giovanni Bellini

was repaired in 1946–50. Its architectural history can be clearly read from the *exterior*. The Gothic façade (1467) of polychrome marble has large blind arches in

its lower section. The *portal* has copies of statues, the originals of which date from 1469. The 11C Romanesque *campanile* stands on the remains of Roman buildings near the *Renaissance apse* (1482–1508) which is articulated by pilasters. The Romanesque *S. portal* (c. 1290) dates from the previous structure, while the *N. portal*, which makes a Palladian impression, dates from 1575.

The single-aisled groin-vaulted *interior* has an elevated choir with red marble steps leading up to it. The so-called 'Madonna Mora' (c. 1450), carved, in a polychrome frame, is in the *crypt* underneath (the crypt was redesigned in 1606–08). The *marble high altar* (1535), richly decorated by Giovanni da Pedemuro and Girolamo Pittoni, stands in the domed sanctuary. The 7th side chapel on the left has a monument (1574) by Girolamo and Giovanni Battista Gualdo. A Gothic marble sarcophagus (1359) forms the altar table in the 4th chapel on the left. The 5th chapel on the

S.Corona, elephant outside side portal   *S.Maria dei Servi*

right has a Byzantine polyptych (Dormition of the Virgin Mary, Crucifixion, Apostles, Evangelists and Saints; 1356) by Lorenzo Veneziano. The 3rd chapel on the right has a painting of the Adoration of the Magi by Francesco Maffei. The 4th chapel on the left has a late work by Bartolomeo Montagna (Virgin Mary with St.Lucy and St.Mary Magdalene). There is a late-Gothic altarpiece of the Coronation of the Virgin (1448) by Niccolò da Venezia in the 5th chapel on the left. The sacristan will take the visitor to see remains of the following structures in the extensive *underground rooms* accessible from the crypt: the 8C Lombard basilica, an 11C early-Romanesque basilica and a Roman road.

The so-called 'Criptoportico Romano', an underground *Roman portico* (1C BC), is in the basement of the Palazzo Proti on the S. side of the Piazza Duomo. Opposite this is the *Oratorio del Gonfalone* (1596), which contains numerous paintings by Palma

Giovane and Andrea Vicentino, as well as many paintings from the Maganza studio.

S.Bernardino (Corso S.Tomaso): This church begun in late-Gothic style in 1451 is also known as *S.Chiara*. It was restored in 1883. An octagonal *centrally planned building*, it has pilaster strips at the corners, Gothic-arch friezes, adjoining chapels and a polygonal drum. The portal has an early-16C relief of St.Bernard of Siena. Inside, the *high altarpiece* of the Holy Family is by Alessandro Maganza.

S.Corona: (Contrà S.Corona): This *Dominican church* (restored) was built to house a thorn relic reputedly from Christ's crown of thorns. Begun in 1261, it was the first Gothic religious building in Vicenza. In 1479–1504 it was given a new choir section designed by Lorenzo da Bologna. Fine features of the *exterior* include the richly decorated terracotta cornice of the choir, the splendid marble portal in the façade (rebuilt in 1888), and the elegant campanile. Gothic arches on massive columns divide the rib-vaulted interior into nave and two aisles. Red marble steps lead up to the elevated sanctuary. Below the sanctuary is the 15/16C *crypt*, from which the 16C *Cappella Valmarana*, designed by Palladio, is accessible. 15/16C *choir stalls*, inlaid by Fra Giorgio Bovio, stand behind the baroque *high altar* (1669–86). The left side chapel contains the sumptuous *Gothic reliquary* (14C) with the thorn relic, which was donated by St. Louis of France. The chief artistic attraction is the 5th altar in the left aisle, whose showpiece 16C altar by Rocco da Vicenza, itself a splendid piece of work, has the Baptism of Christ (*c.* 1500/05), by Giovanni Bellini, the finest work of his later period. Another splendid *altarpiece* is the Adoration of the Magi (1573) by Paolo Veronese in the 4th chapel on the right. *The Palazzo da Monte-Migliorini* (No. 9), said to be built in 1581 to the designs of Andrea Palladio, and the 17C *Palazzo Leoni-Montanari* (No. 21), a baroque palazzo (*c.* 1676–87) with the lavishly stuccoed 'Corridor of Truth' (restored) in the piano nobile, also stand in the Contrà S.Corona.

S.Lorenzo (piazza S.Lorenzo): This *Franciscan church*, begun in early-Gothic style after the previous Romanesque church had been pulled down in 1280, was completed in the 15C. There are seven tall, blind Gothic arches in the lower part of the façade, which also has a splendid 14C *portal baldacchino*, whose columns rest on sculptures of lions. The portal is flanked by two *baldacchino wall tombs* on each side. There is a large round window above the portal and the gable has five smaller round windows with polychrome frames and ascending round-arched friezes. The portal itself has fine *reliefs* on the jambs (twelve patriarchs and prophets) and architrave (God the Father and Saints). Reliefs in the tympanum (Virgin Mary Enthroned with St.Francis of Assisi and St.Laurence, and a small founder figure) are by Andriolo de'Santi.

Round pillars with Attic bases, and early-Gothic lotus capitals divide the rib-vaulted basilican interior into nave and two aisles. Three NW-facing polygonal choir chapels adjoin the two short arms of the transept. There are numerous *Renaissance* and *baroque tombs* commemorating Vicenza's aristocratic families e.g. the baroque wall tomb decorated with military emblems, of

Santuario della Madonna di Monte Bérico, 'Banquet of St.Gregory' by Veronese

General Giambattista da Porto (1661; above the main entrance) and the two sumptuous, richly carved late-Renaissance tombs of Ippolito da Porto (1572) and Leonardo, Pietro and Lodovico da Porto (1555; left wall of the sanctuary). Double windows beside the sanctuary come from the previous Romanesque structure. The black marble altar table (1289), the original altar, is behind the modern high altar. On the right of the *chapel of the Virgin Mary* to the left of the choir there is a good fresco, which has been transferred on to canvas (Beheading of St.Paul, *c.* 1500) by Bartolomeo Montagna. The right transept has a fine Renaissance altar with framed *triptych reliefs* (Christ with angels between St.Francis of Assisi and St.Bernardino of Siena, 1474). The left transept leads into the *chapterhouse,* whose lovely double windows open on to the 15C *cloister;* there is a fountain in the middle.

Opposite the church façade is the *Palazzo Repeta* (today the Banco d'Italia), built by Francesco Muttoni in baroque style in 1701–11. Ornate decorations in the drawing-room include an allegorical marble group (Reason dominating Emotion) by Orazio Marinali.

S.Maria d'Aracoeli (piazza Aracoeli): This early-baroque church was built by Carlo Borella in 1675–80 to plans by Guarino Guarini. It stands at the E. end of the *Giardino Querini,* a large park. The sculptured decorations on the *façade,* which is articulated by columns and pilasters, are by Orazio Marinali's studio. Above the façade rises the drum with a balustrade; the dome is surmounted by a lantern. Around the elliptical *interior* ornate entrances open into the interconnected chapels. The *high altar* (1696) by Tommaso Bezi is the most lavish baroque altar in Vicenza. It is graced by a fine painting (Augustus with the sibyl Tiburtina) by Marco Liberi, and sculptures by Orazio Marinali.

S.Maria dei Servi (piazza delle Biade): The *Servite monastery church* (1407–32) by Giampietro Cermison had three bays added to it in 1490. Its façade (1710) has an elegant *Renaissance portal* (1531) and is adorned with statues by Giovanni Calvi and Orazio Muttoni. The basilican groin-vaulted interior has three rectangular choir chapels at the E. end. Capitals include early-Gothic lotus and crocket capitals and

Santuario della Madonna di Monte Bérico

late-Gothic foliate capitals on the round pillars in the nave. The 2nd *Renaissance altar* (*c.* 1500) in the left aisle is decorated with reliefs and is Lombard in appearance. The 1st altar on the right has a painting (Virgin Mary with Saints who provided relief from the plague) by Benedetto Montagna. A fine Renaissance portal leads from the right aisle into the 15C *cloister*.

S.Maria del Carmine (contrà S.Croce): The neo-Gothic *Carmelite church* (19C) includes the portals and chapel niches (15C) from the previous church of *S.Bartolomeo* (1372/3), which was pulled down. The *chapel niches* are decorated throughout with grotesque and ornamental reliefs (*c.* 1480/90). The 1st chapel on the left has an altarpiece (Virgin Mary with St.Sebastian and St.Antony Abbot, *c.* 1535) by Benedetto Montagna.

S.Nicola da Tolentino (contrà Ponte S.Michele): The *Contrà Ponte S.Michele* leads from the church of *S.Maria dei Servi* across the *Ponte di S.Michele* (the bridge over the Retrone river; built by Giovanni Battista Albanese in Venetian style in 1621–3) to the oratory of *S.Nicola da Tolentino* (16/17C) which has a façade by

Carlo Butiron (1676). Inside there are over 30 stucco-framed *paintings* from the 3rd quarter of the 17C. These are the work of artists from the Veneto, including Giulio Carpioni, Antonio Zanchi, and Francesco Maffei (Angel appearing to St.Nicholas of Tolentino, 1626; Miracle of Córdoba, 1655; Miracles of Perugia and Foligno, 1656; St.Nicholas of Tolentino interceding for the Poor Souls, 1657). The *high altarpiece* of the Holy Trinity (1651) is also by Maffei.

S.Pietro (piazza S.Pietro): This late-Gothic church (15C), with a façade added in 1597, is worth visiting for its *altarpieces* from the 16/17C by: Alessandro (Pietà, Martyrdom of St.Andrew), and Giovan Battista Maganza the younger (St.Maurus and St.Benedict of Nursia), Francesco Maffei (Adoration of the Shepherds), and Giovanni Battista Zelotti (Christ delivering the keys to Peter). The *Ospizio di S.Pietro* to the right of the church is a Benedictine monastery founded in 827. Its 15C cloister has fine terracotta decorations.

SS.Felice e Fortunato (borgo S.Felice): The basilica was founded in 313. When

Santuario della Madonna di Monte Bérico, 'Pietà' by Bartolomeo Montagna

baroque additions were removed in the 20C, Romanesque forms from rebuilding in the 10C and 12C became visible once again. In the 12C, the large round window and the *main portal* were added to the plain brick façade (9/10C). Remains of a 12C fresco (Last Judgement) are to be seen in the tympanum above the portal. The basilica is adjoined in the N. by a *baptistery* (*c.* 1400). The *campanile* (12/13C), a structure of highly original design, leans slightly; it has a 14C wall passage, double arches around the bell chamber and a 15C octagonal crown. The *interior* has a nave, two aisles, columns alternating with pillars, and a raised sanctuary above the *crypt* which contains the 4C tomb of St.Felix Martyr and St.Fortunatus Martyr. Parts of the old *mosaic floor* (4&5C) survive in the nave. The altar to the right of the sanctuary has a statue of the Virgin Mary attributed to Antonino di Nicolò. A door to the right of this leads into the *martyrs' shrine of S.Maria Mater Domini*. Built on a Greek cross ground plan in the 4C, it was later given a dome and narthex.

Large *stone sarcophagi* from the early Christian period are to be seen in the square outside the church.

Santuario della Madonna di Monte Bérico: An arcade 2,230 ft. long, built by Francesco Muttoni in 1746–78 along the *Viale X Giugno*, leads to the rounded hilltop of Monti Bérici in the S. of the city. The Gothic basilica, built in 1428 after two visions of the Virgin Mary, was enlarged in the 15C by Lorenzo da Bologna, who added the monks' choir (1476–80). An annex to the N., built by Andrea Palladio, was pulled down to make way for the present *cruciform domed basilica* (1688–1763) by Carlo Borella. The late-Gothic church's façade, which is topped by spirelets, was rebuilt in the 19C when the tall *campanile* was also erected. Façades in the W., N. and E. are articulated by pairs of columns, and have trefoil windows and rounded gables. The tall dome, with drum and metal roof, is surmounted by a domed lantern. Statues and reliefs both outside and inside the baroque church are from Orazio Marinali's studio. The chapel to the right of the organ gallery (1900) has an *altarpiece* of the Coronation of the Virgin Mary and Saints (1606) by Palma Giovane. The S. transept leads to a *small late-Gothic church* with a statue of 'Madonna di Monte Bérico' (1444) at its modern high altar. The right side altar has

Palazzo del Monte di Pietà

Loggia del Palazzo del Capitano

Piazza

a fine *Pietà painting* which is regarded as the main work of Bartolomeo Montagna (1500). Pier Antonio dall'Abate inlaid the *choir stalls* (1481–8) in the left choir chapel, along with the benches and cupboards in the *sacristy*. The sacristy also has a Pietà fresco by Montagna. A masterly *canvas* (Banquet of St.Gregory, 1572) measuring about 28.9 x 14.8 ft., by Paolo Veronese, hangs in the *refectory* on the E. side of the adjoining late-Gothic *cloister*, whose pointed arches have ornamental terracotta decorations.

Secular buildings

Basilica Palladiana/Palazzo Pubblico (piazza dei Signori): The originally Gothic *Palazzo della Ragione* (1449–94) stands on the S. side of the city's central square (the former Roman forum). The palazzo has an open hall lined with pillars, which was formerly a law court, and a large hall on the upper storey where the Grand Coun-

cil assembled. Andrea Palladio began the conversion of the old palazzo in 1546, but he did not live to see its completion (in 1617). Arcades have double columns on either side of semi-columns; the spandrels are punctured by holes. The ground floor has Doric orders, the upper storey, Ionic. The corners of the buildings are emphasized by joined pairs of semi-columns. Openings in the arcades on the upper storey have balustrades; the cornice balustrade is accentuated by statues on pedestals and these are located directly above the semi-columns throughout the storeys. The Gothic *staircase* by Zanon Marchesini and Bernardino da Milano leads to the *council chamber* ('Salone'), measuring 170 x 70 ft., on the upper storey. This room, which is illuminated by 24 oval windows, has a wooden *keel vault* (restored in the 20C). The *Torre di Piazza*, a slender brick campanile in the NE corner of the building, was a patrician tower which the city took over in 1226. Gothic arches in the bell chamber date from 1311; the octagonal crown from 1444. Lionello Puppi believed the basilica's loggias to be 'Palladio's most celebrated work, which put him on the path to success. They are also to some extent a symbolic work.' Today they are the finest sight in the city. On the N. side of the Piazza dei Signori are the *16C Loggia del Capitano*, which was also designed by Palladio and with three tall arches between four colossal semi-columns with composite capitals, and *Monte di Pietà* (15/16C), the former pawnbroker's shop, which includes the double-storeyed baroque façade (1614–17) of the small church of *S.Vincenzo*.

Casa Pigafetta (9 contrà Pigafetta): This picturesque palazzo, completed in Gothic-Venetian style in *c*. 1480, is the birthplace (1491) of Antonio Pigafetta, the sailor who accompanied Magellan on the first circumnavigation of the world in 1519–22.

Contrà Porti: Many of the interesting patricians' palazzi in Vicenza are to be found in this *contrada* (street) which leads N. from the Corso Palladio. They include the Gothic-Venetian *Palazzo Cavalloni-Thiene* (Nos. 6–10), the splendid *Palazzo*

Porto-Barbaran (No. 11), built in 1569/70 to Palladio's design, the *Renaissance palazzo* (No. 12) of the *Thiene* family, designed by Lorenzo da Bologna (1489; good terracotta portal and fine courtyard), the Gothic *Casa Sperotti-Trissino* (No. 14), the Gothic-Venetian *Palazzo Porto-Breganze* (No. 17) dating from 1481, with a fine Renaissance portal and Renaissance courtyard, the elegant Gothic-Venetian *Palazzo Colleoni-Porto* (No. 19) and the incomplete *Palazzo Iseppo da Porto* (No. 21) dating from 1552 and attributed to Palladio. The *Contrà Zanella* in the E. (see below) leads back to the *Corso Palladio*.

Contrà S.Marco: This street runs N. from the Bacchiglione. On the W. side are the *Palazzo Angaran-Vaccari* (1566) at No. 39, with a partly rusticated façade attributed to Palladio, the *Piovene* (No. 41), a baroque palazzo by Carlo Borella (1676–80) and the classical façade (1756) of the church of *S.Marco degli Scalzi* (15/18C).

Contrà Zanella: Runs parallel to the Contrà Porti (see above). The splendid rear façade (1558) of the *Palazzo Thiene* is by Palladio. The baroque church of *S.Stefano* (1695–1726) has a superb altarpiece (Virgin Mary with St.George and St.Lucy, and an angel making music, *c.* 1528) by Palma Vecchio in the left transept. The Gothic-Venetian *Casa Fontana-Sesso* (No. 2) is charming. *Negri de Salvi* (No. 1), a battlemented Renaissance palazzo, was built in the late 15C.

Corso Andrea Palladio: This central street (the former Roman Decumanus) runs from the medieval *Porta Castello* and the square *Torrione Scaligero* (11–14C) in the W. to the Piazza Matteotti in the E. The *Palazzo Thiene-Bonin* (No. 13) is said to have been started by Palladio and completed by Vincenzo Scamozzi. The *Renaissance palazzo* at No. 45 was inhabited by the *Capra* family. *Palazzi Thiene* (No. 47) is Venetian Gothic. No.67 is known as *Braschi*. The *Palazzo del Comune* (No. 98), which has stuccoes and frescos inside, is

Casa Pigafetta ▷

regarded as Scamozzi's main work (1592). The enchanting Gothic-Venetian *Palazzo da Schio* (No. 147) is also known as *Ca' d'Oro*. The 16C *Casa del Palladio* (No. 165) is reputed to be the house where the great architect lived.

Giardino Salvi (piazzale Roma): This *park* was laid out by Count Giacomo Valmarana in 1552 and has been open to the public since 1592. In it are the Palladian-style *Loggia Valmarana* (1592) near the canal, and the baroque *Loggia Longhena* (1649) by Baldassare Longhena. It has been the city park since 1907, and from its E. section there is a good view of the scant remains of the walls of the former *Scaliger castle* which dates from 1343.

Teatro Olimpico (piazza Mateotti): This is the last work (1580) of Andrea Palladio who designed it shortly before his death for the 'Olympic Academy' of Vicenza, of which he was a founding member. Vincenzo Scamozzi, who was commissioned to carry out the work, built this classical *theatre* with its ascending, semi-elliptical rows of seats and a two-storeyed *backdrop wall* of wood and stucco, enlivened by statues. Scamozzi used the rising floor of the stage and the feigned perspectives to create the illusion that, by looking through the central round-arched portal and the rectangular openings at the sides, the spectator could see the long alleyways of the city of Thebes. 18C statues stand on the balustrade which surmounts the colonnaded passage at the upper end of the rows of spectators' seats. The coffered ceiling over the stage was restored in accordance with the original in 1914.

Villa Almerico-Capra/La Rotonda (33 via della Rotonda): Palladio's most famous villa. Built in 1566/7, it was completed in 1606 by Scamozzi. Outside the façades of this centrally planned square building with its flat *dome,* there are massive external staircases with Ionic *colonnaded porticos* topped by pediments. Walls of the round central *drawing room* are decorated with frescos by Louis Dorigny from Paris. Dome frescos are attributed to Alessandro Maganza. Stuccoes on the vaults and on the fine fireplaces are by Bartolomeo Ridolfi. This villa was the model for numerous Italian and English villas of the 17–19C.

Villa Valmarana ai Nani (8 via S.Bastiano): This villa, named after the dwarf statues (nani) on its surrounding wall, stands a little to the S. of the city on a spur of the Monti Bérici. It comprises the central structure (1668), probably designed by Antonio Muttoni, and the guest house (foresteria), gatehouse and stalls which were built by his son Francesco later than 1725. The villa is famous for its well-preserved frescos (1757) by Giovanni Battista Tiepolo and his son Giandomenico. Rooms around the former loggia (known as the atrium) of the *central structure* are decorated almost exclusively with masterly frescos (scenes from Homer's 'Iliad', Ariosto's 'Orlando Furioso', Virgil's 'Aeneid' and Tasso's 'Jerusalem Liberated') by Giovanni Battista Tiepolo. Apart from the so-called *Stanza dell'Olimpo,*

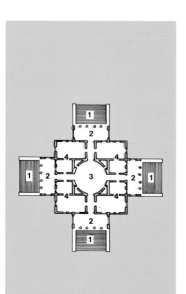

Vicenza, **La Rotonda 1** Steps **2** Ionic colonnaded portico **3** Central drawing room with dome surmounted by a lantern **4** Side rooms

which was also frescoed by the elder Tiepolo (gods of Olympus), the rooms in the *guest house* were painted with frescos of allegories, carnival scenes, people out walking, landscapes and chinoiserie scenes by his son Giandomenico; in this part the individual rooms take their names from frescos.

Museo Civico (piazza Matteotti): The *Palazzo Chiericati,* designed by Palladio and begun in 1550, has a captivating classical façade of original design, with a Doric colonnaded portico on the ground floor and an Ionic colonnaded loggia on the upper storey. The statues on the roof cornice were added in the early 18C. Since 1855 the palazzo has housed the *city museum.*

The *archaeological collection* on the ground floor comprises Stone Age and pre-Roman excavation finds from Vicenza and its environs, including some interesting *votive panels* with human figures (4/3C BC), and Roman and Lombard exhibits, chiefly burial objects, but also remains of a floor mosaic (hunting scene, 4C AD) and items of jewellery. There are stuccoes by Bartolomeo Ridolfi and frescos (Apollo and Diana, signs of the zodiac) by Domenico

Brusasorci on the vault of the 1st room in the *S. wing.* The 2nd room has good frescos (assembly of the gods) by Giovanni Battista Zelotti.

The *picture gallery* on the upper storey is rich in Veneto paintings (14–18C), especially works by the Vicenza school (17/18C). *Room I:* 14C fresco fragments from Vicenza cathedral and a Byzantine-style panel (Death of the Virgin Mary, 1333) by Paolo Veneziano. *Room II:* 15/16C Renaissance paintings, some by Hans Memling (Crucifixion, *c.* 1470). *Room III:* Paintings by Bartolomeo Montagna (several paintings of the Virgin Mary) and Cima da Conegliano (Virgin Mary, St.Jerome and St.James, 1489). *Room IV:* High Renaissance paintings, including works by Giovanni Buonconsiglio (Lamentation, Virgin Mary) and Giovanni Speranza (Ascension). *Room V:* An early work (Virgin Mary and Saints, *c.* 1556) by Paolo Veronese and a painting (St.Augustine healing the plague-sufferers) by Jacopo Tintoretto. *Room VI:* Paintings by Antony van Dyck (Ages of Man), Paolo Veronese (Holy Trinity, 1574) and Lambert Sustris (Flight into Egypt). *Room VII:* Paintings by the Vicenza artists Giovanni Antonio Fasolo

Teatro Olimpico, stage

(Virgin Mary of the Rosary), Alessandro Maganza (portrait of Archbishop Chiericati, portrait of a young nobleman) and Giovan Battista Maganza. *Room VIII:* Paintings from the 17C Venetian school. *Room IX:* Paintings by Jacopo, Francesco and Leandro Bassano, including 'Vicenza priests adoring the Virgin Mary' (1573), a famous work by Jacopo Bassano. *Room X:* Works by Francesco Maffei (including portrait and allegories of Alvise Foscarini, Conversion of the Apostle Paul, Baptism of Christ). *Room XI:* 17C stuccoes, wall paintings from the Carpioni studio, paintings (Artemis and Actaeon, Olindo and Sofronia) by Giovan Battista Pittoni. *Room XII:* 17/18C Veneto landscape paintings by Luca Carlevaris, Marco and Sebastiano Ricci, and Giuseppe Zais. *Room XIII:* Paintings from the church of S.Maria d'Aracoeli (see above) by Giovan Battista Piazzetta (Stigmatization of St.Francis of Assisi, *c.* 1732) and Giovanni Battista Tiepolo (Virgin Mary). *Room XIV:* (Salone): 17/18C paintings by Antonio Bellucci (Judgement of Paris, Family of Darius before Alexander the Great, Continence of Scipio), Luca Giordano (Marriage at Cana, Bathsheba in the bath, Judgement of Paris, Odysseus and

Calypso) and *terracotta statuettes* by Orazio Marinali; 16C *terracotta statue* of the Virgin Mary by Jacopo Sansovino, and a good collection of *drawings* by Andrea Palladio.

Also worth seeing: Apart from the palazzi mentioned above, the following buildings should also be noted: The 16C *Palazzo Angaran* (3 Contrà S.Lucia), with loggias on the façades facing the street and the river. The *Palazzo Civena-Trissino* (12 via Eretenio), built by Palladio in 1540. The Gothic *Palazzo Regaù* (31 via 20 Settembre), with façade paintings. The *Palazzi Trissino-Trento* (*c.* 1558, 10 via Cesare Battisti) and *Valmarana-Braga* (1566, 16 Corso Fogazzaro), both by Palladio. The *Palazzo Trento-Valmarana* (1718, 1 Contrà Cabianca) by Francesco Muttoni, with a magnificent baroque façade.

Environs: Arcugnano (7 km. S.): The classical *Villa Franceschini-Pasini Salasco* (1770) by Ottavio Scamozzi was enlarged in the 2nd half of the 19C. There is an armoury and a good collection of paintings. Outside the tall garden façade there is a well-cultivated park in the Italian style.

Vicenza, Teatro Olimpico

Costozza (12 km. SE): The Gothic-Venetian *Villa Rossi* with good frescos by Zelotti. The 16C *Villa Trento-Carli* with an interesting, partly rusticated façade articulated by semi-columns. The upper storey of the small *Villa Eolia* (today a restaurant) is also decorated with frescos by Giovanni Battista Zelotti. The *Villa Garzadori da Schio* is in a park adorned with statues (Neptune with a dolphin, Andromeda and dwarfs) by Orazio Marinali; the central section of this villa has an Ionic loggia and a sumptuously decorated drawing room. To the right of this is the *Ca'Molino*, with a façade in various styles. The *'Grotta del Marinali' pavilion* (1690), on a higher level, was used as a studio by Orazio Marinali.

Grumolo delle Abbadesse (12 km. E.): The *Villa Capra-Barbaran* consists of a central structure (1672) and guest houses (1782). It has a rusticated portico and a fine octagonal chapel. The *Chiericati-Rigo* (c. 1554) in the Vancimuglio district is a pretty holiday villa with an Ionic colonnaded portico and was built to the plans by Andrea Palladio.

Montegalda (17 km. SE): The former *Castello di Montegalda*, surrounded by tall cypresses and vine-covered slopes, stands on top of a little hill. The castle was founded in the 11C and reinforced in 1176. A number of famous people stayed here, including Emperor Maximilian I, Archduke John, and the unfortunate Mexican 'Emperor' Maximilian of Habsburg. In the 18C the castle was converted into the *Villa Grimani Marcelli* with a fine Italian garden, although the villa was still able to preserve its medieval appearance. Its fortifications consist of grooved battlements, towers and a drawbridge. On the far side of the Bacchiglione river is the *Villa Conti-Campagnolo* (Montegaldella district), known as 'la Deliziosa'. Built in 1622, it was converted in the 18C. An entrance gate with a fine wrought-iron railing leads into the park which is decorated with over 100 statues from Orazio Marinali's studio.

Monteviale (11 km. W.): The *Villa Loschi-Zileri* (Biron), built by Muttoni in 1734, stands in gentle hilly landscape amidst a splendid park itself laid out by Muttoni. There is a fresco cycle (1734) by Giovanni Battista Tiepolo in the grand hall of the villa.

Quinto Vicentino (8.5 km. NE): The *Villa Thiene* in the heart of the town was begun by Palladio in 1545/6 and enlarged

Vicenza, Museo Civico

by Antonio Muttoni in the early 18C. Today it is the office of the 'municipio'. The *Villa Valmarana* was designed by Palladio in *c.* 1563 as a two-storeyed building (now restored). It was completed by the addition of a low attic storey above the Ionic portico on the ground floor. The villa has a chapel (1615), statues, and ornate wrought-iron railings on the garden gates.

37069 Villafranca di Verona

Verona   p.322□B 6

This little town was founded in 1185 under the name of *Borgo Libero* as an outpost of Verona against Mantua. The population withstood a siege of the *Villa Libera* by the Gonzagas in 1404, but the town fell to the Dukes of Ferrara in 1487 and was stormed by Ludovico il Moro, Roberto Sanseverino and the Spanish viceroy in 1493. After a long period of peace, *Villafranca* played an important part in the Italian war of independence, and treaties were concluded here.

Castello: The core of this *Scaliger castle* was built in 1185, but it was only after the battle at the Ponte Molini in Mantua in 1199 that it was reinforced by the addition of seven tall towers and the massive square surrounding wall with its grooved battlements. The height of the central *main tower* was increased in 1243. In 1345, the *Serraglio,* a fortification 16 km. in length, was built to join this castle to the castles of Nogarole (q.v.) and Valeggio sul Mincio (q.v.; see Environs). Of the Serraglio, the bridge across the Mincio river and parts of the wall still survive. After the Venetians rebuilt the Scaliger castle in 1408 Jews who had been expelled from Verona built themselves small houses protected by the walls. Today the large *castle courtyard* is a sports ground.

Villa Gandini Morelli-Bugna (38b via della Pace): Napoleon III and Emperor Franz Josef signed an armistice agreement in this palazzo on 8 July 1859. This agreement led to the conclusion of the peace

of Zurich on 10 November of the same year. The *hall* in which the armistice was signed is still furnished as it was at that time. The adjoining *Museo del Risorgimento* contains weapons, trophies and other material documenting the wars of liberation and the two World Wars.

Environs: Isola della Scala (18 km. SE): The *parish church* in the central Piazza has been rebuilt several times. Its *campanile,* with spire, was begun in 1130 by the architects Hanno and Wariento who are named in an inscription, but it was only completed in 1411.

Nogarole Rocca (8.5 km. SE): The *Castello,* built in 1243, stands not far from the autostrada. In 1345, Mastino II della Scala included it in the Serraglio (see above). Today the castle buildings are used as a farmstead. The imposing 16C *Villa Canossa* (Grezzano district) by Michele Sanmicheli was converted by Adriano Cristofali in the 18C.

Sommacampagna (6.5 km. N.): The Romanesque church of *S.Andrea* (11/12C) stands in the graveyard. The altar consecrated to the 'Dea Leituria' at the base of the last left-hand pilaster inside the church, has an inscription dating from 38 BC from which it can be deduced that the church was built on the site of a heathen temple. The interior has a nave and two aisles, and *fresco decorations* in the Byzantine-Romanesque tradition in the choir apse (two Apostles, 11C), in the side apses and nave (miraculous scenes, 12C), on the right choir wall (St.Zeno, late 13C), and on the inner façade wall (Last Judgement, late 13C). The villas in this little town include the 16C *Villa Fiocco-Masi* built in the style of Sanmicheli.

Sona (10 km. N.): Several 19C *villas* are to be found in this attractive village. In the NW exit road there stands the little church of *SS.Quirico e Giulitta,* built of rough stone in the 15C.

Valeggio sul Mincio (9 km. W.): The 13C *Scaliger castle,* with four defensive towers, was given an additional tall watchtower in the 14C. This tower was designed by Domenico Fiorentino, as was the gigantic *Ponte Rotto* bridge (1339), which is 1,950 ft. long and spans the river Mincio.

Glossary

Acanthus: Decorative element found especially on→Corinthian capitals; it developed from the stylized representation of a sharply serrated, thistle-like leaf.

Aedicule: Wall niche housing a bust or statue; usually with a→ gable,→pillars or→columns.

Aisle: Longitudinal section of a church or other building, usually divided from other such sections by an→arcade.

Altar: Sacrificial table of Greeks and Romans. The Lord's table in the Christian faith. Catholic churches often have several side altars as well as the high altar.

Ambo: Stand or lectern by the choir screen in early Christian and medieval churches; predecessor of the→pulpit.

Ambulatory: A corridor created by continuing the side aisles around the choir; often used for processions.

Ancona: Altarpiece made as a single piece but with several compartments.

Antependium: Covering for the front of the altar.

Apse: Large recess at end of the→choir, usually semicircular or polygonal. As a rule it contains the→altar.

Apsidiole: A small apsidal chapel.

Aquamanile: Pouring-vessel or bowl for ritual washing in the Catholic liturgy.

Aqueduct: Water pipe or channel across an arched bridge; frequently built as monumental structures by the Romans.

Arabesque: Stylized foliage used as a decorative motif.

Arcade: A series of arches borne by columns or pillars. When the arcade is attached to a wall (and is purely decorative), it is called a blind arcade.

Arch: A curved structure of support employed in spanning a space.

Architrave: Main stone member on top of the columns; lowest part of the→entablature.

Archivolt: The face of an arch in Romanesque and Gothic portals; often more than one.

Ashlar: Hewn block of stone (as opposed to that straight from the quarry).

Atrium: In Roman houses a central hall with an opening in the roof. In Christian architecture, a forecourt usually surrounded by columns; also known as a→paradise.

Attic: A (usually richly decorated) storey above the main→entablature; intended to conceal the roof.

Baldacchino: Canopy above altars, tombs, statues, portals, etc.

Baluster: Short squat or shaped column.

Balustrade: Rail formed of→ balusters.

Baptistery: Place of baptism; may be a separate building.

Baroque: Architectural style from c .1600–c .1750. Distinguished by powerfully agitated, interlocking forms.

Bartizan: A small corner turret projecting from the top of a building.

Base: Foot of a column or pillar.

Basket arch: A flattened round arch.

Basilica: Greek hall of kings. In church architecture, a type of church with nave and two or more aisles, the roof of the nave being higher than the roofs above the aisles.

Bay: Vertical division of a building between pillars, columns, windows, wall arches, etc.

Blind arcade:→Arcade.

Blind tracery:→Tracery.

Bosquet: Clumps of trees and bushes, particularly common in French gardens and parks.

Bracket: A projection from the wall used as a support—for a bust, statue, arch, etc.

Calotte: Half dome with no drum.

Calvary: Sculpture of the Crucifixion and Mount Calvary.

Campanile: Bell tower; usually free standing.

Capital: Topmost part of a column. The shape of the capital determines the style or→order.

Cartouche: Decorative frame or panel imitating a scrolled piece of paper, usually with an inscription, coat-of-arms, etc.

Caryatid: A carved figure supporting the entablature.

Cella: Main room of ancient temple containing divine image.

Cenotaph: Monument to dead buried elsewhere.

Chapterhouse: Assembly room in which monks or nuns discuss the community's business.

Charnel house: House or vault in which bones are placed.

Choir: That part of the church in which divine service is sung. Shorter and often narrower than the nave, it is usually raised and at the E. end. In the Middle Ages the choir was often separated from the rest of the church by a screen.

Ciborium: Canopy over high altar; usually in the form of a dome supported on columns.

Classicism: Revival of Greek and Roman architectural principles.

Clerestory: Upper part of the main walls of the nave, above the roofs of the aisles and pierced by windows.

Cloister: Four sided covered walk (often vaulted) and opening inwards by arcades.

Coffered ceiling: A ceiling divided into square or polygonal panels, which are painted or otherwise decorated.

Column: Support with circular cross-section, narrowing somewhat towards the top; the type of column is determined by the→order.→Pillar.

Compound pillar: Often found in Gothic buildings. A central shaft has attached or detached shafts or half-shafts clustered around it.

Conch: Semicircular recess with a half-dome.

Confessio: Chamber or recess for a relic near the altar.

Corinthian order:→Order with richly decorated→capitals; the base has two or more tiers and is similar to that of the→Ionic order.

Cornice: Projecting upper limit of a wall; topmost member of the→ entablature of an→order.

Cosmati work: Decorative technique involving the use of marble inlay, mosaics etc.; many Roman marble workers had the family name Cosma.

Crocket: Gothic leaf-like decoration projecting from the sides of pinnacles, gables etc.

Crossing: The intersection of the nave and transept.

Crypt: Burial place, usually under the→choir. Churches were often built above an old crypt.

Curtain wall: Outer wall of castle.

Cyclops wall: Ancient wall made of large rough blocks of stone of irregular shape.

Dipteros: Temple in which porticoes are connected by a double row of lateral columns.

Diptych: A painted hinged double (altar) panel.

Directoire style: French style under the Directoire (1795–9), influenced by Antiquity.

Dolmen: Chamber tomb lined and roofed with megaliths.

Doric order:→Order in which the columns have a base and bear flat, pad-shaped→capitals.

Dormer window: Window in sloping roof which projects and has its own gabled roof.

Drum: Substructure of a dome; as a rule either cylindrical or polygonal.

Dwarf Gallery: Romanesque feature; wall passage of small arches on the outside of a building.

Empire style: Classical style in France at the beginning of the 19C, with Graeco-Roman and Egyptian models.

Enclos Paroissial: Enclosed churchyard in France, often with a→Calvary.

Entablature: Upper part of an→order; made up of→architrave,→frieze and→cornice.

Eremitage: Pavilion in park or garden, lonely castle or palace.

Exedra: Apse, vaulted with a half-dome; may have raised seats.

Façade: Main front of a building, often decoratively treated.

Facing: Panelling in front of structural components not intended to be visible.

Faience: Glazed pottery named after the Italian town of Faenza.

Fan vault: Looks like a highly decorated rib vault; Concave-sided cone-like sections meet or nearly meet at the apex of the vault.

Filigree work: Originally goldsmith's work in which gold and silver wire were ornamentally soldered on to a metal base. Also used in a more general sense for intricately perforated carvings and stucco.

Finial: Small decorative pinnacle.

Flying buttress: Very large Gothic windows made it necessary to buttress or strengthen the outer walls by half-arches and arches. This support transmitted the thrust of the vault to the buttress.

Foliate capital: Gothic capital in which the basic form is covered with delicate leaf ornaments.

Fosse: Artificially created ditch; often separated castles from the surrounding land with access by a drawbridge.

Fresco: Pigments dispersed in water are appplied without a bonding agent to the still-damp lime plaster. While the mortar dries, the pigments become adsorbed into the plaster.

Frieze: Decorative strips for the borders of a wall. The frieze can be two- or three-dimensional and can consist of figures or ornaments.

Gable: The triangular upper section of a wall. Normally at one end of a pitched roof but it may be purely decorative.

Gallery: Intermediate storey; in a church it is usually for singers and the organ. Arcaded walkway.

Gobelin: Pictorial tapestry woven in the Gobelins factory in Paris.

Gothic: Period in European art and architecture stretching from the mid 12C to the 16C.

Grisaille: Painting in various shades of grey.

Groin vault: Vault in which two→barrel vaults intersect at right angles. The simple groin vault is to be distinguished from the rib vault, in which the intersecting edges are reinforced by ribs.

Half-timbering: Beams are used as supporting parts with an infill of loam or brick.

Hall church: In contrast to the→ basilica, nave and aisles are of equal height; no→transept.

Hermitage: Pavilion in parks and gardens; originally the residence of a hermit.

Holy Sepulchre: Structure representing Christ's tomb as discovered by Constantine, who later encased it in a miniature temple.

Iconostasis: In the Eastern church,

a screen of paintings between the sanctuary and the nave.

Intarsia: Inlaid work in wood, plaster, stone etc.

Ionic order:→Order in which the columns stand on a base of two or more tiers; the→capital has two lateral→volutes.

Jamb: Vertical part of arch, doorway or window.

Keep: Main tower of a castle; last refuge in time of siege.

Lantern: Small windowed turret on top of roof or dome.

Loggia: Pillared gallery, open on one or more sides; often on an upper storey.

Lunette : Semicircular panel above doors and windows, often with paintings or sculptures.

Mandorla: Almond shaped niche containing a figure of Christ enthroned.

Mannerism: Artistic style between→Renaissance and→ baroque (c .1530–1630). Mannerism neglects natural and classical forms in favour of an intended artificiality of manner.

Mansard: An angled roof in which the lower slope is steeper than the upper. The area gained is also called a mansard and can be used to live in. Named after the French architect F.Mansart.

Mausoleum: A splendid tomb, usually in the form of a small house or temple; from the tomb of Mausolus at Halicarnassus.

Menhir: Rough-hewn prehistoric standing stone.

Mensa: Flat surface of the altar.

Mezzanine: Intermediate storey.

Miniature: Small picture, hand illumination in old manuscripts.

Monks' choir: That section of the choir reserved for the monks, frequently closed off.

Monstrance: Ornamented receptacle in which the consecrated Host is shown (usually behind glass).

Mosaic: Decoration for wall, floor or vault, assembled from small coloured stones, pieces of glass or fragments of other materials.

Mullion: Vertical division of a window into two or more lights.

Narthex: Vestibule of basilica or church.

Nave: Central aisle of church, intended for the congregation; excludes choir and apse.

Neo-baroque: Reaction to the cool restraint of→classicism. Re-uses baroque forms; developed in the last part of the 19C as a historicizing, sumptuous style with exaggerated three-dimensional ornamentation and conspicuous colours.

Neo-Gothic: Historicizing 19C style, which was intended to revive Gothic structural forms and decorative elements.

Net vault: Vault in which the ribs cross one another repeatedly.

Nuns' choir: Gallery from which nuns attended divine service.

Nymphaeum: Roman pleasure house, often with statues and fountains.

Obelisk: Free-standing pillar with square ground plan and pyramidal peak.

Odeum: Building, usually round, in which musical or other artistic performances were given.

Onion dome: Bulbous dome with a point, common in Russia and E.Europe; not a true dome, i.e. without a vault.

Opisthodomos: Rear section of Greek temple; behind the cella.

Orangery: Part of baroque castles and parks originally intended to shelter orange trees and other southern plants in winter. However, orangeries often had halls for large court assemblies.

Oratory: Small private chapel.

Order: Classical architectural system prescribing decorations and proportions according to one of the accepted forms:→Corinthian,→ Doric,→Ionic, etc. An order consists of a column, which usually has a base, shaft and capital, and the entablature, which itself consists of architrave, frieze and cornice.

Oriel: Projecting window on an upper floor; it is often a decorative feature.

Pala: Altarpiece.

Palazzo: (Ital) Palace.

Palazzo Vescovile: (Ital) Bishop's Palace.

Pallium: A cloak worn by the Romans; in the Middle Ages, a coronation cloak for kings and emperors, later also for archbishops.

Pantheon: Temple dedicated to all gods; often modelled on that in Rome, which is a rotunda. Building in which distinguished people are buried or have memorials.

Paradise:→Atrium.

Pavilion: Polygonal or round building in parks or pleasure grounds. The main structure of baroque castles is very often linked by corner pavilions to the galleries branching off from the castle.

Pedestal: Base of a column or the base for a statue.

Pendentive: The means by which a circular dome is supported on a square base; concave area or spandrel between two walls and the base of a dome.

Peripteros: Greek temple in which the porticoes are connected laterally by single rows of columns.

Peristyle: Continuous colonnade surrounding a temple or open court.

Piano nobile: The principal floor of a secular building, normally the first floor, on which the public rooms are situated.

Piazza: (Ital) Square.

Pilaster: Pier projecting from a

wall; conforms to one of the→orders.

Pilaster strip: Pilaster without base and capital; feature of Anglo-Saxon and early Romanesque buildings.

Pillar: Supporting member, like a→column but with a square or polygonal cross section; does not conform to any order.

Plinth: Projecting lower part of wall or column.

Polyptych: An (altar) painting composed of several panels or wings.

Porch: Covered entrance to a building.

Portico: Porch supported by columns and often with a pediment; may be the centre-piece of façade.

Pozzo: (Ital) Well.

Predella: Substructure of the altar. Paintings along lower edge of large altarpiece.

Pronaos: Area in front of ancient temple (also of churches); sides enclosed and columns in front.

Propylaeum: Entrance gateway, usually to temple precincts. The Propylaeum on the Acropolis at Athens, 437–432 BC, was the model for later buildings.

Prothyra: Railing before door of Roman house.

Pseudoperipteros: Temple in which porticoes are connected laterally by→pilasters and not→columns.

Pulpit: Raised place in church from which the sermon is preached. May be covered by a→baldacchino or→ sounding board.

Putto: Figure of naked angelic child in→Renaissance,→baroque and→rococo art and architecture.

Pylon: Entrance gate of Egyptian temple; more generally used as isolated structure to mark a boundary.

Quadriga: Chariot drawn by four horses harnessed abreast.

Refectory: Dining hall of a monastery.

Régence style: French style transitional between the→baroque and the→rococo.

Relief: Carved or moulded work in which the design stands out. The different depths of relief are, in ascending order, rilievo stiacciato, bas-relief and high relief or alto-rilievo.

Reliquary: Receptacle in which a saint's relics are preserved.

Renaissance: Italian art and architecture from the early 15C to the mid 16C. It marks the end of the

medieval conception of the world and the beginning of a new view based on classical antiquity.

Retable: Shrine-like structure above and behind the altar.

Rib vault:→Groin vault.

Risorgimento: (Ital) Movement for the unification of Italy (1815–70).

Rocaille: Decorative ornaments adapted from the shell motif; chiefly late→Renaissance and→Rococo.

Rococo: Style towards the end of the→baroque (1720–70); elegant, often dainty, tendency to oval forms.

Romanesque: Comprehensive name for architecture from 1000–c. 1300. Buildings are distinguished by round arches, calm ornament and a heavy general appearance.

Rood screen: Screen between→ choir and→nave, which bears a rood or crucifix.

Rose-window: A much divided round window with rich→tracery; found especially in Gothic buildings, often above the portal.

Rotunda: Round building.

Rustication: Massive blocks of stone separated by deep joints.

Sanctuary: Area around the high altar in a church.

Sarcophagus: Stone coffin, usually richly decorated.

Scroll: Spiral-shaped ornament.

Secularization: Transfer of ecclesiastical possessions to secular use, especially in the Napoleonic period (1803).

Sedilia: Seats for clergy; usually in the wall of the S. side of the choir.

Serliana: Also known as the Palladian or Venetian window. An archway or window consisting of a wide semicircular central arch flanked by a narrower, flat-topped opening on each side.

Sgraffito: Scratched-on decoration.

Sounding board:→Pulpit.

Spandrel: The triangular space between the curve of an arch, the horizontal drawn from its apex, and the vertical drawn from the point of its springing; also the space between two arches in an arcade, and that part of a vault between two adjacent ribs.

Springer: The first stone in which the curve of an arch or vault begins.

Squinch: An arch or system of arches at the internal angles of towers to form the base of a round drum or dome above a square structure.→Pendentive.

Stela: Standing block.

Strapwork: Renaissance carved work modelled on fretwork or cut leather.

Stucco: Plasterwork, made of gypsum, lime, sand and water, which is easy to model. Used chiefly in the 17&18C for three-dimensional interior decoration.

Synagogue: Jewish place of worship.

Tabernacle: Receptacle for the consecrated host.

Tambour: Lower section, or 'drum' of a dome, usually cylindrical or polygonal.

Telamon: Support in the form of a male figure (male caryatid).

Terracotta: Fired, unglazed clay.

Thermal baths: Roman hot-water baths.

Thermal window: Semicircular window divided in three, deriving its name from its use in Roman baths.

Tomba: (Ital) Tomb.

Tracery: Geometrically conceived decorative stonework, particularly used to decorate windows, screens, etc. If it embellishes a wall, it is known as blind tracery.

Transenna: Screen or lattice in openwork found in early Christian churches.

Transept: That part of a church at right angles to the nave;→basilica.

Triforium: Arcaded wall passage looking on to the nave; between the arcade and the clerestory.

Triptych: Tripartite altar painting.

Triumphal arch: Free-standing gateway based on a Roman original.

Trompe l'oeil: Special kind of image which the eye is deceived into viewing as three dimensional.

Tunnel vault: Simplest vault; continuous structure with semicircular or pointed cross section uninterrupted by cross vaults.

Tympanum: The often semicircular panel contained within the lintel of a doorway and the arch above it.

Vedute: Paintings or drawings of a city or landscape.

Via: (Ital) Street.

Volute: Spiral scroll on an Ionic capital; smaller volutes on Composite and Corinthian capitals.

Winged altar: Triptych or polyptych with hinged, usually richly carved or painted, wings.

Index of artists

List of places mentioned in the text

Alphabetical list of the sights of Venice

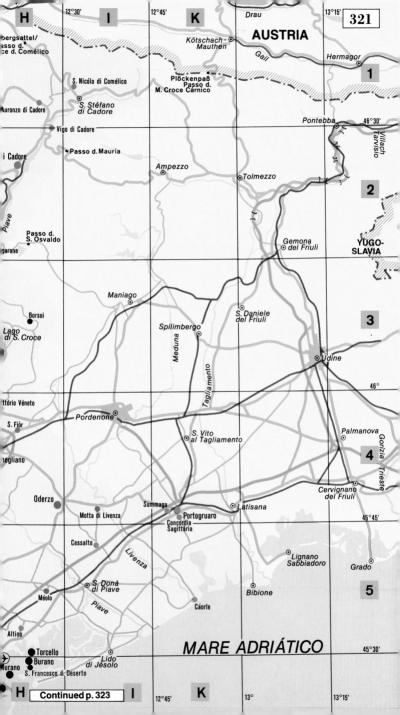

H   12°30'   I   12°45'   K   13°15'

Drau

AUSTRIA

bergsattel/
ce d. Comélico

Kötschach-
Mauthen

Gail

Hermagor

1

S. Nicóla di Comélico

Plöckenpaß
Passo d.
M. Croce Cárnico

S. Stéfano
di Cadore

Pontebba   46°30'

Auronzo di Cadore

Villach
Tarvisio

Vigo di Cadore

i Cadore

Passo d. Mauria

Ampezzo

Tolmezzo

2

Piave

Passo d.
S. Osvaldo

Gemona
del Friuli

YUGO-
SLAVIA

garone

Maniago

Borsoi

S. Daniele
del Friuli

3

Lago
di S. Croce

Spilimbergo

Meduna

Údine

ttório Véneto

Tagliamento

46°

S. Fiòr

Pordenone

egliano

S. Vito
al Tagliamento

Palmanova

Gorizia
Trieste

4

Cervignano
del Friuli

Oderzo

Summaga

Latisana

45°45'

Motta di Livenza

Portogruaro
Concordia
Sagittária

Cessalto

Livenza

Lignano
Sabbiadoro

Grado

S. Donà
di Piave

Bibione

5

Méolo

Piave

Cáorle

Altino

MARE ADRIÁTICO   45°30'

Torcello

Burano

Murano

S. Francesco d. Deserto

Lido
di Jésolo

H   Continued p. 323   I   12°45'   K   13°   13°15'

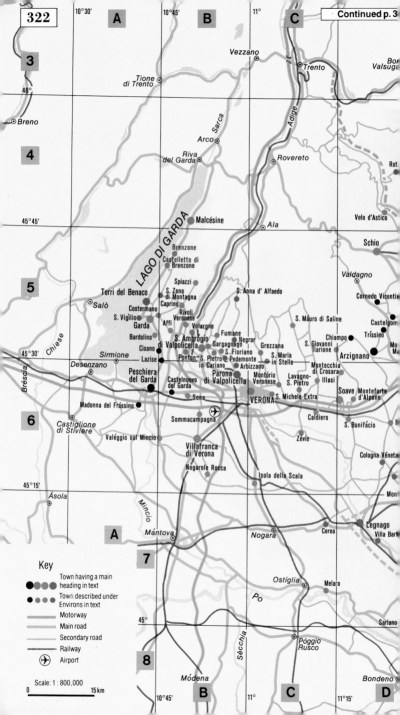

(